GLOBAL ISSUES

WEAPONS OF MASS DESTRUCTION

Michael Kort
Boston University

Foreword by Cathal J. Nolan
Boston University

Facts On File
An imprint of Infobase Publishing

GLOBAL ISSUES: WEAPONS OF MASS DESTRUCTION

Facts On File, Inc.
An imprint of Infobase Publishing
132 West 31st Street
New York NY 10001

Library of Congress Cataloging-in-Publication Data

Kort, Michael, 1944–
Weapons of mass destruction / Michael Kort; foreword by Cathal J. Nolan.
p. cm.—(Global issues)
Includes bibliographical references and index.
ISBN 978-0-8160-7827-1
1. Weapons of mass destruction. 2. World politics—21st century. I. Title.

U793.K67 2010
358'3—dc22 2009024416

Facts On File books are available at special discounts when purchased in bulk quantities for businesses, associations, institutions, or sales promotions. Please call our Special Sales Department in New York at (212) 967-8800 or (800) 322-8755.

You can find Facts On File on the World Wide Web at http://www.factsonfile.com

Text design by Erika K. Arroyo
Illustrations by Dale Williams
Composition by Mary Susan Ryan Flynn
Cover printed by Art Print, Taylor, PA
Book printed and bound by Maple Press, York, PA
Date printed: April 2010
Printed in the United States of America

10 9 8 7 6 5 4 3 2 1

This book is printed on acid-free paper and contains 30 percent postconsumer recycled content.

CONTENTS

PART II: PRIMARY SOURCES

PART III: RESEARCH TOOLS

List of Maps, Graphs, and Tables

Foreword

Weapons of mass destruction (WMD) comprise the most destructive and deadly weapons conceived by modern science and engineering. Whether nuclear, chemical, or biological, they pose a severe threat to all countries. Nor is this threat just theoretical: All types of WMD were used in real wars during the 20th century. All modern militaries therefore must seek countermeasures to potential enemy use of WMD in battle. Some efforts have been made to negotiate elimination of WMD from major military arsenals, but confidence in verification of arms control agreements across the globe remains weak. As a result, most major military powers have concluded that the best method of security from enemy WMD that is currently available is to keep stockpiles of their own WMD as a deterrent threat. However, stockpiles encourage states still without WMD to try to acquire them, which then makes arms control even harder.

The greatest threat from WMD in the 21st century is to civilians. Unlike other modern weapons (the so-called conventional weapons), most modern WMD are not designed or built principally for use in war. They are kept at hand in national arsenals first and foremost to induce fear in opposing countries and populations. This might be done defensively to deter a potential enemy from attacking, or offensively, to coerce an enemy into doing something politically that they do not wish to do. All the major military powers of the early 21st century—China, Russia, the United States, India, Great Britain, and France—and a number of smaller powers maintain stocks of WMD for both purposes: to deter and to impress potential opponents. So far the states have maintained their stocks without major incident. However, the potential remains great for misunderstanding or a severe shift in political relations that will raise temptations for use of WMD in an as yet unforeseen crisis or future war.

A growing, more imminent, and lasting threat is the potential for use of WMD by determined terrorist groups beyond the control of any state, either through their own research efforts or more directly from a supplier rogue government. WMD under the control of rogue regimes that disdain international treaties—notably but not exclusively the quixotic family dictatorship that rules North Korea—vastly increase this threat of the use of WMD as terror weapons. If terrorist groups ever obtained WMD or the knowledge to produce them, there is a great danger that the weapons would be used in terror attacks against "soft targets" such as malls, airports, subway systems, and defenseless cities. This threat is real, immediate, and urgent. It will also remain with us for decades, if not forever.

Advancing technologies of miniaturization and bioengineering, combined with mass transportation networks and daily international movements by millions of people, make secret transport of WMD to soft targets a rising threat, while hampering detection and interception. Although not inevitable, it is now highly probable that a terrorist group will eventually succeed in deploying some kind of WMD in a major city. No one knows if that city will be New York, New Delhi, Beijing, Moscow, or Paris. That this threat is real was demonstrated by the use of poison gas by a Japanese religious cult in 1995, when its members spread the nerve gas Sarin in the Tokyo subway to kill ordinary people. Al-Qaeda is known to be researching dirty radiation bombs and nerve and chemical weapons. Rogue governments and individual rogue scientists are actively proliferating nuclear and missile technology.

Wars between states armed with WMD remain a real concern. However, the possibility that small groups of terrorists with bizarre political or social ambitions will gain access to WMD is the main current concern. Of the three types of WMD—nuclear, chemical, and biological—the use of biological weapons poses the greatest threat in the foreseeable future since nuclear weapons so far remain controlled by a handful of states and chemical weapons are harder to use as terror weapons and also less deadly. Biological weapons can be used to attack people directly or—potentially far more damaging—indirectly by striking global food supplies. Anthrax spores, hoof and mouth cultures, wheat rust, and other animal or plant diseases in the hands of terrorists have the potential to wipe out massive herds of domestic animals and entire food crops. There is historical precedent for concern in the Japanese effort during World War II to burn down the forests of North America and destroy U.S. food supplies using high altitude balloons (*fugo*) carrying incendiary bombs and Japan's plans to carry various plagues across the Pacific. Today, balloons would not be needed: It is possible to enter almost every country by normal commercial aircraft while carrying disease spores, to then rent a car and simply drive to the countryside to carry out a terror plan to infect crops or animals as a means of wrecking an enemy's economy. Such an attack, if successful, would drive food prices beyond reach, cause panic buying and hoarding, and wreck the food supply system for millions.

Both the number of states with ongoing conflicts that have WMD and the potential for terrorists to attack defenseless civilian populations with some form of WMD are higher than ever. So are the stakes. Understanding WMD and the issues that surround them are critical for the 21st century. This book is the best place to start your journey to understanding. Professor Michael Kort has written a highly accurate and reliable guide to WMD. The work is carefully documented and sourced. It is scholarly, yet written in accessible and plain prose that is readily understandable by high school students and all others searching for a clear introduction to a complex subject. It is up-to-date, conversant with both traditional and online resources, and authoritative without being overbearing in the assessments it makes and conclusions it draws. It is equally good at explaining technical issues about how WMD are designed and work and the political and historical contexts in which the different classes of WMD have been developed and deployed.

Part I is divided into three chapters that provide an outstanding introduction to the problem of WMD. The first chapter is a global survey of the history of development of WMD. The second focuses on various issues surrounding WMD from the point of view of the United States, including a comprehensive history of policy changes, arms control efforts, and counter-proliferation programs. The next chapter applies the same rigorous analysis to the role of WMD in contemporary global affairs, providing a country-by-country survey of several major state players: Russia, Israel, India, Pakistan, and North Korea. All subjects are handled with scholarly depth and facility, but also a natural teacher's deft touch at level-appropriate explanation. The historical analysis is accurate, the judgments are sound, and the presentation of supporting material is clear and concise.

What marks off this guide from others and gives it special strength and utility is the inclusion of important documents and other tools to aid students in their research and allow them to draw their own informed conclusions about the issues raised. Through direct access to annotated primary documents, teachers and students alike will be able to formulate comparative judgments and delve deeper into controversies confident that they are becoming conversant with the real facts and important questions at issue. They will also find highly useful the thoughtful section How to Research Weapons of Mass Destruction. In this admirable supplement to the main guide, Professor Kort provides an outstanding guide to basic research derived from his many years of undergraduate and other teaching. The advice he provides to students on how to research a complex and dense subject is clear, helpful, unbiased, and wise. The book closes with a set of useful appendixes on basic facts and figures about WMD, a brief listing of key historical players, a guide to relevant international organizations, a chronology, a glossary, and an especially useful and fully up-to-date annotated bibliography.

—Cathal J. Nolan
Boston University

List of Acronyms

ABM	antiballistic missile
AEC	Atomic Energy Commission
BARC	Bhabha Atomic Research Center
BDA	Bilateral Destruction Agreement
BSL	Biosafety Level
BWC	Biological Weapons Convention
CDC	Centers for Disease Control
CIA	Central Intelligence Agency
CTBT	Comprehensive Nuclear Test Ban Treaty
CTRP	Cooperative Threat Reduction Program (Nunn-Lugar)
CWC	Chemical Weapons Convention
CWS	Chemical Warfare Service
DHS	Department of Homeland Security
DSP	Defense Support Program
EPA	Environmental Protection Agency
ERW	Enhanced Radiation Weapon
EU	European Union
GTRI	Global Threat Reduction Initiative
H-2	deuterium
H-3	tritium
HEMED	Science Corps (according to Hebrew words)
HEU	highly enriched uranium

HHS	Department of Health and Human Services
IAEA	International Atomic Energy Agency
IAEC	Israel Atomic Energy Commission
ICBM	intercontinental ballistic missile
IDF	Israel Defense Forces
IIBR	Israel Institute for Biological Research
INF	Intermediate Nuclear Forces
KGB	Committee for State Security (according to Russian words)
LEP	life extension program
LEU	low-enriched uranium
LTBT	Limited Test Ban Treaty
MIRV	multiple independently targeted reentry vehicle
MOU	Memorandum of Understanding
NATO	North Atlantic Treaty Organization
NNSA	National Nuclear Security Administration
NPT	Nuclear Nonproliferation Treaty
NSC	National Security Council
NSCWM	National Strategy to Combat Weapons of Mass Destruction
NTI	Nuclear Threat Initiative
OPCW	Organization for the Prohibition of Chemical Weapons
PAEC	Pakistan Atomic Energy Commission
PRC	People's Republic of China
Pu-239	plutonium 239
RRW	Reliable Replacement Warhead Program
SAFE	Security and Accountability for Every Port
SALT I	Strategic Arms Reduction Talks I
SALT II	Strategic Arms Reduction Talks II
SBIRS	Space Based Infrared System
SDI	Strategic Defense Initiative
SLBM	submarine-launched ballistic missile
SNS	Strategic National Stockpile
SORT	Strategic Offensive Reduction Treaty

List of Acronyms

START I	Strategic Arms Reduction Talks I
START II	Strategic Arms Reduction Talks II
THAAD	Terminal High Altitude Area Defense
TNT	trinitrotoluene
U-235	uranium 235
U-238	uranium 238
WMD	weapons of mass destruction

PART I

At Issue

1

Introduction

OLD AND NEW WEAPONS OF MASS DESTRUCTION

About 2,500 years ago, a nomad people called the Scythians controlled a vast territory north of the Black Sea and Caucasus Mountains stretching from central Europe well into Asia. The Scythians were famous as warriors. They were superb riders who fought on horseback with bows and arrows and light swords. Masters of cavalry tactics, when facing a larger or more powerful army they would retreat, drawing their enemy onto the limitless plain that was their homeland before counterattacking at just the right moment. Scythian warriors were feared both because of their skills and their gruesome custom of cutting the heads off their slain enemies and turning the skulls into leather-lined drinking cups. Perhaps ironically for a warrior people, the Scythians also were known for their artistic talents. They created exquisite jewelry and ornaments, which they wore but also used to decorate their saddles and weapons. So the Scythians were famous, and feared, for fighting their wars not only with great skill and ferocity, but also with considerable style.

There is something else about the Scythians and how they fought that is less well known. These fierce warriors were among the pioneers in developing a primitive version of what we now call biological weapons. Today, biological weapons, along with nuclear and chemical weapons, are classified as a special category of weapons called weapons of mass destruction, or WMD.[1] They are considered a special category of weapon because they can kill far greater numbers of people than any other types of weapons. Modern biological weapons, as well as nuclear and chemical weapons, require a highly sophisticated technology to develop and build. The technology available to the Scythians trailed well behind that of some of their neighbors to the south, such as the ancient Greeks and Persians. But the Scythians used powers of observation, their skills as archers, and well-built bows for shooting arrows long distances to create a simple, low-tech weapon that used biology to kill with frightening effectiveness. According to ancient Greek sources, the Scythians mixed together the bodies of decomposed poisonous snakes, human blood, and manure and then stored this mixture underground for a while in sealed containers. The mixture itself was dangerous because it contained deadly snake poison; by allowing it time to decay in a sealed container the foul-smelling concoction became even more dangerous because it provided an environment for the growth of bacteria that in turn caused deadly infections in humans. The Scythians did not know how this happened; all they really knew was that arrows tipped with their rotting mixture did not have to hit a vital organ in order to kill an enemy soldier. The slightest wound was enough because either an infection from the bacteria, which led to gangrene or tetanus, or the effects of the snake venom the arrow carried eventually caused death.[2] And that made these arrows far more deadly than ordinary arrows, which had to be more perfectly aimed to achieve the same results.

Today, a Scythian poisoned arrow, even though technically a biological weapon, would not qualify as a weapon of mass destruction. Nor would primitive forms of chemical weapons qualify, which were also used in ancient times, such as when the Spartans used sulfur and other materials to create poisonous smoke during the Peloponnesian War (431–404 B.C.E.). WMD in the hands of many nations today—whether they are nuclear, biological, or chemical—are the products of modern science. They are infinitely more lethal than anything ancient warriors had and capable of causing death on a terrifying mass scale. As such, their very existence makes them a threat to every nation on Earth. Even worse, some WMD already are in the hands of countries, such as North Korea, Iran, or Pakistan, that threaten international stability. There is also the danger that international terrorist groups such as al-Qaeda might acquire these weapons or, in the case of nuclear weapons, the materials needed to make a weapon. It therefore is vital for each of us to understand what these weapons are, how they work, how to find out who has them, how to prevent their spread, what can be done to prevent their use, and how to defend against them. It also is important to understand the serious health and environmental problems involved in destroying these weapons. Our future in many ways depends on how we cope with the challenges WMD pose.

WHAT ARE WEAPONS OF MASS DESTRUCTION?

The premier weapons of mass destruction are nuclear weapons. They either split or fuse atoms to release enormous amounts of energy that cause explosions of catastrophic dimensions, explosions far more powerful than can be achieved by conventional means using chemical reactions. Chemical and biological weapons constitute the second tier of WMD. They use chemical or biological substances to poison people. In either case, the ability of a small arsenal of these weapons to kill vast numbers of people distinguishes them from conventional weapons.

Conventional modern weapons such as guns, artillery, bombs, and other explosives can, and have, caused mass destruction in terms of both physical property and human casualties, especially during the wars of the 20th century. For example, the losses on both sides during World War I (1914–18)—in single, drawn-out battles that lasted for months—reached the hundreds of thousands as huge armies fought each other from opposing lines of trenches, battering each other with artillery and shooting each other to pieces with machine guns. Thus, in February 1916, the Germans began the Battle of Verdun against the French with a bombardment from 1,400 artillery pieces along an eight-mile front that lasted for 12 hours. The battle that followed lasted almost until the end of the year. By the time it was over, the two sides had suffered a combined total of about 750,000 casualties, one-third of them deaths. Even worse was the horrific First Battle of the Somme, fought from July through November 1916 between the British and French on one side and the Germans on the other. On the *first day* of their infantry assault against the German lines, charging into a storm of machine-gun fire, the British lost almost 20,000 dead and another 40,000 wounded, making that July 1 the bloodiest day in British military history. By the time the fighting along the Somme River had ended, the British, French, and German armies had lost more than 1.2 million men, about a third of them dead. During World War II (1939–45), the British and American air forces bombed German and Japanese cities in an effort to disrupt industrial production and their overall war effort and thereby shorten the war. Hundreds of bombers took part in individual attacks, some of which killed thousands of people, and in several cases tens of thousands, in a single day. Those raids also leveled large parts of those cities.

Weapons of mass destruction are different from conventional weapons in that this level of damage can be achieved, at least in the case of nuclear weapons, with just a single weapon and quite literally in an instant. In the cases of chemical and biological weapons, more than one weapon and more time would be required, but the number of weapons would still be small and the attack would be over quickly in comparison to the enormous number of conventional weapons used and the duration of the battles in which they were used during World War I and World War II.

The second key point about weapons of mass destruction is that they fall into two subcategories: nuclear weapons on the one hand and chemical and biological weapons on the other. Or, as Allison Macfarlane, a specialist on

WMD, expressed it in the title of an article, "All Weapons of Mass Destruction Are Not Equal."[3] Nuclear weapons are far more destructive and certain as killers than either biological or chemical weapons. A single nuclear bomb based on World War II–era technology could wipe out an entire city, and modern nuclear weapons are many times more powerful than what was available six or seven decades ago. There also are extremely accurate and reliable methods for delivering nuclear weapons to their targets. Indeed, the first time the U.S. government ever used the term *weapons of mass destruction* in an official policy document, in 1950 in a top-secret document issued by the National Security Council (NSC), it was in reference to nuclear weapons. The broader context was the threat posed by the Soviet Union's development of those weapons and its first test of an atomic bomb.[4]

This is not the case with biological and chemical weapons. Even the most deadly chemical weapons do not come close to nuclear weapons in killing potential. On top of that, effectively delivering them to their target can depend on factors, such as the weather, an attacker cannot control. Biological weapons are potentially many times more deadly than chemical weapons. However, the complicating factors involved in their use, from the climatic conditions at the time of attack to the length of time it takes them to become effective, make them less suitable as battlefield weapons than chemical weapons. In addition, while nuclear weapons, like bombs and other explosives, destroy buildings and all types of infrastructure, chemical and biological weapons do not. It therefore is possible to defend against chemical and biological weapons with gas masks, protective clothing, shelters, rapid response by public health personnel, and decontamination procedures. Biological weapons also can be countered or limited in their impact by vaccination campaigns.

In dealing with chemical and biological weapons, it is also essential to understand the difference between what are called agents and actual weapons. Biological and chemical agents are the toxic materials that go into weapons. Agents are what distinguish one type of chemical or biological weapon from another. Chemical or biological agents do not become weapons until they have been weaponized, that is, placed in some kind of device that allows them to be delivered to the target population. That can be a bomb, artillery shell, a machine that disperses the agent, or some other device. In a sense, the same applies to nuclear weapons. Every nuclear weapon has two parts: the atomic warhead, bomb, or artillery shell that actually causes damage when it detonates, and the airplane, missile, or artillery piece—in other words some kind of machine—that delivers the explosive component to its target. The airplane or a missile is referred to as a delivery vehicle.

CHEMICAL WEAPONS

There is no single definition of what exactly constitutes a chemical weapon. That is because not all experts and institutions concerned with the issue agree on the definition of a chemical agent, which is the material that is used to make chemical weapons. The North Atlantic Treaty Organization (NATO), a defensive military alliance the United States was instrumental in founding in 1949, defines a chemical agent as a "chemical substance which is intended for use in military operations to kill, seriously injure, or incapacitate people because of its physiological effects."[5] NATO specifically excludes from this category "riot control agents, herbicides, smoke, and flame." This volume will follow the NATO definition. Some chemicals are explosives and therefore used to make conventional weapons. The difference between these chemicals and chemical agents is that chemical weapons do not use explosions but rather the poisonous qualities of their chemical agents to kill or incapacitate. Chemical weapons are not the only weapons that kill and maim by means of poison. Biological weapons do the same thing. The difference between chemical and biological weapons is that the agents used to make the former are created by human beings in laboratories while agents used to make the latter are organisms that exist in nature or poisons produced by those organisms.

Chemical Agents

There are four main types of chemical agents, defined according to how they do their damage: choking agents, blistering agents, blood gasses, and nerve gasses. All are combinations of two or more substances called precursors and can be gasses, liquids, or solids. Chemical weapons can be directed against a target population by a range of methods. They can be sprayed as aerosols, spread by explosive devices, or just be allowed to evaporate naturally. They can also be dumped into water supplies. Spraying can be done by agricultural sprayers, crop dusters, or special tanks attached to aircraft. Airplanes or missiles can deliver explosive bombs or warheads. Chemical weapons do their damage when they are absorbed into the body through the skin, by the respiratory tract, by the eyes, through a wound, or in some other way.[6]

CHOKING AGENTS

Choking agents, also called lung-damaging agents, damage tissue in the lungs, making it impossible to breathe and ultimately causing suffocation. They are gasses that must be inhaled in order to take effect. Two of the best-known choking agents, and the ones with the longest history, are chlorine and phosgene. Both gasses were used during World War I. Because they are heavier than air, they sink to ground level, which is why during that war they were effective against soldiers in trenches or foxholes. Once choking agents are inhaled, they cause a fluid buildup in the lungs so that the victim suffocates by drowning.

BLISTERING AGENTS

A second category of chemical agents are blistering agents, whose use also dates from World War I. Blistering agents, except in very large doses, usually do not cause death. Rather, they incapacitate enemy soldiers by causing extremely painful injuries. They burn and cause large watery blisters on any part of the body they contact. The skin, eyes, mucous membranes, lungs, and blood-forming organs are all vulnerable to blistering agents. They can damage the respiratory tract if inhaled and cause vomiting and diarrhea when swallowed. Mustard gas, which was used extensively during World War I, is the best-known blistering agent. Blistering agents can be spread as aerosols, liquids, or vapors. They also can be thickened so that they contaminate ships, aircraft, and other equipment for extended periods of time.

BLOOD AGENTS

Blood agents kill by interfering with the ability of red blood cells to transmit oxygen from the lungs to other parts of the body. The gas hydrogen cyanide, a blood agent occasionally used in World War I, has the most horrible history by far of any chemical weapon and, for that matter, of any weapon of mass destruction. It alone has killed millions of people, although not as a weapon of war and not on a battlefield. Between World War I and World War II, German scientists working for the I. G. Farben chemical company developed a formulation of hydrogen cyanide in which the poison, combined with a stabilizer, could be kept in solid form by being impregnated into small earthen pellets. As long as the pellets were kept in sealed containers and not exposed to air, the hydrogen cyanide would not escape and therefore could be safely stored. Before World War II, this formulation, known as Zyklon B, was used commercially as a pesticide to kill rodents in buildings and ships. During World War II, however, Germany's Nazi regime found another, indescribably evil use for Zyklon B: It was the poison used to murder millions of Jews in gas chambers at Auschwitz and other death camps during the Holocaust. A weapon of war during World War I, hydrogen cyanide killed thousands of times more people during World War II as an agent of genocide.

NERVE AGENTS

Nerve agents constitute the most recently developed category of chemical weapons, and the most deadly. All of them are liquids. They block an enzyme essential to the working of the central nervous system, eventually causing death. Nerve agents were first discovered and produced in Germany during the 1930s by scientists working on the development of insecticides. The first nerve agent, called tabun and developed in 1936, was many times more powerful than any of the chemical weapons used during World War I.[7] Sarin, developed two years later, was five times more deadly than tabun; a single droplet the size of a pinprick could kill a human. A third agent, soman, developed in 1944, was more lethal still. Of these agents, during World War II only tabun actually was weaponized. About 2,000 tons of tabun, out of 12,000 produced, were put into artillery shells, rockets, and bombs. Fortunately, these weapons were never used, most likely because the leaders of Nazi Germany feared how the Allies might retaliate if they were the first to use chemical weapons. Tabun, sarin, and soman all are classified as G-agents (respectively: GA, GB, and GD), in contrast to even more lethal nerve agents—V-agents—developed after World War II. The V-agents were discovered originally by British scientists, but they later were developed and produced by both the Soviet Union and the United States. More than 50 V-series agents were developed by the United States alone, although the U.S. government ultimately decided to focus on the version called VX. When inhaled, VX is three times more toxic than sarin; when absorbed through the skin, VX is 1,000 times more toxic than sarin. A Soviet version of VX called R-33 is more deadly and less treatable than VX.[8]

BIOLOGICAL WEAPONS

Biological weapons are used to infect large numbers of people with deadly or debilitating germs and cause epidemics. These weapons are made from naturally occurring pathogenic microorganisms, that is, organisms that cause disease. These agents make biological weapons unique because they can be used to cause casualties over a wide area without the need to move large amounts of equipment and do so in ways that are extremely difficult to trace. Because biological weapons do not cause immediate visible damage—the diseases they cause must incubate for days or weeks before symptoms appear—by the time they are discovered the attackers can easily have made their escape. And once biological weapons have started to act on a target population, they spread the damage they do on their own because, as with any disease, people who have been infected can infect others. As the military specialist Robert Hutchinson has put it, biological weapons do their terrible work "silent and unseen."[9]

These advantages have a corollary that distinguishes biological weapons from other WMD: Because they do not have an immediate effect on the people they target, biological weapons are not suited for the battlefield. Their real effective use is against civilian populations. While biological agents obviously exist in nature, it takes a modern laboratory to grow enough of them to produce weapons and prepare them so they have the strength necessary to fulfill their intended purpose. One of the main problems in weaponizing biological agents is that as living creatures they can die or weaken—lose their ability to do damage—outside the lab. They must be kept alive and sufficiently virulent from the time they are produced until the time they actually are used.

Biological Agents

Although there is no agreement on how many different types of organisms actually are biological weapons agents, four types of organisms lead the list of microbes that have or can be used to produce biological weapons: bacteria, viruses, rickettsiae, and toxins.

BACTERIA

Bacteria are microscopic single-cell organisms. Although some are poisonous, they are essential to life; none of us could survive without the bacteria in our bodies or in the world around us. Bacteria have been around for billions of years and in fact were the earliest form of life on Earth. Some bacteria are extremely durable. As a group, they can survive extreme conditions from subfreezing to above the boiling point of water and make use of a huge variety of substances to get the energy they need to live. Poisonous bacteria do their damage either on their own or by producing substances called toxins, which sicken or kill the host organism. Among the bacteria that can be used to make biological weapons are those that cause deadly diseases such as anthrax, cholera, bubonic plague, and tularemia. The bubonic plague has been responsible for some of the worst epidemics—called pandemics because they killed so many people—in history, including the epidemic known as the Black Death that killed one-third of the population of Europe during the 14th and 15th centuries. Today, diseases caused by bacteria often can be treated with antibiotics.

VIRUSES

Viruses are considered biological agents even though they technically are not living creatures. Instead, they are collections of genetic material that require a living host cell in order to reproduce. Viruses are much smaller than bacteria, and the diseases they produce usually do not respond to antibiotics. The common cold is caused by viruses. Far more ominously, so are deadly diseases such as smallpox, Ebola, yellow fever, and Venezuelan equine encephalitis. Smallpox, one of the most deadly human diseases, finally was eradicated about 30 years ago. The last known case occurred in Africa in

1977. During the 20th century alone, smallpox is estimated to have killed about 500 million people.[10]

RICKETTSIAE

If viruses are at the boundary between the living and nonliving, rickettsiae have characteristics of both viruses and bacteria. While ranging in size between the two, over all rickettsiae are similar to bacteria; however, like viruses they can only reproduce inside other living cells. Rickettsiae cause diseases such as typhus, Q fever, and Rocky Mountain fever. As with bacterial diseases, illnesses caused by rickettsiae often can be treated with antibiotics.

TOXINS

Toxins are poisons produced by living organisms such as bacteria, fungi, or plants rather than living organisms themselves. Some toxin molecules contain protein, but others do not. Toxins cannot reproduce and therefore cannot spread like bacteria, viruses, or rickettsiae. Making matters even more complicated, some toxins can be produced by chemical processes. Probably the best-known and most feared disease caused by toxins is botulism, which is found on poorly preserved food.

Categories of Threat

Each category of agents mentioned above contains organisms of varying danger. That is why the U.S. Centers for Disease Control and Prevention (CDC) has grouped the different biological agents, irrespective of what type or organism each is, into three categories of threat. Category A contains the most dangerous current agents, "high-priority agents that pose a risk to national security" because they can be easily transmitted from person to person, have high mortality rates, could cause a public panic, and require special preparation by public health officials. They include the agents that cause anthrax (bacteria), bubonic plague (bacteria), smallpox (virus), Ebola (virus), and botulism (toxin). Category B agents are "moderately easy to disseminate," have moderate or low mortality rates, and require increases in the CDC's ability in detection and diagnosis. Category B includes the agents that cause typhus (rickettsiae), Q fever (rickettsiae), and the toxin ricin. Category C agents are "emerging pathogens" with potentially high mortality rates that might be developed in the future.[11] One of these new threats is called the Nipah virus, which was first identified in 1999 after causing a number of deaths in Malaysia.[12]

NUCLEAR WEAPONS

Primitive forms of chemical and biological weapons have existed since ancient times and were used throughout the history of warfare before the

20th century. This is not true of nuclear weapons. They are strictly the product of discoveries in atomic physics made in the 20th century, and they could not be built without modern engineering and manufacturing techniques that first became available in the mid-1940s. The atomic bomb was developed during World War II by the United States because it believed that Nazi Germany was building nuclear weapons. The Manhattan Project, as the effort was called, was a project with the very highest priority at a time of many competing needs. Germany surrendered before the atomic bomb was ready, but the weapon was used nonetheless on two occasions three days apart in August 1945 to force Japan's unconditional surrender and finally end the most devastating war in human history. Since being used on August 6 against Hiroshima and August 9 against Nagasaki—and bringing about Japan's surrender on August 14—atomic weapons have never again been used in war.

Nuclear weapons, like conventional bombs, do their damage by exploding; all nuclear weapons, regardless of how they are delivered to their target, are in fact bombs. The difference between a conventional bomb and a nuclear bomb is that explosions in conventional bombs are caused by rapid chemical reactions while explosions in nuclear bombs are caused by atomic reactions. Because atomic reactions yield vastly greater amounts of energy than chemical reactions, nuclear bombs, per unit of material, produce explosions thousands, or even millions, of times more powerful than conventional bombs. In addition, because nuclear explosions cause radioactive fallout that is dangerous to all life, nuclear explosions continue to kill and maim for years after they take place.

Fission and Fusion

There are two basic processes that cause nuclear explosions: fission and fusion. They are opposites, as fission is when a single atom is split and fusion is when two atoms are combined into one. Fission bombs commonly are called atomic bombs; fusion bombs are called thermonuclear or hydrogen bombs.

In order for fission to occur, a nucleus of an atom must absorb a neutron from outside, become unstable, and split into two smaller parts. This process releases a great deal of energy, as well as more neutrons that can cause other atoms to split. If enough neutrons are absorbed by other nuclei so that more fissions occur, the result is a continuing process called a chain reaction. If the mass and density of fissionable nuclei are enough, an explosion will occur.

All this is much easier said than done, as only a few elements are fissile; that is, only a few types of atoms, after being bombarded by slow-moving neutrons, fission readily and give off enough neutrons to cause further fission and therefore sustain a chain reaction. One is uranium, the heaviest naturally occurring element, and another is plutonium, an element that aside from a few minute traces does not exist in nature and therefore must be artificially produced in a complex device called an atomic reactor. However, not all the isotopes of these two elements are fissile and can sustain a chain reaction. In fact, U-238, the isotope that makes up more than 99 percent of all naturally occurring uranium, does not meet that standard. Of all naturally occurring uranium, only the isotope U-235, which accounts for less than 1 percent (about .7 percent) of the total, is fissile and therefore suitable for building an atomic bomb. Although U-238 cannot sustain a chain reaction, it can be converted in an atomic reactor to the artificial element plutonium 239 (Pu-239), which like U-235 is fissile. Finally, it takes a certain amount of U-235 or Pu-239—which must be sufficiently pure and dense, have the correct shape, and meet other precise specifications—to cause an explosive chain reaction. This required amount of fissile material under the required conditions is called a supercritical mass. Small amounts of other fissile isotopes of plutonium or artificially created uranium sometimes are used to make nuclear bombs. The exact amount of fissile material needed in turn depends on complex technical factors.[13]

Fusion produces even more energy than fission. For example, while the power of the largest fission bombs is measured in kilotons, or thousands of tons of TNT, fusion bombs have been built and tested whose power was measured in megatons, or millions of tons of TNT.[14] Light atoms must be used to produce fusion. In order to fuse their nuclei, immense heat is needed, which can only be achieved by means of a fission explosion. Fusion bombs therefore involve both fission—to create the necessary conditions for fusion—and fusion itself. The power of the bomb comes from both types of reaction. Two isotopes of hydrogen—deuterium (H-2) and tritium (H-3)—are used in fusion bombs. They are gasses in nature that must be compressed at very high temperatures to produce fusion.

Materials for an Atomic (Fission) Bomb

Before an atomic bomb can be built, it is necessary to produce enough fissile material to make it work. This was a major challenge during World War II, when the first atomic bombs were developed, and it remains a significant obstacle today. In fact, it is the most technically difficult part of the overall process of building an atomic bomb and the single most important factor that keeps terrorists from building one. Terrorist organizations do not control the industrial infrastructure or have the scientific skills necessary to produce fissile material. Basically, producing fissile material means producing relatively pure U-235 from uranium ore that is about 99 percent U-238 or artificially creating relatively pure Pu-239.

The process separating U-235 from U-238 so that the U-235 is sufficiently pure for use in an atomic bomb is called enrichment. The purer the U-235, the less is needed to build a bomb. During World War II, the United States used a process called electromagnetic isotope separation, but it was abandoned after the war because it was so energy intensive. Currently, there are two main methods, both of which originated in the U.S. wartime nuclear bomb program, used to enrich U-235: gaseous diffusion and a process using machines called centrifuges. Both separate lighter U-235 gas from slightly heavier U-238 gas. However, the centrifuge process is more efficient and economical and is gradually displacing the gas diffusion process. Gas centrifuges look relatively simple when viewed as a diagram, but they are very difficult to build and operate successfully. Manufacturing them requires special high-tech metal alloys, and they must be perfectly balanced because they spin at such high speeds. Thousands of centrifuges must operate together in what are called cascades to produce usable amounts of enriched U-235. Once the uranium gas has the desired percentage of U-235, it is passed through a series of compressors and put into special containers. The gas is then cooled until it solidifies on the walls of these containers. It takes U-235 enriched to at least 20 percent to make a nuclear weapon, but U-235 used for this purpose normally is enriched to at least 85 to 90 percent. Uranium that has been enriched to 20 percent U-235 is called highly enriched uranium (HEU). Uranium that has been enriched to 85 or 90 percent U-235 is called weapons-grade uranium. In the United States, weapons-grade uranium must be at least 93 percent U-235. These grades of uranium are very different from low-enriched uranium (LEU), which is used for peaceful purposes in research reactors or in civilian power plants. While some low-enriched uranium used in research reactors can be from 12 to almost 20 percent U-235, the material used in civilian reactors to produce power is about 3.5 percent U-235. Methods of enrichment using lasers that are more efficient and produce less waste than the current processes are being developed.[15]

Plutonium is easier to produce than highly enriched U-235. Plutonium is created when U-238 captures one or more neutrons and thus is transformed into Pu-239, one of 15 isotopes of plutonium. This transformation occurs in nuclear reactors, but the creation of Pu-239 is only the beginning of the process of producing a material that can be used in an atomic bomb. The plutonium produced in a reactor must be separated from other waste products, many of which are highly radioactive and extremely dangerous. This process begins by removing the used-up—or spent—nuclear fuel from the reactor. This fuel is in the shape of long rods. These fuel rods are sent to a reprocessing plant, where they are chopped into small pieces. Then a series of chemical processes separates the plutonium from the fuel rod casings and other waste products. This is done under strict safety procedures that include the use of heavy lead shielding. The plutonium is then reduced to metal form, at which point it is ready to be used in a nuclear bomb.[16]

Two Types of Fission Bombs

There are two types of fission bombs, both of which were developed by the Manhattan Project: the so-called gun-type bomb and the implosion bomb. These terms refer to how the bombs cause a chain reaction in their nuclear material, and thereby an explosion. There are two types of fission bombs because of an important difference in how U-235 and plutonium behave. In a gun-triggered bomb, a small amount of U-235 is literally shot by a gunlike device down a tube into a larger mass of subcritical U-235. When that happens, the subcritical mass becomes supercritical, a fission reaction begins, and the bomb explodes. This was the type of bomb used at Hiroshima.

However, this process does not work for plutonium, a fact that was not known to scientists working on the first atomic bomb until 1944. This is because of what scientists call spontaneous fission, the tendency of atoms to fission on their own—although not nearly fast enough to cause a chain reaction—without outside intervention. As the historian Richard Rhodes describes it, because of plutonium's rate of spontaneous fission, in a gun-type bomb "the plutonium bullet and target would melt down and fizzle before the two parts had time to join."[17] In other words, the effort to bring two pieces of plutonium together would not produce a supercritical mass, and therefore no explosion. The problem of spontaneous fission arises not because of Pu-239 but because of the isotope Pu-240; both of these isotopes are formed in atomic reactors, and for a variety of reasons separating them is not a practical option. Therefore, in order to create a supercritical mass of plutonium, a given quantity of that element that is subcritical must be compressed extremely rapidly in what is called an implosion. In an atomic bomb a sphere of plutonium is imploded using high explosives. The explosives must be perfectly calibrated to create an inward-directed shock wave that compresses the subcritical mass of plutonium to the point where it becomes so dense that it reaches a supercritical mass, at which point a nuclear explosion takes place.[18] The type of fission bomb that uses this method is called an implosion-type bomb. It involves a much more complicated design than a gun-type bomb. During the Manhattan Project, scientists, confident their design would work the first time, decided they did not need to test their uranium gun-type bomb before using it in combat; they did have to test their plutonium implosion bomb. That test, on July 16, 1945, at the Alamogordo bombing range in New Mexico, was the first atomic explosion in history. It produced an explosion that measured about 18 kilotons, equal to the power of 18,000 tons of TNT. A plutonium implosion bomb of similar size was dropped on Nagasaki.

Fusion Bombs

Fusion, or thermonuclear, bombs are both far more powerful and considerably more complicated and difficult to build than fission weapons. Aside from the nuclear materials they contain, they also are made up of thousands of non-nuclear parts: batteries, cables, capacitors, detonators, fuses, and the like. The first thermonuclear device ever tested—it weighed more than 60 tons and was much too large to be a deliverable bomb—exploded with the power of 10 million tons of TNT. In other words, it was more than 500 times stronger than the first fission bomb test and more than 800 times more powerful than the bomb that destroyed Hiroshima. The entire coral island in the Pacific Ocean on which the test took place literally disappeared. Shortly after that test took place, a worried U.S. president Dwight D. Eisenhower, who had been the supreme commander of all Allied forces in Europe during World War II, stated, "War no longer has any logic whatsoever."[19] By that he meant a war in which thermonuclear weapons were used would destroy everyone involved and most likely all civilized life on Earth. The most powerful explosion ever produced by human beings was a Soviet test of a nuclear device in 1961. It had the power of 58 million tons of TNT (58 megatons). That made it almost 5,000 times as powerful as the atomic bomb that destroyed the city of Hiroshima with a force of 12 kilotons in August 1945.

Fusion bombs actually involve two sets of virtually simultaneous nuclear explosions in two separate parts of the bomb.[20] That is why they are called two-stage thermonuclear weapons. The first set of events takes place in the spherical top part of the bomb known as the shell. As in a plutonium fission bomb, conventional explosions implode a subcritical mass of Pu-239 to a supercritical state and create a fission explosion. In order to make a thermonuclear bomb work and ignite the next stage, this explosion must be boosted by the presence of hydrogen gas consisting of both deuterium and tritium isotopes. This happens when the fission explosion of Pu-239 causes the deuterium and tritium stored in the shell to undergo fusion, which in turn releases energy in the form of high-energy neutrons and thereby causes further fissioning of Pu-239. This complex combination of events is called the primary explosion.

The main part of the bomb is a cylinder known as the secondary. It contains a hollow rod of Pu-239 or U-235 called the spark plug. The rod is surrounded by a substance called lithium deuteride, which is actually deuterium that has been put into solid form by chemically combining it with the silvery metallic element lithium. This is the main fuel of the fusion bomb. The tritium necessary for the secondary to produce a fusion explosion is produced when neutrons from the primary explosion are absorbed by the lithium atoms, which then emit a helium nucleus. The lithium deuteride in turn is surrounded by a casing of U-238. At the top of the cylinder is a shield, also made of U-238, which prevents the lithium deuteride from becoming heated prematurely after the primary explosion.

The primary fission explosion in the shell generates the heat, pressure, and high-energy neutrons necessary to cause a fusion reaction in the secondary. The fission explosion compresses the lithium deuteride, in turn causing the plutonium or uranium spark plug to reach a supercritical mass and fission, which in turn heats the lithium deuteride from the inside so that fusion begins. In this environment of superheat and super-pressure, the U-238 casing also fissions, releasing yet more energy and increasing the explosive power of the bomb. At the point where the bomb explodes, called the hypocenter, temperatures reach hundreds of millions of degrees.

Neutron Bombs and Radiological Weapons

Most of the energy from nuclear explosions, whether from fission or fusion reactions, is released in the form of a blast—or shock wave—and heat. The shock wave and heat kill people and destroy physical objects such as buildings or bridges much like conventional weapons, only on an exponentially greater scale. However, nuclear explosions also emit about 15 percent of their energy in the form of radiation. Some of the radiation is emitted at the time of the explosion in the form of gamma rays and neutrons. The rest comes somewhat later from objects that are made radioactive by the effect of the nuclear explosion. Either way, radiation is harmful to humans and other forms of life and will sicken and kill people for days, weeks, months, and even years after the explosion itself. This is what happened in the wake of the explosions at Hiroshima and Nagasaki.[21]

The exception to this is a so-called enhanced radiation weapon (ERW), or neutron bomb. It is a very small thermonuclear weapon that has been engineered to release about half of its energy in the form of radiation, mainly neutrons. Because of its small size and the low proportion of energy it releases in the form of blast and heat, the neutron bomb causes damage to houses and other structures only within a radius of a few hundred yards from where it explodes. In fact, even the danger from radiation is limited to a small area. This means a neutron bomb could be used against tanks and infantry but would not damage nearby cities and towns where civilians lived.[22] During the cold war, the United States developed the neutron bomb to counter the enormous advantage the Soviet Union and its allies had in Europe in terms of conventional armored forces. Its purpose was to stop Soviet conventional forces without killing nearby civilians and destroying the territory the United States and its NATO allies were trying to protect.

In military doctrine, a neutron bomb is considered a tactical weapon, which means it is a smaller weapon with limited destructive power designed for battlefield use. In that sense, it can be argued that a neutron bomb is not a weapon of mass destruction, although since a neutron bomb is a fusion weapon the opposite can be argued as well. Most nuclear weapons, precisely because they are designed to cause destruction on a mass scale, are known as strategic weapons. However, in many cases strategic weapons are defined more narrowly. This is the case in international treaties involving the United States and the Soviet Union (after 1991, Russia). Those treaties have defined strategic nuclear weapons as weapons that can reach their targets more than 3,440 miles (5,500 km) away from the country that uses them.

At the other end of the technological spectrum, a radiological weapon, or "dirty bomb," is not a nuclear weapon but uses radioactive materials to do its damage. A dirty bomb is a conventional explosive combined with radioactive material. When the bomb explodes, it spreads the radioactive material, contaminating any area that material manages to reach. Dirty bombs can be fearsome and spread terror and are therefore potentially weapons of choice for terrorist groups since they do not involve complicated technology. However, the damage they can do is limited and falls far short of what is considered mass destruction. The good news, at least up until now, is that the materials that would make a dirty bomb most effective, such as spent nuclear fuel from an atomic reactor, are precisely the materials that are most difficult for terrorists to buy or steal. At the same time, it also is possible for terrorists to turn nuclear reactors or spent-fuel storage facilities into radiological weapons by attacking those facilities and blowing them up. That is one reason security at these facilities is so vital.[23]

IMPACT OF A NUCLEAR BOMB: IF A NUCLEAR BOMB HIT NEW YORK

What would happen if an atomic bomb exploded in New York City? The full extent of the loss of life and destruction would depend on many factors, including the size and type of the bomb, the altitude at which the bomb detonated, and the time of day. The actual results are therefore very difficult to predict. No matter what, however, the results would be catastrophic, as the following possible scenario suggests. A 150-kiloton bomb—more than a dozen times as powerful as the bomb dropped on Hiroshima but small by current standards—is detonated by terrorists at noon on a clear day at the base of the Empire State Building in Manhattan, the most densely populated of New York City's five boroughs. Manhattan is a long, narrow island with an area of about 24 square miles and a population of about 1.5 million people. (New York City is home to about 8 million people.) Within one second, the shock wave and intense heat from the explosion will have killed everyone within a distance of four-tenths of a mile in every direction from ground zero, or more than 75,000 people. The Empire State Building and every major building within that zone will be reduced to rubble. Within four seconds, as the shock wave and heat spread in all directions, the impact area of the explosion will be as wide as Manhattan at its widest point (about 2 miles), and about an additional 300,000 people will be dead. Within several more seconds, the damage will extend to the boroughs of Brooklyn and Queens on Long Island on the far side of the East River and to New Jersey on the west bank of the Hudson River. By then, most of Manhattan will be without utilities. As rescue efforts begin, all surviving hospitals and other medical facilities will be overwhelmed with severely injured people. Access to or exit from the island via the tunnels and bridges that survived the explosion will be limited, as they will be damaged and partially blocked. People will die from their injuries and from the effects of radioactive fallout. According to this scenario, the final toll will be about 800,000 dead, 900,000 injured, and significant property destruction within an area of 20 square miles. The city will take years to recover. All this is only a possible scenario, but it is a likely one.[24]

WMD USE IN WARFARE THROUGH WORLD WAR II

Before the Twentieth Century

The Scythians and Spartans were not the only groups to use biological or chemical agents in warfare before the development of modern WMD. There are many reports before the 20th century of similar attempts in many parts of the world. During the sixth century B.C.E., the Assyrians, the most powerful military power in the Middle East, attempted to use a plant disease called rye ergot to poison the wells of their enemies. China's Song dynasty (960–1279) used arsenic smoke against enemy forces. In one of the more notorious examples of premodern biological warfare, Mongols besieging the city of Caffa (modern Feodosiya, Ukraine) on the shores of the Black Sea in 1346 used catapults to hurl corpses infected with the deadly bubonic plague over the city walls. Not only was the city forced to surrender after an epidemic broke out, but people fleeing the city who reached Italy may have contributed to the plague pandemic that swept across much of continental Europe in the decades that followed. Russian forces attacking the Swedish-held town of Revel on the shores of the Baltic Sea may have used a similar tactic in 1710. In another notorious incident, British forces fighting a Native American rebellion in western Pennsylvania gave infected blankets that had been used by smallpox patients to their adversaries during truce negotiations. The impact of this effort is uncertain since the smallpox epidemic that ravaged the local Native American population in 1763 and 1764 probably began several months earlier. Other Native Americans may have used a similar tactic against British forces five decades earlier by poisoning the British water supply with dead animals. British forces may also have attempted to spread smallpox to American troops during the Battle of Yorktown at the close of the Revolutionary War.[25]

World War I

Early in the evening of April 22, 1915, French soldiers in their trenches near the small town of Ypres saw something strange moving toward them from the German lines. It was not what they might have expected eight months into World War I, by which time the fighting along what was called the western front had reached a stalemate along opposing lines of trenches that extended across northern France from the Swiss border to the North Sea. Rather than an artillery barrage or an attack by infantry troops, French troops saw a green cloud close to the ground. They had no idea what it was until it was too late. The cloud was chlorine gas, which had been released from more than 5,700 cylinders positioned in front of the German trenches as the wind began to blow from the north toward the French lines. More than 160 tons of the highly poisonous gas were released, with devastating effect. As the cloud enveloped the French trenches, men everywhere suddenly gasped for breath, shook with violent spasms, and collapsed. They had breathed in the chlorine gas, and it was destroying their lungs. More than 600 soldiers died horrible deaths, and many more suffered debilitating injuries.[26]

The Ypres attack marked the first large-scale use of modern chemical weapons in history and therefore the first use of weapons of mass destruction. The British and French soon retaliated, the first British attack using chlorine coming in late September 1915. The use of poison gas quickly escalated. In December 1915, the Germans fired artillery shells filled with phosgene, a poison 18 times more deadly than chlorine; the French retaliated with the same gas in February 1916. In July 1917, the Germans used mustard gas for the first time, delivering it inside artillery shells in fighting that once again took place at Ypres. That attack caused 20,000 casualties, and by the end of the war mustard gas had caused 400,000 casualties. Both sides used mustard gas, which became known as the king of war gasses and was the most feared chemical agent in the World War I arsenals. American soldiers sent to fight in Europe after the United States entered the war on the Allied side in April 1917 were unprepared for the horrors of gas warfare. They had to count on gas masks provided by the British and French. By the end of the war, the major powers had fired about 125,000 tons of poison gas at each other, most of which was delivered by 66 million artillery shells. Thirty-nine different agents were used. This deadly rain of gas killed 90,000 soldiers and injured 10 times that number. Almost half of the casualties and more than half of the deaths were Russian soldiers fighting against Germany on the war's eastern front. Although the Russians also used poison gas during the war, their soldiers were especially vulnerable because they had neither the equipment nor training they needed to protect themselves. Chemical weapons accounted for a quarter of all American casualties in the war but were responsible for only about 2 percent of the deaths.[27]

Immediately after the war, the British used poison gas against the Bolshevik forces during their intervention in the Russian civil war. The Bolsheviks meanwhile used poison gas against peasant rebels fighting their dictatorial regime.[28]

Chemical and Biological Weapons from the 1920s through World War II

After World War I, all of the major powers maintained an interest in chemical or biological weapons. France kept a stockpile of mustard gas and phosgene and for several years during the 1920s and again in the 1930s investigated biological weapons. Britain did the same, while the United States maintained its Chemical Warfare Service, originally set up in June 1918, which in 1920 became a specialized branch of the U.S. Army.[29] Germany and Japan put significantly greater resources into WMD. After its defeat in World War I, Germany had been forbidden by the Treaty of Versailles of 1919 from importing or manufacturing chemical weapons. It got around that ban several years later by reaching a secret agreement with the Soviet Union under which the two countries cooperated in developing a range of weapons, including chemical weapons. The work on these weapons was done deep inside the Soviet Union, far away from prying Western eyes. After Adolf Hitler and the Nazi Party came to power in 1933, Germany ended its cooperation with the Soviet Union and developed the world's most deadly chemical weapons at home.

In 1936, German scientists developed tabun and in 1938 sarin. Meanwhile, in the Far East, Japan began a major chemical weapons program in 1921; 10 years later it began a biological weapons program.[30]

At the same time, there was a renewed effort to control the use of WMD. The first international attempt to control WMD was the Hague Convention of 1899. This agreement banned the use of "poison or poisoned weapons." A separate document signed at the time, the Hague Declaration, banned the use of "projectiles" whose sole purpose was "the diffusion of asphyxiating or deleterious gasses." A Second Hague Convention in 1907 reaffirmed these pledges. Unfortunately, that is all they were since these agreements had no enforcement mechanisms. All the major European powers that subsequently used chemical weapons during World War I were parties to these agreements. The postwar effort to control WMD rested on the Geneva Protocol for the Prohibition of the Use in War of Asphyxiating, Poisonous or Other Gasses, signed in 1925. Although the main focus of the Geneva Protocol was chemical weapons, it also contained a clause that extended its prohibitions to "bacteriological methods of warfare." The protocol was sponsored by the League of Nations. Over the course of the next decade, the Geneva Protocol was signed and ratified by 40 countries, including all the great powers with the exception of the United States (which signed but did not ratify the protocol) and Japan.[31]

The Geneva Protocol, which like the Hague Conventions had no enforcement procedures, did not prevent the use of poison gas in warfare or combat during the 1920s or 1930s. Spain, which bought its materials from Germany, used poison gas against rebels in Spanish Morocco during the mid-1920s, while Italy made extensive use of mustard gas in its conquest of Ethiopia in 1935 and 1936. By far the most massive use of chemical or biological WMD, however, was by Japan, which used both forms of weapons against soldiers and civilians when it invaded China in 1937. The Japanese use of these weapons continued through the end of World War II. Biological weapons were developed by the notorious Unit 731, a special unit based in the northeastern area of China known as Manchuria, which the Japanese had occupied in 1931. Unit 731 worked on bombs and other means of delivering biological agents—including releasing plague-infected fleas in populated areas—throughout the war. It also conducted horrific experiments on thousands of prisoners of war, most of them Chinese although some were Americans. At least 10,000 individuals died terrible deaths as victims of those experiments, which resembled some of the barbaric experiments with disease agents done by the Nazis in their death and concentration camps during World War II. The number of Chinese civilians and soldiers killed or maimed by Japanese chemical and biological weapons is unknown. As Sheldon Harris, one of the leading experts on Unit 731, has put it, "Even to the most dispassionate observer, the Japanese biological warfare programme seems astounding in its scale and cruelty."[32]

Japan was the only belligerent power to use biological or chemical weapons on the battlefield during World War II. Although the Germans had large supplies of the newly developed nerve gas, they did not use it in combat, most probably because of fears of how the Allies, who also had stocks of poison gas, would respond. The United States and Great Britain produced phosgene, mustard gas, and another powerful agent called lewisite, while Canada produced its own agents and also purchased some from the United States. Britain's prime minister Winston Churchill broadcast a specific warning to Germany in 1942 that the Allies would retaliate "on the largest possible scale" if the Nazis resorted to poison gas weapons. When Germany finally was defeated in 1945, the Allies, who had feared for much of the war that the Germans were building an atomic bomb, were shocked to find the enemy had developed and produced large supplies of nerve gasses far more deadly than anything in the Allied arsenal.[33] There was some talk late in the war in American military circles about using poison gas in the Pacific theater against Japanese troops, who in battle after battle refused to surrender and fought to the death at a terrible cost to American soldiers and marines. However, this idea was emphatically rejected by President Franklin D. Roosevelt, who was willing to consider using these weapons only in retaliation for Japanese first use.[34]

The Allies did not ignore biological weapons during the war. The Soviet Union continued its biological warfare program, which dated from 1926, as did the British, whose program dated from 1936. British tests during 1942 and 1943 with weaponized anthrax on an island off Scotland had to be halted after heavy storms spread anthrax spores to the mainland, where they infected dozens of local sheep and caused widespread alarm. The United States maintained a program centered at Camp Detrick in Maryland beginning in 1942.[35]

The Atomic Bomb

Many new weapons involving scientific breakthroughs were developed and deployed during World War II. However, none involved fundamentally new science or had such serious and dangerous implications for the future as the atomic bomb. As U.S. secretary of war Henry Stimson explained about six weeks before the bomb was successfully tested, its invention involved "a new relationship of man to the universe." Stimson added, "It must be controlled if possible to make it an assurance of future peace rather than a menace to civilization."[36]

The American program to build an atomic bomb was started because President Roosevelt and his top advisers feared that Nazi Germany would build such a weapon, a terrifying prospect given the murderous nature of that regime. After several years of investigating the scientific and technological challenges involved, the Manhattan Project to build an atomic bomb was organized in mid-1942. Notwithstanding daunting and unprecedented scientific and technical problems, the Manhattan Project took less than three years to fulfill its assigned task. By the summer of 1945, it had designed and built two types of atomic bomb: a gun-type bomb using enriched U-235 and an implosion bomb using plutonium.

There never was any question among America's civilian and military leaders that the atomic bomb, if it actually worked, would be used if necessary to end the war. This assumption was reinforced by the situation in the summer of 1945. Germany had surrendered on May 8 and leaders in Washington knew the American people were war weary and increasingly upset about mounting casualties their fathers, sons, and husbands were suffering in ferocious battles against Japanese troops, who in battle after battle refused to surrender and fought to the last man. All the available evidence indicated that, like Nazi Germany, Japan would fight to the bitter end. President Harry S. Truman, who came into office when Roosevelt died in April 1945, and his advisers were determined to end the war as soon as possible. They were not at all sure the atomic bomb alone could force a Japanese surrender, only that it would put considerably more pressure on the Japanese and thereby hasten the heretofore unattainable surrender. Above all, America's leaders dreaded the enormous casualties they expected their soldiers would suffer in the planned invasion of Japan, which was scheduled to take place in the fall of 1945.

The two atomic explosions that ended World War II each destroyed a huge part of a city. No one knows exactly how many people died. A reasonable guess is that almost 80,000 people died on August 6 in Hiroshima and between 25,000 and 40,000 on August 9 in Nagasaki. Tens of thousands more, possibly driving the total to 200,000 or even higher, died from radiation and burns in the aftermath of the bombings. The bombs achieved their objective: Japan announced its surrender on August 14, ending the most destructive war in human history. The new weapons also left a world living under a cloud of dread about what might happen in the future long after the mushroom clouds that covered Hiroshima and Nagasaki had dissipated.

WMD USE SINCE WORLD WAR II

Biological and Chemical Weapons

The postwar era began with a multinational effort to destroy the huge stocks of captured German chemical weapons. In the years immediately after the war, tens of thousands of tons of chemical munitions were dumped at sea by the

United States, Britain, and the Soviet Union. The United States and Britain continued this practice, disposing both of German chemical materials as well as some munitions of their own, until the early 1970s. Finally, in 1974 (United States) and 1975 (Britain), the countries signed the 1972 London Convention on the Prevention of Marine Pollution banning that practice. This dumping was done at a time when there was less concern about the environment than there is today, and some experts are worried about what might happen if these poisonous chemicals leak from their containers. According to one estimate, at present almost 500,000 tons of chemical munitions lie at the bottom of the North Sea, the Baltic Sea, the Adriatic Sea, the Atlantic Ocean, the Pacific Ocean off the coast of Japan, and in other places. Since 1946, an estimated 500 people, mainly fishermen who have brought contaminated objects to the surface in their fishing nets, have been injured by these weapons.[37]

While the Allied victory in World War II brought with it the end of the German and Japanese WMD programs, in the decades following the war both the United States and the Soviet Union continued to expand their chemical and biological weapons programs. (See "Focus on the United States" and "Global Perspectives" for details.) Canada, shortly after the war, and Britain, in the mid-1950s, abandoned them, as did France by the 1980s. At the same time, as scientific and technical knowledge spread, other countries set up chemical and biological weapons programs. Experts admit that it is extremely difficult to know which countries have biological and chemical weapons since these programs are kept secret and are relatively easy to hide. One problem is that many of the chemicals or biological agents used to make weapons also have legitimate civilian uses. They are, in other words, dual-use substances. Once they are produced for legitimate purposes, they can be diverted and secretly made into deadly weapons. The evidence suggests that after World War II at least two dozen countries set up chemical and/or biological weapons. This list includes—but is not limited to—the People's Republic of China (PRC), the Republic of China (Taiwan), Cuba, Egypt, Iran, Iraq, Israel, Libya, North Korea, Pakistan, South Africa, South Korea, Sudan, and Syria. Of these countries, only South Africa, Iraq, and Libya no longer have programs. Iraq was disarmed of all its WMD in a lengthy process that lasted years after the Gulf War of 1991, while South Africa voluntarily ended its WMD efforts (including a nuclear program) in the early 1990s. Libya gave up its chemical and nuclear programs in 2004, at which time inspectors found no evidence of an existing biological program.[38]

While there is no verifiable evidence of the use of biological weapons in warfare since World War II, there are several documented instances of chemical weapons use, all by Muslim states in the Middle East. During the mid-1960s, Egypt intervened in a civil war in Yemen and used mustard gas and phosgene against royalist forces attempting to restore the country's monarchy, which had been overthrown in a military coup. In 1987, Libyan forces attempting to take control of neighboring Chad used mustard gas supplied by Iran against Chadian troops. By far the most extensive and deadly use of chemical weapons was by the Iraqi dictator Saddam Hussein, who used them between 1983 and 1988 in Iraq's war with Iran. These weapons accounted for thousands of Iranian casualties, perhaps 3 to 5 percent of the hundreds of thousands of casualties Iran suffered during the war. Iran eventually responded with chemical weapons of its own, although it did not use them as effectively as Iraq. Iraq used both mustard and nerve agents, while Iran's arsenal was limited to mustard agents. In 1988, Hussein turned his chemical weapons against his own country's Kurdish minority, attacking a number of villages with both mustard and nerve agents. The largest of these attacks, all against civilians, killed 4,000 people in the village of Halabja.[39]

While these events took place, other countries made an effort to control and reverse the spread of chemical and biological weapons. In late 1969, the U.S. president Richard Nixon announced that the United States was renouncing the offensive use of biological weapons and changing its policy regarding chemical weapons. This new stance was unilateral, that is, the United States was going to act without requiring other nations to do the same. The United States promised to destroy its stocks of biological weapons and pledged that all future research in this area would be strictly for defensive purposes. The president reaffirmed U.S. policy that deadly chemical weapons would be kept for retaliatory purposes only and extended that policy to chemicals that incapacitate rather than kill. He also urged that an international treaty be negotiated to ban these weapons entirely. In 1975, the United States officially became a party to the 1925 Geneva Protocol, thereby making itself legally bound to use chemical weapons for retaliation purposes only.[40]

Meanwhile, international efforts produced major agreements negotiated about 20 years apart: the Biological Weapons Convention (BWC) and the Chemical Weapons Convention (CWC). Negotiations for the BWC were completed in 1972, and it officially took effect in 1975. The BWC banned the possession of biological weapons, making it the first international agreement to prohibit the possession of an entire class of weapons. The problem with the BWC is that it is vague on key points—for example, the difference between offensive and defensive research—and, most important, has no enforcement mechanism. That is why, although the agreement to date has been signed and ratified by more than 160 countries, there has been significant cheating. Most seriously, the Soviet Union signed the agreement in 1972 and then violated it for two decades by carrying out the most extensive biological weapons program of any country in history. Not until the 1990s, by which time the

Soviet Union had collapsed, did this program come to light. Several countries known to have biological weapons programs have not ratified the BWC.[41]

The CWC was negotiated in the early 1990s and officially took effect in 1997. To date, it has been signed and ratified by more than 180 countries. The CWC prohibits the development, production, and stockpiling of chemical weapons. Those countries ratifying the agreement that have these weapons must destroy them. As with the BWC, several countries known to have chemical weapons programs have not signed or ratified the CWC. The CWC created an international body—the Organisation for the Prohibition of Chemical Weapons (OPCW)—to inspect sites where chemical weapons might be produced or stored and undertake their destruction. As of 2009, the OPCW reported that member nations had destroyed about 43 percent of the world's declared chemical weapons stocks. However, there is a huge potential difference between what has been declared by member states and what they actually have. For example, during the 1990s, the United States, with good reason, suspected that Russia's declaration regarding its chemical weapons was incomplete. Beyond that, the destruction of chemical weapons is a dangerous and environmentally threatening activity, and that has slowed up the process of destruction.[42]

Nuclear Weapons

World War II was followed by a long period of conflict and competition between the United States and the Soviet Union known as the cold war. The United States was the leader of an alliance that included many of the world's democratic countries, while the Soviet Union led a bloc of Communist states. The cold war, which began almost immediately after World War II ended and lasted until about 1990, led to a Soviet-American nuclear arms race that left each country with the power to destroy the world many times over. Each country's nuclear arsenal so exceeded that of any other country that the term *superpower* was used to describe their standing in the world. During the 1950s, both the United States and the Soviet Union developed thermonuclear, or hydrogen, weapons. As they were developing these weapons, other countries also acquired nuclear weapons. Eventually, some of those countries also developed thermonuclear weapons. Finally, with the world living under a cloud of potential nuclear destruction, an effort began to curb the nuclear arms race. Over time, from the late 1960s through the 1990s, that effort led to a series of important arms control treaties.

NUCLEAR ARMS RACE DURING THE COLD WAR

The United States was the world's only nuclear power for four years. Then, in August 1949, the Soviet Union tested its first nuclear bomb. In January 1950, the U.S. president Harry S. Truman ordered the United States to proceed with development of the hydrogen bomb, which in those days often was called the superbomb. The first U.S. test of a thermonuclear device—it was too large to be a deliverable bomb—took place in November 1952, exploding with a force of 10 megatons. In August 1953, the Soviet Union successfully tested its first hydrogen bomb. That bomb actually was not a fully thermonuclear two-stage weapon but rather one whose design permitted the use of a limited amount of thermonuclear fuel. It had an explosive yield of about 400 kilotons. In March 1954, the United States tested its first deliverable hydrogen bomb. The Soviet Union successfully tested its first fully thermonuclear bomb in November 1955.[43]

The first American and Soviet nuclear weapons were designed to be delivered by large bombers. This provided some possibility of defense, as both aircraft and ground-based missiles could be used to shoot bombers down. However, during the late 1950s and 1960s, both sides developed guided missiles capable of delivering nuclear weapons. The two main types of missiles were intercontinental ballistic missiles (ICBMs), which were based on land, and submarine-launched ballistic missiles (SLBMs), which could be launched from submarines. This made them virtually undetectable. In the late 1960s, both sides developed the ability to put more than one atomic warhead on a guided missile. The top part of a guided missile that can carry more than one atomic warhead is called a MIRV, which stands for multiple independently targeted reentry vehicle. While constantly improving their long-range ballistic missiles, both sides also developed shorter range missiles capable of carrying nuclear warheads; they also developed cruise missiles, highly accurate jet-powered missiles that could fly at low altitudes and therefore beneath the range of the radar used to detect high-flying aircraft or guided missiles.

NUCLEAR WEAPONS PROLIFERATION

Meanwhile, what came to be known as the nuclear or atomic club grew. Great Britain tested its first atomic bomb in 1952 and its first thermonuclear weapon in 1957. France did the same, respectively, in 1960 and 1968, while the People's Republic of China tested its first atomic bomb in 1964 and its first hydrogen bomb in 1967. Israel became an unofficial nuclear power in the late 1960s. Unlike the other nuclear states, Israel has never officially admitted that it has nuclear weapons. In the early 1980s, South Africa also secretly became a nuclear power, but it gave up its program and dismantled its weapons in the 1990s. Meanwhile, India in 1974 (with the test of a nuclear device, not a weapon) and Pakistan in 1998 openly became nuclear powers. Finally, North Korea probably became a nuclear power shortly after the turn of the 21st century. However, it did not publicly announce it had nuclear weapons until 2005 and did not test a nuclear device until 2006. There also are more than 30 countries, including all the nuclear powers, that have ballistic missiles. These missiles, because they are so difficult to defend against, are the most likely way one country would attack another with a nuclear weapon.[44]

NONPROLIFERATION EFFORTS

By the 1960s, three issues dominated the thinking about nuclear weapons. First, there was great concern that the Soviet-American arms race would lead to a catastrophic nuclear war. Second, people worried that many countries would acquire nuclear weapons, which in turn could lead to nuclear war on a smaller but still disastrous scale. Third, it was clear that nuclear testing, especially in the atmosphere, was releasing radioactive materials that could harm the health of millions of people even without a nuclear war.

Over time, a series of international agreements attempted to address these concerns, achieving varying degrees of success. In 1963, the United States, the Soviet Union, and Great Britain signed the Limited Test Ban Treaty (LTBT), banning nuclear tests in the atmosphere, under water, and in outer space. While it has since been signed by more than 116 countries, non-signatories include France and the People's Republic of China, both major nuclear powers. The last nuclear test violating the LTBT limits was in 1992 by the PRC. The Comprehensive Nuclear Test Ban Treaty, banning all nuclear tests and dating from 1996, has been ratified by 145 states. However, that treaty has not entered into force because nine states—the United States, India, Pakistan, Egypt, Iran, Israel, Indonesia, North Korea, and the PRC—whose ratification is required to bring the treaty into force either have not signed or not ratified the treaty.[45]

In 1968, an international effort produced the Treaty on the Non-Proliferation of Nuclear Weapons (NPT); since then 189 countries have become parties to the treaty. This includes the five countries—the United States, Russia (in those days, part of the Soviet Union), Britain, France, and the PRC—that were nuclear powers in 1968 and that according to the treaty are the only countries permitted to have these weapons. That said, they must be committed to eventually eliminating their nuclear arsenals. All other countries are prohibited from having nuclear weapons.

The NPT has had its successes. It is credited with convincing some potential nuclear powers such as Argentina and Brazil to give up their programs. In 1993, two years after joining the NPT, South Africa completed the destruction of its six nuclear weapons. Another success linked with the NPT occurred in the early and mid-1990s when Ukraine, Belarus, and Kazakhstan, all of which inherited Soviet nuclear weapons after the Soviet Union collapsed in 1991, agreed to give up their nuclear weapons and then transferred them to Russia. But it has also had important failures. During the 1980s and 1990s, Iraq, Iran, and North Korea—all NPT parties at the time—successfully hid their programs from inspectors sent by the International Atomic Energy Agency (IAEA), which under the NPT has authority to inspect the nuclear facilities of member states. Iraq had its nuclear and other WMD programs closed down after its defeat in the Gulf War of 1991 when the UN Security Council imposed far more thorough inspections than those carried out under the NPT. But North Korea, which renounced the NPT in 2003, now almost certainly has nuclear weapons, and the evidence is overwhelming that Iran is continuing its nuclear weapons program. In addition, an international black market in nuclear technology run by Abdul Qadeer Khan, head of Pakistan's nuclear program, existed for years before finally being uncovered in early 2004. Libya, an NPT party and also for many years a supporter of Arab terrorist organizations such as the Abu Nidal Organization and the Palestinian Islamic Jihad, for 10 years secretly attempted to acquire fissile material and nuclear weapons technology before agreeing to give up its nuclear program in December 2003. It did so only after being caught red-handed attempting to import centrifuge parts several months earlier, a discovery that exposed Libya's nuclear program to the world.[46] In short, the NPT worked when countries acted in good faith; those that did not were able to violate the NPT and get away with it. In addition, India, Pakistan, and Israel, all of which have nuclear weapons, have refused to join the NPT.

A notable success in scaling back nuclear weapons resulted from a series of arms control agreements between the United States and the Soviet Union between 1972 and 1991 and further agreements between the United States and Russia after the collapse of the Soviet Union. The first agreement was the SALT I (Strategic Arms Limitation Talks) treaty signed in 1972, which limited the number of nuclear missiles each side could have. It also strictly limited the number of antiballistic missiles (ABMs)—missiles used to defend against nuclear missiles—each side could have. (The SALT II treaty was signed in 1979 but never ratified by either side.) After signing the INF (Intermediate Nuclear Forces) treaty of 1987, both sides eliminated all of their ground-launched intermediate-range nuclear missiles. In 1991, the two sides went further in START I (Strategic Arms Reduction Treaty), which required substantial reduction in the parties' nuclear arsenals. (A second arms reduction treaty—START II—signed after the Soviet Union's collapse between the United States and Russia in 1993 never entered into force.) Both sides pledged further reductions in the SORT (Strategic Offensive Reductions Treaty) agreement signed in 2002. Although the accounting process is very complicated, it is reasonable to say that since the mid-1980s the nuclear arsenals of the United States and Russia (which inherited the defunct Soviet Union's arsenal) have decreased by about 50 percent.[47]

However, that positive development does not negate the reality that not only the United States and Russia, but countries in some of the world's most unstable regions, have either nuclear arsenals or other weapons of mass destruction. The nuclear arsenals represent the biggest threat. Among the dangers they pose is that terrorist organizations such as al-Qaeda could steal either a completed weapon or the fissile materials needed to construct a weapon. This is most likely to happen in Russia, where corruption has reached epidemic proportions and where dozens of the sites holding nuclear weapons or tons of fissile material are not adequately guarded. Another danger involves both powers. Because the United States and Russia keep so many of their weapons on high alert so they can be launched within 15 minutes, the danger of an accidental launch remains very real.[48] Beyond the United States and Russia, regional tensions could lead to nuclear disaster, as they nearly did when India and Pakistan went to the brink of war in 2002. The world's biological and chemical weapons arsenals, while less menacing than nuclear arsenals, pose serious threats of their own. The following two chapters examine the nature of these WMD arsenals, the problems they pose, and what is being done to address these issues.

---

[1] This is the definition used in the U.S. government's *National Strategy to Combat Weapons of Mass Destruction,* issued in 2002. According to the highly respected Nuclear Threat Initiative (NTI) Web site, this is also the most widely used definition in other official U.S. documents. Available online. URL: http://www.nti.org/f_wmd411/fla1.html. Accessed July 28, 2009.

[2] Adrienne Mayor. *Greek Fire, Poison Arrows, and Scorpion Bombs: Biological and Chemical Warfare in the Ancient World.* Woodstock, N.Y.: Overlook Duckworth, 2003, pp. 77–79; Thomas J. Johnson. "A History of Biological Warfare from 300 B.C.E. to the Present." Johnson is associate professor of respiratory care and health sciences, School of Health Professions, Long Island University. Available online. URL: http://www.aarc.org/resources/biological/history.asp. Accessed June 6, 2008.

[3] Allison Macfarlane. "All Weapons of Mass Destruction Are Not Equal." *Audit of the Conventional Wisdom.* MIT Center for International Studies. Available online. URL: http://www.alternet.org/world/31510/. Accessed July 28, 2009.

[4] Joseph M. Siracusa. *Nuclear Weapons: A Very Short Introduction.* London: Oxford University Press, 2008, p. 57.

[5] *NATO Handbook on the Medical Aspects of NBC Operations AMedP-6(B).* Washington, D.C.: Departments of the Army, Navy, and the Air Force, 1996, Part III—Chemical, Chapter 1, Introduction, 101. Definition. Available online. URL: http://www.fas.org/nuke/guide/usa/doctrine/dod/fm8-9/toc.htm. Accessed June 16, 2008.

[6] Joseph Cirincione, Jon B. Wolfsthal, and Miriam Rajkumar. *Deadly Arsenals: Nuclear , Biological, and Chemical Threats,* Second Edition, revised and expanded. Washington, D.C.:

Carnegie Endowment for International Peace, 2005, pp. 62–63; *NATO Handbook on the Medical Aspects of NBC Operations AMedP-6(B),* Part III—Chemical, Chapter I, Introduction, 106. Routes of Absorption.

[7] Federation of Atomic Scientists. "Introduction to Chemical Weapons." Available online. URL: http://www.fas.org/programs/ssp/bio/chemweapons/introduction.html. Accessed March 18, 2009.

[8] Jonathan B. Tucker. *War of Nerves: Chemical Warfare from World War I to al-Qaeda.* New York: Pantheon Books, 2006, pp. 158–159, 181–182, 215; Robert Hutchinson. *Weapons of Mass Destruction: The No-Nonsense Guide to Nuclear, Chemical, and Biological Weapons Today.* London: Weidenfeld and Nicolson, 2003, pp. 215–217.

[9] Hutchinson. *Weapons of Mass Destruction,* p. 236.

[10] Hutchinson. *Weapons of Mass Destruction,* p. 237.

[11] Centers for Disease Control and Prevention. "Bioterrorism Agents/Diseases." Available online. URL: http://www.bt.cdc.gov/agent/agentlist-category.asp. Accessed June 21, 2008.

[12] World Health Organization. "Nipah virus." Available online. URL: http://www.who.int/meciacentre/factsheet/fs262/en/. Accessed June 22, 2008.

[13] *NATO Handbook on the Medical Aspects of NBC Operations AMedP-6(B),* Part I—Nuclear, Chapter 1—General Information, Chapter 2—Conventional and Nuclear Weapons—Energy Production and Atomic Physics, Section 2—Mechanisms of Energy Production, 201–206; Cirincione, Wolfsthal, and Rajkumar. *Deadly Arsenals,* pp. 46–47.

[14] TNT, or trinitrotoluene, is an extremely powerful explosive invented in 1863. Nuclear bombs, which are far more powerful, are measured according to the explosive force that would be generated by thousands or even millions of tons of TNT. A thousand pounds of TNT is called a kiloton; a million pounds of TNT is called a megaton.

[15] United States Nuclear Regulatory Commission. "Uranium Enrichment." Available online. URL: http://www.nrc.gov/reading-rm/doc-collections/fact-sheets/enrichment.html. Accessed June 25, 2008; World Nuclear Association. "Uranium Enrichment." Available online. URL: http://www.world-nuclear.org/info/inf28.html. Accessed June 25, 2008; Cirincione, Wolfsthal, and Rajkumar. *Deadly Arsenals,* p. 47; Federation of American Scientists. *Special Weapons Primer.* "Uranium Production." Available online. URL: http://www.fas.org/nuke/intro/nike/uranium.htm. Accessed June 25, 2008.

[16] Federation of American Scientists. *Special Weapons Primer.* "Plutonium Production." Available online. URL: www.fas.org/nike/intro/nike/plutonium.htm. Accessed June 25, 2008; Cirincione, Wolfsthal, and Rajkumar. *Deadly Arsenals,* pp. 51–52.

[17] Richard Rhodes. *The Making of the Atomic Bomb.* New York: Simon and Schuster, 1986, p. 548.

[18] *NATO Handbook on the Medical Aspects of NBC Operations AMedP-6(B),* Part I—Nuclear, Chapter 2—Conventional and Nuclear Weapons—Energy and Atomic Physics, Section II—Mechanisms of Energy Production, 210. Critical Mass; Owen T. Cote, Jr. "Appendix B: P Primer on Fissile Materials and Nuclear Weapons Design." In Graham T. Allison, Owen Cote, Jr., Richard A. Falkenrath, and Steven Miller. *Avoiding Nuclear Anarchy: Containing the Threat of Loose Russian Nuclear Weapons and Fissile Material.* Cambridge, Mass.: MIT Press, 1996. Available online. URL: http://www.pbs.org/wgbh/pages/frontline/shows/nukes/readings/appendixb.html. Accessed June 27, 2008.

[19] Quoted in Siracusa. *Nuclear Weapons,* p. 59.

[20] The material in the next three paragraphs is drawn from numerous sources, but primarily from the following two sources: Union of Concerned Scientists. "Nuclear Weapons: How They Work." Available online. URL: http://www.ucsusa.org/global_security/nuclear_weapons/nuclear-weapons-how-they.html? Accessed June 26, 2008; Owen T. Cote, Jr. "Appendix B: P Primer on Fissile Materials and Nuclear Weapons Design."

[21] Atomic Archive. "The Energy of a Nuclear Weapon." Available online. URL: http://www.atomicarchive.com/Effects/effects1.shtml. Accessed June 18, 2008; Federation of American Scientists. *Special Weapons Primer.* "Nuclear Weapons Radiation Effects." Available online. URL: http://www.fas.org/nuke/intro/radiation.htm. Accessed June 27, 2008.

[22] Global Security. Weapons of Mass Destruction. "Neutron Bomb/Enhanced Radiation Weapon." Available online. URL: http://www.globalsecurity.org/wmd/intro/neutron-bomb/htm. Accessed June 22, 2008; Atomic Archive. "The Neutron Bomb." Available online. URL: http://www.atomicarchive.com/Fusion/Fusion5.shtml. Accessed June 27, 2008; NuclearFiles.org. Project of the Nuclear Age Peace Foundation. "The Neutron Bomb." Available online. URL: http://www.nuclearfiles.org/menu/key-issues/nuclear-weapons/basics/neutron-bomb.htm. Accessed June 27, 2008.

[23] The Online News Hour. Tracking Nuclear Proliferation. "Types of Nuclear Bombs." Available online. URL: http://www.pbs.org/newshour/indepth_coverage/military/proliferation/types.html. Accessed June 27, 2008; New York City Department of Health and Mental Hygiene. Public Health Emergency Preparedness. "Dirty Bombs." Available online. URL: http://www.nyc.gov/html/doh/html/bt/bt_fact_dirtybombs.shtml. Accessed June 23, 2008.

[24] Atomic Archive. "New York City Example." Available online. URL: http://www.atomicarchive.com/Example/Example1.shtml. Accessed June 23, 2008; Siracusa. *Nuclear Weapons,* pp. 7–8. A more recent scenario suggests similar results. See Graham Allison. *Nuclear Terrorism: The Ultimate Preventable Catastrophe.* New York: Times Books, 2004, pp. 3–4. This scenario involves a 10-kiloton bomb detonated in Times Square and predicts 500,000 people would be killed and all buildings within a third of a mile completely destroyed.

[25] James Martin Center for Nonproliferation Studies. "Chronology of State Use and Biological and Chemical Weapons Control." Available online. URL: http://cns.miis.edu/research/cbw/pastuse.htm. Accessed June 30, 2008; Elizabeth A. Fenn. "Biological Warfare in Eighteenth-Century North America: Beyond Jeffrey Amherst." *Journal of American History* (March 2000): parts 1–7, 26, 42–43. Available online. URL: http://www.historycooperative.org/journals/jah/86.4/fenn.html. Accessed June 6, 2008; L. Szinicz. "History of Chemical and Biological Warfare Agents." *Toxicology* 214 (2005): pp. 167–181. Available online. URL: http://www.sciencedirect.com. Accessed June 30, 2008.

[26] Hutchinson. *Weapons of Mass Destruction,* pp. 197–206; Tucker. *War of Nerves,* p. 15.

[27] Tucker. *War of Nerves,* pp. 15–20; Szinicz. "History of Chemical and Biological Warfare Agents," p. 170; Thomas Graham, Jr. *Commonsense on Weapons of Mass Destruction.* Seattle and London: University of Washington Press, 2008, pp. 118–119; Eric Croddy. *Chemical and Biological Warfare: A Comprehensive Survey for the Concerned Citizen.* New York: Copernicus Books, 2002, p. 150.

[28] James Martin Center for Nonproliferation Studies. "Chronology of State Use and Biological and Chemical Weapons Control." Available online. URL: http://cns.miis.edu/research/cbw/pastuse.htm. Accessed June 30, 2008; Michael Kort. *The Soviet Colossus: History and Aftermath.* Armonk, N.Y.: M. E. Sharpe, 2006, p. 143.

[29] Jeanne Guillemin. *Biological Weapons: From the Invention of State-Sponsored Programs to Contemporary Bioterrorism.* New York: Columbia University Press, 2005, pp. 24–27, 44; James Martin Center for Nonproliferation Studies. "Chemical and Biological Weapons:

Possession and Programs Past and Present." Available online. URL: http://cns.miis.edu/research/cbw/possess.htm. Accessed May 23, 2008; Tucker. *War of Nerves*, p. 21.

[30] Tucker. *War of Nerves*, pp. 22–23; Hutchinson. *Weapons of Mass Destruction*, pp. 210–217; James Martin Center for Nonproliferation Studies. "Chemical and Biological Weapons: Possession and Programs Past and Present."

[31] Tucker. *War of Nerves*, pp. 10–11, 21–22; The quotation from the Geneva Protocol is in Croddy. *Chemical and Biological Warfare*, pp. 170–171, 238.

[32] James Martin Center for Nonproliferation Studies. "Chronology of State Use and Biological and Chemical Weapons Control"; Sheldon Harris. "The Japanese Biological Warfare Programme: An Overview." In *Biological and Toxin Weapons: Research, Development and Use from the Middle Ages to 1945.* SIPRI Chemical and Biological Warfare Studies no. 18, edited by Erhard Giessler and John Ellis van Courtland Moon. Oxford: Oxford University Press, 1999, p. 151.

[33] James Martin Center for Nonproliferation Studies. "Chronology of State Use and Biological and Chemical Weapons Control"; Croddy. *Chemical and Biological Warfare*, pp. 152–155; Hutchinson. *Weapons of Mass Destruction*, pp. 212–214; Tucker. *War of Nerves*, pp. 84–86.

[34] Gerhard L. Weinberg. *A World at Arms: A Global History of World War II.* Cambridge and New York: Cambridge University Press, 1994, pp. 867, 885; Croddy. *Chemical and Biological Warfare*, pp. 157–158.

[35] James Martin Center for Nonproliferation Studies. "Chemical and Biological Weapons: Possession and Programs Past and Present"; Johnson. "A History of Biological Warfare from 300 B.C.E. to the Present"; Guillemin. *Biological Weapons*, pp. 54–56.

[36] "Notes of the Interim Committee Meeting, Thursday, 31 May 1945." In Michael Kort. *The Columbia Guide to Hiroshima and the Bomb.* New York: Columbia University Press, 2007, pp. 181–183.

[37] Hutchinson. *Weapons of Mass Destruction*, pp. 223–225; Monterey Bay Aquarium Research Institute. "Dangerous Unknowns: MBARI Researcher Points Out the Lack of Information on Chemical Weapons Dumped at Sea." Available online. URL: http://www.mbari.org/news/homepage/2008/chemweapons.html. Accessed July 2, 2008.

[38] James Martin Center for Nonproliferation Studies. "Chemical and Biological Weapons: Possession and Programs Past and Present." Accessed May 23, 2008; ———. "Weapons of Mass Destruction in the Middle East: Libya." Updated April 2006. Available online. URL: http://cns.miis.edu/research/wmdme/libya.htm. Accessed July 5, 2008.

[39] Croddy. *Chemical and Biological Warfare*, pp. 160–166; James Martin Center for Nonproliferation Studies. "Reported Use of Chemical Weapons, Ballistic Missiles, and Cruise Missiles in the Middle East." Available online. URL: http://cns.miis.edu/wmdme/use.htm. Accessed May 24, 2008.

[40] Tucker. *War of Nerves*, pp. 216–217, 235; Guillemin. *Biological Weapons*, pp. 125–126; Croddy. *Chemical and Biological Warfare*, p. 238; Judith Miller, Stephen Engelberg, and William Broad. *Germs: Biological Weapons and America's Secret War.* New York: Simon and Schuster, 2001, p. 63.

[41] Miller, Engelberg, and Broad. *Germs*, pp. 63–64; Croddy. *Chemical and Biological Warfare*, pp. 238–239; Center for Defense Information. Chemical and Biological Weapons Site. "Biological Weapons Convention Overview." Available online. URL: http://www.cdi.org/issues/cbw/bwc.html. Accessed May 15, 2008.

[42] Organization for the Prohibition of Chemical Weapons. "The Chemical Weapons Ban: Facts and Figures." Available online. URL: http://www.opcw.org/publications/facts-and-figures/. Accessed April 12, 2009; Tucker. *War of Nerves,* pp. 320–323; Croddy. *Chemical and Biological Warfare,* pp. 181–187; Daniel Feakes. "Getting Down to the Hard Cases: Prospects for CWC Universality." Available online. URL: http://www.armscontrol.org/act/2008_03/Feakes. Accessed July 6, 2008; Croddy. *Chemical and Biological Warfare,* p. 176.

[43] David Holloway. *The Soviet Union and the Arms Race.* New Haven, Conn.: Yale University Press, 1983, p. 24.

[44] Siracusa. *Nuclear Weapons,* pp. 59–60; Cirincione, Wolfsthal, and Rajkumar. *Deadly Arsenals,* pp. 5–8; Graham. *Commonsense on Weapons of Mass Destruction,* pp. 10–11; Nuclear Threat Initiative. WMD411. "Missiles." Updated November 6, 2008. Available online. URL: http://www.nti.org/f_WMD411/fla5.html. Accessed July 28, 2009.

[45] Atomic Archive. "Limited Test Ban Treaty (1963)." Available online. URL: http://www.atomicarchive.com/Treaties/Treaty3.shtml. Accessed July 7, 2008; Cirincione, Wolfsthal, and Rajkumar. *Deadly Arsenals,* p. 455; Federation of American Scientists. "Burundi Signs the Comprehensive Nuclear-Test-Ban Treaty." Available online. URL: http://www.fas.org/irp/news/2008/09/burundi.html. Accessed July 28, 2009.

[46] George Bunn. "The Nuclear Nonproliferation Treaty: History and Current Problems." Arms Control Association. (December 2003). Available online. URL: http://www.armscontrol.org/act/2003_12/Bunn.asp?print. Accessed July 7, 2008; Cirincione, Wolfsthal, and Rajkumar. *Deadly Arsenals,* pp. 5–8, 24; David E. Sanger. "The Khan Network." Available online. URL: http://iis-db.stanford.edu/evnts/3889/Khan_network-paper.pdf. Accessed June 16, 2008; Nuclear Threat Initiative. "Proliferation and Use of Nuclear Weapons." Updated March 2008. Available online. URL: http://nti.org/f_WMD411/fla4_1.html. Accessed June 5, 2008; U.S. Department of State. "Patterns of Global Terrorism: 1997. Overview of State-Sponsored Terrorism." Available online. URL: http://www.state.gov/www/global/terrorism/1997Report/sponsored.html. Accessed April 15, 2009.

[47] Joseph Cirincione. *Bomb Scare: The History and Future of Nuclear Weapons.* New York: Columbia University Press, 2008, p. 86; Cirincione, Wolfsthal, and Rajkumar. *Deadly Arsenals,* pp. 124, 210–211; Graham. *Commonsense on Weapons of Mass Destruction,* pp. 42–44.

[48] Cirincione. *Bomb Scare,* pp. 87–102.

2

Focus On The United States

KEY ISSUES

The key issues for the United States regarding WMD have changed over the years. At first, the concern was to develop these weapons because other countries already had them or, in the case of nuclear weapons during World War II, might develop them. After the war, the competition with the Soviet Union dominated American thinking about WMD. Then, beginning in the 1960s, new issues emerged. The United States increasingly became concerned with stopping the spread of WMD to countries that did not have them and reducing or eliminating the arsenals of countries that already had these weapons. At the same time, the spread of WMD increased the urgency of developing countermeasures against these weapons. Another issue that gradually emerged was how to deal with the environmental impact involved in the production, testing, and destruction of these weapons.

HISTORY AND CURRENT ARSENALS

On April 24, 1863, almost four months after issuing the Emancipation Proclamation and seven months before his Gettysburg Address, President Abraham Lincoln signed a document officially issued by the U.S. War Department called General Orders No. 100. The order was a code of military conduct designed to set standards for how Union troops should deal with the enemy. It had been drawn up on the president's instructions by Francis Lieber, law professor at Columbia University, and therefore is also known as the Lieber Code. General Orders No. 100 contained more than 150 specific instructions, or articles, that Union troops were required to follow. It has been called "the first modern military field manual." Among many other things, it prohibited leaving wounded enemy soldiers to die on the field of battle, killing enemy soldiers attempting to surrender, and mistreatment of prisoners of war. General Orders No. 100 covered a wide range of subjects beyond the treatment of individual enemy soldiers. Thus, Article 70 stated: "The use of poison in any manner, be it to poison wells, or food, or arms, is wholly excluded from modern warfare. He that uses it puts himself out of the pale of the law and the usages of law."[1]

During the Civil War, many of the provisions of General Orders No. 100 were ignored by commanders in the field. Nonetheless, its language influenced subsequent efforts in Europe to establish norms for modern warfare during the late 19th and early 20th centuries, such as the Hague Conventions of 1899 and 1907. These agreements did nothing to prevent the use of chemical weapons by the European belligerents during World War I. The United States, which officially entered the war on the Allied side in April 1917, was totally unprepared for chemical warfare when its troops reached the European battlefields in the summer of 1917, even though deadly chemical weapons had been in use on those battlefields for more than two years. At that point, General John J. Pershing, the commander of all American forces in Europe, ordered General Amos Fries to form a unit to train American troops to defend themselves against chemical weapons and to develop the ability to use chemical weapons offensively. Fries organized the First Gas Regiment to deal with the emergency. In June 1918, the War Department in Washington established the Chemical Warfare Service (CWS). The United States quickly built several factories, which produced about 1,600 tons of mustard, phosgene, and other agents by war's end. None of that material, however, was ever shipped overseas. When American forces in Europe finally responded to German gas attacks against them, they used materials and equipment supplied by Britain and France.[2]

This involvement with chemical weapons marked the start of America's WMD programs. During World War II, biological and nuclear programs would be added to the list. The United States is one of fewer than a dozen countries that at one time or another in the 20th or 21st centuries has possessed all three types of weapons of mass destruction.

The U.S. Chemical Weapons Program

After a debate on the future of the CWS, Congress in 1920 made it a permanent part of the U.S. Army, mainly out of fear that other nations would develop chemical weapons. However, the CWS did not receive much funding and had a staff of only 500 military and 1,000 civilian personnel, much smaller than its wartime strength. Its status was not affected when the United States signed the 1925 Geneva Protocol banning chemical and biological weapons, as the Senate did not ratify the agreement. It would not ratify the protocol until 1974. Meanwhile, the CWS continued to work on chemical weapons agents and on improving artillery shells and bombs with which to deliver them against enemy forces.[3]

Despite the existence of the CWS, during the 1930s the U.S. Army focused on developing better conventional weapons and tactics. The outbreak of World War II once again found the United States unprepared to deal with or wage modern chemical warfare. American policy during the war was clear: This country would only use chemical weapons in retaliation if another power used them first. As President Franklin D. Roosevelt stated in 1943, "We shall under no circumstances resort to the use of such [chemical] weapons unless they are first used by our enemies."[4] At the same time, the fear of what those enemies might do led to a massive expansion of the CWS's activities. Its budget rose from $2 million to $1 billion between 1940 and 1942 alone, and by the end of the war new factories in several states had produced more than 146,000 tons of chemical agents such as chlorine, lewisite, and mustard gas. One facility established at the Massachusetts Institute of Technology did some of the world's most advanced research on gas masks and other methods of defending against chemical weapons. Although the United States stuck to its no-first-use policy and in fact never used chemical weapons during the war, the army did prepare its troops to deal with chemical weapons. More than 60,000 personnel served in over 400 specially trained and equipped chemical units. Troops were issued gas masks and other equipment, and when U.S. forces landed in Europe to liberate the continent from German occupation the troops hitting the beaches were followed by decontamination units in case the Germans counterattacked with chemical weapons.[5] Fortunately, Germany did not resort to these weapons, probably because of fear of Allied retaliation. American forces in the Pacific also did not face chemical weapons. The Japanese, who used them in China, did not use them against American or other Allied forces elsewhere in Asia or in the Pacific.

U.S. CHEMICAL WEAPONS POLICIES FROM WORLD WAR II TO 2009

As World War II in Europe was drawing to a close, America and its allies were shocked to discover that Germany had developed chemical agents far more deadly than anything in their arsenals. It was a stunning intelligence failure. The Allies had nothing to match tabun, to say nothing of sarin and soman. Fortunately, German intelligence also had failed—they were not aware of the advantage they possessed. A British study done several years later concluded that had German forces used tabun against Allied soldiers or put it in rockets used to attack British cities late in the war the casualties would have been enormous. As soon as the war was over, hundreds of tons of German chemical agents, as well as thousands of artillery shells and bombs containing those agents, were sent to the United States for study.[6]

While the United States investigated Germany's nerve agents and other advanced weapons programs in areas such as rocketry and jet aircraft development, it (and Britain) knew that the Soviet Union was doing the same. This is why Congress decided to continue chemical weapons research, turning the job over to the Chemical Corps, as the CWS was renamed in 1946. By then, the Soviet Union's policies in Eastern Europe had led to the cold war and with that growing concerns about further aggressive Soviet intentions. In August 1949, the Soviets tested their first atomic bomb, several years earlier than expected. The outbreak of the Korean War (1950–53) in June 1950 raised tensions to a new level, especially given the assumption in Washington—which turned out to be correct—that the Soviets were behind the North Korean invasion of South Korea. In 1950, President Harry S. Truman reaffirmed America's "retaliation only" policy regarding chemical weapons. However, he also received intelligence estimates that the United States lagged badly behind the Soviet Union in chemical weapons development and stockpiling. This led to a dramatic increase in the budget of the Chemical Corps, which made the decision to focus on the production and weaponization of sarin. The factories to produce sarin were completed by 1952. During the 1950s, the United States produced both bombs and artillery shells to deliver sarin against enemy targets.[7]

Soon, chemical weapons development moved to a more advanced level. During the early 1950s, British scientists produced a new class of even more deadly chemicals, the so-called V- (for "venomous") agents. American work on V-agents began in the mid-1950s, and more than 50 different V-agents were produced and examined before the decision was made to concentrate on a compound known as VX. Production of VX and artillery shells, bombs, and short-range rockets to deliver it began in the early 1960s. One reason the United States focused on VX was to deter the Soviet Union from using its superiority in conventional forces to attack Western Europe. American strategists wanted to avoid using nuclear weapons if the Soviets attacked, since that would inevitably lead to a catastrophic nuclear war. Using VX and other chemical weapons to stop Soviet forces was viewed as a way to effectively stop the Soviets without sparking a nuclear war. At the same time, American scientists worked to develop chemical antidotes against VX, as well as portable machines that could be used on the battlefield to detect nerve agents.[8]

During the late 1960s, opinions within the government shifted regarding the usefulness of chemical weapons. In part, this was due to public pressure. Developing, testing, and storing chemical weapons were all dangerous. In

1968, an open-air test of VX in a remote section of Utah killed more than 4,000 sheep when equipment failure and unexpected wind patterns blew the VX, which had been sprayed as an aerosol from an airplane, beyond the intended test area. The next year, there was an accidental release of a small amount of sarin gas at a storage facility on the island of Okinawa. Both of these incidents were widely reported by the news media. There was also public concern that the policy of sinking chemical agents at sea would do environmental harm and become a long-term health hazard. Meanwhile, the government undertook a detailed study of chemical and biological weapons, as a result of which President Richard M. Nixon made policy changes, some of which were announced on November 25, 1969. Nixon reaffirmed America's "retaliation only" policy regarding lethal chemical weapons and extended that ban to chemical weapons that incapacitate rather than kill. He called for an international ban of these weapons. In the same statement, Nixon declared that the United States was renouncing the use of biological weapons and called for U.S. ratification of the Geneva Protocol of 1925, which banned both chemical and biological weapons, a step the Senate took in 1974. An important policy change not mentioned in the November 25 announcement was Nixon's decision to ban the production of poisonous chemical agents. Any new chemical weapons the United States developed would be what are called binary weapons. Binary chemical weapons—as opposed to unitary weapons—consist of two agents, neither of which alone is poisonous. They are combined into a poisonous agent only when the shell or bomb they are stored in is fired or released on a target. American scientists had built the first version of these weapons—it contained the VX nerve agent—during the early 1960s. However, binary chemical weapons were not put into production, at first because of technical problems and later because it was assumed that American restraint regarding chemical weapons would be met with Soviet restraint. That assumption turned out to be incorrect. (See the section on Russia in "Global Perspectives" for details.) Meanwhile, the government turned to chemical neutralization and incineration to destroy obsolete chemical agents, rather than dumping them at sea.[9]

Although enthusiasm for chemical weapons waned in the late 1960s and early 1970s, new concerns about advancements in the Soviet weapons program emerged beginning in 1973. The evidence came from Israel, which after its 1973 war with Egypt and Syria turned over captured Soviet tanks and other equipment to the United States. The information Israel provided was extremely valuable, and very worrisome. It turned out that Soviet armored vehicles provided to the Arabs had sophisticated anti–chemical weapons defenses. The Soviets also had supplied Egypt and Syria with other materials, including antidotes for nerve gas and decontamination equipment. This intelligence information contributed to a reevaluation of how Soviet forces in Europe were prepared not only for chemical warfare but also for biological and radiological warfare. They clearly were far better prepared than the American forces that would have to fight them in the event of war. News from other world trouble spots added to these concerns. Soon after the Soviet invasion of Afghanistan in December 1979, there were unconfirmed reports from refugees that Soviet troops were using chemical weapons against antigovernment guerrillas. In 1982, Iraq began using chemical weapons in its war against Iran. By that time, the United States had intensified its effort to develop defensive equipment against chemical weapons such as protective masks and clothing and detection and decontamination equipment. In 1985, after a long debate, the U.S. Congress approved the production of binary chemical weapons. The United States produced binary weapons only until 1990, after which it ceased the production of chemical agents and weapons. At that time, the chemical components of binary weapons were only a small fraction of the total U.S. arsenal: Of the total U.S. stockpile of almost 32,280 tons of chemical agents, 680 tons were for use in binary weapons.[10]

One result of the preparations made during the 1980s was that the American forces that fought in the Gulf War against Iraq in 1991 had advanced defensive equipment for protection against chemical weapons. Although the Iraqi dictator Saddam Hussein had been expected to use these weapons, he did not. There are several possible reasons for this. Hussein and his commanders may have feared how the United States and its allies might retaliate, or U.S. bombing may have made it impossible to move chemical weapons into position where they could be used. After the war, work continued on defensive equipment, and, by the mid-1990s, the United States had developed new equipment, including an infrared sensor that could detect nerve agents at a distance of three miles.[11]

THE CHEMICAL WEAPONS CONVENTION

Meanwhile, the United States and other countries moved forward with efforts to eliminate the threat of chemical weapons. Negotiations on this issue began around 1980, and in 1993 it was announced that the Chemical Weapons Convention (CWC) was ready for signing. The CWC entered into force in 1997, having been signed and ratified by 65 countries. At that point, the Organization for the Prohibition of Chemical Weapons (OPCW) was established to inspect and verify that parties to the CWC were carrying out their obligations.[12]

The CWC requires that member nations declare their chemical weapons facilities and destroy their weapons stockpiles. The largest burden of destroying chemical weapons fell on the United States and Russia, which in the 1990s between them had declared more than 70,000 tons of chemical agents. The United States, with good reason given the available evidence, doubted the Russian declaration was complete. (See "Global Perspectives" for details on the Soviet chemical weapons program.) Nonetheless, in compliance with the CWC, the United States began destroying its agents, a process that necessarily was slow because of the dangers involved. Significant progress was made, and in September 2006 the U.S. Army announced it had destroyed half of the American chemical weapons stockpile. Even with that achievement, the United States could not meet its original CWC deadline for destroying all its chemical weapons. It therefore requested that the deadline be extended from 2007 to 2012. According to the U.S. Defense Department, it will take until 2023 for the United States and Russia to finish destroying their chemical weapons stockpiles.[13]

The U.S. Biological Weapons Program

The United States began to take an interest in biological weapons just before the outbreak of World War II in 1939. Until then, American leaders had believed that effective public health programs and proper sanitation could deal with biological weapons. However, intelligence reports about German and Japanese activities raised concerns that these methods would not suffice. Discussion and preliminary research into the newly recognized threat went on for about three years before President Roosevelt ordered that work begin on both defensive measures and potential offensive agents. This decision was made after British tests on an island off the coast of Scotland demonstrated that bombs loaded with anthrax spores could kill at a distance downwind of several hundred yards. The newly established War Research Service, until it was dissolved in 1944, was given responsibility for coordinating the biological warfare program, while the CWS was charged with building and running the necessary research and production facilities.[14]

The funds devoted to biological warfare grew rapidly in 1943 and 1944, and by 1944 almost 4,000 people at the CWS were working on biological weapons. They focused mainly on two agents, anthrax and botulinum toxin. However, a large factory built in Indiana to make biological agents ultimately only produced what are called simulants, relatively harmless bacteria that can be used to study how deadly agents might spread. About 8,000 pounds of one of those agents (called BG) was produced by the end of the war. Shortly after the war, the Indiana facility was closed and then sold to a commercial drug company, which to this day produces veterinary antibiotics there.

Immediately after the war, biological warfare work was limited to laboratory research under the auspices of the Chemical Corps. Then, cold war tensions and concerns changed that policy. During 1948 and 1949, two studies by the Defense Department concluded that the United States was vulnerable to biological warfare and that its defenses had to be improved. The outbreak of the Korean War led to a dramatic expansion of the U.S. biological warfare program, as it did with most other weapons programs. A new research laboratory was built at an army base in Maryland and a large production facility at another base in Arkansas. New pathogens were studied, including those that cause plague, cholera, and Q fever, in an effort to find agents suitable for weaponization. One problem during the 1950s and 1960s involved testing. In an effort to understand the vulnerability of civilian populations, open-air testing was done over American cities, including New York City, San Francisco, and Minneapolis. This testing, it must be stressed, always involved simulants rather than the deadly agents themselves. Even so, there is evidence that these simulants were not entirely safe and may have caused disease in some people. The only open-air testing with deadly agents was done in the mid- and late 1960s on a remote coral atoll about 800 miles west of Hawaii; monkeys were exposed to these agents. As the 1960s drew to a close, the U.S. biological weapons arsenal was based on seven main agents, two of which—anthrax and tularemia—were deadly. The other agents caused diseases that normally were not fatal.

Meanwhile, opinion in the United States was turning against biological weapons. Both the dangers involved in developing and storing them and their actual usefulness were being debated. In the spring of 1969, congressional hearings focused attention on these problems, as well as on similar issues related to chemical weapons. At about the same time, and less than five months after taking office, President Richard M. Nixon ordered the National Security Council to reevaluate biological and chemical weapons. On November 25, 1969, in the same announcement in which he dealt with chemical weapons, the president renounced the offensive use of biological weapons. He stated that the United States no longer would develop, produce, or stockpile these weapons and would destroy its arsenal of these weapons. Further research in biological warfare would be for defensive purposes only, such as developing vaccines and other countermeasures to protect the country against biological attack. The United States completed the job of destroying its biological weapons arsenal in 1972.[15] After about three decades, its offensive biological weapons program was over.

The American renunciation of biological weapons helped pave the way for the successful negotiation in 1972 of the Biological and Toxins Weapons

Convention (BWC). The United States signed the BWC that year, and the Senate ratified the convention in 1975.

The U.S. Nuclear Weapons Program

THE ATOMIC BOMB AND HIROSHIMA

The American program to build an atomic bomb originated with a series of decisions made by President Franklin D. Roosevelt between the fall of 1939 and early 1942 that culminated in the establishment of the Manhattan Project. Roosevelt and his top advisers feared that Nazi Germany, a world leader in science and technology and the country where nuclear fission was first achieved, would build such a weapon. In light of the tyrannical nature of the Nazi regime and its unmistakably aggressive intentions, Roosevelt considered a nuclear-armed Germany to be a direct threat to the United States, even before the outbreak of World War II. That threat loomed even larger and more menacing after Germany began the war in September 1939 and, during the next two years, scored a succession of major military victories.

The United States entered the war on the Allied side in December 1941, after Japan's surprise attack on America's Pearl Harbor naval base in Hawaii and Germany's declaration of war against the United States a few days later. The Manhattan Project finally was organized in mid-1942. General Leslie Groves, the officer who had been in charge of building the Pentagon, was put in charge of the vast effort in the fall of that year. The Manhattan Project was the most closely held American military secret of the war; in fact, virtually none of the 125,000 people who worked on the bomb in dozens of locations across the country knew what they were working on. They only knew their specific tasks, whether developing new, high-precision parts for machines, finding materials that could resist corrosion, or solving any of a vast host of other problems. In fact, most of the country's leaders, including top civilian officials and military officers, did not know such a project existed. Roosevelt made his decision to develop the bomb without consulting Congress and hid the Manhattan Project budget inside the overall military budget funding the war effort. Of course, none of this secrecy prevented spies working for the Soviet Union from penetrating the project and, in the end, learning and forwarding to Moscow many of the key secrets needed to build an atomic bomb.

The epicenter of the project was a special laboratory build in a remote part of the New Mexico desert called Los Alamos. This is where the first atomic bombs were designed and built. Los Alamos became home to hundreds of distinguished scientists, many of them Nobel Prize winners, and their families. It eventually grew into a community of 6,000 people, including many children born between 1943 and 1945. Some of the Los Alamos scientists, as well as scientists working at other Manhattan Project locations, were refugees who had fled the Nazi tyranny in Europe and come to the United States. The man in charge at Los Alamos, personally chosen by Groves, was a brilliant young physicist from the University of California at Berkeley named J. Robert Oppenheimer. The Manhattan Project also included two gigantic production facilities—in Oak Ridge, Tennessee, and Hanford, Washington—respectively built from the ground up to produce enriched U-235 and Pu-239. The Oak Ridge site contained a gaseous diffusion plant— four stories high and almost half a mile long—that was the largest building in the world. Although it was the most automated plant in the world, it nonetheless employed 3,000 workers on each of its three shifts. Important work for the Manhattan Project also went on at about a dozen other major locations scattered across the country.

Notwithstanding daunting and unprecedented scientific and technical problems, the Manhattan Project took less than three years to fulfill its assigned task. During that time, there never was any question among America's civilian and military leaders—first under Roosevelt and after April 1945 under Truman—that the atomic bomb would be used if needed to end the war. This may seem surprising, especially given the reluctance of these same decision makers to resort to chemical weapons that in fact were much less destructive, but there are good reasons for it. The radically new nature of the weapon played a part. Not until the plutonium implosion bomb was first tested on July 16, 1945, was the power of the new weapon fully appreciated. In a betting pool arranged just before the New Mexico test, no less an expert than Oppenheimer himself guessed the test would yield an explosion of 300 tons of TNT; the actual explosion yielded 18,000 tons, or 60 times Oppenheimer's guess. Nor was the impact radioactivity would have on people exposed to an atomic blast sufficiently understood. A few days *after* both Hiroshima and Nagasaki had been bombed, an official Manhattan Project statement maintained that very little radioactive waste would reach the ground because both bombs exploded high in the air over the two cities. In fact, a great deal of radioactivity fell to the ground. America's leaders, even as they understood the revolutionary nature of the atomic bomb, also saw it, as Secretary of War Henry L. Stimson put it, as an explosive weapon "much more powerful than any of its predecessors." It seemed reasonable that the United States should make use of this new explosive weapon.[16]

More fundamentally, by the summer of 1945 the people of the United States, soldiers and civilians alike, were war weary, and their leaders knew it. Germany had surrendered in May, but Japan continued to fight on. Casualties in recent battles against entrenched Japanese forces on islands such as Iwo Jima and Okinawa had been shockingly high: almost 26,000 dead and wounded on Iwo Jima, a tiny volcanic rock only eight miles square, and more than 80,000 total casualties, including almost 10,000 navy personnel offshore, in the battle for Okinawa. All intelligence, which included intercepts of Japanese diplomatic and military communications, overwhelmingly indicated that Japan was not prepared to surrender on terms remotely acceptable to the United States and its Allies. The invasion of Japan, scheduled to begin in November 1945, promised casualties of staggering proportions. Estimates that reached President Harry S. Truman went as high as 500,000 or more before a final victory could be achieved. It was against this background that the atomic bomb was used as soon as it was ready. On July 26, 1945, Japan was warned in the Potsdam Declaration, a statement jointly issued by the United States, Britain, and China, that it faced "prompt and utter destruction" if it did not surrender. The Potsdam Declaration also promised Japan that after a period of occupation and reform its sovereignty would be restored under a government "established in accordance with the freely expressed will of the Japanese people."[17] On July 28, Japan rejected the Allied demands. Nine days later, on August 6, 1945, an American B-29 bomber named the *Enola Gay* dropped an atomic bomb on the city of Hiroshima.

When Japan made no move toward surrender in the days immediately after Hiroshima, a second American atomic bomb was dropped on Nagasaki on August 9. By then, the Soviet Union, which had not been involved in the Pacific War, had declared war on Japan. On August 10, the Japanese government stated it was prepared to surrender, but it took until August 14 before crucial differences between the two sides were worked out. Japan officially announced its surrender on Allied terms just before midnight Tokyo time, at last ending World War II. August 9, 1945, marks the last time the United States ever used an atomic bomb as a weapon of war.

THE THERMONUCLEAR (HYDROGEN) BOMB

After World War II, the United States drastically cut its armed forces and its military budget. Although some leaders worried that these cuts went too far, the American people, having lived through the Great Depression and then the war, were determined to get their fathers, sons, and husbands home, get on with their lives, and enjoy the peace. In 1946, the Atomic Energy Act created the civilian Atomic Energy Commission (AEC) to run the U.S. nuclear program, a job it took over from the U.S. Army on January 1, 1947. At that point the army's bomb assembly teams were dispersed. This was an important development, as putting together an atomic bomb was a complex operation requiring a highly trained team of 24 specialists. The task itself took almost two days. Once assembled, the bombs still needed maintenance—essential batteries had to be recharged every 48 hours, for example—to remain usable.

Given all these complications, it is possible that in early 1947 the United States, in a total arsenal of fewer than a dozen nuclear weapons, had only one usable bomb. David E. Lilienthal, the first head of the AEC, who checked the bomb storage area at Los Alamos in 1947, noted, "I was shocked what I found out. . . . Actually we had one [bomb] that probably was operable when I first went off to Los Alamos, one that had a good chance of being operable."[18] This quickly changed over the next two years, especially after serious tension developed with the Soviet Union in Europe during 1948; by late 1949 the United States had an arsenal of about 200 atomic bombs. Testing since 1946 also made these bombs more efficient and powerful than the 1945 bombs.[19]

The Soviet test of an atomic bomb in August 1949 came as a shock to the United States. The Soviets had not been expected to develop a bomb for several more years. It was assumed that the Soviets had succeeded so early because their spies had stolen American secrets. We now know that this assumption was correct, and that Soviet spying on the Manhattan Project probably advanced their program by two years.

The Soviet test immediately led to a debate, both within the Truman administration and in the media, about whether the United States should build a hydrogen bomb. Many people, including experts in the field such as Robert Oppenheimer, opposed development of what they often called the "superbomb," or, simply, the "super." They believed the Soviet Union would follow suit. The result would be an arms race that would create weapons literally capable of destroying all civilized life on the planet. What Oppenheimer and other opponents of the hydrogen bomb did not know—what no one in the West knew—was that the race for a hydrogen bomb was already on, and had been for several years. The Soviet Union actually began working on a design for a thermonuclear bomb in 1946, and by 1948 they had what the historian David Holloway, the leading expert on the early Soviet nuclear program, calls "the basic design concept for a workable thermonuclear bomb."[20]

More than a year later, in January 1950, President Truman knew nothing of this development as he faced the decision about what the United States should do. Truman did know that the Soviet Union had tested an atomic bomb in August 1949. He knew that although expert opinion on what to do was divided, several of his top advisers were warning that the Soviet Union would forge ahead and build a hydrogen bomb, even if the United States did not. This would have created a situation General Omar Bradley, the chairman of the Joint Chiefs of Staff and therefore the country's top military officer, called "intolerable." Truman also knew that the British had just arrested Klaus Fuchs, a prominent physicist who had spied for the Soviet Union while working at Los Alamos during World War II. Fuchs also had taken part in important scientific discussions about the development of the hydrogen bomb. On January 31, 1950, meeting with a special three-person committee he had appointed to advise him about whether to develop the hydrogen bomb, the president asked, simply and directly, "Can the Russians do it?" Everyone at the meeting agreed that they could. Truman responded, "In that case we have no choice. We'll go ahead."[21] The decision was announced that day.

Four decades later in his memoirs, Andrei Sakharov, the designer of the Soviet Union's first hydrogen bomb, offered an answer to the question of whether an American decision not to build that weapon would have affected the Soviet program. President Truman, who died almost 20 years before Sakharov was free to write truthfully about Soviet nuclear policies, would have appreciated hearing what the great Soviet physicist had to say. According to Sakharov, "Any U.S. move toward abandoning work on a thermonuclear weapon would have been perceived as a cunning, deceitful maneuver, or as evidence of stupidity or weakness."[22]

In the race for the hydrogen bomb that followed, both sides could claim at least one victory. The first significant technological advance was actually part of the American effort to improve its fission bombs. In May 1951, the United States tested what was called a "boosted" fission bomb. It was a fission bomb that included a tiny amount of thermonuclear fuel to increase the power of the fission explosion, in this case to more than 45 kilotons. The thermonuclear threshold was crossed on November 1, 1952, when the United States tested a huge device, not a deliverable bomb, that weighed 60 metric tons. It exploded with a force of 10 million tons of TNT, almost 1,000 times more powerful than the Hiroshima bomb, completely obliterating the Pacific coral atoll on which it was detonated. The fireball alone would have engulfed all of Manhattan; the blast would have destroyed the rest of New York City. However, it was the Soviet Union, on August 12, 1953, that tested the first deliverable hydrogen bomb. The so-called layer cake bomb, conceived by Andrei Sakharov, was not a full two-stage thermonuclear device, as its design limited the amount of thermonuclear fuel that could be used and hence the size of the explosion that could be achieved. Still, a significant proportion of its explosive yield of about 400 kilotons came from fusion reactions, which is why it is considered a thermonuclear bomb. It is worth noting that just two months earlier, the U.S. Central Intelligence Agency (CIA) reported that it had "no evidence" that the Soviet Union was working on thermonuclear weapons.[23] The first American deliverable bomb was detonated on a Pacific atoll in February 1954 with a yield of 15 megatons. The first fully thermonuclear Soviet bomb, in November 1955, produced an explosion of 1.6 megatons.[24]

FROM ARMS RACE TO ARMS CONTROL

The Nuclear Arsenal at Mid-Century

By the mid-1950s, the nuclear arms race between the United States and the Soviet Union was well under way. There are many factors that must be considered in measuring the size of a nuclear arsenal, including how many nuclear warheads or bombs[25] that arsenal contains and the number of missiles and bombers of various sorts available to deliver them. The total explosive force of an arsenal's weapons and the accuracy with which they can be delivered also are crucial factors in evaluating a nuclear arsenal. That said, between 1954 and 1966, the U.S. stockpile of nuclear warheads and bombs grew from about 2,000 to more than 32,000. Thereafter, that number declined gradually for 25 years as the arsenal was modernized, falling to 21,000 in 1990, the year before the START I (Strategic Arms Reduction Treaty) agreement with the Soviet Union led to much deeper reductions.[26]

The United States relied on what it called a triad of systems to deliver nuclear weapons against targets in the Soviet Union. This triad consisted of intercontinental ballistic missiles (ICBMs), submarine-launched ballistic missiles (SLBMs), and long-range bombers, which could deliver bombs and, after they were developed, highly accurate cruise missiles. The first modern jet bomber designed to deliver nuclear weapons was the B-52, which first entered service in 1954. Over time, newer versions of the B-52 entered service, as did two entirely new bombers: the supersonic B-1B, which entered service in the mid-1980s, and the B-2, which entered service in the early 1990s and has a special stealth design that makes it very difficult for enemy radar to detect. The first ICBM, the Atlas, became operational in 1959, while the first submarine capable of firing Polaris missiles entered service in 1960. In the decades that followed, the original versions of these weapons were replaced by more advanced and reliable versions. The cumbersome liquid-fueled Atlas, later joined by the larger and even more complex Titan missile, gave way to the solid-fueled Minuteman and MX missiles that could be launched from their silos within minutes. The solid-fueled Minuteman and MX also were more accurate and much safer and easier to maintain than their liquid-fueled predecessors. At sea, Polaris missiles were replaced by Poseidon missiles. They in turn gave way to Trident missiles, which were carried on the newly developed Ohio class submarines. However, the basic concept of a triad was retained.[27] The United States also deployed a variety of shorter range nuclear weapons outside its borders, including ballistic and cruise missiles in Europe to deter any Soviet attack against members of the NATO alliance.

Nuclear Tests

The United States required many nuclear tests to develop its arsenal. Between 1946 and 1962, it conducted 1,054 tests, 24 of which were done jointly with Great Britain. Of these, 210 were in the atmosphere, 839 (including the 24 conducted jointly with Great Britain) were underground, and five were underwater. The last non-underground test was in 1962, while the last American nuclear test of any kind was in 1992. Since then, the United States has conducted 23 of what the government calls "subcritical experiments" at its Nevada test site, most recently in 2006. Because these experiments were not capable of producing a self-sustaining chain reaction, the American position was that these experiments were not nuclear tests.[28]

One problem with nuclear tests is that they are dangerous, especially aboveground tests that release radioactive materials into the atmosphere. An example was the test of the first deliverable American hydrogen bomb conducted on a Pacific atoll in 1954. The February explosion turned out to be twice as powerful as expected, and shifting winds brought radioactive fallout to inhabited islands whose population had not been evacuated. Hundreds of people were showered by nuclear fallout. The fallout also poisoned the crew of a Japanese fishing boat, one of whose members died. Even underground nuclear tests pose risks. In 1970, radioactivity from an underground test at the Nevada Test Site, the main U.S. site for underground tests, escaped into the atmosphere. Today, that area, where about 100 atmospheric and 800 underground tests took place, is still scarred by those tests. More than 300 square miles beneath the site is contaminated, and more than 30,000 acres aboveground have contaminated soil whose use must be permanently restricted.[29]

Nonproliferation Efforts

The accelerating nuclear arms race was a major concern in capitals throughout the world, including Washington and Moscow. Developing ever more advanced missiles, warheads, and related systems was extremely expensive, but, more than that, the buildup of nuclear weapons left the United States, the Soviet Union, and their allies in a very dangerous position. A crisis could push the two countries into a nuclear war, something that almost happened during the Cuban missile crisis of 1962. It was conceivable that a nuclear war could begin by accident if one side or the other mistakenly thought it was under attack and therefore attacked the other with its bombers or missiles.

The two sides began discussing limiting their nuclear arms in the late 1960s. In 1972, the world's two nuclear superpowers signed SALT I, which actually consisted of two treaties. The Anti-Ballistic Missile Treaty (ABM Treaty) limited the number of antiballistic missiles each country was permitted to have to 100 each for two sites—such as a city or a military base;

in 1974, that number was further reduced to 100 for one site. In effect, the ABM Treaty was a relief to both sides for two reasons. First, any effort to build a missile defense that could protect an entire country would be prohibitively expensive. Second, given the technology available at that time, it was impossible for either side to protect itself against the other's huge missile arsenal. The second SALT I treaty was the Interim Agreement, which put limits on how many ICBMs and SLBMs each side could have. The agreement allowed the Soviet Union a slightly larger number of both missiles because of America's technological advantages. However, it did not cover bombers, an area where the United States had a numerical advantage. More significantly, the Interim Agreement counted missiles, not warheads. This left both sides free to develop technologies that would allow them to put more than one warhead on each missile. These new warheads were called MIRVs (multiple independently targeted reentry vehicle) and were another area in which the United States had a technological lead: The United States deployed its first MIRV warheads in 1970, five years ahead of the Soviet Union.[30]

In short, SALT I put some brakes on the arms race, but did not keep it from moving forward. The SALT II agreement of 1979 had an expanded scope to include bombers and MIRVs, but it was never ratified by either side. It nonetheless was unofficially observed by both countries until the United States withdrew from the agreement in 1986. The next year, the United States and the Soviet Union signed the INF (Intermediate-Range Nuclear Forces) Treaty, under which over the next several years they destroyed all of their ground-launched nuclear ballistic and cruise missiles with ranges between 300 and 3,300 miles. That treaty included extensive on-site inspections and other means of verification to make sure its terms were carried out.[31]

In 1991, the United States and the Soviet Union finally reached an agreement that reduced the number of strategic nuclear weapons, the most destructive weapons in their arsenals that were aimed at each other. The term *strategic* refers to land-based ballistic missiles with a range of more than 3,440 miles (5,500 km), ballistic missiles launched from submarines, and long-range bombers, as well as the nuclear warheads designed for those delivery vehicles. START I—along with its various annexes, protocols, agreements, and understandings—was a complicated document hundreds of pages long with elaborate provisions for on-site inspections and verification by other means such as spy satellites. It required the United States and the Soviet Union to reduce their total strategic nuclear warhead stockpiles to 6,000. This figure refers to nuclear warheads actually deployed and ready for use. It does not include those in storage or nonstrategic (short-range) weapons. START I therefore required the United States to cut its arsenal of strategic nuclear weapons almost in half, something it achieved, on schedule, in 2001. Russia, which inherited most of the Soviet nuclear arsenal when that country collapsed, met its obligations as well.[32]

START II, signed by the United States and Russia in 1993 and intended to reduce strategic warheads to about 3,000–3,500 per nation, never entered into force. The Russian parliament did not ratify the treaty until 2000, and then did so with conditions unacceptable to the United States. In 2002, the United States pulled out of the 1972 ABM Treaty. The reason, as explained by President George W. Bush, was that the treaty did not allow the United States to build defenses against new nuclear missile threats—from countries such as North Korea and Iran—that did not exist in 1972. As the president put it, "The ABM Treaty hinders our government's ability to develop ways to protect our people from future terrorist or rogue state missile attacks."[33] Meanwhile, in 2002 the United States and Russia signed SORT (Strategic Offensive Reductions Treaty), also known as the Moscow Treaty. Under SORT, the United States and Russia pledged to reduce their strategic nuclear arsenals to 1,700–2,200 deployed warheads each. The short treaty—it is less than two pages long—contains no inspection or other verification provisions. This caused concern because all U.S.-Russian inspection and verification procedures depended on START I, which was scheduled to expire in December 2009. Beyond that, the newly signed SORT extended only until the last day of 2012. This meant that unless new agreements were negotiated, as of 2010, when START I expired, there would be no verification procedures in place, and as of 2013, when SORT expired, the United States and the Soviet Union would be free to add warheads to their nuclear arsenals. Nevertheless, after signing SORT the United States continued to reduce its nuclear arsenal, and by early 2009 it officially passed the halfway mark in meeting its obligations under that treaty. In December 2009, when START I expired, Russia and the United States agreed to respect the terms of that treaty, including its vital inspection provisions, while they continued negotiations on a new treaty.[34]

THE CURRENT U.S. NUCLEAR WEAPONS ARSENAL

The nuclear forces of the United States are in a state of flux. In compliance with its treaty obligations, the United States is continuing to reduce its arsenal of nuclear warheads. It has also phased out some of the missiles built during the cold war to deliver them. At the same time, it is attempting to modernize its remaining arsenal so that it remains effective for deterring aggression or, if necessary, responding to WMD attacks.

As of early 2009, the United States had a stockpile of about 5,200 nuclear warheads. This stockpile included 2,700 operational warheads and 2,500 being held in reserve. Of the operational warheads, about 2,200 are for strategic—that is, long-range—missiles or bombers. The others, about 500 warheads, are designed for short-range (tactical) air-launched or submarine-launched cruise missiles or for delivery by various types of aircraft such as the F-16 N/D and F-15E. An additional 4,200 warheads were scheduled to be dismantled, meaning that the United States actually had a total of 9,400 warheads. As in the past, the strategic nuclear warheads could be delivered by a triad of weapons: land-based ICBMs, SLBMs, and bombers. The ICBMs were all Minuteman III missiles; the last MX missiles were retired in 2005. The SLBMs are Trident II missiles. The bombers were the most advanced version of the B-52—the B-52H—and the B-2. (The B-1B no longer was assigned to carry nuclear weapons.) The B-52H bombers carry two types of nuclear bombs as well as cruise missiles equipped with nuclear warheads, while the B-2 stealth bombers carry three types of nuclear bombs. The United States also had more than 4,000 strategic warheads awaiting dismantlement.[35]

The U.S. nuclear arsenal, like that of any other country, must be maintained in order to remain reliable and therefore effective as a deterrent against aggression. This is a serious problem because nuclear weapons deteriorate over time. In 2009, the average American nuclear warhead, built during the cold war, was more than 20 years old. Most were between 30 and 40 years old. This is longer than their intended lifetimes when they were designed and built; during the cold war, nuclear weapons generally were replaced by newer and more modern designs every 10 to 15 years. This is a major concern of the National Nuclear Security Administration (NNSA), which was established within the U.S. Department of Energy in 2000 and is responsible for the management and security of the nation's nuclear weapons. To maintain America's nuclear weapons—without resorting to nuclear testing—the NNSA operates the Stockpile Stewardship Program, which currently receives about $6 billion per year in funding. That overall effort includes keeping nuclear warheads and bombs in working order through what the NNSA calls life extension programs (LEPs). Each different type of weapon has its own LEP, which involves careful inspection of warheads and bombs and replacement of components as needed. This is a painstaking and expensive job. Warheads and bombs, each of which contains thousands of parts, must be disassembled, as must many of their key components, and new components must be manufactured that work exactly like the old ones. As the NNSA has pointed out, this allows the United States to extend the life of its nuclear arsenal for 20 to 30 years without producing new weapons or conducting nuclear tests.[36]

In 2005, the NNSA concluded that additional measures were necessary to properly maintain the U.S. nuclear stockpile. It argued that even with the LEPs it is not possible to prevent nuclear warheads from deteriorating over the long term. It therefore recommended what it calls the Reliable Replacement Warhead (RRW) program. Under this program, the NNSA will go beyond checking older warheads and replacing their parts as needed. Instead, it will design, produce, and deploy an entirely new generation of warheads to provide the United States with a safer and more reliable stockpile of nuclear weapons. When the NNSA proposed the RRW program, its administrator Linton Brooks added a second reason to rebuild America's nuclear stockpile: the need to train a new generation of nuclear weapons designers and engineers before the current generation retires. Since 2005, Congress has provided limited funding to start the RRW program. In early 2007, it selected a design team from the Lawrence Livermore National Laboratory and the Sandia National Laboratories to develop a RRW warhead for U.S. submarine-based missiles. However, significantly larger funding will be required to carry out the RRW program. In addition, some scientists oppose the RRW program because they are concerned it may lead to nuclear testing. Others have a very different, and opposite, concern: They want to go beyond the LEP and RRW programs and resume nuclear testing on the grounds that only testing can guarantee a reliable nuclear arsenal over the long term. It therefore remains a matter of debate whether the RRW is the best way to proceed.[37]

U.S. STRATEGIES FOR COMBATING WMD

In December 2002, about 15 months after Islamic terrorists destroyed the World Trade Center in New York City and damaged the Pentagon in Washington, D.C., the White House issued its National Strategy to Combat Weapons of Mass Destruction (NSCWMD). It warned that weapons of mass destruction "in the possession of hostile states and terrorists represent one of the greatest security challenges facing the United States." The document noted that several countries that have supported international terrorism already possess WMD and "are seeking even greater capabilities." These states intend to use these weapons to prevent the United States from responding to aggression "against our friends and allies in regions of vital interest." The NSCWMD also warned that terrorists are attempting to acquire WMD "with the stated purpose of killing large numbers of our people and those of our friends and allies—without compunction and without warning." It then listed three pillars, or broad approaches, that form the basis of the effort to protect the United States against WMD: counter-proliferation, nonproliferation, and WMD consequence management. Counter-proliferation means preventing the use of WMD that are in the hands of hostile forces. Among other things, this involves military, intelligence, law enforcement, and other agencies preventing WMD materials, technology, and expertise from reaching hostile states or terrorist groups. It also includes destroying WMD in hostile hands before they can be used. Nonproliferation is the effort to prevent the spread of WMD, often through international cooperation. This includes strengthening international organizations such as the International Atomic Energy Agency (IAEA) and international treaties such as the Treaty on the Non-Proliferation of Nuclear Weapons (NPT). It also includes actions the United States can take on its own, such as improving export controls on materials that can be used to produce WMD. Consequence management means minimizing the impact of WMD if they are used against civilians at home or American military personnel abroad.[38]

In practice, these broad categories tend to overlap, and specific programs that are put into place often apply to more than one of the NSCWMD pillars. What follows therefore will be an overview of the most important current national programs and policies, rather than a pillar-by-pillar summary of the NSCWMD.

Countering Biological and Chemical Weapons

Measures against biological and chemical weapons deal primarily with the threat of terrorism. An essential part of that effort is detecting either biological or chemical agents before they can do extensive damage. In 2007, the Department of Homeland Security (DHS) reported that between 2001 and 2007 various agencies in the federal government had spent $32 billion on detection systems and other programs related to bio-defense alone. This included the BioSense program run by the Centers for Disease Control (CDC) that collects data from federal, state, and local agencies in order to detect and identify public health emergencies. The DHS, along with the Environmental Protection Agency (EPA) and the CDC, operates BioWatch, which monitors atmospheric sensors in 30 American cities. These sensors are designed to detect and analyze dangerous biological agents. Equally important are measures to combat these agents. To that end, the DHS, along with the Department of Health and Human Services (HHS), manages Project BioShield, established in 2004. BioShield provides funding to develop medical measures against attacks by biological, chemical, and radiological weapons. These countermeasures include vaccines, drugs, and diagnostic equipment and are held in the Strategic National Stockpile (SNS) for emergency use. In 2004, DHS was given $5.6 billion over 10 years to purchase these countermeasures. In mid-2008, the HHS reported progress in several areas, including having delivered 10 million doses of anthrax vaccine and antibiotics to be used following exposure to anthrax to the SNS.[39]

The federal government has also organized and trained dozens of National Guard civil support teams to assist local authorities in the event of a WMD attack. The civil support teams undergo 15 months of training and have the skills and equipment to detect chemical, biological, and even nuclear agents. As of mid-2008, three dozen of the planned 55 teams were certified to carry out their missions.[40]

The federal effort to improve defenses against the most deadly biological agents took on additional urgency after 2001, when five people died and 17 became sick after receiving or handling anthrax-contaminated mail. Several of these letters were sent to the offices of U.S. senators, and Senate offices had to be shut down. The others were sent to members of the news media. It took five months to decontaminate one government building, the Hart Senate Office Building. It took until the summer of 2008 to close the case, when the government identified a top-level researcher at the government's bio-defense labs at Ft. Detrick, Maryland, as the culprit. However, since he committed suicide just before he was about to be indicted, unresolved questions about the nature and extent of his guilt remain.[41]

Research on the most dangerous agents is done in ultrahigh-security facilities called Biosafety Level 4 (BSL-4) laboratories, the facilities with the highest available level of lab security. In 2001, there were only five of these labs in the United States; by 2007, after a massive increase in funding, there were 15. These laboratories are surrounded by fences, guards, closed-circuit TVs, alarms, and other devices. Workers must pass strict background checks. In the buildings that house the labs, the air is filtered, and staff must wear special gear and follow strict decontamination procedures. Nonetheless, the BSL-4 labs are controversial because they still have safety problems, such as deadly materials being misplaced or workers in the labs accidentally becoming infected despite stringent security procedures. During 2007 and 2008, the Government Accountability Office (GAO) examined perimeter security procedures at five of the country's leading BSL-4 labs and found that three of them had poor security. That said, the government views the research these labs do as vital to defending the country against biological weapons that might fall into terrorist hands.[42]

Other aspects of defensive research include understanding the effectiveness of weapons that terrorists might get their hands on. For example, the CIA at one point built and tested a Soviet-designed germ bomb it feared might be sold to terrorists. In another project, military experts built a germ factory using only products available for commercial uses. The project revealed how easy it would be for a terrorist organization or a hostile nation, by using ordinary commercial materials, to build a facility to produce biological weapons without being detected.[43]

The United States also has cooperated with countries that formerly were part of the Soviet Union to eliminate threats left by cold war era Soviet biological weapons program. Funds for this effort have been provided by the Nunn-Lugar Cooperative Threat Reduction (CTR) Program (see "Countering Nuclear Weapons" below). Under that program, beginning in the 1990s, the United States destroyed former Soviet facilities for making biological weapons in Kazakhstan and Uzbekistan. It also decontaminated an island in the Aral Sea shared by the two countries where 150 tons of anthrax had been buried. Before burying the anthrax, the Soviet government had attempted to decontaminate it, but it was later discovered that the Soviet effort had failed. The United States therefore had to finish the job.[44]

Countering Nuclear Weapons

Whereas U.S. measures against biological and chemical weapons focus primarily on terrorist organizations, the country's measures against nuclear weapons must take into account a broader range of threats. They must focus on terrorists, unfriendly countries that already have nuclear weapons, and countries that are attempting to acquire these weapons.

One of the most effective American measures against nuclear weapons has been the Nunn-Lugar CTR Program, designed to prevent fissile materials necessary for making nuclear weapons from getting into the wrong hands. The program is named for Sam Nunn and Richard Lugar, who were its main sponsors in the U.S. Senate. Enacted into law in 1991, the CTR provides U.S. funds and expert help for Russia to dismantle its nuclear stockpile according to its treaty agreements and to safeguard its remaining nuclear materials. Along with dismantling actual nuclear weapons, it is vital to secure the fissile materials of which they are made. Russia has a huge amount of fissile nuclear material that terrorists could use to make atomic weapons, if they could steal or illegally buy it. The CTR therefore provides funds and equipment to secure sites at which nuclear weapons and materials are stored. By 2008, more than 2,000 Russian ICBMs had been dismantled and 7,200 of its nuclear warheads deactivated. The CTR also provided funds and expertise to remove nuclear materials from the former Soviet states such as Ukraine, Kazakhstan, and Belarus. For example, during 1994 in a top-secret operation almost 600 kilograms of weapons-grade uranium were removed from Kazakhstan and shipped to the United States. Some of the CTR's activities ranged beyond the borders of the former Soviet Union, as in 2002 when enough weapons-grade uranium to make two atomic bombs was removed from Serbia. A private organization known as the Nuclear Threat Initiative (NTI) participated in that operation by providing Serbia with $5 million for environmental cleanup. Along with its anti-nuclear efforts, the CTR provides U.S. funds and other assistance to eliminate Russia's chemical and biological stockpiles. Additional CTR funds are used to employ scientists who formerly worked in Soviet WMD programs for peaceful purposes. This is to discourage them from working for countries secretly attempting to develop those weapons or providing their expertise to terrorist groups.[45]

In 2004, the United States launched another program to secure the world's nuclear materials from terrorists, the Global Threat Reduction Initiative (GTRI). The GTRI is run by the U.S. Department of Energy's NNSA and cooperates with other nations, including Russia, concerned with preventing terrorists from getting their hands on nuclear material. For example, in 2005, the United States and Russia cooperated in the removal of 14 kilograms of highly enriched uranium (HEU) from the Czech Republic to Russia. By 2008, enough HEU to make five nuclear bombs had been removed from countries that either formerly were part of the Soviet Union or Soviet-dominated states of Eastern Europe. The latter group included Poland, from which 8.8 kilograms of HEU was returned to Russia in 2007. As part of its GTRI mission, the NNSA works worldwide to protect nuclear materials at a variety of sites, to remove them from other sites, and to convert HEU to low-enriched uranium (LEU) that can be used to fuel nuclear power plants but not to build nuclear weapons. Although there is a great deal more to be done, NNSA's progress in these areas is substantial.[46]

Another way the United States supports the fight against nuclear weapons its endorsement of the international NPT. Nonproliferation depends on international cooperation for enforcement, and it has worked, such as when the United States worked together with Russia between 1992 and 1994 to get Ukraine, Belarus, and Kazakhstan to give up the former Soviet nuclear weapons based on their territories. International cooperation ended Iraq's nuclear weapons programs (as well as its biological and chemical weapons programs) after the Gulf War of 1991. In this case, the international community first defeated Iraq in battle before Iraq agreed to conditions that enabled UN inspectors to find and dismantle those programs. Even then, it took more than four years for those inspectors to discover the extent of the Iraqi nuclear program, aided by Saddam Hussein's son-in-law who defected to the United States and revealed the location of key information, including computer diskettes, photographs, and hardware components. He also provided important information on Iraq's chemical and biological weapons programs. Sanctions, diplomatic pressure, and fear of U.S. military action after the United States and its allies had removed Saddam Hussein from power in Iraq likely led the Libyan dictator Muammar Qaddafi to give up his country's secret nuclear program in 2004, along with its chemical weapons and missile programs. However, neither the NPT nor international pressure prevented North Korea from developing and testing a nuclear weapon in 2006, nor have they stopped Iran's nuclear enrichment program, which is intended to create material that can be used to build nuclear weapons.[47]

U.S. countermeasures also include preventing nuclear or radiological weapons that are already in the hands of terrorists or hostile countries from reaching the United States. One way to get a nuclear weapon into the United States, especially for terrorists, is to ship it into the country and then set it off by remote control. That is why since 2001 the United States has spent billions of dollars to develop high-tech inspection equipment to check containers coming into its seaports. In October 2006, this effort was reinforced by the Security and Accountability for Every Port (SAFE) Act, which was designed to keep nuclear, chemical, and biological weapons from entering the country in any of the 11 million containers shipped to the United States each year. The act also reinforced the program under which U.S. inspectors check cargo in foreign ports before it is shipped to this country.[48]

A long-standing U.S. measure for countering nuclear weapons is its system of early warning satellites, called the Defense Support Program (DSP). The first DSP launch was in 1970, and since then more than 20 of these satellites have been put into orbit. Five of those satellites were still operational when the last of the DSP series launched in November 2007. Plans call for replacing the DSP system with a more advanced system of satellites called the Space-Based Infrared System (SBIRS). The SBIRS satellites, which will be in a high Earth orbit, in turn will be part of a larger warning system that includes low-orbit satellites and ground- and sea-based radars.[49]

Another countermeasure that is more controversial is the development of a missile defense system. From 1983 to 1993, the United States had a project called the Strategic Defense Initiative (SDI) that researched the possibility of building a defense against Soviet ballistic missiles. However, the system the United States is developing is not designed to defend against Russian missiles. That in fact would be impossible. Even with the reduction in its number of nuclear weapons, Russia will continue to have more than enough nuclear-armed missiles to overwhelm any system the United States could build. Nor is Russia likely to attack the United States with nuclear missiles. Despite tensions between the two countries, they do not consider themselves enemies. Beyond that is the certainty that any attack on the United States will be followed by retaliation that Russia cannot survive.

Instead, the U.S. missile defense program is directed against countries with small nuclear arsenals such as North Korea and, potentially, Iran, which might resort to nuclear blackmail or may not be deterred by the threat of retaliation. It is designed to protect not only the United States but also its allies and friends and involves a variety of missiles with different capabilities. The United States currently has what the Defense Department's Missile Defense Agency calls "a limited defense against ballistic missile attack." It consists primarily of ground-based missiles based in Alaska and California designed to defend against long-range missiles; Aegis missiles based on warships designed to defend against short- to intermediate-range missiles; and PAC-3 missiles designed to defend against short- and medium-range missiles. Other systems are under development, such as the truck-based portable Terminal High Altitude Area Defense (THAAD) system, which had its fifth consecutive successful test in mid-2008. Overall, between 2001 and 2008, the Missile Defense Agency was successful in 35 of the 43 tests it conducted in which it used one missile to hit and shoot down another. The agency calls these tests "hit-to-kill intercepts."[50]

Missile defense is controversial. Some weapons experts such as Joseph Cirincione believe it is not possible to build a system that is sufficiently reliable. Others, such as Loren B. Thompson, Ph.D., the former deputy director of the security studies program at Georgetown University, strongly disagree, and there is an ongoing debate on the subject. Several countries are currently partnering with the United States in building missile defenses. Japan has worked with the United States since 1999 and plans to deploy four warships with Aegis missiles. NATO allies such as Great Britain, Denmark, the Netherlands, and the Czech Republic all support American missile defense efforts. Israel's Arrow missile defense system, which the United States co-funded and developed, has been deployed since 2000. A more advanced version of the Arrow, again with U.S. assistance, is being developed. India is another country that has worked on developing a missile defense system.[51] All of this means that missile defense is going to continue to be a central part of the U.S. effort to protect itself and its allies and friends against nuclear weapons that are in the hands of hostile countries.

1 Alex Markels. "Will Terrorism Rewrite the Laws of War." Available online. URL: http://www.npr.org/templates/story/story.php?storyId=5011464. Accessed July 15, 2008; "General Orders No. 100: Instructions for the Government of Armies of the United States in the Field." The Avalon Project at Yale Law School. Available online. URL: http://avalon.law.yale.edu/19th_century/lieber.asp. Accessed March 25, 2008.

2 Al Mauroni. "The US Army Chemical Corps: Past, Present, Future." Army History Research Web site. Available online. URL: http://www.armyhistory.org/armyhistorical.aspx?pgID=868&id=1 33excompID=32. Accessed July 14, 2008; Jonathan B. Tucker. *War of Nerves: Chemical Warfare from World War I to al-Qaeda.* New York: Pantheon Books, 2006, pp. 20–21.

3 Mauroni. "The US Army Chemical Corps: Past, Present, Future."

4 Quoted in Joseph Cirincione, Jon B. Wolfsthal, and Miriam Rajkumar. *Deadly Arsenals: Nuclear, Biological, and Chemical Threats,* Second Edition, revised and expanded. Washington, D.C.: Carnegie Endowment for International Peace, 2005, p. 213.

5 Mauroni. "The US Army Chemical Corps: Past, Present, Future"; Tucker. *War of Nerves,* p. 89.

6 Tucker. *War of Nerves,* pp. 86–90 (Details on the British War Office study conducted in 1951 can be found on page 86.).

7 Tucker. *War of Nerves,* pp. 122–134, 140–141.

8 Tucker. *War of Nerves,* pp. 158–164, 165–170; Cirincione, Wolfsthal, and Rajkumar. *Deadly Arsenals,* p. 213.

[9] Tucker. *War of Nerves,* pp. 180–181, 212–218; Mauroni. "The US Army Chemical Corps: Past, Present, Future."

[10] Mauroni. "The US Army Chemical Corps: Past, Present"; Tucker. *War of Nerves,* pp. 226–230, 240–242, 262–266, 302.

[11] Jeffrey K. Smart. "History of Chemical and Biological Warfare: An American Perspective." In *Medical Aspects of Chemical and Biological Warfare.* Bethesda, Md.: Office of the Surgeon General, Department of the United States Army, 1997, 72–74. Available online. URL: www.bordeninstitute.army.mil/published_volumes/chemBio/chembio.html. Accessed July 17, 2008.

[12] Center for Defense Information. Chemical and Biological Weapons Site. "Chemical Weapons Convention Overview." Available online. URL: http://cdi.org/issues/cbw/chem.html. Accessed June 22, 2008. Tucker. *War of Nerves,* p. 320.

[13] Tucker. *War of Nerves,* pp. 292–295, 317–324; Eric Croddy. *Chemical and Biological Warfare: A Comprehensive Survey for the Concerned Citizen.* New York: Copernicus Books, 2002; p. 176; U.S. Army Chemical Materials Web site. "U.S. Army Chemical Materials Agency Destroys Half of Total Number of Munitions in National Stockpile." August 30, 2006. Available online. URL: http://www.cma.army.mil/fndocumentviewer.aspx?docid=003675943. Accessed July 16, 2008; Nuclear Threat Initiative. United States Profile. "Introduction." Updated May 2008. Available online. URL: http://www.nti.org/e_research/profiles/USA/index.html. Accessed July 14, 2008.

[14] The material in this and the following two paragraphs is based on the following sources: Croddy. *Chemical and Biological Warfare,* pp. 227–232; Henry L. Stimson Center. "History of the U.S. Offensive Biological Warfare Program (1941–1973)." Available online. URL: http://www.stimson.org/cbw/?sn=CB2001121275. Accessed July 18, 2008; Cirincione, Wolfsthal, and Rajkumar. *Deadly Arsenals,* pp. 211–212; Jeanne Guillemin. *Biological Weapons: From the Invention of State-Sponsored Programs to Contemporary Bioterrorism.* New York: Columbia University Press, 2005, p. 110.

[15] Henry L. Stimson Center. "History of the U.S. Offensive Biological Warfare Program (1941–1973)." Available online. URL: http://www.stimson.org/cbw/?sn=CB2001121275. Accessed July 18, 2008; Croddy. *Chemical and Biological Warfare,* pp. 232–233; Guillemin. *Biological Weapons,* pp. 124–125; Cirincione, Wolfsthal, and Rajkumar. *Deadly Arsenals,* p. 212.

[16] Michael Kort. *The Columbia Guide to Hiroshima and the Bomb.* New York: Columbia University Press, 2007, p. 24; Michael D. Gordin. *Five Days in August: How World War II Became a Nuclear War.* Princeton, N.J.: Princeton University Press, 2007, pp. 52–58. The Stimson quote is in *Five Days in August,* p. 57.

[17] Kort. *The Columbia Guide to Hiroshima and the Bomb,* pp. 40–44, 226–228.

[18] Robert H. Ferrell. *Harry S. Truman and the Cold War Revisionists.* Columbia and London: University of Missouri Press, 2006, pp. 49–51. The chapter where this information appears has the telling title "Diplomacy without Armaments."

[19] Joseph Cirincione. *Bomb Scare: The History and Future of Nuclear Weapons.* New York: Columbia University Press, 2008, p. 21; McGeorge Bundy. *Danger and Survival: Choices about the Atomic Bomb in the First Fifty Years.* New York: Random House, 1988, p. 203.

[20] David Holloway. *Stalin and the Bomb.* New Haven, Conn., and London: Yale University Press, 1994, pp. 294–299.

[21] Bundy. *Danger and Survival,* pp. 211–213.

[22] Quoted in Holloway. *Stalin and the Bomb,* p. 318.

[23] Holloway. *Stalin and the Bomb,* pp. 299–300, 307, 310; Richard Rhodes. *Dark Son: The Making of the Hydrogen Bomb.* New York: Simon and Schuster, 1995, p. 510.

[24] David Holloway. *The Soviet Union and the Arms Race.* New Haven, Conn.: Yale University Press, 1983, p. 24.

[25] Following conventional usage, the term *warhead* will be used to apply to warheads that are fitted on missiles or bombs dropped by aircraft.

[26] "Global Nuclear Stockpiles, 1945–2006." *Bulletin of Atomic Scientists* (July/August 2006): p. 66

[27] Atomic Forum. "U.S. Nuclear Weapons Program." Available online. URL: www.atomicforum.org/usa/usa.html. Accessed July 21, 2008; U.S. Navy Fact File. "Fleet Ballistic Missile Submarines—SSBN." Available online. URL: www.navy.mil/data/fact_display.asp?cid=4100&tid=200<0x0026 >ct=4. Accessed July 23, 2008; Natural Resources Defense Council. "Issues: Nuclear Weapons, Waste and Energy." Available online. URL: www.nrdc.org/nuclear/nudb/data5.asp. Accessed July 23, 2008; National Park Service. "History of Minuteman Missile Sites." Available online. URL: www.nps.gov/archive.mimi/history/srs/history.htm. Accessed July 23, 2008.

[28] Nuclear Weapon Archive. "Gallery of U.S. Nuclear Tests." Available online. URL: www.nucleararchive.org/Usa/Tests/index.html. Accessed July 22, 2008; Jonathan Medalia. "CRS Report for Congress. Comprehensive Nuclear Test-Ban Treaty: Background and Current Developments." Updated May 28, 2008. Congressional Research Service. Available online. URL: http://opencrs.cdt.org/document/RL33548. Accessed July 25, 2008.

[29] Gerard J. DeGroot. *The Bomb: A Life.* Cambridge, Mass.: Harvard University Press, 2005, pp. 196–198; "Nevada Natural Resources Status Report." Available online. URL: http://dcnr.nv.gov/nrp01/env10.htm. Accessed April 9, 2009.

[30] Michael Kort. *The Columbia Guide to the Cold War.* New York: Columbia University Press, 1998, pp. 65–66.

[31] Thomas Graham, Jr. *Commonsense on Weapons of Mass Destruction.* Seattle and London: University of Washington Press, 2004, pp. 41–42; Cirincione, *Bomb Scare,* p. 40.

[32] Graham. *Commonsense on Weapons of Mass Destruction,* pp. 42–43; Cirincione, Wolfsthal, and Rajkumar. *Deadly Arsenals,* p. 210.

[33] CNN.com. "U.S. Quits AMB Treaty." December 14, 2001. Available online. URL: http://archives.cnn.com/2001/ALLPOLITICS/12/13/rec.bush.abm/. Accessed July 23, 2008.

[34] Arms Control Association. "Text of the Treaty Between the United States of America and the Russian Federation on Strategic Offensive Reductions." (5/24/02). Available online. URL: www.armscontrol.org/docments/sort.asp. Accessed July 23, 2008; Cirincione, Wolfsthal, and Rajkumar. *Deadly Arsenals,* pp. 210–211; Robert S. Norris and Hans Kristenson. "U.S. Nuclear Forces, 2009." *Bulletin of the Atomic Scientists* (March/April 2009), p. 59.

[35] Norris and Kristensen. "U.S. Nuclear Forces, 2009." *Bulletin of the Atomic Scientists* (March/April 2009): pp. 60–64; Anatoli Diakov, Eugene Miasnikov, and Mimur Kadyshev. *Non-Strategic Nuclear Weapons: Problems of Control and Reduction.* Moscow: Center for Arms Control, Energy, and Environmental Studies of the Moscow Institute of Physics and Technology, 2004, p. 29.

[36] National Nuclear Security Administration. "Life Extension Programs." Available online. URL: http://nnsa.energy.gov/defense_programs/print/life_extension_programs.htm. Accessed July 25, 2008; ———. "The Stockpile." Available online. URL: http://nnsa.energy.gov/defense_programs/print/The_Stockpile.htm. Accessed July 25, 2008; Jonathan Medalia. "CRS Report for Congress. The Reliable Replacement Warhead Program: Background and Current Developments." Updated May 19, 2008. Congressional Research Service. Available online. URL: www.fas.org/sgp/crs/nike/RL32929.pdf. Accessed July 24, 2008; National Nuclear Security Administration. "Stockpile Stewardship Plan Overview." Fiscal Years 2007–2011. (11/13/06). Available online. URL: http://nnsa.energe.gov/defense_programs/documents/Stockplie_Overview_November_13_20 06pdf. Accessed July 27, 2008; Cirincione, Wolfsthal, and Rajkumar. *Deadly Arsenals,* p. 208.

[37] Jonathan Medalia. "CRS Report for Congress. The Reliable Replacement Warhead Program: Background and Current Developments." Updated May 19, 2008. Congressional Research Service. Available online. URL: www.fas.org/sgp/crs/nike/RL32929.pdf. Accessed July 24, 2008; Eli Kintisch. "Livermore Lab Dips into the Past to Win Weapons Design Contest." *Science* (March 9, 2007). Available online. URL: www.sciencemag.org/cgi/content/full/315/5817/1348. Accessed July 30, 2008.

[38] White House. *National Strategy to Combat Weapons of Mass Destruction.* (December 2002). Available online. URL: www.whitehouse.gov/news/releases/200212/WMDStrategy.pdf. Accessed June 15, 2008.

[39] Barry Rosenberg. "Bolstering Bio-Defense." *Homeland Security* (June 2004). Available online. URL: www.mcgrawhillhomelandsecurity.com. Accessed July 28, 2008; John Marburger. "Keynote Address on National Preparedness." October 20, 2003. Office of Science and Technology Policy. Available online. URL: www.ostp.gov/pdf/10_20_30_JHM_biosecurity_2003.pdf. Accessed July 28, 2008. Marburger is the director, Office of Science and Technology Policy; Kumal Ramphia. "Annual Report on BioShield Released to Congress." (7/11/08). Center for Biosecurity. Available online. URL: www.upmcbiosecurity.org/website/biosecurity_briefing/archive/countmeasr_dev/2. Accessed July 29, 2008.

[40] Global Security.org. "Weapons of Mass Destruction Civil Support Teams." Available online. URL: www.globalsecurity.org/military/agency/army/wmd_cst.htm. Accessed July 23, 2008; Gerry J. Gilmore. "Guard-Staffed WMD Civil Support Teams Slated for Increase." (1/20/04). American Forces Press Service. Available online. URL: www.defenselink.mil/bews/newsarticle.aspx?ud=27474. Accessed July 29, 2008; Jim Kouri. "National Guard Teams Prepare for Terrorist WMD Attacks." (7/27/08). Canada Free Press. Available online. URL: www.canadafreepress.com/index.php/article/4143. Accessed July 29, 2008.

[41] "Scientist Suspected in 2001 Anthrax Attacks Dead in Apparent Suicide." Foxnews.com. Available online. URL: www.foxnews.com/story0.2933395723,00.html. Accessed August 1, 2008.

[42] Guillemin. *Biological Weapons,* pp. 175–178; Mike Mitka. "Congress Queries Need for and Safety of High-Containment Research Laboratories." *Journal of the American Medical Association* 298, no. 20 (11/28/07): 2,359–2,360; Eric Lipton and Scott Shane. "Anthrax Case Renews Questions on Bioterror Effort." *New York Times* (8/3/08). Available online. URL: www.nytimes.com/2008/08/03/us/03anthrax.html?hp#. Accessed August 3, 2008; National Institute of Allergy and Infectious Diseases. "Biodefense: Biosafety Level 4 Laboratory Tour." Available online. URL: http://www3.niaid.nih.gov/topics/BiodefenseRelated/Biodefense/PublicMedia/labtour/. Accessed April 17, 2009; Mickey McCarter. "Two of Five BSL-4 Labs Flunk Security Test." *HS Today* (10/17/08). Available online. URL: http://www.hstoday.us/content/view/5659/128/. Accessed April 17, 2009.

[43] Judith Miller, Stephen Engelberg, and William J. Broad. "U.S. Germ Warfare Research Pushes Treaty Limits." *New York Times* (9/4/01).

[44] Toggzhan Kassenova. "Biological Threat Reduction in Central Asia." *Bulletin of Atomic Scientists* (6/18/08). Available online. URL: http://'thebulletin.org/web-edition/features/biological-threat-reduction-central-asi. Accessed September 14, 2008.

[45] Richard Lugar. "Lugar Speech at Conference on Defense against Weapons of Mass Destruction." Web site of Richard G. Lugar, U.S. senator from Indiana. Available online. URL: http://lugar.senate.gov/press/rcord.cfm?id=291461. Accessed July 28, 2008; ———. "The Next Step in U.S. Nonproliferation Policy." *Arms Control Today* (December 2002). Available online. URL: www.armscontrol.org/act/2002_12/lugar_dec02. Accessed August 1, 2008; Nuclear Threat Initiative. "The Nunn-Lugar Cooperative Threat Reduction (CTR) Program." Available online. URL: www.nti.org/db/nisprofs/russia/forasst/nunn_lug/overview.htm. Accessed August 1, 2008; Cirincione. *Bomb Scare,* pp. 141–143.

[46] National Nuclear Security Administration. "Working to Prevent Nuclear Terrorism." Available online. URL: http://nnsa.energy.gov/news/print/982htm. Accessed July 24, 2008; "US-Russian Agreement Repatriates Highly Enriched Uranium from Poland." June 9, 2007. Bellona. Available online. URL: www.bellona.org/articles/articles2007/ebrd_grants?printerfriendly=yes. Accessed August 1, 2008.

[47] Thom Shanker. "U.S. Says Iran Has Material for an Atomic Bomb." *New York Times* (3/2/09). Available online. URL: http://www.nytimes.com/2009/03/02/washington/02military.html. Accessed April 18, 2009.

[48] Center for Defense Information. "Port and Maritime Security in the United States: Reactions to an Evolving Threat." (1/21/03). Available online. URL: www.cdi.org/terrorism/maritimesecurity-pr.cfm. Accessed August 2, 2008; "Bush Signs U.S. Port Security Act: Contains Ban on Internet Gambling." (10/23/06). Available online. URL: www.foxnews.com/story/0,2033,220496,00.html. Accessed August 2, 2008.

[49] Air Force Space Command. "USAF Launches last DSP (early warning) Satellite." Available online. URL: http://afspc/af.mil/news/story.asp?id=123075609. Accessed April 20, 2009; John Watson and Keith P. Zondervan. "Missile Defense Agency's Space Tracking and Surveillance System." *Crosslink* 9, no. 1 (Spring 2008). Available online. URL: http://www.aero.org/publications/crosslink/spring2008/03.html. Accessed April 20, 2009.

[50] Missile Defense Agency, Department of Defense. *Missile Defense-Worldwide* (2008): pp. 1, 4–7; ———. "Successful Missile Defense Intercept Test Takes Place Off Hawaii." (6/25/08). Available online. URL: www.mda.mil/mdaLink/pdf/08news/0074.pdf. Accessed August 1, 2008; Jim Garamone. "Iranian Threat Justifies Missile Defense, General Says." American Forces Press Services News Articles. Available online. URL: www.defenselink.mil/news/newsarticle.aspx?id=50511. Accessed July 28, 2008.

[51] Joseph Cirincione. "7/24/08—Bush Seeks $12 Billion to Waste on Obsolete Missile Defense." Peninsula Peace and Justice Center. Available online. URL: http://peaceandjustice.org/article.php?story=20080724091446943. Accessed July 28, 2008; Loren B. Thompson. "Why Missile Defense Makes More Sense Today Than During the Cold War." Available online. URL: http://lexingtoninstitute.org/printer_1285.shtml. Accessed July 21, 2008; Wade Boese. "More States Step Up Anti-Missile Work." *Arms Control Today* (January/February 2008). Available online. URL: www.armscontrol.org/act/2008_01-02/stepup.asp. Accessed July 28, 2008; GlobalSecurity.org. "Arrow TMD." Available online. URL: www.globalsecurity.org/space/systems/arrow.htm. Accessed August 2, 2008.

3

Global Perspectives

In the decades that followed World War II, at least two dozen countries established chemical and/or biological weapons programs, and most of those countries now have those weapons or the ability to produce them. Between 1945 and 2006, the nuclear club grew to nine.[1] Today, aside from the United States in North America, countries in Europe, Asia, and Africa have weapons of mass destruction (WMD). Only South America, the single-country continent of Australia, and uninhabited Antarctica are free of these weapons. This chapter will focus on Russia, the largest country in the world and the only nuclear power whose nuclear arsenal matches that of the United States; Israel, a tiny Middle Eastern country with a small nuclear arsenal and a uniquely dangerous security problem; India and Pakistan, nuclear powers living side by side in South Asia with a long history of conflict; and North Korea, a communist dictatorship in northeast Asia that is one of the most repressive and politically isolated countries in the world.

RUSSIA

Key Issues

In addition to its formidable nuclear arsenal, Russia also has chemical weapons and probably a significant stock of biological agents. Russia's military might is growing. Its leadership is trying to reclaim the international influence once enjoyed by the former Soviet Union, the country that in reality was an empire controlled by Russia before it collapsed in 1991. Russia's leaders consider the United States to be the main obstacle in achieving that goal. In order to deal with the United States as an equal, Russia is committed to being America's military equal. This means having a nuclear arsenal that is competitive in every way, offensively and defensively, with the U.S. arsenal. At the same time, Russia's leaders understand that their country's security is enhanced by nuclear arms control and by international efforts to eliminate biological and chemical weapons. Aside from the problems posed by these weapons themselves, there also are serious questions about the security of non-weaponized fissile materials stored in Russia. These are materials that terrorist groups such as al-Qaeda could use to build nuclear weapons.

History and Current Arsenals

Russia was the core of the Soviet Union, which existed from November 1917 until its collapse in December 1991. The Soviet Union itself was the successor state to the Russian Empire, whose autocratic monarchy collapsed in March 1917 as World War I raged. The democratic government that replaced Russia's monarchy survived only eight months. It was overthrown by a small group of militant Marxist socialists who seized power in a coup in November 1917 and founded a state they eventually called the Union of Soviet Socialist Republics, or Soviet Union. The Soviet Union soon became a totalitarian dictatorship whose stated goal was to bring about a world communist revolution. After World War II, the Soviet Union stood as one of the world's two military superpowers, along with the United States. The two countries also became the leaders of rival alliances, the United States heading an alliance of democratic, capitalist states and the Soviet Union in control of a group of communist dictatorships. As leaders of these two blocs with fundamentally different types of political and economic systems, the Soviet Union and the United States competed for influence on a worldwide scale in a struggle known as the cold war. Although they never directly faced each other in war, as part of their cold war struggle the United States and the Soviet Union engaged in a massive arms race. That competition included the development and production of WMD, among them chemical and biological weapons, but, most important, nuclear weapons. Given the real danger that a nuclear war could destroy all civilized life on Earth, the two sides negotiated several agreements to limit the size of their respective nuclear arsenals and control the spread of nuclear weapons to other countries. They also signed agreements involving chemical and biological weapons.

At the time it collapsed in 1991, the Soviet Union had huge chemical, biological, and nuclear arsenals, and the Russian Federation—usually called Russia—that emerged from that collapse with about three-quarters of the former Soviet Union's territory inherited most of those weapons. During the 1990s, it was hoped that Russia would develop into a democratic country. That has not happened. Although not nearly as repressive as the Soviet Union, Russia today is an authoritarian country whose people do not have the power to change their government through free elections.

THE SOVIET/RUSSIAN CHEMICAL WEAPONS PROGRAMS

Origins

During World War I—the conflict that saw the largest use of chemical weapons in history—almost half of all casualties from chemical weapons were Russian soldiers. Not only were the Russian soldiers unprepared to defend themselves against chemical weapons, but they were unprepared to use them effectively. Thus, when the Russians first tried to use them against the Germans in July 1916, they delayed too long and the Germans were able to prepare defensive measures. Russian officers failed to take note of changing wind conditions and as a result gassed their own troops stationed in forward positions. German artillery then hit the Russian trenches where gas-filled canisters were stored, killing hundreds of surprised men who could not put on their gas masks in time. The entire operation was a disaster.[2]

The new Soviet regime that came to power in November 1917 soon demonstrated it could use chemical weapons more effectively. However, it did so by using them against its own people: peasants who opposed the Soviet dictatorship and rebelled against it in late 1920. The use of chemical weapons was part of an extraordinarily brutal military campaign launched in June of that year. It included widespread public shooting of hostages, deportations of entire families, and the seizure of all possessions of families who fled the battle zone. Along with these policies, the commander of the Soviet army, Mikhail Tukachevsky, ordered that forests where peasants were hiding should be cleared by poison gas. The gas was to be used to "kill everyone hiding there." The overall campaign of which the use of poison gas was a part continued until mid-July, when it was ended because of high-level opposition in the government to its extreme methods.[3]

The Soviet government also began studying defense against chemical weapons in 1921 at an institute called the Higher Military-Chemical School of the Red Army. During the 1920s, the Soviet Union secretly worked with Germany to develop and test chemical weapons, a partnership that lasted until Adolf Hitler ended it when he came to power in 1933. The first modern factory to produce chemical weapons—the factory also produced chemicals for ordinary civilian use—began production in 1929. Called Chemical Works No. 91 and later renamed Khimprom, it was located deep in the Russian heartland in the city of Stalingrad (since 1961, Volgograd) on the banks of the Volga River. The Soviet army meanwhile established a site near the Volga, called Polygon, where chemical weapons could be tested. It was enlarged in the late 1930s, requiring the evacuation of four towns, and expanded again during World War II to an area of 1,000 square kilometers (383 sq. m.). Immediately after the war, the Soviets were able to obtain German chemical weapons factories; equipment for producing both sarin and tabun was disassembled and shipped to Chemical Works No. 91, along with some leading German chemists and engineers.[4]

Soviet Chemical Weapons Programs during the Cold War

After World War II, the Soviet Union began producing both tabun and sarin. That was followed by a lengthy effort to master the difficult process of manufacturing soman, which led to soman's large-scale manufacturing beginning in 1967. The Soviet chemical weapons program took a major step forward in the late 1950s when a successful spying operation obtained the formula for VX developed in the West. Soviet scientists then developed their own version of VX. Known as R-33, it was more deadly and more difficult to treat than the American compound on which it was based. Large-scale production of R-33 began in 1972 in an enormous new factory in the town of Novocherboksarsk, on the Volga River about 400 miles east of Moscow. V-agents and numerous other chemicals such as lewisite were produced at dozens of factories and stored in specially built facilities in several cities, including Volgograd. The Soviets developed a variety of ballistic missiles, rockets, bombs, and mines to deliver these deadly chemicals. They also made battle plans to use these weapons against the United States and its NATO allies in the event of war in Europe.[5]

The Soviet chemical weapons program came at a high environmental price. For example, in 1965 a flood washed wastewater from the production of chemical weapons into the Volga River. The poisons killed huge numbers of sturgeon, the fish whose eggs are the valuable delicacy known as caviar. The dead fish, lying belly up in the water, turned the river white for a distance of 50 miles.[6]

Finally, during the early 1970s, the Soviet Union began a massive effort, code-named "Foliant," to develop an entirely new generation of nerve gasses even more powerful than V-agents. The goal was to develop agents that were more poisonous, more stable and therefore easier to store, and easier to produce. The research was centered at a scientific institute in Moscow and carried out under the highest level of security. The institute, whose main job was to develop chemical warfare agents, employed more than 3,500 people, including 500 scientists. Eventually it produced two agents, labeled A-230 and A-232, that were produced in small quantities in a factory in Volgograd. In 1976, a series of tests were conducted, first on animals and then in the open air. The new agents turned out to be five to eight times more deadly than VX.[7]

By the 1980s, the Soviet Union was working on binary versions of its chemical agents. This work focused both on V-agents and on the new generation of agents developed in the 1970s. Unlike in the United States, where the question of developing binary agents was openly discussed and debated in Congress, in the Soviet Union all discussions and work took place in extreme secrecy. Soviet scientists developed binary versions of both R-33 (called Novichok) and A-232 (Novichok-5). Significantly, the Soviet Union continued to work on these new agents, even after officially announcing in 1987 that it had stopped all manufacture of chemical weapons. In 1989–90, Soviet scientists conducted open-air tests of Novichok-5 in a remote desert region of Central Asia in what today is Uzbekistan.[8]

By the end of the 1980s, the Soviet Union had produced at least 40,000 metric tons of chemical nerve, blister, and choking agents and had the largest chemical weapons arsenal in the world. According to the Federation of American Scientists, some reports put that figure at more than 50,000 tons. About 80 percent of that arsenal consisted of nerve agents such as sarin, soman, and VX. The rest were blistering agents such as mustard gas, lewisite, a mustard-lewisite mixture, and phosgene. The nerve agents all were weaponized: that is, they were stored in artillery shells, rocket warheads, and similar weapons. One storage site alone, about 1,000 miles from Moscow in the western Siberian town of Shchuch'ye, contained almost 2 million of these weapons, mainly artillery shells but also warheads that can be fitted on guided missiles. In contrast, much of the blister agent material was stored in bulk containers. In fact, it is not known even today how large the Soviet chemical agent stockpile was by the late 1980s, when the cold war finally began to wind down.[9]

The program continued despite a Soviet-American agreement signed in September 1989 known as the Wyoming Memorandum of Understanding (Wyoming MOU). The agreement called for the two sides to exchange information on their chemical agent stockpiles, including the types of agents they had, the size of their stockpiles, and where they were stored. However, the Soviets continued to hide the Foliant program and its new nerve agents. The United States did not learn about the Foliant weapons program until October 1991, during the Soviet Union's last days, when Vil Mirzayanov, a chemist who had worked in the Soviet chemical weapons program for 25 years, described its existence in an article in a Moscow newspaper. His claims later were confirmed by two other scientists, including one who had worked on the development of A-232. Within months after Mirzayanov's article was published, the Soviet Union collapsed, and the matter became the concern of the new Russian government. The Russians claimed that the Wyoming MOU did not cover the new agents because they had been produced in small amounts for testing only, an explanation that did not satisfy the United States. The episode left the United States with questions about the chemical agents the Russians actually had that have never been completely answered. It did not help that in the fall of 1992 Mirzayanov was arrested and charged with divulging state secrets. U.S. protests helped get the charges against him dismissed in early 1994.[10]

Russian Chemical Weapons: Stockpile and Destruction

Russia is party to two agreements that require it to destroy its chemical weapons and agents: the Bilateral Destruction Agreement (BDA), which the Soviet Union signed with the United States in June 1990, and the Chemical Weapons Convention (CWC), which Russia signed in 1993 and ratified in 1997.[11] The actual process of destruction has been going on for more than a decade. Russia has received foreign assistance both in terms of funding and technical aid. Both the U.S. government's Cooperative Threat Reduction (CTR) Program and the private Nuclear Threat Initiative (NTI) have been involved, as have various organizations associated with the European Union (EU) and individual countries such as Germany and the Netherlands.[12]

Destruction of chemical weapons involves many technical difficulties and environmental hazards, and, in 2006, Russia, like the United States, received a five-year extension to 2012 under the CWC to destroy those weapons. Having met its 2003 deadline to destroy 1 percent of its declared 40,000 tons of chemical agents, Russia in 2007 met its revised deadline by destroying 20 percent of them. It also destroyed major production facilities in Volgograd and Novosherboksarsk, the former task being completed in 2005 and the latter in mid-2007. In June 2008, a new facility for destroying chemical weapons was opened at a storage facility near the city of Penza, about 350 miles southwest of Moscow. It was the fourth of seven that were planned, each of which is located next to a chemical weapons storage facility because the chemicals involved are considered too dangerous to move. Perhaps the most important single destruction facility, built with $1 billion in American aid, was opened in May 2009 in Shchuch'ye, just east of the Ural Mountains. It was important because so much of the nerve gas stored in Shchuch'ye is in artillery shells, and the site is very close to Russia's border with Kazakhstan. The difficulties in developing a safe method for destroying the nerve gas and the delays in getting the Shchuch'ye facility built illustrated the problems involved in destroying chemical weapons. As Igor V. Rybalchenko, a leading scientific adviser to the Russian government, put it, "It turns out that it is a lot easier to produce chemical weapons than to destroy them." All seven destruction facilities were expected to be operating by the end of 2009, and Russia's next deadlines were to destroy 45 percent of its chemical weapons by the end of 2009 and 100 percent by 2012. As of early 2009, Russia had destroyed 30.1 percent of these weapons. However, because Western countries contributing to the program have not provided the expected funding, the head of Russia's state commission on chemical disarmament reported it would be difficult to meet those goals. At the same time, the question remains whether Russia in fact has chemical weapons that it has not declared.[13]

THE SOVIET/RUSSIAN BIOLOGICAL WEAPONS PROGRAM

Origins

The Soviet biological weapons program dates from the 1920s, when it was set up following the model of the country's chemical weapons program. It was expanded during the 1930s as new institutes were established near Moscow and elsewhere. During 1936 and 1937, Soviet scientists conducted open-air experiments of biological weapons in Central Asia. The experiments took place on Vozroshdeniye (Renaissance) Island in the middle of the Aral Sea, which today stands astride the border of Kazakhstan and Uzbekistan. Both ships and aircraft were used in these experiments. Additional biological weapons facilities were built during World War II.

The Soviet Biological Weapons Program during the Cold War

Soviet biological weapons research continued and expanded after World War II, with work being done by about 25,000 people working in facilities controlled by the Ministry of Defense and in several agricultural laboratories. By far the most important expansion of research and development took place in the early 1970s. A decision was made to begin a massive new secret program in 1973, four years after the United States publicly renounced the use of biological weapons. It also was only one year after the Soviet Union had signed the Biological Weapons Convention and two years before it formally ratified the agreement. In other words, the Soviet Union acted in direct violation of an international agreement it had just signed. While many motives certainly were involved, it appears that Soviet leadership did not believe the United States was being truthful when it renounced biological weapons in 1969 and was convinced the United States had an offensive program. Soviet leaders also apparently feared that their country lagged far behind the West in genetics and molecular biology and therefore had to catch up.[14]

The expanded Soviet biological weapons program was carried out by the newly created Chief Directorate for Biological Preparations, or Biopreparat, which worked directly under the Council of Ministers. It was headed by a general who had direct access to the Soviet Union's top political leadership and ties with the secret police (KGB) as well as many important Soviet scientific institutions, including the Academy of Sciences and the Ministries of Health and Agriculture. Biopreparat included about 50 sites and at its peak probably employed at least 40,000 people, 9,000 of whom were highly trained scientists and technicians. These facilities were hidden from foreign intelligence by being placed inside civilian biotechnology and pharmaceutical enterprises. Biopreparat's most important research center was the Obolensk State Research Center for Applied Microbiology, an enormous compound about 50 miles south of Moscow where Soviet scientists developed dozens of strains of bacteria for use in biological weapons. Its equipment included at least 40 two-story fermentation tanks that were maintained at Biosafety Level 4 (BSL-4) security standards. The Obolensk complex, described by Professor Jeanne Guillemin, an expert on biological weapons, as the "size of a small city," was modeled on centers the Soviets had built in the 1940s and 1950s to develop and produce nuclear weapons. Other important Biopreparat facilities were scattered across the country from Estonia on the Baltic Sea in the west, to the city of Sverdlovsk (renamed Ekaterinburg after the fall of the Soviet Union) on the eastern slopes of the Ural Mountains, to Central Asia and Siberia.[15]

Biopreparat scientists weaponized a wide range of agents, including brucellosis, Marburg virus, tularemia, typhus, Q fever, smallpox, plague, and anthrax. Altogether, they studied more than 50 biological agents. Genetic engineering was used to develop new generations of biological weapons agents more deadly and better suited for weapons use than anything known in the West. Their new strains of anthrax and plague bacteria, for example, were resistant to antibiotics available to the United States and its allies. Tons of smallpox agents were produced and weaponized by placing them in intercontinental missiles capable of reaching the United States. Anthrax and plague agents also were prepared for use against the United States and its allies.[16]

The Soviet Union succeeded in keeping the Biopreparat program secret for almost two decades despite a major environmental and health disaster that eventually became public knowledge. The incident occurred at a biological weapons facility in Sverdlovsk. Although many details remain unknown to this day, in April 1979 the Sverdlovsk facility released deadly anthrax spores into the atmosphere. More than 90 people became ill, and 64 of them died, the first within four days and the last about six weeks later. Neither Western intelligence agencies nor the mainstream press found out about the event. Instead, a Russian-language newspaper in West Germany serving the Russian émigré community in Europe broke the story in October 1979, providing additional details in January 1980. The Soviet government denied the story, claiming instead that the anthrax outbreak in Sverdlovsk was caused by tainted meat. Among the denials was an article published by the official government news agency called "A Germ of Lying." However, various forms of American intelligence evidence, including satellite photographs, strongly supported the biological weapons facility thesis. Despite further investigation, during the 1980s expert opinion remained divided. Douglas J. Feith, a senior Pentagon official, told Congress that the Soviets had developed "new means of biological warfare" and had made "stunning advances" in biotechnology. However, Matthew Meselson, a prominent Harvard University biologist who was consulted by the CIA, found the Soviet explanation of tainted meat "completely plausible."[17]

A few years later, it became indisputably clear that those who had believed the Soviets had been, as Meselson admitted, "entirely wrong."[18] Vladimir Pasechnik, a biologist who headed one of Biopreparat's most important secret laboratories, and Kanatjan Alibekov (he later Americanized his name to Ken Alibek), who had served as Biopreparat's first deputy director, described the extent of the Biopreparat program after defecting to the West. Pasechnik defected in 1989 while on a trip to Great Britain. Despite Pasechnik's revelations, in the face of questioning by both the American and British governments the Soviet leader Mikhail Gorbachev denied the program existed. Then in 1992, the year after the Soviet Union's collapse, Alibek defected from what was now Russia. Before becoming Biopreparat's deputy director, Alibek had been the head of the project's huge anthrax-production facility in the town of Stepnogorsk in what today is the independent country of Kazakhstan. His information about the extent and sophistication of Biopreparat's operations shocked Western intelligence officials, whose job it was to be informed about such things. Finally, in February 1992, the Russian president Boris Yeltsin, who at the time of the Sverdlovsk anthrax disaster 23 years earlier had been the Communist Party official in charge of that city, publicly confirmed that the program had existed. He also maintained that it had been ended and that the dismantling of offensive biological weapons facilities had begun in 1986.[19]

The Biopreparat program left behind at least three major problems: an urgent security threat, a huge environmental menace, and a series of worrisome unanswered questions. The security issue had two parts. First, there was genuine fear that biological agents in storage were not adequately protected and could be stolen, either by terrorist groups or by agents of countries seeking these weapons. Perhaps even more worrisome, there was the real possibility that thousands of Russian scientists thrown out of work by the end of the Biopreparat program would work for other countries seeking to develop WMD. Of special concern was Iran, especially after reports suggested in 1995 that Iran was trying to recruit former Soviet scientists. China was another country rumored to be in the market for these scientists.[20]

The environmental menace caused by Biopreparat existed in many areas across the vast expanse of the former Soviet Union. One of the most polluted places that program left behind, and one that became a symbol of the problem, was an island in the middle of the Aral Sea, a salty lake on the border between Kazakhstan and Uzbekistan. Called Vozrozhdeniye (Renaissance or Rebirth) Island, it had been considered a secure place for various biological weapons activities because it was remote and surrounded by water. In 1988, the Soviet government decided it had to destroy a huge stock of anthrax bacteria that had been produced and was being stored in Sverdlovsk. The goal was to destroy these materials before Western intelligence services could find them. Therefore, tons of anthrax bacteria from Sverdlovsk was decontaminated, packed into steel containers, and shipped 850 miles east for burial on Vozrozhdeniye. Unfortunately, the decontamination process was not successful, a fact that was not known until after the anthrax was buried. Making matters worse, the Aral Sea was drying up, which meant the distance between the island and the mainland was shrinking. The anthrax on Vozrozhdeniye remained there for more than a decade. It was left for the United States to clean up the deadly mess. As part of the Nunn-Lugar Cooperative Threat Reduction Program, an American team successfully decontaminated the anthrax, an extremely dangerous job that was completed in 2002.[21]

Finally, there is concern in the West that the Russians are not telling the truth about having destroyed all their biological agents and stopped their research and development. To be sure, the massive former Soviet facility in a town called Stepnogorsk has been destroyed under CTR. However, Stepnogorsk is in Kazakhstan, and the facility there was dismantled in cooperation with that country, not Russia. In Russia itself, three of its most important military biological weapons facilities—which are run by the Ministry of Defense—are still off-limits to Western experts. In short, it is impossible to verify that some part of the largest and most dangerous biological weapons program in history is not still operating in secret.[22]

THE SOVIET/RUSSIAN NUCLEAR WEAPONS PROGRAM

Origins and the First Weapons

The Soviet nuclear weapons program began during World War II when intelligence information reached Moscow about the American Manhattan Project. The Soviet effort to build a nuclear bomb drew on a long Russian tradition of excellence in physics that dated from czarist times—that is, from the era before 1917 when Russia was ruled by a monarch called a czar—and which the Soviet regime continued to promote. Soviet physicists did significant work in nuclear fission and published important papers on their work in 1939–41, immediately after the first groundbreaking work in Germany. An actual program was set up in 1943, under the leadership of the distinguished physicist Igor Kurchatov. However, the war effort against Nazi Germany absorbed almost all the Soviet Union's resources, and the program remained small. Not until the United States successfully developed an atomic bomb and used it to force a Japanese surrender and end World War II did the Soviet project become an all-out effort. Beginning in the summer of 1945, it became a priority program with Kurchatov receiving all the resources he required.[23]

As the Soviets began to build the industrial infrastructure needed to develop a nuclear weapon, Soviet scientists already had the blueprints for a plutonium implosion bomb from spies inside the American project, some of whom were working at Los Alamos. However, building a bomb still required ultramodern facilities, the most up-to-date knowledge of nuclear physics, and solving many complicated engineering and technical problems. Nevertheless, most experts agree that the information from the Manhattan Project saved Kurchatov and his colleagues two years.[24]

The Soviet effort took place under the direction of Lavrenty Beria, one of the Soviet dictator Joseph Stalin's closest aides and from the late 1930s through World War II the head of the Soviet secret police. The secret police in turn controlled a vast network of slave labor camps called the Gulag. Millions of Gulag inmates had previously been used in all areas of the Soviet economy, including many of its most difficult and dangerous mining and construction projects. Now, Gulag prisoners did most of the mining and construction for the atomic bomb program, unprotected from radioactivity and other dangers. More than 450,000 people worked on the project, more than half of them in mining. They mined uranium in several parts of the Soviet Union and in Eastern Europe under terrible conditions and without safety precautions. Tens of thousands of Gulag prisoners worked in construction, including 70,000 who worked on the huge nuclear facility called Chelyabinsk-40, which was built at breakneck speed on the eastern slopes of the Ural Mountains. Many of these people, both in mining and construction, were exposed to dangerous and often lethal doses of radiation. Even many of the 10,000 skilled scientists and engineers who worked on the project were prisoners, although they were housed in special prisons where they lived under tolerable conditions. Fully half the research on the Soviet Union's early nuclear program, until the Gulag was dismantled after Stalin's death in 1953, was conducted in prison laboratories.[25]

The most important work in designing and building nuclear weapons was done at a newly established laboratory called Arzamas-16. It was set up in the spring of 1946 about 240 miles east of Moscow in a small town that previously had been best known for its monastery. Arzamas-16 was a secret nuclear weapons research facility that became home to top nuclear physicists, including Andrei Sakharov, and slowly grew into a small city. Because

"Arzamas" sounded a bit like "Los Alamos," Soviet scientists sometimes called it by the nickname "Los Arzamas."[26]

The first Soviet nuclear reactor, which may have been based on an American design, was completed in Moscow and produced its first controlled chain reaction on December 25, 1946. Three years later, on August 29, 1949, the Soviet Union successfully exploded its first atomic bomb, a plutonium bomb that was a close copy of the bomb the United States had exploded barely four years earlier. It took two more years for Soviet scientists to test a second bomb, a plutonium bomb of their own design that was a significant improvement on the American design. The bomb tested in 1951 weighed about half as much as the older bomb and exploded with twice the yield. Meanwhile, the Soviets also had a high-priority program to develop guided missiles to deliver those bombs. Its engineers at first worked to improve and extend the range of the German V-2 rocket used during World War II. By the early 1950s, they were working on their own designs, including one that in 1957 became the world's first intercontinental missile and the first rocket capable of launching an artificial satellite into orbit.[27]

Thermonuclear Weapons

Like their American counterparts, Soviet physicists in 1945 understood that it might be possible to use an atomic bomb to ignite nuclear fission. In 1946, Klaus Fuchs, who was still spying on behalf of Moscow, provided Soviet scientists with information on work related to thermonuclear explosions being done in the West. Among other things, Fuchs had attended a conference at Los Alamos in April 1946 whose participants had concluded that "it is likely that a super-bomb can be constructed and will work." That same year, Soviet scientists began working to design a thermonuclear bomb.[28]

By 1948, two years before the United States made its decision to build this weapon, the Soviets had a design for a workable hydrogen bomb, Andrei Sakharov's "layer cake" design. Although this design was not a fully two-stage thermonuclear weapon, it nonetheless was a fusion bomb able to produce a far greater explosion than a fission bomb. It was tested successfully in August 1953 and produced an explosion of about 400 kilotons. This success came almost a year after the United States tested a 10-megaton nuclear device. The Soviet advantage was that their bomb actually was small enough to be used as a weapon, unlike the enormous American device. The American advantage was that its scientists had developed a genuine two-stage thermonuclear device whose potential size was virtually unlimited. By early 1954, the United States had built and successfully tested a deliverable bomb, the test itself producing the astounding yield of 15 megatons. During that same year, the Soviet scientists finally unraveled the scientific mysteries of how to produce a two-stage thermonuclear explosion. They successfully tested their bomb in November 1955. The Soviet bomb exploded with a force of 1.6 megatons, about one-tenth of the recently tested U.S. bomb. However, it was dropped from an airplane, the first time that feat was ever achieved with a fusion bomb.[29]

One of the more interesting facts about the first air-dropped fusion bomb is that it also produced the first landing of an airplane carrying an atomic bomb. That occurred when the original test had to be cancelled because of a change in weather conditions after the bomber scheduled to drop the bomb had taken off. Making matters worse, the airfield where the bomber had to land had iced over. The runway was cleared and, on Kurchatov's orders, the landing was made.[30]

Not every problem in the Soviet nuclear weapons program turned out as well as the situation just described. It was a program plagued with accidents. The worst accident probably occurred in September 1957 when a tank containing highly radioactive wastes from a nuclear weapons plant exploded. The incident contaminated an area of about 15,000 square kilometers (5,800 square miles) in the Ural Mountains in central Russia. More than 10,000 people had to be evacuated from their homes, and the area remains contaminated to this day. Far worse than any single accident has been the cumulative radioactive legacy of Soviet nuclear testing. Between 1949 and 1989, more than 450 nuclear tests—116 in the atmosphere—were conducted in the northeast part of what today is Kazakhstan. Aside from the radioactivity spread by the atmospheric tests, about half of the underground tests released radioactivity into the atmosphere. The Soviet testing left behind a grim legacy of cancer, other diseases, and birth defects that are still passed down from generation to generation, with the impact actually getting worse in the third and fourth generations born since those tests.[31]

"Tsar Bomba": The King of Bombs

The Soviet thermonuclear program also produced the largest man-made explosion in history, a colossal 57 megatons. The bomb that produced that explosion was detonated on October 30, 1961, at a Soviet test site on an island north of the Arctic Circle. It remains unclear why the Soviets built such a gigantic bomb, which was far too large and powerful to serve as a military weapon. No Soviet bomber carrying the bomb—it was 25 feet long, more than six feet wide, and weighed more than 20 tons—could reach the United States, and, had it been dropped on a western European country, deadly fallout would have been carried eastward to Soviet allies in eastern Europe and even the Soviet Union itself.

Original plans called for a 100-megaton bomb, but in the end that fortunately was scaled down by about half. The bomb was so large that it could not fit into any Soviet bomber; it had to be suspended beneath a Tu-95, the largest bomber in the Soviet air force. The flash from the explosion could be seen 600 miles away, and windowpanes the same distance away broke. The explosion caused an atmospheric disturbance that circled the Earth three times. A cameraman who witnessed the blast described the fireball as "powerful and arrogant like Jupiter. . . . It seemed to suck the whole Earth into it." A visitor to ground zero a while after the blast found everything was gone, not only the snow and ice of the frozen landscape but the rocks as well. He reported that "the ground of the island had been *leveled,* swept and licked so that it looks like a skating rink. . . . Everything in this area has been swept clean, scoured, melted, and blown away." According to one estimate, had the Soviets exploded a 100-megaton bomb it would have created a firestorm the size of the state of Maryland. The designers called their bomb "Big Ivan" (Ivan is a common Russian name). Others nicknamed the 57-megaton monster "Tsar Bomba" (the King of Bombs), a reference to the Russian tradition of building enormous devices—such as the world's largest bell and cannon, both on display in Moscow—that are impressive to look at but also completely useless.[32]

Nuclear Arms Control

The Soviet Union and, after its fall in 1991, the Russian Federation, became a party to the same agreements regarding nuclear weapons as the United States. Soviet atmospheric and underwater testing ended with the 1963 Nuclear Test Ban Treaty. In 1996, Russia signed the Comprehensive Nuclear-Test-Ban Treaty (CTBT). The last Soviet nuclear test had taken place six years earlier, bringing its total to 715. Since some of those tests involved more than one device, between 1949 and 1990 the Soviet Union actually tested 969 nuclear devices. The Soviet government claimed that 124 of those tests were for peaceful purposes. The Russian Federation that succeeded the Soviet Union did not conduct any tests between 1990 and the signing of the CTBT.[33]

Like the U.S. arsenal, the Soviet Union's nuclear arsenal was subject to the limits imposed by the SALT (Strategic Arms Limitation Talks) I agreement of 1972, the unratified SALT II of 1979 (which both sides observed into the mid-1980s), and the 1987 INF (intermediate-range nuclear forces) agreement. The Soviet arsenal of nuclear warheads and missiles that could reach the United States finally began to shrink under the 1991 START I (Strategic Arms Reduction Treaty) agreement. Under that agreement, the Soviet Union had to reduce its number of deployed strategic nuclear warheads to 6,000. They, in turn, could be deployed on 1,600 delivery vehicles: ICBMs (intercontinental ballistic missile), SLBMs (submarine-launched ballistic missile), or bombers. Along with the United States, Russia met its treaty obligations on time in December 2001.[34]

The START II agreement signed by Russia and the United States in 1993 never went into force, even though the United States ratified the treaty in 1996 and Russia did the same in 2000. The Russian ratification included conditions unacceptable to the United States regarding missile defense. When the United States withdrew from the 1972 Anti-Ballistic Missile Treaty (ABM) in 2002, Russia withdrew from START II. Finally, Russia joined the United States in signing the Treaty of Moscow, or Strategic Offensive Reductions Treaty (SORT) in 2002. Both sides ratified the treaty the next year. It calls for each country to reduce its number of deployed nuclear warheads to between 1,700 and 2,200 by 2012.[35]

The Current Russian Nuclear Arsenal

Like the United States, Russia continues to reduce its nuclear arsenal while at the same time modernizing it. However, as of 2009, Russia had by far the world's largest arsenal of nuclear warheads. It included about 4,830 operational warheads of various types and 8,130 being held in reserve or scheduled to be dismantled, a total of about 13,000 warheads.[36] This compares to the U.S. arsenal of about 2,700 operational warheads and a total of about 9,400 warheads.[37]

Russia has also shut down nuclear reactors that produce plutonium. As of 2008, there were three reactors in Russia still producing plutonium. Two of them, both in the Siberian town of Seversk, were shut down in 2008, the first in April and the second in June. Under an agreement reached in 2003, U.S. observers were able to visit these reactors, which during the Soviet era were highly secret facilities. Shutting down the two Seversk reactors was the work of a joint program between the U.S. government's National Nuclear Security Administration (NNSA) and Rosatom, Russia's state nuclear power monopoly. Because those facilities produced energy for civilian use, the United States provided a large amount of aid to help Russia build conventional power plants to make up for the lost electricity. Russia's one remaining reactor producing plutonium, also located in Siberia, is expected to be shut down in 2010.[38]

As of 2009, the Russian arsenal had about 1,350 nuclear warheads deployed on 383 ICBMs. Some of those missiles were based in underground silos, while others were mounted on mobile launchers. A fleet of 10 nuclear submarines was supplied with 160 SLBMs that carry a total of 576 warheads. Russia also had 77 strategic bombers that can carry either long-range cruise missiles or nuclear bombs. The bomber force was equipped with a total of about 850 warheads. In addition, Russia had about 5,390 warheads designed to be delivered by shorter range, or nonstrategic, aircraft and missiles. A total of about 1,800 were operational; the rest were held in reserve or scheduled to be dismantled. The operational warheads were held by various branches of the Russian military. Short- and midrange aircraft equipped with missiles or bombs carried about 650 of these operational warheads. Submarines, surface ships, and naval aircraft armed with cruise missiles, rockets, and other weapons were equipped with just under 700 warheads. Various antimissiles or air defense missiles carried between 600 and 700 operational warheads.[39]

Meanwhile, Russia is modernizing its nuclear forces and developing new weapons. For example, the first of a new class of nuclear submarine will become operational in 2008. It is expected to be equipped with a new SLBM with a range of 5,000–6,000 miles. During 2007 and 2008, Russia also tested an updated version of its most advanced ICBM, a weapon designed to evade antimissile systems. The new missile, called the RS-24, has the additional advantage of being road mobile: that is, it can be moved from place to place by specially designed vehicles rather than being based in a fixed silo. The RS-24 is expected to become operational by the very end of 2009.[40]

Russian Strategies for Combating WMD

The Russian government, while not as secretive as the Soviet government, is not as open about its actions in many fields as the U.S. government. That means much less is known about its programs to counter WMD. Like the United States, Russia is concerned with protecting itself against a nuclear missile attack. It has an antimissile defense system to protect Moscow. This system, called the A-135, consists of both long-range and short-range missiles, both armed with nuclear warheads. This means the missiles do not have to hit their targets directly but can destroy them by exploding nearby. Russia tested its system three times between 2004 and 2007 as part of its program to modernize and upgrade it. It also has modern antiaircraft weapons that can be used to defend against cruise missiles and short-range ballistic missiles as well as aircraft. Until 2007, the most advanced system of this kind was called the S-300. However, that year the Russians announced they would begin deploying the more advanced and effective S-400 system. Russia also has a system of early-warning satellites to detect ballistic missile launches. In December 2008, a new and advanced satellite was added to that system, which now has a total of five satellites. Meanwhile, in April 2008, Russia announced a new program to create what officials call a unified national defense to better combine and coordinate its air defense and antimissile capabilities.[41]

To help secure the stockpile of fissile materials from getting into the wrong hands, Russia and the United States have worked together under the Treaty on the Non-Proliferation of Nuclear Weapons (NPT) to remove former Soviet nuclear weapons from Ukraine, Belarus, and Kazakhstan and transfer them for destruction to Russia. Another ongoing Russian/American cooperative effort is the U.S.–funded Global Threat Reduction Initiative (GTRI). Under this program, highly enriched uranium has been moved from former Soviet satellite countries such as the Czech Republic and Poland and shipped to Russia. Russia also has accepted American help to secure its own stocks of fissile material held in many storage sites, especially under the Nunn-Lugar CTR Program.[42]

Efforts to combat chemical weapons date from the Soviet era, at least in terms of providing soldiers with defensive weapons. By the early 1970s, the Soviet Union had tanks and armored personnel carriers equipped with seals, filters, and other systems to keep out poison gas. Soviet forces also had gas masks, automatic detector alarms, injectors equipped with nerve gas antidote, and portable shelters, as well as wash-down equipment for decontaminating tanks and aircraft.[43] As mentioned, Russia has been working to destroy its declared chemical weapons stockpile, work that has been going on with the aid and cooperation of the United States and other Western powers. Until 2004, much of this work, as well as work to meet Russia's obligations under the Biological Weapons Convention (BWC), was done by the Russian Munitions Agency. Then its responsibilities were transferred to the Ministry of Industry and Energy. Another agency involved in protecting Russia from chemical and biological weapons is the Ministry for Civil Defense, Emergency Situations, and Disaster Management. While that ministry's main concern is natural disasters, its special unit of civil protection troops are equipped with equipment that protects against radiation, biological, and chemical hazards.[44]

ISRAEL AND THE MIDDLE EAST

The Unstable Middle East

The Middle East—which includes Libya and Egypt in North Africa, the seven countries of the Arabian Peninsula, as well as Jordan, Israel, Lebanon, Syria, Turkey, Iraq, and Iran—has been the scene of numerous wars since the end of World War II. The area holds the largest reserves of crude oil worldwide and has thus been critically important to the industrial powers. Most of the countries at the heart of the Middle East became independent of European powers only in the 1940s. Israel, most of whose people are Jewish, is the only country in the Middle East that does not have a majority Muslim population. It is also the region's only democracy. Since World War II, Israel and Arab states that refuse to recognize Israel's right to exist have fought four wars. In addition, Israel has fought two wars against heavily armed militias controlled by non-state Arab organizations committed to its destruction. Arab states have fought against each other since World War II, such as when Egypt intervened in a civil war in Yemen in the 1960s and when Iraq, under Saddam Hussein, attacked and overran Kuwait in 1990. Iraq's aggression spread fear throughout the region and convinced Egypt and 11 other Arab states to join in a U.S.–led military effort in 1991 that drove Iraq from Kuwait. Nations from several continents participated in that campaign, which is known as the 1991 Gulf War.

The longest and most destructive recent war in the Middle East pitted Iraq against Iran. Most of Iran's people are ethnically Persians rather than Arabs. Furthermore, while most Arabs belong to the majority Sunni branch of Islam, most Iranians belong to the minority Shii branch. Iran itself is controlled by a Shii theocracy. The Iran-Iraq war, also instigated by Saddam Hussein, began in 1980 when Iraq invaded Iran because of a border dispute. The war lasted until 1988; as many as 1 million people may have died in that long, bloody struggle.

One notable, and ominous, fact about some of the wars in the Middle East is that in two of them at least one side used weapons of mass destruction, specifically chemical weapons. Between 1963 and 1967, Egypt used mustard and phosgene gas while fighting in Yemen. Iraq introduced chemical weapons into its war with Iran when it used mustard and nerve gasses against Iranian forces in 1983. The next year Iran retaliated with mustard gas, and both sides used these weapons as the war dragged on. A third case of chemical weapons use by a Middle Eastern state involved Libya. It used mustard gas against its southern neighbor Chad, a country that is not considered a Middle Eastern state. Libya used mustard gas supplied by Iran during 1986–87 when it attacked Chad and attempted to occupy some of its territory, which contained uranium deposits Libya wanted for itself.[45]

During their eight-year war, Iran and Iraq also attacked each other's nuclear facilities, although in neither case were these facilities completed and operating. Iran used warplanes to bomb Iraq's Osirak nuclear reactor in September 1980, just a week after being attacked by Iraqi troops. That attack was not successful. It was left to Israel, which feared that it would be in mortal danger if Iraq developed nuclear weapons, to destroy the nearly completed reactor, a task it carried out in June 1981. Between 1984 and 1987, Iraqi warplanes attacked Iran's uncompleted Bushehr nuclear reactor four times without significant success.[46]

Egypt, Syria, and Iran

Because so much is kept secret, it is extremely difficult to be certain which nations in the Middle East are developing or already have WMD. Nor is it certain how advanced or large any WMD arsenals in the Middle East are. That said, experts generally agree on several points. Libya and Iraq, which both at one time had extensive WMD programs, have given them up. Iraq was forced to do so after its defeat in the 1991 Gulf War. Libya voluntarily did so under considerable international pressure after 2003 when its secret nuclear program was conclusively exposed.

Syria has an advanced chemical weapons program, with production facilities in several cities. It has not signed the CWC. Some experts consider Syria's program to be the most advanced program in the Middle East. Syria has hundreds of tons of chemical agents, including sarin, VX, and mustard gas. It has missiles that can carry chemical warheads for several hundred miles, as well as bombs that can be delivered by aircraft. It is believed that Russia, China, and several European countries have aided Syria in its chemical program. Syria also has a biological weapons program but probably is not yet able to produce those weapons. It has signed but not ratified the BWC.[47] In September 2007, Israel bombed and destroyed a nuclear reactor to produce plutonium Syria was secretly building with North Korean and Iranian help. In that project, Syria was providing the territory to locate the reactor, Iran the funds to pay for it, and North Korea the technical expertise to build it. Syria is on the U.S. State Department list of countries that promote terrorism.

Egypt probably was the first country in the Middle East to obtain chemical weapons, and it used them during the 1960s in Yemen. It has not signed the CWC. It also supplied Iraq with chemical weapons agents and technology during the 1980s. Egypt currently has a stockpile of chemical agents that includes nerve agents and mustard gas. It has signed but not ratified the BWC. The United States believes Egypt has produced biological weapons agents and probably still has them. Although in 2007 and again in 2009 traces of weapons-grade uranium were found at a site where Egypt has two small research reactors, experts do not believe that Egypt has a nuclear weapons program. Egypt has an arsenal of several different types of ballistic missiles that can deliver chemical weapons.[48]

Iran is developing biological weapons and possesses chemical weapons and ballistic missiles to deliver them. During its 1980s war with Iraq, Iran began stockpiling phosgene, mustard gas, and other agents and probably began production of nerve agents in the mid-1990s. Despite the fact that Iran has ratified the CWC, the United States believes that it has weaponized blister, blood, and choking agents. Iran ratified the BWC in 1973, before the revolution that brought its current radical Islamic regime to power. However, experts believe that Iran has a biological weapons program, which includes research on anthrax, and that it has both produced and weaponized a small quantity of these agents.[49]

Far more important, in direct violation of its international agreements, Iran is developing nuclear weapons. Iran publicly insists that its extensive nuclear program is for peaceful purposes only, but no informed observer takes those claims seriously. Iran's nuclear facilities include a large plant to enrich U-235 that has been operating for several years. Its existence was a secret until revealed by an Iranian oppostion group in 2002. Recently, Iranian scientists installed more advanced centrifuges in that facility. As of mid-2009, experts believed that Iran had 7,000 centrifuges enriching uranium there. A second secret enrichment site, still under construction, was revealed in fall 2009 after intensive intelligence efforts by the United States, Britain, France, and Israel. Built into a mountain and carefully disguised, it is too small to house the needed number of centrifuges to produce enough enriched uranium for peaceful industrial purposes. It is, however, exactly the right size, if equipped with advanced centrifuges, to produce highly enriched uranium for nuclear bombs. Iran also has a facility to produce heavy water, as well as numerous facilities throughout the country for nuclear research and related activities. A large light-water nuclear reactor built by Russia is nearing completion; the Russians already have delivered the fuel for that reactor. Although the reactor supposedly is designed to produce electricity for peaceful purposes, many experts are convinced that Iran intends to extract plutonium from its spent fuel to use in nuclear bombs. Iran also is known to be working on designs for nuclear warheads, almost certainly with foreign help.[50]

Iran has an extensive arsenal of ballistic missiles to deliver its WMD, along with aircraft and cruise missiles. It is working intensively on developing ballistic missiles able to carry heavier payloads for longer distances. Iran's most advanced missile already has a range of about 1,200 miles, which brings most of the Middle East and some targets in Europe into range.

Iran's WMD program, and especially its nuclear program, is a direct threat to Israel, a country Iran's leaders repeatedly and in the most violent language have threatened to destroy. Nor is Iran just a threat to Israel. Iran's nuclear program may well cause Arab countries in the region to acquire these weapons. This would cause a regional nuclear arms race whose final outcome could be catastrophic. Iran also has been repeatedly designated by the U.S. State Department as the world's "most active sponsor of state terrorism." Iran's growing global ambitions, its threats to disrupt the shipment of oil from the Persian Gulf, and its nuclear program make Iran a threat to U.S. interests worldwide.[51]

In 2005, the International Atomic Energy Agency (IAEA) found Iran to be in noncompliance with the NPT. Yet both before and since then, all international efforts based on sanctions and other peaceful methods to get Iran to stop developing nuclear weapons have failed. In late 2008, the IAEA reported that Iran had produced enough low-enriched uranium to build a nuclear bomb. Some intelligence estimates projected that Iran would have enough uranium for three weapons by the end of 2009. Although that uranium would have to be enriched further to be used in a nuclear bomb, the IAEA report was ominous.[52]

WMD in Israel: Key Issues

Israel faces a threat to its national security more dangerous and constant than any country in the world. In fact, Israel is virtually unique in the world in that its very right to exist is denied by many of its neighbors. It was invaded by armies from five Arab states—Egypt, Syria, Iraq, Jordan, and Lebanon—when it declared its independence in 1948. The goal, only three years after the Holocaust, was to carry out what the head of the Arab League called a "war of extermination."[53] In June 1967, after Egypt moved thousands of heavily armed troops to the Egyptian/Israeli border and its president announced that his country's "basic objective will be the destruction of Israel," Israel was forced to fight a defensive war against Egypt and its two allies, Syria and Jordan.[54] Israel was attacked again by Egypt and Syria in 1973. Israel avoided destruction only by costly victories in these three wars. Throughout its history, Israel also has had to deal with terrorist attacks launched from Arab-controlled territory along its borders. One reason Israel attacked Egypt in 1956 was to end terrorist attacks from Egypt's Sinai Peninsula into southern Israel. In 1982 and again in 2006, to eliminate terrorist bases just beyond its northern border, Israel had to send its army into neighboring Lebanon.

Israel has signed peace treaties with two Arab countries, Egypt in 1979 and Jordan in 1994. However, those treaties were signed with leaders who are now dead, and neither treaty was ever popular with most Egyptians or Jordanians. To this day, most of the Arab world remains extremely hostile toward Israel, as the constant drumbeat of anti-Israel propaganda from those countries demonstrates.

Meanwhile, after its Islamic revolution in 1979, Iran joined the campaign to destroy Israel. Iran is 80 times the size of Israel and has 10 times its population. It also has great oil wealth and large, modern military forces. It has chemical weapons, ballistic missiles that can reach Israel, and a program to develop nuclear weapons. Iran's leaders, who are bitterly anti-American as well as violently anti-Semitic, have repeatedly stated they intend to wipe Israel "off the map." The language they use to describe Israel, and Jewish people in general, is identical to the language heard in Nazi Germany before and during the Holocaust, when the Nazis murdered 6 million Jews. Iran's top leaders have called Israel a "cancerous tumor," a "dead fish," and a "stinking corpse." In 2006, as a huge crowd shouted "death to Israel," Iran's president questioned whether Israelis are human beings. Iran is the world's leading sponsor of international terrorism and provides modern weapons and training to terrorist organizations committed to Israel's destruction. Israelis have every reason to believe that the Iranian leaders who pledge to destroy their country mean exactly what they say.[55]

All this hostility is especially worrisome because Israel's geography makes it unusually vulnerable to nuclear attack. It is a small country—about the size of New Jersey—and most of its population is concentrated in a narrow strip of land about 100 miles long along the Mediterranean coast. Israel's national survival depends on stopping a nuclear attack before it happens, and it must be prepared to deal with chemical and biological weapons as well. This security situation, plus the memory of the Holocaust and the world's failure to do anything to stop that genocide, governs many Israeli defense policies.

Among those policies is Israel's approach to WMD in general and nuclear weapons in particular. Israel has developed WMD, and especially nuclear weapons, so it can defend itself. Israel's primary objective is known as deterrence: to be so strong that your enemies will not dare to attack you. If that does not work and war comes, Israel must be powerful enough to defeat any combination of enemies that attack it, using whatever weapons it must to assure its survival.

History and Current Arsenal

ISRAEL'S CHEMICAL AND BIOLOGICAL WEAPONS PROGRAMS

Many key facts about Israel's chemical and biological weapons programs remain shrouded in secrecy. There is general agreement, however, that Israel has developed, produced, and stockpiled chemical weapons. At some point in its history, it may have also deployed them, especially during wartime. There is less agreement about Israel's biological program. It is assumed that Israel has done extensive work in this area, especially regarding defensive measures, but most experts believe that Israel is not producing or stockpiling biological agents. As of 2009, Israel had signed but not ratified the CWC and neither signed nor ratified the BWC.[56]

Israel's chemical and biological programs date from several months before the country's founding in 1948. With World War II and the Holocaust only three years in the past, the people who soon would be leading Israel knew that when they declared independence their new country would be invaded by surrounding Arab countries. David Ben-Gurion, Israel's founding prime minister, was convinced that to survive Israel had to become one of the world's most advanced scientific and technological countries. Science and technology would enable the country to advance and prosper. More urgently, only with the most modern weapons would Israel be able to defend itself from its neighbors, who vastly outnumbered it in population and exceeded it in every measure of national strength.

At least some of Israel's scientific and technological expertise would have to be used to develop and build weapons of mass destruction. Ben-Gurion and his advisers hoped that these weapons, and the threat they represented, would serve their purpose as deterrence simply by being in Israel's hands and therefore would not have to be used. However, if war came and Israel was on the verge of defeat, they would be used as a last resort. Armed only with conventional weapons, Israel managed to defeat the invading Arab armies in 1948–49 in a bloody struggle Israelis call the War of Independence. But the continued Arab refusal to make peace or accept Israel's right to exist reinforced Ben-Gurion's outlook and commitment to building WMD.[57]

Ben-Gurion and his closest advisers believed that only nuclear weapons could provide Israel with the security it sought. However, during its first years of independence the country did not have the resources and expertise needed to develop nuclear weapons. Thus, Israel's first WMD program, established during the 1948–49 war, focused on chemical and biological weapons. In his planning, Ben-Gurion worked closely with two key assistants: science adviser Professor Ernst David Bergmann, an organic chemist, and Shimon Peres, who decades later would himself become prime minister. The first institution to work on WMD was called the Science Corps, better known by the Hebrew acronym HEMED. It was attached to Israel's military, the Israel Defense Forces (IDF), and staffed by a small but outstanding group of chemists and biologists. Within HEMED, a second supersecret laboratory called HEMED BEIT was established to work on biological warfare.[58]

After the war a reorganization took place, and in 1952 the Israel Institute for Biological Research (IIBR) was established. It was housed in a building surrounded by an orange grove outside the small town of Ness Ziona, which today is an upscale suburb of Tel Aviv, Israel's largest city. From the start the IIBR had a so-called dual identity. Officially, it was under the jurisdiction of the prime minister's office, and part of it did civilian work. Scientists doing that work have published papers and discussed their work in conferences all over the world. However, the IIBR also worked on top-secret projects involving chemical and biological weapons under the supervision of Israel's Ministry of Defense. It did its work with a surprisingly small budget, a tiny fraction of Israel's military research and development budget. Over the years, the IIBR's facility in Ness Ziona grew into a significant research complex surrounded by a concrete wall equipped with the most modern electronic sensors for protection against intruders.[59]

During the 1950s and 1960s, Israel did not place the same value on chemical and biological weapons. Although biological weapons had to be studied and even kept in reserve to deter enemies from using them, they were not viewed as useful battlefield weapons. In contrast, chemical weapons could be used on the battlefield, which meant that Israel's Arab enemies someday might use them against Israeli troops.[60]

Chemical Weapons

In 1955, with the threat of another war looming with Egypt, Israel launched what Ben-Gurion called a "crash program" to move beyond research to producing chemical weapons and making them operational. Ben-Gurion was worried that Israel's very existence was threatened. The urgency came not only from the threat of war but from Israel's fear that Egypt had chemical weapons and would use them, either on the battlefield or against civilians. In fact, Egypt as yet did not have a chemical weapons program, although it might have had some old British weapons abandoned after World War II. As part of its effort to develop chemical weapons, during the early 1960s Israel worked together with France. Some Israeli scientists visited France's main chemical weapons testing site in the Sahara in what was then the French colony of Algeria.[61]

By the mid-1960s, Israel knew that Egypt had chemical weapons. Beginning in 1963, Egyptian forces fighting in Yemen's civil war had used bombers to drop bombs filled with mustard and phosgene gasses. The bombers were supplied by the Soviet Union; the chemical weapons were either World War II leftovers or new weapons Egypt had acquired from the Soviet Union. Concern that these weapons would be used against Israel mounted in the spring of 1967 amid a rising drumbeat of threats when tens of thousands of Egyptian troops moved to Israel's southern border and two of Israel's other Arab neighbors, Syria and Jordan, prepared for war. Israel prepared not only for war but to defend itself against chemical warfare. In May, Israeli intelligence discovered that the Egyptians had a small number of artillery shells filled with sarin gas just south of the Israel/Egypt border. There were not enough of them to make a significant difference if fighting broke out, but more than enough for Israel to take emergency measures. It immediately bought 20,000 gas masks in the United States and another 20,000 in West Germany. It also bought thousands of doses of antidotes against nerve agents. A few days later, in early June, the 1967 Six-Day War began. In this war, Israel had three opponents: Egypt, Syria, and Jordan. Experts believe that Israel deployed its chemical weapons during the war, but when Egypt did not use its chemical weapons, neither did Israel.[62]

In 1973, Israel faced a much more serious chemical weapons threat, even though it had to fight only Egypt and Syria in what Israelis call the Yom Kippur War. Egypt had dozens of aircraft armed with sarin-filled bombs and Soviet-made missiles able to carry chemical warheads about 185 miles. Syria had chemical weapons as well, which it had bought from Egypt. They included sarin-filled artillery shells and missile warheads and spray tanks that could be fit on airplanes. Both countries also had Soviet-made tanks and other armored vehicles designed to protect their operators against chemical weapons. The Israelis captured some of these and turned them over to the United States. During the fighting, the Israelis also intercepted messages by Egypt putting its units with chemical weapons on alert. These units were not ordered into action, perhaps because of fear of Israeli retaliation.[63]

Just as the United States was surprised by the Soviet Union's chemical warfare equipment, Israel was shocked by the weapons and equipment Egypt and Syria had. After the war, the Israeli government took a major step to protect its civilian population by ordering 1 million gas masks. They were designed and manufactured in Israel. A special air-filtration device similar to a crib was designed for infants too small to wear a gas mask. These protective devices were not given to the population at large but held in reserve to be distributed if a serious threat arose.[64]

Despite Egypt and Syria's improved chemical arsenals, by the 1970s Israel placed less value on those weapons for its own arsenal. The reason was that by then Israel had developed nuclear weapons. Still, Israel maintained its research and development effort to defend against chemical weapons and, if necessary, to use them in retaliation for a chemical attack so it would not have to resort to nuclear weapons. The importance of that policy was demonstrated in 1990 when Iraqi dictator Saddam Hussein threatened to use chemical weapons "to make fire burn half of Israel." Although Israel did not take part in the 1991 Gulf War, Iraq fired several dozen missiles at Israel during that conflict. At the request of the United States, Israel did not retaliate. The great concern was that Iraq's missiles were armed with chemical warheads, as Iraq was known to have a chemical weapons arsenal. The Iraqi barrage forced millions of Israelis to retreat to shelters and specially prepared rooms that were sealed with tape and plastic sheeting. There they put on gas masks that had been distributed to every citizen and waited for the all clear signal. Sometimes that took hours. As it turned out, none of the Iraqi missiles had chemical warheads. Nonetheless, the tension took its toll; two civilians died and almost 1,000 were hospitalized for a variety of conditions. Some people hurt themselves when they did not use their gas masks properly. Others panicked and took a nerve gas antidote that is poisonous if a person has not been exposed to nerve gas. Others experienced extreme anxiety or suffered heart attacks.[65]

Biological Weapons

Although Israel's leaders never considered biological weapons to be practical for the battlefield, they understood very well the potential role they could play as terror weapons. Therefore, Israel had to be able to defend against them. Exactly what was done at the IIBR is not known, but Israel undoubtedly worked on many biological agents and how to defend against them. In a rare public statement, in 2001 the IIBR announced that it had developed an anthrax vaccine that can be administered in a single injection. This was a significant improvement over the vaccine used by the U.S. Department of Defense, which required three injections.[66]

Current Israeli Chemical and Biological Weapons and Countermeasures

Most experts agree that Israel continues to do advanced research involving chemical and biological weapons and has the ability to produce them. It is uncertain whether Israel currently has stockpiles of chemical and/or biological agents. The best guess is that it does not have biological agents and has not weaponized any chemical agents it might have.[67]

Much more is known about Israel's countermeasures regarding these weapons. As its announcement in 2001 about an anthrax vaccine makes clear, Israel continues to work on antidotes. It also has a program to provide modern gas masks to its entire population. In 2006, the government began collecting the old gas masks held by the public so they could be repaired and upgraded. This process went more slowly than planned, but by mid-2009 almost 80 percent of the gas masks had been refurbished. However, while the redistribution of the gas masks was scheduled to begin in November, it was expected to take two years to complete. As a stopgap measure, Israel's army has an emergency plan to distribute gas masks to most of the public within 48 hours. The army also is training some officers to assist local mayors and other officials in running their communities during wartime. They will assist with many urgent tasks, including protecting the civilian population against WMD. Israel also has a special office in the defense ministry to manage the home front if the country goes to war.[68]

ISRAEL'S NUCLEAR PROGRAM: "THE BOMB IN THE BASEMENT"

Origins and the Struggle to Maintain Secrecy

When people speak of Israel's "bomb in the basement," they obviously are not referring to where Israel keeps its atomic weapons. To be sure, they certainly are stored in underground bunkers so that they will be safe from attack. But "bomb in the basement" refers to the official status of Israel as a nuclear power. It means that while Israel has developed nuclear weapons, and that everyone knows it, the Israeli government has never officially announced the fact. Israel has not signed the NPT.

In 1963, Shimon Peres, at the time Israel's assistant minister of defense, stated that Israel "will not introduce nuclear weapons to the region, and certainly will not be the first."[69] At the time, Israel had a nuclear program but had not succeeded in building an atomic bomb. That has changed, but not

Israel's official position regarding atomic weapons. Israel does not deny it has them, but does not officially admit it either. This so-called nuclear ambiguity is designed to impress Israel's enemies with its power and deter them from attack. It also is intended to try to avoid a nuclear arms race in the Middle East. At the same time, Israel adopted its nuclear ambiguity policy to avoid pressure to give up its nuclear arsenal from the countries promoting nuclear nonproliferation. The most important of these countries by far is the United States, Israel's most consistent friend. By officially maintaining its nuclear ambiguity, Israel enables the United States to support nuclear nonproliferation and at the same time accept the fact that Israel needs and has nuclear weapons for self-defense.

Given its limited resources, Israel was unable to begin its nuclear program immediately after independence. Nonetheless, it did do what it could to prepare the way. In 1949, Israeli scientists searched the Negev, the country's desert region in the south, looking for uranium deposits. They found some low-grade deposits, but nothing more. In 1952, the Israeli Atomic Energy Commission (IAEC) was set up under the chairmanship of Ernst David Bergmann, the same scientist who had been advising Prime Minister Ben-Gurion on other WMD projects since 1948. Its existence was not announced until 1954. From the start, the IAEC had two functions. Publicly, it worked under the prime minister's office to explore peaceful uses of nuclear energy. Secretly, it worked under the ministry of defense to develop nuclear weapons.[70]

In light of the complexity and huge costs involved in developing nuclear weapons, Israel knew it could not undertake the project without outside help. During the mid-1950s, Israel turned to France for help. France also was trying to develop an atomic bomb. The two countries at the time saw eye to eye on a number of international issues. French leaders also knew their program was making slow progress. One difficulty they were having involved complex mathematical calculations related to the implosion process. As one government official told the Israelis, the French program had "holes in it." Israel had computer technology that could help fill those holes. It also was able to provide France with valuable intelligence information on other matters. Mutual need brought the two countries together, and in 1957 they signed a secret agreement. France agreed to build a powerful nuclear reactor for Israel, supply Israel with enriched uranium, and build a plant that would enable Israel to extract plutonium from the waste produced by the reactor. The deal was completed under such secrecy that some of its most important parts were only verbal understandings. To this day, many of the key details are still classified.[71]

French help was crucial to Israel's completing its nuclear program successfully. Israeli scientists and technicians were able to train at France's nuclear facilities. Israeli and French scientists worked together designing nuclear weapons, and Israeli scientists were present at several French nuclear tests, including the first test in 1960. However, in the mid-1960s, France ended this nuclear cooperation, largely because French president Charles de Gaulle was unsympathetic to Israel. From then on Israel had to develop its nuclear arsenal alone.[72]

Israel's other crucial need was to keep the program secret. That was not easy once construction started in the mid-1960s several miles south of the small town of Dimona on the northern edge of the Negev desert. It was an enormous project that included not only a nuclear reactor but four underground facilities: a plutonium separation plant, a plant to store used uranium fuel rods, a laboratory to test the purity of uranium samples, and a waste treatment plant. Fifteen hundred Israelis worked on the project, as did dozens of technical experts from France. The project used so much cement that there was a shortage in the housing construction industry.[73]

Israel managed to keep what it was doing at Dimona secret from foreign intelligence agencies, including those of the United States. The United States became aware of the Dimona project in 1960, although it was not sure exactly what type of nuclear facility the Israelis were building. Between 1961 and 1963, President John F. Kennedy put pressure on Israel to allow American experts to visit the Dimona reactor. There were several visits by American inspectors in the mid-1960s during the presidency of Lyndon Johnson, but Israel succeeded in concealing key parts of the Dimona facility from them. Experts agree that out of sympathy for Israel's grave security problems, a matter of particular importance to President Johnson, the United States did not push as hard as it could have. In the end, the United States did not approve of Israel's effort to build nuclear weapons, but it did not really try to stop it.[74]

By the early 1960s, Israel was totally committed to developing nuclear weapons. Its determination had been reinforced when in the late 1950s and early 1960s the United States refused to guarantee Israel's security. Israel wanted the same guarantees that the United States had provided to its NATO allies, a guarantee backed by American nuclear weapons. Japan, not a NATO member, had received a similar U.S. guarantee. Still, American concerns influenced how Israel handled its atomic program. Israel developed atomic weapons but never admitted it. That way, it avoided openly violating American nonproliferation policies. This position eventually was spelled out in a secret 1969 agreement between Israel's prime minister Golda Meir and U.S. president Richard M. Nixon.[75]

Meanwhile, well before any agreement with the United States, Israel worked to acquire other materials it needed. One of them was heavy water, or water that contains a deuterium atom (O_2) rather than a simple oxygen atom.

In a nuclear reactor, heavy water is the "moderator," the material that controls the chain reaction. Nuclear reactors that use heavy water as a moderator do not require enriched uranium as their fuel because heavy water is more effective than regular water in slowing down neutrons from fission reactions. So-called light water reactors, which use regular water as a moderator, require enriched uranium. In 1959, Israel ordered 20 tons of heavy water from Norway; it was delivered in two shipments, one in mid-1959 and the other in 1960.[76]

Uranium came from various sources. Israel's Negev desert supplied about 10 tons per year after an Israeli physicist developed an inexpensive way of extracting the uranium from the phosphate deposits in which the uranium was found. A large shipment was smuggled to Israel from a stockpile in the Netherlands in an undercover operation that included transferring the uranium from one ship to another in the middle of the Mediterranean Sea. The most important country among Israel's other uranium sources was South Africa.[77]

Israel Becomes a Nuclear Power

It is generally believed that Israel achieved the ability to build a nuclear bomb in late 1966. The reactor at Dimona probably went into operation in 1964 and the plutonium separation plant shortly thereafter. By 1966, Israel had produced enough weapons-grade plutonium, perhaps four kilograms, to build a nuclear weapon. It had designed a bomb but did not dare test it, since a test would have announced its program to the world. Instead, it conducted what is known as a cold test, in which each critical part of the weapon is tested by a simulation. That cold testing was completed in November 1966.[78]

All that remained was to make the decision to actually build a bomb. That decision was made during the tension-packed days of May 1967, as Israel faced a threat of war from the combined forces of Egypt, Syria, and Jordan. Just days before the war broke out, Israeli engineers and technicians working under enormous pressure assembled two nuclear bombs. Some Israeli leaders wanted to openly declare that their country had nuclear weapons in order to intimidate their enemies and avoid war. That proposal was rejected. Meanwhile, Israel strengthened the defenses around Dimona against both air and ground attack. The nuclear weapons were put on operational alert but never used, as Israel's conventional armed forces scored a decisive victory over the Egyptians, Syrians, and Jordanians in six dramatic but very costly days.[79]

It is believed that during the early 1970s Israeli scientists developed an advanced method of enriching U-235 using lasers and that Israel began using that system as well as centrifuges for that purpose. Israel's nuclear capability played an important role in the 1973 Yom Kippur War. The Israelis were surprised by the Egyptian and Syrian attacks and suffered early defeats. Israel's leaders, as deputy chief of staff General Israel Tal later put it, feared the country faced "a war for our very national and physical existence." However, Egyptian war aims did not go that far, and Egypt was the dominant country in the Egyptian-Syrian partnership and determined its objectives. One reason was that Egypt's president Anwar Sadat was convinced that Israel had a nuclear arsenal and would use it if its existence was threatened. Experts do not agree about what Israel did with its nuclear weapons during the war. Most observers believe that when Israel suffered costly defeats on the ground during the first days of the war, Moshe Dayan, its defense minister, ordered nuclear bombs to be loaded on airplanes and warheads on Israel's Jericho guided missiles. Those missiles were placed on high alert. Experts do not agree about whether Prime Minister Golda Meir canceled that order. In any event, Israel's army and air force turned the tide of the battle, defeated the Egyptian and Syrian forces, and Israel's atomic weapons remained unused and went back into the basement.[80]

Nuclear Test beneath the Seas

In September 1979, an American VELA spy satellite detected a flash in the Indian Ocean. The flash was similar to those observed from space when France and China conducted unannounced nuclear tests. The test remains a mystery to this day. However, most observers believe it was an Israeli nuclear test of some sort carried on in cooperation with South Africa. It may, in fact, have been the third such test, with the first two hidden from spy satellites by cloud cover. One possibility is that it was the test of a fission trigger for a thermonuclear device.[81]

In 1986, some of Israel's nuclear secrets were revealed when an Israeli technician who had been dismissed from his job at Dimona turned over photographs he had secretly taken and other information to a British newspaper. The technician's revelations, which included pictures of warheads, suggested that Israel had between 100 and 200 weapons. The technician also revealed that Israel had produced tritium and lithium deuteride. That suggested that Israel had the ability to build boosted nuclear weapons, which are considerably more powerful than ordinary fission weapons. Although experts disagreed about exactly what weapons Israel had, they did agree that by the mid-1980s the Israelis had a highly advanced nuclear program.[82]

Israel's Nuclear Arsenal Today

Despite the information that got out in 1986, the exact size and nature of Israel's nuclear arsenal remains a tightly held secret. The most common estimate offered by experts is that Israel has between 100 and 200 nuclear bombs and warheads. It is producing enough nuclear material to add several new weapons each year. Some of the devices in the arsenal may be thermonuclear weapons. Israel has a variety of modern aircraft that can deliver these weapons. It also has between 50 and 100 Jericho-1 missiles with a range of 300 to 600 miles, as well as more advanced Jericho-2 missiles with a range of about 1,000 miles. Israel also developed the three-stage Shavit rocket, which it has used since the late 1980s to put spy satellites into orbit.[83]

In addition, Israel has three submarines built in Germany capable of firing cruise missiles. It is widely believed that Israel has modified cruise missiles it bought from the United States so that they can carry nuclear warheads and that the submarines mentioned above carry those missiles. Israel itself has developed and produced much of the key technology and equipment for those submarines, including the equipment that enables the submarines to launch missiles with nuclear warheads. This small fleet gives Israel the ability to retaliate against any nuclear attack by an Arab nation or Iran. In late 2005, Israel ordered two more submarines capable of firing cruise missiles from Germany. Those submarines will be delivered in 2012.[84]

Israeli Strategies for Combating Nuclear Weapons

Israel has worked very hard and invested significant resources in developing countermeasures against nuclear weapons. In cooperation with the United States, it developed the Arrow antiballistic missile defense system, which is based on the Arrow 2 interceptor missile. Israel has tested the Arrow 2 successfully 13 times and deployed two batteries of the missiles to defend the country. These batteries, with about 100 missiles each, give Israel the world's only operational antiballistic missile system. A third Arrow 2 battery is planned.[85]

In August 2008, the United States announced it would help Israel develop a more advanced antimissile system, the Arrow 3. Meanwhile, the United States agreed to base its FBX-T radar system in Israel. This radar will extend Israel's ability to detect incoming missiles from 600 to 1,300 miles, thereby significantly increasing the warning time Israel will have to use its Arrow missiles to defend itself against a missile attack from Iran. Still, the Israelis will have only a few minutes to act, as Iran's Shehab-3 missile can reach their country in only 11 minutes. The FBX-T radar relies in part on satellites in fixed orbit over Iran and can pick up and detect and notify Israel about an Iranian launch in about 90 seconds.[86]

Israel also has used other means to protect itself against nuclear weapons. In August 2007, seven Israeli warplanes bombed and destroyed a nuclear reactor under construction in Syria. The reactor was being built in a remote area in the northeastern part of the country with North Korean help and was modeled on the reactor the North Koreans use to produce plutonium for nuclear weapons. Iran also was involved in the project.[87]

INDIA AND PAKISTAN

Key Issues

South Asia is the only region in the world with two nuclear powers that have gone to war with each other in recent times, although these wars occurred before either power had developed nuclear weapons. The two countries are India and Pakistan, and they have fought three wars since they both became independent in 1947. Because of conflict between the region's Hindu and Muslim populations, when Great Britain gave up its control of the Indian subcontinent after two centuries of colonial rule two new countries emerged: predominantly Hindu India and overwhelmingly Muslim Pakistan. India was by far the larger of the two, with more than four times Pakistan's area and almost four times its population. Reflecting the uneven distribution of the subcontinent's Muslim population, Pakistan was divided into two parts, West Pakistan and East Pakistan, separated by about 1,000 miles of Indian territory. Because of dreadful violence between Hindus and Muslims, including widespread massacres of defenseless people, at least 10 million people fled their homes to live in the country where they would be the majority. An estimated 1 million people died in the violence and mass migrations, adding new bitterness to the centuries-old legacy of deep hostility between the two communities.

India and Pakistan's first two wars, in 1947–48 and in 1965, were over Kashmir, a picturesque mountainous region in the northwestern part of the Indian subcontinent claimed by both sides. The fighting in 1947–48 left India in control of two-thirds of Kashmir, a situation that remained the same after the 1965 war. The third war, in 1971, grew out of an internal Pakistani issue: the campaign by the people of East Pakistan to win more autonomy for their region. The Pakistani army brutally suppressed the autonomy movement, killing at least 200,000 people and possibly many more. An estimated 8 million people became refugees when they fled from East Pakistan into India. India then intervened in the fighting, partly for humanitarian reasons and partly to weaken Pakistan. After the Indian army defeated the Pakistanis, East Pakistan became the independent country of Bangladesh.

Since 1971, India has had good relations with Bangladesh, but Indian-Pakistani relations have remained very tense. There have been several military clashes along their long border, and Kashmir remains as bitterly contested as ever. The fact that both countries tested nuclear weapons in 1998 has increased the urgency of keeping the tension between them from erupting into another war. That nearly happened in 1999, when militant Islamic forces backed by Pakistan infiltrated Indian-held territory in Kashmir. Serious fighting, including heavy artillery barrages between the two sides and eventually air strikes by India, lasted for more than two months before Pakistani forces withdrew. During the fighting there were fears that a miscalculation by either side could lead to nuclear war. The two countries again came dangerously close to war after Islamic terrorists attacked the Indian parliament in December 2001, killing a dozen people.

India and Pakistan, bitterly divided by religion, are also very different politically. India is a stable democracy, the world's largest in terms of population. Pakistan is an authoritarian and unstable country that has experienced several periods of military rule. Aside from Pakistan, India is concerned by the power of China, its huge neighbor to the northeast. India and China, the world's two most populous countries with populations of more than 1 billion each, are Asia's two emerging great powers. China traditionally has supported Pakistan in its rivalry with India.

India's WMD Programs

BIOLOGICAL AND CHEMICAL WEAPONS

India is a technologically advanced country with well-developed chemical and biological industries. It has many highly skilled scientists and well-equipped facilities for cutting-edge research and development. The government actively promotes the further development of these industries.

India's chemical industry has a long history, and today Indian factories produce more than 70,000 commercial products. These civilian products include pharmaceutical drugs, plastics, petrochemicals, dyes and pigments, and a wide variety of chemicals that are used for pesticides, fertilizers, and other agricultural purposes. In terms of volume, India ranks 12th in the world as a producer of chemicals. India is the world's 13th largest exporter of pesticides and disinfectants. Those exports include chemicals that in addition to their civilian applications can be used to make deadly chemical agents. More than 16 percent of India's manufacturing exports are chemicals. Indian companies also manufacture and export dual-use equipment, which means equipment that can be used for military as well as civilian purposes. India's chemical industry produces $28 billion worth of chemicals each year, which amounts to 12.5 percent of the country's industrial production.[88]

Although India has been secretive about its chemical and biological weapons programs, it did declare in 1997 that it possessed a stockpile of chemical weapons. This was something it had not admitted in 1993 when it signed the CWC or in 1996 when it ratified the CWC. India then began destroying its chemical weapons in accordance with its CWC obligations. By

January 2008, India reported that it had destroyed more than 90 percent of its most deadly chemical agents, a category that includes agents such as VX and sarin. In March 2009, India informed the Organisation for the Prohibition of Chemical Weapons (OPCW) that it had destroyed all of its declared chemical weapons stockpile, making it the third country—after Albania and South Korea—to do so. At the same time, experts point out that India has the scientific knowledge and industrial capacity to produce these agents in the future should it choose to do so.[89]

India's biotechnology industry has developed significantly during the past 20 years. In terms of civilian uses, India has become a leader in using genetic engineering to improve crop yields. It ratified the BWC in 1974. Nonetheless, some intelligence specialists believe that India has biological weapons, although there is no clear evidence that India has an offensive biological weapons program. However, there is no doubt that it has the capacity to make these weapons. India has worked on defensive measures against biological attacks, including research on combating diseases such as smallpox, plague, cholera, and botulism. Much of that research is conducted by a government agency called the Defence Research and Development Organisation. Other research is done by various branches of India's military. In addition, India has set up an elite force to serve as first responders in the event of a nuclear or biological attack. India has been the victim of a number of attacks by Islamic terrorists with links to Pakistan, most recently in November 2008 when almost 200 people were murdered in the city of Mumbai. While these attacks were carried out with conventional weapons, India fears that Islamic terrorists could carry out attacks using biological agents.[90]

INDIA'S NUCLEAR WEAPONS PROGRAM: 1947–1998

When the Indian Atomic Energy Commission was established in 1948, the primary objective was to use atomic energy for peaceful purposes. However, India's leaders already were thinking about nuclear weapons, and Jawaharlal Nehru, India's first prime minister, did not rule out building them. By the mid-1950s, India took its first steps toward building nuclear weapons, including establishing a Department of Atomic Energy. There were at least three reasons India eventually decided to develop nuclear weapons: to deter Pakistan from hostile actions; to protect India from China, a country whose growing power was already a concern in the 1950s and which became a nuclear power in the 1960s; and to achieve recognition as an international great power.

By 1956, India had two atomic reactors: Apsara, a small light-water research reactor built with British help, and Cirus, a much larger heavy-water reactor supplied by Canada. When Apsara went critical in 1957, it became the first operating nuclear reactor on the continent of Asia outside the Soviet Union. The United States supplied heavy water for Cirus in 1956 under its Atoms for Peace program, which provided small nuclear reactors and training to dozens of countries so they could carry out research for peaceful purposes. Apparently, at the time neither Canada nor the United States believed that India was interested in building atomic weapons. They were mistaken. In order to free itself from outside control or supervision, India did not accept uranium fuel for Cirus from Canada. Instead, India decided to produce its own natural uranium fuel. In 1958, using plans supplied by an American company, India began building a reprocessing center to separate plutonium from the spent fuel of the Cirus reactor, a project completed in 1964. The Cirus reactor, which began operation in 1960, eventually produced the plutonium for India's first atomic test. In the decades that followed, it became the source of half of India's current supply of weapons-grade plutonium. Today, both the Cirus reactor and the reprocessing plant are part of India's most important nuclear research and development center. Located in Trombay, a suburb of the city of Mumbai on India's western coast, it is called the Bhabha Atomic Research Centre (BARC). BARC is named in honor of Homi Jehangir Bhabha, the scientist who was its founding director and who for many years argued that India should develop atomic weapons.[91]

During the mid-1960s, India's nuclear program was held up for several reasons. There were technical problems with its nuclear facilities, and the country's political leadership was divided about whether India should develop a nuclear bomb. That indecision did not last. Aside from its long-standing problems with Pakistan, India was very concerned that China had tested atomic bomb in 1964 and a thermonuclear weapon in 1967. By the late 1960s, India made the decision to move ahead, refusing in 1968 to sign the NPT. Every effort was made to keep the program secret. In 1972, Prime Minister Indira Gandhi told scientists at BARC to build a nuclear device and ready it for a test. In 1974, in a test called "Smiling Buddha," India detonated a plutonium device with an explosive force of about eight kilotons. The device was not a deliverable bomb, and India officially claimed that the test was designed to learn how to use nuclear explosions for peaceful purposes.[92] Knowledgeable observers did not take that claim seriously, fully understanding that India had established the foundation it needed to build an atomic bomb within a relatively short period of time.

In fact, India did not build a deliverable atomic weapon for more than a decade. Technical assistance and supplies that India had counted on in its nuclear program were cut off, making it more difficult for local scientists and engineers to make progress. These sanctions affected India's civilian nuclear power program as well as its military efforts. In 1977, a new prime minister, Morarji Desai, who opposed India's nuclear weapons program took office. This further slowed down nuclear weapons progress. However, by the late 1970s, the news leaked out that Pakistan had a large and advanced nuclear program. When Indira Gandhi once again became prime minister in 1980, work on building a workable bomb was speeded up. Despite pressure from her top military officers, Gandhi did not allow India's scientists to conduct a nuclear test. Her government was trying to improve relations with the United States, which supported nonproliferation and therefore opposed an Indian nuclear test. Nonetheless, Gandhi not only authorized work on building an actual bomb but also efforts to develop hardware and techniques so that the bomb could be delivered to a target by aircraft and missiles. Work also began on developing ballistic missiles. Eventually, that program led to the development of the short-range Prithvi and the medium-range Agni missiles that today are the backbone of India's ballistic missile arsenal.[93]

Indira Gandhi was assassinated in 1984, but her son and successor as prime minister, Rajiv Gandhi, also strongly supported India's nuclear weapons program. Against the background of Pakistani advances in nuclear technology, in 1989 Rajiv Gandhi ordered that India manufacture nuclear weapons. Although Gandhi was voted out of office later that year, the work he had ordered continued under his successors. By 1990, India had about two dozen weapons, although they remained unassembled. In addition, India still had not perfected the hardware and operational techniques necessary for aircraft or ballistic missiles to carry atomic bombs or warheads to a target. Finally in 1994, India had both nuclear weapons and the hardware and systems necessary to deliver them to a target. Proof came in a test conducted that year when a French-built fighter-bomber successfully dropped a dummy bomb, which was complete except for its plutonium core. Although it had not conducted a nuclear test since 1974, India was a nuclear power.[94]

When India finally conducted a new test in May 1998, it conducted not one but five over a period of a few days, three on May 11 and two on May 13. The May 11 tests reportedly involved three devices: a 12-kiloton fission device, a 43-kiloton thermonuclear device, and a so-called sub-kiloton device (a device with a yield of less than a kiloton). On May 13, two sub-kiloton devices were tested. From the start, there was disagreement over whether India's claims about the yield of its thermonuclear tests were accurate. Today, U.S. government experts believe that the thermonuclear explosion was much smaller than India claimed. This in turn suggests that one of the two stages of the device did not operate as planned and that the overall test was a failure.[95]

In August 1999, more than a year after its series of tests, India in effect formally announced its status as a nuclear power by issuing an eight-part document detailing the purposes of its nuclear arsenal. This type of statement is known as a nuclear doctrine. It said that India's nuclear arsenal was designed to deter attacks. India would only build enough nuclear weapons to achieve what it called a "credible minimum nuclear deterrence." At the same time, the document said that the size of India's nuclear arsenal would be determined by the country's overall security needs. Further, India would never attack first with nuclear weapons, but only use them in response to an attack. In 2003, India officially reaffirmed its nuclear doctrine. Significantly, it added that it might use nuclear weapons in retaliation for biological or chemical attacks.[96]

India's nuclear tests of May 1998 are especially important because during that month India did not test alone. Between May 28 and May 30, just weeks after India's last test, Pakistan conducted six nuclear tests. Two nuclear powers now faced each other in South Asia, separated only by a long line on a map.

INDIA'S NUCLEAR ARSENAL TODAY

The exact size and composition of India's nuclear arsenal are a closely held secret. Experts estimate that India has produced between 300 and as much as 600 tons of weapons-grade plutonium and may be producing an additional 20 to 40 kilograms per year. That is enough to build between 40 and 120 weapons. A reasonable estimate is that India has between 50 and 60 assembled warheads. That arsenal may include some fusion-boosted plutonium bombs. India has several types of aircraft that can deliver nuclear bombs as well as short-range (100 miles/150 km) Prithvi I missiles and medium-range Agni missiles. The Agni I missile has a range of about 420 miles (700 km), while the more advanced Agni II missile can deliver a nuclear weapon to a target more than 1,200 miles (2,000 km) away. The Agni II has another advantage: It uses solid fuel and can be launched in 15 minutes, unlike the Agni I, whose upper stage is liquid-fueled and requires half a day to launch. The Agni II is capable of reaching any place in Pakistan. India is working to develop the Agni III missile, with a range of up to 3,000 miles (5,000 km). This new missile will be rail-mobile: That is, it will be launched from a platform that can be moved from place to place on railroad tracks. The Agni III is intended as a weapon against China. India also is developing a nuclear submarine capable of firing nuclear-tipped missiles. This will give it the ability to retaliate against a nuclear attack even if an enemy were to attack first and destroy its land-based nuclear weapons.[97]

Pakistan's WMD Programs

CHEMICAL AND BIOLOGICAL WEAPONS

Pakistan has the technical ability to produce chemical warfare agents, but there is no evidence that it has a chemical warfare program. It has signed and ratified the CWC. Yet some observers remain suspicious that Pakistan has a secret chemical warfare program. It has imported dual-use chemicals and equipment such as chemical and biological weapons protection suits that could be used to produce chemical weapons. Nonetheless, as of 2008, the OPCW considers Pakistan to be a country in good standing. However, Pakistanis acting on their own may be involved in chemical warfare–related activity. It has been reported that two leading Pakistani scientists may have helped al-Qaeda learn about how to disperse chemical and biological warfare agents through the air. In 2002, Pakistani police discovered chemical laboratories belonging to an Islamic terrorist organization based in Pakistan. That organization, Lashkar-e-Jhangvi, is known to have ties to al-Qaeda.[98]

In 1998, after Pakistan's nuclear tests, the U.S. Department of Commerce imposed sanctions on Pakistani government and private agencies or companies it suspected were involved in the country's nuclear weapons programs. At the time, the U.S. government also imposed sanctions on several Pakistani facilities it suspected might be involved in chemical or biological warfare programs. Since the 1990s, Pakistan has been accused of doing biological warfare research. However, although Pakistan has biotechnology skills and facilities, there is no verifiable evidence that it has an offensive biological warfare program.[99]

PAKISTAN'S NUCLEAR PROGRAM, ORIGINS TO 1998

Pakistan's nuclear program in many ways mirrors India's. One difference is that while India relied on plutonium in its nuclear bomb program, Pakistan relied on enriched uranium. The main reason Pakistan decided to develop nuclear weapons was as a lever against India, whose power in every other way far exceeded its own. Like India, Pakistan began with research into using nuclear power for peaceful purposes, setting up the Pakistan Atomic Energy Commission (PAEC) in 1956. In the early 1960s, the United States supplied Pakistan with its first nuclear reactor, a small light-water research reactor. In 1972, a much larger reactor to produce electric power built by a Canadian company began operation. That facility has always been under the supervision of the IAEA, which means it is unlikely that Pakistan could have used its spent fuel for its nuclear weapons program.

Pakistan began its program to develop nuclear weapons in early 1972. The decision was a reaction to their disastrous defeat by India in the war of 1971 that led to East Pakistan establishing its independence as the country of Bangladesh. Pakistan's prime minister at the time was Zulfikar Ali Bhutto, who in the mid-1960s had stated, "If India builds the Bomb, we will eat grass or leaves, even go hungry, but we will get one of our own."[100] The program was Pakistan's most closely held secret. Since poverty-stricken Pakistan lacked the resources to pay for the program, it required secret funding from outside sources. That initially came from two oil-rich Muslim countries, Libya and Saudi Arabia, both of which were ready to help build what Bhutto called an "Islamic bomb." Pakistan's nuclear program also required a massive smuggling operation to get everything from designs to high-tech components Pakistan could not make itself. This became a major challenge after 1975, when in response to India's 1974 nuclear test the United States and six other technologically advanced countries formed the Nuclear Suppliers Group (NSG). Its job was to support nonproliferation by controlling the export of technology and equipment that could be used to develop nuclear weapons.[101]

Pakistan's smuggling operations extended to more than half a dozen countries, from the United States and Canada to several countries in western Europe. However, the most important cog in that huge operation was a metallurgist named Abdul Qadeer Khan. Because of the skills and technology he brought with him, Khan played a key role in Pakistan's decision to use enriched uranium rather than plutonium to build its atomic bomb. Born in what was then British-controlled India, Khan moved to Pakistan after India's partition. Khan was a metallurgical engineer, who had first studied in Pakistan and then received advanced training in West Germany and Belgium. In 1972, he took a position at a uranium enrichment plant in Belgium run by a British-Dutch-West German company. In 1974, he secretly began supplying information about uranium enrichment to Pakistan. When he returned to Pakistan in 1975, he brought with him a vast store of knowledge as well as stolen plans for advanced centrifuges, which Pakistan then used to develop a program to enrich uranium. He then headed Pakistan's enrichment facility in Kahuta, in northeast Pakistan. Today that facility is named the Khan Research Laboratory in his honor.[102]

Khan's contributions to the Pakistani nuclear bomb program were immense, and he is considered the father of Pakistan's nuclear bomb. But he was much more than that. Within a few years after beginning work in Pakistan, Khan established a black market network that trafficked in nuclear technology and hardware. Khan provided secret assistance to countries such as Iran, North Korea, and Libya, in exchange obtaining resources Pakistan needed for its program. This network, which Khan set up in the late 1970s, was not exposed until 2003, despite suspicions that Pakistan was exporting nuclear technology and equipment. The Khan network severely undermined international efforts at nonproliferation by providing enrichment equipment and technology to Libya, North Korea, and Iran. In return, Pakistan earned millions of dollars, as did Khan personally. Equally important, North Korea provided Pakistan with medium-range missiles that significantly advanced Pakistan's ability to deliver its nuclear weapons. In exchange, North Korea received Pakistani technology for producing highly enriched uranium. Despite denials by the Pakistani government, there is no doubt that Khan did not operate alone. For example, Pakistani military cargo planes flew North Korean missiles to Pakistan.[103]

Another country that secretly aided Pakistan's nuclear program was China. China provided Pakistan with components essential to centrifuges that helped Pakistan enrich uranium, missile technology that was used in several types of ballistic missiles, and even the design for an advanced nuclear warhead. During the 1990s, China also helped Pakistan build a nuclear reactor that has enabled Pakistan to produce plutonium.[104]

Experts agree that by 1985 or 1986 Pakistan had produced enough enriched uranium to build an atomic bomb. American pressure, and Pakistan's desire to buy advanced American aircraft and other weapons, seems to have caused Pakistan to slow its production of highly enriched uranium (HEU) in the late 1980s. However, that changed after 1990. It was then that Pakistan probably used the HEU it had already produced to put together several cores for atomic bombs, although it did not build fully assembled weapons. The pace of enrichment increased further after 1994 when Pakistan bought 5,000 ring magnets, which are vital components for centrifuges, from China. Finally, on May 28, 1998, Pakistan conducted five nuclear tests. One was a device with an estimated yield of between nine and 12 kilotons. The others were sub-kiloton devices. Two days later, Pakistan conducted another test of a four-to-six-kiloton device.[105]

PAKISTAN'S CURRENT NUCLEAR ARSENAL

Experts estimate that Pakistan has produced enough HEU to build between 50 and 110 nuclear weapons. It also probably has enough plutonium for 10 to 20 weapons. A reasonable guess is that Pakistan actually has a stockpile of about 60 warheads. However, some of them are stored in the form of components and therefore have to be assembled, which can be done in a matter of days. To deliver these weapons, Pakistan has U.S.-made jet aircraft, as well as aircraft from France and China. It also has ballistic missiles for the job. They include the short-range Ghaznavi, a solid-fuel missile with a range of about 250 miles (400 km) derived from a missile supplied by China in the 1990s. The Ghaznavi has the advantage of being road-mobile; it is launched from specially built transporters. The solid-fueled Shaheen I, another road-mobile missile derived from a Chinese design, has a range of between 280 and 435 miles (450 km to 700 km). A longer-range two-stage version of that missile, the Shaheen II, will have a range of about 1,555 miles (2,500 km) when it is fully developed. Pakistan also has the Ghauri missile, which has a range of about 840 miles (1,200 km). This is a local version of the North Korean Nodong missile. In addition to ballistic missiles, Pakistan is developing the Babur air-launched cruise missile, with a range of about 310 miles (500 km). It has been tested several times and is similar to a Chinese cruise missile but is not yet operational.[106]

Along with its missile buildup, Pakistan is expanding its ability to make nuclear weapons. It is building two plutonium reactors, which are among the largest in the developing world. Each of these reactors will produce enough plutonium for Pakistan to build four to five nuclear weapons per year. In addition, Pakistan is upgrading its centrifuge program, which will enable it to produce more weapons-grade uranium. This program makes Pakistan the only country in the world that is rapidly building up its nuclear forces. According to David Albright, a former UN weapons inspector, Pakistan is "building a capability beyond any reasonable requirement." That new capability may well include an effort to develop thermonuclear weapons.[107]

Pakistan's political instability makes its nuclear buildup all the more dangerous. Radical Islamic groups are deeply entrenched in Pakistan, and many important government agencies have been infiltrated by Islamic militants. These agencies include not only Pakistan's army and its main intelligence service but also its nuclear establishment. Indeed, as the former CIA head George Tenet has written, just weeks before the September 11, 2001, al-Qaeda attacks on the World Trade Center and the Pentagon, two leading Pakistani nuclear officials met in Afghanistan with al-Qaeda leader Osama bin Laden. All this makes the security of Pakistan's nuclear weapons and facilities a matter of urgent concern in Washington and other world capitals. It also explains why the United States reportedly has a detailed plan to infiltrate Pakistan and seize control of its nuclear warheads if the country falls under the control of Islamic militants.[108]

Indian and Pakistani Strategies for Combating WMD

India's efforts to combat WMD are a response to two types of threats: the arsenals of Pakistan and China and terrorist attacks by Islamic militants supported by Pakistan or Islamic groups based in Pakistan. Thus far, all terrorist attacks against India have involved only conventional weapons, including the most recent incident in November 2008 when 10 gunmen killed 165 people in the city of Mumbai. The threat posed by Islamic terrorism is one reason India has been working closely with Israel since the 1990s on a variety of military projects.

That cooperation was demonstrated in April 2009 when India used one of its own rockets to place an all-weather Israeli-made spy satellite into orbit. The satellite was ordered and delivered on a rush basis after the Mumbai attack. The next month Israeli military instructors participated in the Indian army's biggest ever antiterror exercise. Some of the combat vehicles used in that exercise were developed in Israel.[109]

Meanwhile, India has been developing its own means of defending against chemical and biological weapons. India's army and other defense agencies have developed special clothing such as masks and suits and equipment such as detectors to protect the country's soldiers against chemical and biological weapons as well as against nuclear hazards. These agencies are also doing research on antibodies against bacterial, viral, and chemical agents. Responses are being prepared against diseases such as anthrax, smallpox, plague, and botulism. India produces small quantities of nerve gasses to test its protective equipment.[110]

India's program to defend against nuclear weapons is focused on developing an antiballistic missile defense system. It is intended to defend against potential attacks from both Pakistan and China. India is developing its own missiles to shoot down incoming ballistic missiles but is also cooperating with Israel on important aspects of the overall system. For example, the radars used to track incoming missiles are based on equipment previously imported from Israel that originally was designed for Israel's Arrow antimissile system.[111]

Very little is known about Pakistan's program to combat WMD. Pakistan is openly seeking to acquire an antiballistic missile system and at various times has discussed its needs with the United States.

NORTH KOREA

Key Issues

North Korea, officially known as the Democratic Republic of North Korea, is a communist dictatorship whose methods of leadership are as brutal as those used by the Soviet dictator Joseph Stalin during the 1930s and 1940s. The country was established in 1948 as a result of the Soviet Union's occupation of the northern half of the Korea Peninsula after World War II. When the Soviets removed their troops, they left behind a communist regime under a dictator named Kim Il Sung. The southern part of the peninsula, occupied after the war by the United States, became the Republic of Korea, or South Korea. Kim in 1950 tried to conquer South Korea. His invasion of South Korea began the Korean War. Backed by the United Nations, the United

States sent troops to help South Korea, which was unprepared for war. Several months later, the People's Republic of China intervened on the North Korean side. The Korean War lasted until 1953, ending about where it began at the 38th parallel in the middle of the peninsula. Most of the peninsula, north and south of the 38th parallel, was in ruins. Because the fighting was ended by an armistice rather than a peace treaty, even today North and South Korea technically are at war. Their border is the most highly militarized border in the world.

After the Korean War, with American help, South Korea prospered and eventually became a democracy. North Korea remained a rigid communist dictatorship, almost entirely isolated from the rest of the world. Most of North Korea's resources went into building a huge military machine. Nothing changed when Kim Il Sung died in 1994; he was succeeded by his equally ruthless and fanatical son, Kim Jong Il, and today the 1.2 million-man army is the fourth largest in the world. During the 1990s, North Korea, with its inefficient state-controlled farming system, experienced a terrible famine. Although international aid provided about $1 billion worth of food, most of that went to soldiers and government officials, while mass starvation occurred among the civilian population. North Korea's economic collapse, extreme isolationist policy, and ruthless leadership make it especially volatile. The countries it considers its two main enemies, South Korea and Japan, have abstained from developing nuclear weapons, but both possess the technical capability to build those weapons. Both countries also are allies of the United States, whose troops stationed in South Korea were equipped with tactical nuclear weapons from 1958 until the last of them were withdrawn in 1991. As early as the 1950s, North Korea began research on WMD. Its success in that area has become a major source of instability in northeast Asia and especially a direct threat to South Korea and Japan. Beyond that, North Korea has played a major role in spreading both nuclear and military technology to countries such as Pakistan, Iran, and Syria, making its WMD programs a major concern to countries around the world.

Biological and Chemical Weapons

North Korea's chemical weapons program dates from the mid-1950s. Originally, it relied on help from China, but beginning in the mid-1960s, the North Koreans turned to the Soviet Union for assistance. It appears that through the 1970s the North Koreans had only defensive capabilities, but by the mid-1980s they probably had 250 tons of chemical agents, including both mustard and nerve agents. By 2006, according to South Korean intelligence estimates, North Korea had between 2,500 and 5,000 tons of chemical agents. These include all of the major classes of agents: blister, choking, blood, and nerve. However, experts believe that most of the North Korean chemical weapons agents are blister, choking, and blood, rather than some of the most deadly nerve agents. North Korea probably does have stocks of the nerve agent sarin and has the ability to produce V-agents, but it is uncertain whether it can manufacture large quantities of these agents.[112]

Experts believe that a significant percentage of North Korea's chemical agents already are weaponized, that is, stored in artillery shells and rocket warheads. North Korea has thousands of artillery shells, mortars, and rockets that can be weaponized with chemical agents, as well as hundreds of short-range ballistic missiles. All of these can easily be positioned near the border with South Korea. More than half of North Korea's army is deployed within 90 miles of the border with South Korea, along with thousands of guns and artillery pieces of all kinds. In the event of war, North Korea could use its chemical weapons against both soldiers—along with South Korean forces, there are more than 30,000 U.S. troops stationed in South Korea—and millions of South Korean civilians within the range of its guns. North Korea has not signed the CWC.[113]

North Korea's biological weapons program is shrouded in secrecy. Both U.S. and South Korean intelligence agencies are convinced that North Korea has biological weapons agents, despite the fact that it ratified the BWC in 1987. Available evidence indicates that North Korea's biological weapons program is far less advanced than its chemical weapons program. The program dates from the 1960s. At that time, the North Koreans investigated diseases such as anthrax, cholera, smallpox, and yellow fever. By the 1980s, the North Koreans probably had produced agents for several diseases, including anthrax. South Korea's defense ministry believes that North Korea's biological weapons arsenal includes anthrax, smallpox, and cholera. It may also include cultures of the agent that produces smallpox. U.S. military intelligence believes that some of these agents have been weaponized. It is likely that North Korea has between 10 and 20 facilities doing biological weapons research.[114]

Nuclear Weapons

The North Korean nuclear weapons program is one of the urgent threats facing the United States and other countries attempting to prevent the proliferation and use of WMD. North Korea's nuclear weapons are a direct threat to two American allies in northeast Asia, South Korea and Japan. In addition, North Korea has been directly involved in spreading nuclear weapons or missile technology to countries such as Pakistan, Iran, and Syria. There is also the fear that North Korea under certain circumstances would sell WMD to terrorist organizations.

North Korea began a program of nuclear research in the mid-1950s with Soviet help. According to the North Koreans, the program was intended to develop nuclear energy for peaceful uses. North Korean scientists and technicians received training in the Soviet Union, and in the mid-1960s, the Soviet Union provided North Korea with a small light-water nuclear reactor fueled by HEU. Its small size meant it was suited for research only, not producing power. The reactor, which became fully operational in 1967, nonetheless produced plutonium that potentially could be used to make nuclear weapons. Additional help in developing nuclear technology came from China. Having learned about nuclear technology and received equipment essential to getting started, North Korea began research into building nuclear weapons on its own. It also relied on its own technological knowledge and resources to develop ballistic missiles. North Korea's first reactor and most of its major nuclear facilities are located in the city of Yongbyon, in the western part of the country about 60 miles north of the capital of Pyongyang.[115]

During the 1970s, North Korea acquired from the Soviet Union technology for reprocessing spent nuclear fuel from nuclear reactors. In 1977, North Korea signed an agreement with the IAEA to allow inspection of its Soviet-supplied nuclear reactor. In 1985, after being pressured by the Soviet Union, North Korea became a party to the NPT.

Neither the agreement with the IAEA nor the signing of the NPT prevented North Korea from secretly beginning a program to develop nuclear weapons during the 1980s. There were two major reasons for this. First, the Soviet-supplied reactor was not under close and continuous IAEA supervision, which may have allowed North Korean scientists to divert some of the plutonium it produced to the country's weapons program. Second, between 1979 and 1985, North Korea built a second nuclear reactor, the 5-MW(e) reactor. This five-megawatt (electrical) reactor was not under IAEA supervision. After becoming operational in 1986, the 5-WM(e) reactor produced enough plutonium each year to make one nuclear weapon. Meanwhile, North Korea built a plant to reprocess spent nuclear fuel into weapons-grade plutonium. In 1989, North Korea shut down the 5-MW(e) reactor for about 70 days, enough time to remove its spent fuel rods. This in turn made it possible to extract plutonium from those rods and reprocess it to create the weapons-grade material used in nuclear bombs. Two other shutdowns of the 5-MW(e) reactor, respectively for 30 days and for about 50 days, followed in 1990 and 1991, once again allowing the North Koreans to extract and reprocess more plutonium for nuclear weapons. Not until 1992, under the terms of North Korea's acceptance of the NPT, was the 5-MW(e) reactor inspected by the IAEA. Inspectors found that North Korea had been untruthful in its declarations about its nuclear materials. By then, it was clear to expert observers that North Korea had enough weapons-grade plutonium for several weapons.[116]

An urgent international effort followed to convince North Korea not to build nuclear weapons and give up its nuclear weapons program. In October 1994, the United States and North Korea reached an agreement brokered by former U.S. president Jimmy Carter. Under this Agreed Framework, North Korea was to freeze its nuclear program, dismantle facilities that could be used for making weapons, and allow the IAEA to monitor its actions to assure it was complying with its obligations. In return, the United States agreed to organize a consortium of nations that would provide North Korea an aid package worth billions of dollars. That package included building two modern light-water nuclear power plants and providing an annual supply of fuel oil until those plants could be built.

The agreement failed as North Korea secretly continued its nuclear program. Its secret operations included getting technology to produce HEU from Pakistan in exchange for ballistic missiles. In January 2003, North Korea withdrew from the NPT. A few months later, U.S. intelligence discovered that North Korea was secretly reprocessing thousands of plutonium fuel rods that previously had been in storage. That year, North Korea announced it had enough plutonium for six nuclear bombs. Once again, international negotiations began. Eventually they involved six countries: North Korea, the United States, Russia, China, Japan, and South Korea. In the end, after several stops and starts, these negotiations also failed. North Korea announced that it had nuclear weapons on February 10, 2005. On October 9, 2006, North Korea tested a plutonium nuclear device. The exact yield of the test is unknown. North Korea announced the test would have the force of four kilotons, but Western experts agree it was almost certainly less than one kiloton.[117] In fact, while the test apparently was not completely successful, it was generally agreed that it was enough to make North Korea the world's ninth nuclear power.

Meanwhile, North Korean engineers were hard at work developing ballistic missiles. That program was aided by rockets and missiles supplied by the Soviet Union and especially by technical help from China beginning in the late 1970s. In the early 1980s, North Korea obtained a Soviet Scud missile with a range of about 180 miles (300 km) from Egypt. This advanced its program because the Scud was more advanced than anything the North Koreans had received from the Soviet Union. North Korean engineers were able to copy the missile—a process known as reverse engineering—and even slightly extend its range. North Korea's missile program had the bonus of earning some money. During the 1980s, North Korea sold many of its improved missiles to Iran; Iran used these missiles during its war with Iraq. North Korea eventually also sold missiles to Libya, Pakistan, Syria, and probably Egypt, making it the leading exporter of missiles to the developing world.[118]

North Korea's Nuclear Arsenal

North Korea has an unknown number of nuclear weapons, possibly as many as nine. It has more than 20 nuclear facilities, including uranium mines and facilities for processing uranium. Along with its stock of plutonium, North Korea probably has some HEU. It is likely that vital technology for enriching uranium came from Pakistan in return for North Korean missiles. North Korea also has an arsenal of ballistic missiles. This includes about 600 to 800 missiles derived from Soviet Scud missiles. These are short-range weapons with a range of between 180 and 360 miles (300–600 km). North Korea has between 150 and 200 medium-range Nodong missiles capable of hitting targets about 780 miles (1,300 km) distant. It also probably has about 10 Taepodong I missiles. This two-stage missile has a range of about 1,200 miles (2,000 km). North Korea is also developing a long-range missile with three stages—the Taepodong II—that potentially could reach the United States. Despite its formidable missile arsenal, most experts initially doubted that North Korea had a nuclear device small enough to be fitted on a missile. In other words, it would have to use an airplane to launch a nuclear attack on another country. By early 2009 that assessment had changed, as intelligence agencies in the United States and other countries, as well as the IAEA, concluded that North Korea had succeeded in miniaturizing its nuclear warheads. These warheads can be fitted on medium-range missiles, which means North Korea is capable of launching nuclear attacks against major cities in South Korea and Japan.[119] In May 2009, North Korea conducted a second nuclear test. Again, Western experts were unsure of its yield and exactly how successful it was. Nonetheless, the consensus was that the test had a larger yield than the 2006 test and demonstrated North Korea had made progress in designing nuclear warheads.[120]

The countries discussed in this chapter are very different from one another. The only features they share are that they are nuclear powers and have the capacity to make other types of WMD. That alone makes them major players on the international stage and countries well worth careful study by anyone interested in world affairs.

---

[1] The nine countries are the United States, Russia, Great Britain, France, the People's Republic of China, India, Pakistan, Israel, and North Korea.

[2] Jonathan B. Tucker. *War of Nerves: Chemical Warfare from World War I to Al-Qaeda.* New York: Pantheon Books, 2006, p. 20; Eric Croddy. *Chemical and Biological Warfare: A Comprehensive Survey for the Concerned Citizen.* New York: Copernicus Books, 2002, p. 32.

[3] Quoted in Nicholas Werth. "A State Against Its People: Violence, Repression, and Terror in the Soviet Union." In *The Black Book of Communism: Crimes, Terror, Repression,* edited by Stéphane Courtois, pp. 117–118. Cambridge, Mass.: Harvard University Press, 1999.

[4] Tucker. *War of Nerves,* pp. 106–107, 146; Croddy. *Chemical and Biological Warfare,* p. 33.

[5] Tucker. *War of Nerves,* pp. 180–189, 230–231; Federation of American Scientists. WMD Around the World. "Chemical Weapons." Available online. URL: http://www.fas.org/nuke/guide/russia/cbw/cw.htm. Accessed July 15, 2008.

[6] Tucker. *War of Nerves,* pp. 186–187.

[7] Tucker. *War of Nerves,* pp. 232–236.

[8] Tucker. *War of Nerves,* pp. 299–300, 315.

[9] Federation of American Scientists. WMD Around the World. "Chemical Weapons." Available online. URL: http://www.fas.org/nuke/guide/russia/cbw/cw.htm. Accessed July 15, 2008; Joseph Cirincione, Jon B. Wolfsthal, and Miriam Rajkumar. *Deadly Arsenals: Nuclear, Biological, and Chemical Threats,* Second Edition, revised and expanded. Washington, D.C.: Carnegie Endowment for International Peace, 2005, pp. 139–140; Peter Eisler. "Plan to Destroy Russian Weapons Nears Collapse." *USA Today* (10/01/02). Available online. URL: http://www.usatoday.com/news/world/2002-09-30-russian-weapons-1acover_x.htm. Accessed September 14, 2008.

[10] Tucker. *War of Nerves,* pp. 315–317, 332–334; Federation of American Scientists. WMD Around the World. "Chemical Weapons." Available online. URL: http:// www.fas.org/nuke/guide/russia/cbw/cw.htm. Accessed July 15, 2008.

[11] "Agreement Between the United States of America and the Union of Soviet Socialist Republics on Destruction and Non-Production of Chemical Weapons and on Measures to Facilitate the Multilateral Convention on Banning Chemical Weapons." Available online. URL: http://www.fas.org/nuke/control/bda/text/bda.html. Accessed September 14, 2008; Cirincione, Wolfsthal, Rajkumar. *Deadly Arsenals,* p. 140.

[12] Nuclear Threat Initiative. Russia Profile. "Chemical Overview." Available online. URL: http://www.nti.org/e_research/profiles/Russia/Chemical/index.html. Accessed September 14, 2008.

[13] Arms Control Association. "Chemical Weapons Deadlines Extended." (January/February 2008). Available online. URL: http://www.armscontrol.org/act/2007_01-02/CWDeadlines. Accessed September 14, 2008; Defense Threat Reduction Agency. Maj. Adam S. Talkington. "Chemical Weapons Production in Russia Is Closer to Being a 'Cold' Idea." *Combating WMD Journal* 2. Available online. URL: http://www.cbrniac.apgea.army.mil/Products/Documents/USANCA%20Journals%20and%20Reports/CWMD_Journal_No_2_Mar08.pdf. Accessed October 20, 2008; "Russia Opens Fourth Chemical Weapons Destruction Plant."

International Herald Tribune (6/17/08). Available online. URL: http://www.iht.com/articles/apl/2008/06/17/news/Russia-Chemical-Weapons.php. Accessed September 14, 2008; Deutsche Welle. "Germany to Help Russia Destroy Chemical Weapons Stockpile." (6/10/08). Available online. URL: http://www.dw-world.de/dw/article/0,2144,3401229,00.html. Accessed September 14, 2008; Nuclear Threat Initiative. Russia Profile. "Chemical Overview." Available online. URL: http://www.nti.org/e_research/profiles/Russia/Chemical/index.html. Accessed September 14, 2008; Clifford J. Levy. "In Siberia, the Death Knell of a Complex Holding a Deadly Stockpile." *New York Times* (5/27/09). The quotation from Igor V. Rybalchenko is from this article; Nuclear Threat Initiative. "Russia Faces Chemical Weapons Disposal Funding Challenges." (4/13/09). Available online. URL: http://www.globalsecuritynewswire.org/gsn/nw_20090413_2704.php. Accessed April 12, 2009.

[14] The information in the previous two paragraphs is taken from the following sources: Christopher J. Davis. "Nuclear Blindness: An Overview of the Biological Weapons Programs of the Former Soviet Union and Iraq." *Emerging Infectious Diseases* 4, no. 4 (July–August 1999), pp. 509–512. Available online. URL: http://www.cdc.gov/ncidod/EID/vol5no4/davis.htm. Accessed September 17, 2008; Jeanne Guillemin. *Biological Weapons: From the Invention of State-Sponsored Programs to Contemporary Bioterrorism.* New York: Columbia University Press, 2005, pp. 134–147; Judith Miller, Stephen Engelberg, and William Broad. *Germs: Biological Weapons and America's Secret War.* New York: Simon and Schuster, 2001, pp. 95–97, 136–137, 220–221, 284–286; Croddy. *Chemical and Biological Warfare,* pp. 34–35. The discussion in the next several pages relies heavily on these sources.

[15] The quote is from Guillemin. *Biological Weapons,* pp. 136–137. See also Miller, Engelberg, and Broad. *Germs,* p. 205; Davis. "Nuclear Blindness," p. 3; GlobalSecurity.org. "Obolensk NPO Biointez State Research Center for Applied Microbiology." Available online. URL: http:// www.globalsecurity.org/wmd/world/russia/obolensk.htm. Accessed September 20, 2008; Federation of American Scientists. "Biopreparat." Available online. URL: http://www.fas.org/nuke/guide/russia/agency/bw.htm. Accessed September 21, 2008; Arms Control Association. "Building a Forward Line of Defense: Securing Former Soviet Biological Weapons." Available online. URL: http://www.armscontrol.org/act/2004_07-08/Luongo. Accessed April 22, 2009. Because of Soviet/Russian secrecy, it is impossible to be sure of the exact number of people who worked on biological weapons. The most common estimate is a total of 60,000–65,000.

[16] David Brand. "CU's Vogel: Russian Biological Warfare Plans Still Pose Global Threat." *Cornell Chronicle* (2/22/01). Available online. URL: http://www.news.cornell.edu/chronicle/01/2.22.01/AAAS_Vogel.html. Accessed September 14, 2008. Kathleen Vogel, the subject of this article, holds a Ph.D. in chemistry; Arms Control Association. "Chemical and Biological Weapons Proliferation at a Glance." (September 2002). Available online. URL: http://www.armscontrol.org/factsheets/cbwprolif. Accessed September 14, 2008; Croddy. *Chemical and Biological Warfare,* p. 35; Davis. "Nuclear Blindness," p. 3; Miller, Engelberg, and Broad. *Germs,* p. 136.

[17] Miller, Engelberg, and Broad. *Germs,* pp. 76–79, 82–83, 93–94, 143–144; Davis. "Nuclear Blindness," pp. 3–4; National Security Archive. *Volume V: Anthrax at Sverdlovsk, 1979.* Available online. URL: http://www.gwu.edu/~nsarchive/NSAEBB/NSAEBB61/. Accessed September 20, 2008.

[18] Miller, Engelberg, and Broad. *Germs,* pp. 76–79, 93–94, 143–144; Davis. "Nuclear Blindness," pp. 3–4; National Security Archive. *Volume V: Anthrax at Sverdlovsk, 1979.* Available online. URL: http:// www.gwu.edu/~nsarchive/NSAEBB/NSAEBB61/. Accessed September 20, 2008.

[19] National Security Archive. *Volume V: Anthrax at Sverdlovsk, 1979.* Available online. URL: http:// www.gwu.edu/~nsarchive/NSAEBB/NSAEBB61/. Accessed September 20, 2008; Miller, Engelberg, and Broad. *Germs,* pp. 136–137; Guillemin. *Biological Weapons,* pp. 134–135, 145; Croddy. *Chemical and Biological Warfare,* pp. 34–35; Arms Control Association. "Chemical and Biological Weapons Proliferation at a Glance." Available online. URL: http://www.armscontrol.org/node/2473/print. Accessed September 14, 2008.

[20] Croddy. *Chemical and Biological Warfare,* p. 35; Cirincione, Wolfsthal, and Rajkumar. *Deadly Arsenals,* p. 142.

[21] The drying up of the Aral Sea, itself a massive environmental disaster, was caused by ill-conceived Soviet irrigation policies, under which most of the water in the two rivers feeding the sea was diverted to irrigate cotton fields. Today, Vozrozhdeniye Island is a peninsula, having become joined to the mainland in 2001. Judith Miller. "Poison Island: A Special Report; At Bleak Asian Site, Killer Germs Survive." *New York Times* (6/2/99). Available online. URL: http://query.nytimes.com.gts/fullpage.htm?res=9507E1D81030F931A35755C 0A96 F9582. Accessed September 20, 2008; CRS Report for Congress. Jim Nichol. "Central Asia: Regional Developments and Implications for U.S. Interests," pp. 23–34. Available online. URL: http://www.dtic.mil/cgi-bin/GetTRDoc?AD=ADA475033&Location<0x00 3D> U2&doc=GetTRDoc.pdf. Updated July 5, 2007.

[22] Arms Control Association. "Chemical and Biological Weapons Proliferation at a Glance." Available online. URL: http://www.armscontrol.org/node/2473/print. Accessed September 14, 2008; Guillemin. *Biological Weapons,* p. 146; Cirincione, Wolfsthal, and Rajkumar. *Deadly Arsenals,* p. 141; Toggzhan Kassenova. "Biological Threat Reduction in Central Asia." *Bulletin of Atomic Scientists* (6/18/08). Available online. URL: http://thebulletin.org/web-edition/features/biological-threat-reduction-central-asia. Accessed September 14, 2008; Nuclear Threat Initiative. Russia Profile. "Biological Overview." Available online. URL: http://www.nit.org/e_research/profiles/russia/biological/index.html. Accessed September 14, 2008.

[23] Nuclear Weapons Archive. "The Soviet Nuclear Weapons Program." Available online. URL: http://www.nuclearweaponsarchive.org/Russia/Sovwpnprog.html. Accessed July 14, 2008.

[24] Gerard J. DeGroot. *The Bomb: A Life.* Cambridge, Mass.: Harvard University Press, 2005, pp. 127–128.

[25] David Holloway. *The Soviet Union and the Arms Race.* New Haven and London: Yale University Press, 1984, pp. 21–23; David Holloway. *Stalin and the Bomb: The Soviet Union and Atomic Energy, 1939–1956.* New Haven and London: Yale University Press, 1994, pp. 172–173, 184–185, 193–194; DeGroot. *The Bomb,* 134–135.

[26] Nuclear Weapons Archive. "The Soviet Nuclear Weapons Program." Available online. URL: http://www.nuclearweaponsarchive.org/Russia/Sovwpnprog.html. Accessed July 14, 2008; Holloway. *Stalin and the Bomb,* pp. 196–197.

[27] Holloway. *The Soviet Union and the Arms Race,* pp. 22–23; Holloway. *Stalin and the Bomb,* pp. 181–187; DeGroote. *The Bomb,* p. 135; Nuclear Weapons Archive. "The Soviet Nuclear Weapons Program." Available online. URL: http://www.nuclearweaponsarchive.org/Russia/Sovwpnprog.html. Accessed July 14, 2008.

[28] Holloway. *Stalin and the Bomb,* pp. 294–295; DeGroote. *The Bomb,* pp. 166–168. The quotation is from Holloway.

[29] Holloway. *Stalin and the Bomb,* pp. 295–317; Nuclear Weapons Archive. "The Soviet Nuclear Weapons Program." Available online. URL: http://www.nuclearweaponsarchive.org/Russia/Sovwpnprog.html. Accessed July 14, 2008.

[30] Holloway. *Stalin and the Bomb,* pp. 314–315.

[31] John C. K. Daly. "Analysis: Kazakhs to Boost Uranium Output." SpaceDaily. Available online. URL: http://www.spacedaily.com/reports/Analysis_Kazakhs_to_boost_uranium_output_999.html. Accessed April 23, 2009; Robert Elegant. "Fallout: In Kazakhstan, the Human Wreckage of Soviet Nuclear Tests." *National Review* (9/02/02). Available online. URL: http://findarticles.com/p/articles/mi_m1282/is_16_54/ai_90570245/pg_2/?tag=content;col1. Accessed April 23, 2009; Mike Edwards. "A Broken Empire." *National Geographic* (March 1993), p. 23.

[32] Quoted in DeGroote. *The Bomb,* pp. 252–253; John Lewis Gaddis. *Now We Know: Rethinking Cold War History.* Oxford and New York: Clarendon Press, 1997, pp. 255–256; Nuclear Weapons Archive. "*Big Ivan,* The Tsar Bomba ('King of Bombs')." Available online. URL: http://nuclearweaponsarchive.org/Russia/TsarBomba.html. Accessed September 28, 2008.

[33] Nuclear Weapons Archive. "Soviet Nuclear Test Summary. Last updated, October 7, 1997. Available online. URL: http://nuclearweaponsarchive.org/Russia/Sovtestsum.html. Accessed September 30, 2008.

[34] Cirincione, Wolfsthal, and Rajkumar. *Deadly Arsenals,* p. 126; Graham. *Commonsense on Weapons of Mass Destruction,* pp. 42–43.

[35] Cirincione, Wolfsthal, and Rajkumar. *Deadly Arsenals,* p. 128; Joseph Cirincione. *Bomb Scare: The History and Future of Nuclear Weapons.* New York: Columbia University Press, 2008, p. 42.

[36] Robert S. Norris and Hans M. Kristensen. "Russian Nuclear Forces, 2008." *Bulletin of the Atomic Scientists* (May/June 2009), p. 55–56.

[37] See chapter 2.

[38] FoxNews.com. "Report: Russia Shuts Down Nuclear Reactor Producing Weapons-Grade Plutonium." Available online. URL: http://www.foxnews.com/story/0,2933,351880,00.html. Accessed April 20, 2008; National Nuclear Security Administration. "NNSA Announces the End of Plutonium Production in Seversk, Russia." (6/05/08). Available online. URL: http://nnsa.energy.gov/news/2041.htm. Accessed September 30, 2008; Tomsknews.com. "Sibirskii khimicheskii kombinat zaglushil atomnyi reaktor ADE-4." (Siberian chemical enterprise closed the atomic reactor ADE-4) (4/20/08). Available online. URL: http://tomsknews.com/news/?id=5189. Accessed September 30, 2008; Russian Strategic Nuclear Forces. "One Plutonium Production Reactor in Seversk to Be Shut Down." Available online. URL: http://russianforces.org/blog/2008/04/one_plutionium_production_react.shtml. Accessed September 30, 2008.

[39] Robert S. Norris and Hans M. Kristensen. "Russian Nuclear Forces, 2009." *Bulletin of the Atomic Scientists* (May/June 2009), p. 61; Russianforces.org. Russian Strategic Nuclear Forces. "Current Status." (June 2008). Available online. URL: http://russianforces.org/current. Accessed September 7, 2008.

[40] Norris and Kristensen. "Russian Nuclear Forces, 2008." *Bulletin of the Atomic Scientists* (May/June 2008), p. 56; "Russia Test-Fires Topol Missile, Georgia Desperately Cries for NATO Membership." *Pravda* (6/28/08). Available online. URL: http://english.pravda.ru/russia/politics/28-08-2008/106240-russia_topol_missile-0. Accessed September 30, 2008; Russian Strategic Nuclear Forces. "Strategic Fleet." Available online. URL: http://russianforces.org/navy/. Accessed April 17, 2009; ———. "Strategic Rocket Forces." Available online. URL: http://russianforces.org/missiles/. Accessed April 17, 2009.

[41] Norris and Kristensen. "Russian Nuclear Forces, 2008." *Bulletin of the Atomic Scientists* (May/June 2008), p. 57; MISSILETHREAT.com "System 135." Available online. URL: http://

www.missilethreat.com/missiledefensesystems/id7,page.1,css.print/system_detail/system_detail.asp. Accessed October 1, 2008; GlobalSecurity.org. "Russia develops defense program against high-precision strikes." Available online. URL: http://www.globalsecurity.org/wmd/library/news/russia/2008/russia-080429-rianovosti02.htm. Accessed July 4, 2008; RIA Novosti. "Russia to Deploy S-400 Air Defense Systems around Moscow Aug. 6." Available online. URL: http://en.rian.ru/russia/20080121/97447013.html. Accessed October 1, 2008; Russian Strategic Nuclear Forces. "Launch of Cosmos-2446, a New First-Generation Early-Warning Satellite." Available online. URL: http://russianforces.org/blog/2008/12/launch_of_cosmos-2446_a_new_fi.shtml. Accessed April 20, 2009; GlobalSecurity.org. "Russia Develops Defense Program against High-Precision Strikes." Available online. URL: http://www.globalsecurity.org/wmd/library/news/russia/2008/russia-080429-rianovosti02.htm. Accessed July 4, 2008.

[42] See chapter 2.

[43] Tucker. *War of Nerves,* pp. 227–228. This all became known to the United States when Israel captured Soviet weapons and equipment supplied to Egypt during the 1973 Yom Kippur War. Israel passed all this information on to the United States.

[44] Nuclear Threat Initiative. "Russia: Government and Selected Ministries." Available online. URL: http://www.nti.org/db/nisprofs/russia/govt/ministry.htm#mie. Accessed April 22, 2009; Federation of American Scientists. "Ministry for Extraordinary Situations [EMERCOM]." Available online. URL: http://fas.org/nuke/guide/russia/agency/emercom.htm. Accessed April 22, 2009; Bettina Renz. "Crisis Response in War and Peace: Russia's 'Emergencies' Ministry and Security Sector Reform." *World Defense Systems* 16. Available online. URL: http://www.sovereign-publications.com/wds-articles/Renz.pdf. Accessed July 23, 2009.

[45] James Martin Center for Nonproliferation Studies. "Reported Use of Chemical Weapons, Ballistic Missiles, and Cruise Missiles in the Middle East." Available online. URL: http://cns.miis.edu/wmdme/use.htm. Accessed May 8, 2009.

[46] James Martin Center for Nonproliferation Studies. "Reported Conventional Military Attacks on NBC Facilities in the Middle East." Available online. URL: http://cns.miis.edu/research/wmdme/prempt.htm. Accessed May 22, 2008.

[47] James Martin Center for Nonproliferation Studies. "Syria: Weapons of Mass Destruction Capabilities and Programs." Updated April 2006. Available online. URL: http://cns.miis.edu/research/wmdme/syria.htm. Accessed May 24, 2008; Carnegie Endowment for International Peace. "Summary of Syria's Chemical and Biological Weapons Programs." Available online. URL: http://www.carnegieendowmend.org/publications/index.cfm?fa=print&id<0x003D>13695. Accessed July 17, 2008.

[48] James Martin Center for Nonproliferation Studies. "Egypt: Weapons of Mass Destruction Capabilities and Programs." Available online. URL: http://cns.miis.edu/research/wmdme/egypt.htm. Accessed May 24, 2008; Carnegie Endowment for International Peace. "Summary of Syria's Chemical and Biological Weapons Programs." Available online. URL: www.carnegieendowmend.org/publications/index.cfm?fa=print&id<0x003 D>13695. Accessed July 17, 2008; "U.N. Watchdog: Weapons Grade Uranium Found in Egypt." FoxNews.com (5/06/09). Available online. URL: http://www.foxnews.com/story/0,2933,519120,00.html. Accessed May 13, 2009.

[49] James Martin Center for Nonproliferation Studies. "Iran: Weapons of Mass Destruction Capabilities and Programs." Available online. URL: http://cns.miis.edu/research/wmdme/iran.htm. Accessed May 24, 2008.

[50] Elaine Sciolino. "Atomic Monitor Signals Concern over Iran's Work." *New York Times* (5/27/08); ———. "Nuclear Agency Says Iran Has Improved Enrichment." *New York Times* (5/27/08); James Martin Center for Nonproliferation Studies. "Iran: Weapons of Mass Destruction Capabilities

and Programs." Available online. URL: http://cns.miis.edu/research/wmdme/iran.htm. Accessed May 24, 2008; GlobalSecurity.org. "Iran Expects Russia to Complete Bushehr Power Plant on Schedule" (10/18/08). Available online. URL: http://www.globalsecurity.org/wmd/library/news/iran/2008/iran-081018-irna01.htm. Accessed October 31, 2008; FoxNews.com. "Report: Iran Began Building Uranium Enrichment Facility Seven Years Ago." Available online. URL:www.foxnews.com/story/0,2933,574526,00.html. Accessed November 12, 2009.

51 U.S. Department of State. "Chapter 3—State Sponsors of Terrorism Overview." *Country Reports on Terrorism* (4/30/08). Available online. URL: http://www.state.gov/s/ct/rls/crt/2007/103711.htm. Accessed November 1, 2008; Michael Rubin. "Iran's Global Ambition." *Middle Eastern Outlook* (3/17/08). Available online. URL: http://www.aei.org/outlook/27658. Accessed November 1, 2008; Nimrod Raphaeli. "The Middle East Ventures into Nuclear Energy." MEMRI Inquiry and Analysis Series—No. 467. Available online. URL: www.memri.org/bin/latestnews.cgi?ID=IA46708. Accessed October 9, 2008.

52 William J. Broad and David Sanger. "Iran Said to Have Nuclear Fuel for One Weapon." *New York Times* (11/20/08). Available online. URL: www.nytimes.com/2008/11/20/world/middleeast/20nuck.html?_r=1&ref<0 x003D>todayspa. Accessed November 20, 2008.

53 Quoted in Abba Eban. *My Country: The Story of Modern Israel.* New York: Random House, 1972, p. 48.

54 Quoted in Martin Gilbert. *The Arab-Israeli Conflict: Its History in Maps.* London: Weidenfield and Nicolson, 1974, p. 68. Egypt's president at the time, Gamal Abdul Nasser, was the most influential leader in the Arab world.

55 "Wipe Israel 'Off the Map' Iranian Says." *International Herald Tribune* (10/27/05). Available online. URL: http://www.iht.com/articles/2005/10/26/news/iran/php. Accessed October 10, 2008; Joshua Teitelbaum. "Analysis: Iran's Talk of Destroying Israel Must Not Get Lost in Translation." *Jerusalem Post* Online Edition (6/22/08). Available online. URL: http://www.jpost.com/servlet/Satellite?cid=1213794295236&pagename<0x003D>JPost%2FJPArticle%2FPrinter. Accessed June 22, 2008; Y. Mansharof and A. Savyon. "Iran." MEMRIE-mail Newsletter (6/6/08). All the quotations are from statements by Iranian president Mahmoud Ahmadinejad except for the "cancerous tumor" remark, which was made by Iran's supreme leader Ayatollah Ali Khamenei.

56 Avner Cohen. "Israel and Chemical/Biological Weapons: History, Deterrence, and Arms Control." *The Nonproliferation Review* (Fall/Winter 2001), pp. 39–40; Cirincione, Wolfsthal, and Rajkumar. *Deadly Arsenals,* p. 261.

57 Cohen. "Israel and Chemical/Biological Weapons," pp. 27–30.

58 Cohen. "Israel and Chemical and Biological Weapons," pp. 31–33.

59 Cohen. "Israel and Chemical and Biological Weapons," pp. 33–34.

60 Cohen. "Israel and Chemical and Biological Weapons," p. 42; Nuclear Threat Initiative. Israel Profile. "Biological Overview." Available online. URL: http://www.nti.org/e_research/profiles/Israel/Biological/index.hmtl. Accessed October 12, 2008.

61 Cohen. "Israel and Chemical and Biological Weapons," pp. 40–41; Tucker. *War of Nerves,* pp. 191, 195.

62 Tucker. *War of Nerves,* pp. 195–196.

63 Tucker. *War of Nerves,* pp. 227–228.

64 Tucker. *War of Nerves,* p. 228.

65 Nuclear Threat Initiative. Israel Profile. "Chemical Overview." Available online. URL: http://www.nti.org/e_research/profiles/Israel/Chemicall/index.hmtl. Accessed July 17,

2008; Tucker. *War of Nerves,* pp. 308–309. The quote is from the Nuclear Threat Initiative Web site.

[66] Nuclear Threat Initiative. Israel Profile. "Biological Chronology." Available online. URL: http://www.nti.org/e_research/profiles/Israel/Biological/3652.hmtl. Accessed October 14, 2008; United States Department of Defense. "Anthrax Vaccination Program Questions and Answers." Updated June 18, 1998. Available online. URL: http://www.defenselink.mil/other_info/qanda.html. Accessed October 17, 2008.

[67] Cirincione, Wolfsthal, and Rajkumar. *Deadly Arsenals,* p. 261; James Martin Center for Nonproliferation Studies. "Weapons of Mass Destruction in the Middle East. Israel: Weapons of Mass Destruction Capabilities and Programs." Available online. URL: http://cns.miis.edu/research/wmdme/israel.htm. Accessed May 24, 2008.

[68] Yaakov Katz. "Gas Mask Handout Delayed to Late 2009." *Jerusalem Post* Online Edition. Available online. URL: http://www.jpost.com/servlet/Satellite?cid=1222017545320$pagename=J Post%2FJPArti. Accessed October 16, 2008; Yakov Katz. "Gas Mask Redistribution to Take 2 Years." *Jerusalem Post* Online Edition. Available online. URL: http://www.jpost.com/servlet/Satellite?cid=1239710711570&pagename<0x003D>JPost%2FJPArticle%2FShowFull. Accessed May 13, 2009.

[69] Quoted in Avner Cohen. *Israel and the Bomb.* New York: Columbia University Press, 1998, p. 119.

[70] Nuclear Threat Initiative. Israel Profile. "Israel Nuclear Facilities." Available online. URL: http://www.nti.org/e_research/profiles/Israel/Nuclear/3583/html. Accessed October 19, 2008.

[71] Michael Karpin. *The Bomb in the Basement: How Israel Went Nuclear and What That Means for the World.* New York: Simon and Schuster, 2007, pp. 80, 91; Nuclear Threat Initiative. Israel Profile. "Nuclear Overview." Available online. URL: http://www.nti.org/e_research/profiles/Israel/Nuclear/index.html. Accessed October 19, 2008.

[72] Warner D. Farr. "The Third Temple's Holy of Holies: Israel's Nuclear Weapons," p. 8. Available online. URL: http://www.fas.org/nuke/guide/israel/nuke/farr.htm. Accessed June 10, 2008; Karpin. *The Bomb in the Basement,* pp. 92, 168–175; Cirincione, Wolfsthal, and Rajkumar. *Deadly Arsenals,* p. 264.

[73] Karpin. *The Bomb in the Basement,* pp. 108–110.

[74] Nuclear Threat Initiative. Israel Profile. "Nuclear Overview." Available online. URL: http://www.nti.org/e_research/profiles/Israel/Nuclear/index.html. Accessed October 19, 2008; Federation of American Scientists. WMD Around the World. "Nuclear Weapons." Available online. URL: http://www.fas.org/nuke/guide/israel/nuke. Accessed July 9, 2008.

[75] Nuclear Threat Initiative. Israel Profile. "Nuclear Overview." Available online. URL: http://www.nti.org/e_research/profiles/Israel/Nuclear/index.html. Accessed October 19, 2008; Farr. "The Third Temple's Holy of Holies: Israel's Nuclear Weapons," p. 7.

[76] Hyperphysics. Hosted by the Department of Physics and Astronomy, Georgia State University. Available online. URL: http://hyperphysics.phy-astr.gsu.edu/Hbase/NucEne/ligwat.html. Accessed October 22, 2008; Karpin. *The Bomb in the Basement,* pp. 143–145.

[77] Karpin. *The Bomb in the Basement,* p. 140; Farr. "The Third Temple's Holy of Holies: Israel's Nuclear Weapons," p. 8.

[78] Farr. "The Third Temple's Holy of Holies," p. 12; Karpin. *The Bomb in the Basement,* pp. 268–269; GlobalSecurity.Org. "Dimona Nuclear Research Reactor." Available online. URL: http://www.globalsecurity.org/wmd/world/israel/dimona.htm. Accessed October 26, 2008.

[79] Karpin. *The Bomb in the Basement,* pp. 279–284; Cirincione, Wolfsthal, and Rajkumar. *Deadly Arsenals,* p. 264.

[80] Nuclear Threat Initiative. Israel Profile. "Nuclear Overview." Available online. URL: http://www.nti.org/e_research/profiles/Israel/Nuclear/index.html. Accessed October 19, 2008; Karpin. *The Bomb in the Basement,* pp. 323–330. The quote from General Tal is on page 326.

[81] Cirincione, Wolfsthal, and Rajkumar. *Deadly Arsenals,* p. 265; Karpin. *The Bomb in the Basement,* p. 343.

[82] Federation of American Scientists. WMD Around the World. "Nuclear Weapons." Available online. URL: http://www.fas.org/nuke/guide/israel/nuke. Accessed July 9, 2008; Cirincione, Wolfsthal, and Rajkumar. *Deadly Arsenals,* p. 262.

[83] James Martin Center for Nonproliferation Studies. "Weapons of Mass Destruction in the Middle East. Israel: Weapons of Mass Destruction Capabilities and Programs." Updated April 2006. Available online. URL: http://cns.miis.edu/research/wmdme/israel.htm. Accessed May 24, 2008; Cirincione, Wolfsthal, and Rajkumar. *Deadly Arsenals,* pp. 262–263; Nuclear Threat Initiative. Israel Profile. "Missile Overview." Available online. URL: http://www.nit.org/e_research/profiles.Israel/Missile/index.html. Accessed October 19, 2008.

[84] Cirincione, Wolfsthal, and Rajkumar. *Deadly Arsenals,* p. 263.

[85] Nuclear Threat Initiative. Israel Profile. "Missile Overview." Available online. URL: http://www.nit.org/e_research/profiles/Israel/Missile/index.html. Accessed October 19, 2008.

[86] DEBKAfile. "American Crews Will Control US FBX-Band Radar Granted Israel" (8/19/08). Available online. URL: http: www.debka.com/headline.php?hid=5518. Accessed August 21, 2008; Jewish Telegraphic Agency. "Israel, U.S. Reportedly Close Radar Deal" (8/19/08). Available online. URL: http://www.jta.org/cgi-bin/iowa/breaking/109991.html. Accessed August 19, 2008; *Jerusalem Post* Online Edition. "US Defense Department Pledges Support for Arrow 3" (8/08/08). Available online. URL: http://www.jpost.com/servlet/Satellite?cid=1215331213785&pageneme-JPost%2FJPArticl. Accessed August 6, 2008.

[87] Leonard S. Spector and Avner Cohen. "Israel's Airstrike on Syria's Reactor: Implications for the Nonproliferation Regime." Arms Control Association. Available online. URL: http://www.armscontrol.org/act/2008_07-08/SpectorCohen. Accessed October 29, 2008.

[88] Nuclear Threat Initiative. India Profile. "Chemical Overview." Available online. URL: http://www.nti.org/e_research/profiles/India/Chemicals/index.html. Accessed October 17, 2008; Nuclear Threat Initiative. India Profile. "Biological Overview. Available online. URL: http://www.nti.org/e_research/profiles/India/Biological/index.html. Accessed October 17, 2008.

[89] Nuclear Threat Initiative. India Profile. "Chemical Overview." Available online. URL: http://www.nti.org/e_research/profiles/India/Chemicals/index.html. Accessed October 17, 2008; Ritu Sharma. "India Destroys Its Chemical Weapons Stockpile." Thaindian News (5/14/09). Available online. URL: http://www.thaindian.com/newsportal/uncategorized/india-destroys-its-chemical-weapons-sto ckpile_100192355.html. Accessed May 14, 2009.

[90] Nuclear Threat Initiative. India Profile. "Biological Overview. Available online. URL: http://www.nti.org/e_research/profiles/India/Biological/index.html. Accessed October 17, 2008.

[91] Nuclear Weapon Archive. "India's Nuclear Weapons Program. The Beginning: 1944–1960." Available online. URL: http://nucleararchive.org/India/IndianOrigin.html.Accessed October 17, 2008; Cirincione, Wolfsthal, and Rajkumar. *Deadly Arsenals,* p. 225.

92 Nuclear Weapons Archive. "India's Nuclear Weapons Program. On to Weapons Development: 1960–1967." Available online. URL: http://nucleararchive.org/India/IndianWDevelop.html. Accessed November 27, 2008; Nuclear Weapons Archive. "India's Nuclear Weapons Program. Smiling Buddha: 1974." Available online. URL: http://nucleararchive.org/India/IndianSmiling.html. Accessed November 27, 2008.

93 Nuclear Weapons Archive. "India's Nuclear Weapons Program. The Long Pause: 1974–1989." Available online. URL: http://nucleararchive.org/India/IndiaPause.html. Accessed November 27, 2008.

94 Nuclear Weapons Archive. "India's Nuclear Weapons Program. The Momentum Builds: 1989–1998." Available online. URL: http://nucleararchive.org/India/IndiaMomentum.html. Accessed November 27, 2008.

95 Cirincione, Wolfsthal, and Rajkumar. *Deadly Arsenals,* p. 225; Federation of American Scientists. WMD Around the World. "Nuclear Weapons." Available online. URL: http://www.fas/org/nuke/guide/india/nuke/. Accessed October 17, 2008.

96 Cirincione, Wolfsthal, and Rajkumar. *Deadly Arsenals,* pp. 226–227; Nuclear Weapons Archive. "India's Nuclear Weapons Program. India as a Nuclear Power: 1998–2001." Available online. URL: http://nucleararchive.org/India/IndiaNPower.html. Accessed November 27, 2008.

97 Robert S. Norris and Hans M. Kristensen. "India's Nuclear Forces, 2007." *Bulletin of the Atomic Scientists* (July/August 2007), pp. 74–77; Nuclear Threat Initiative. India Profile. "Nuclear Overview." Available online. URL: http://www.nit.org/e_research/profiles/India/Nuclear/index.html. Accessed October 17, 2008; Cirincione, Wolfsthal, and Rajkumar. *Deadly Arsenals,* pp. 221, 229; Nuclear Weapons Archive. "India's Nuclear Weapons Program: Present Capabilities." Available online. URL: http://nucleararchive.org/India/India Arsenal.html. Accessed November 27, 2008.

98 Cirincione, Wolfsthal, and Rajkumar. *Deadly Arsenals,* p. 240; Nuclear Threat Initiative. Pakistan Profile. "Chemical Overview." Available online. URL: www.nti.org/e_research/profiles/Pakistan/Chemical/index.hmtl. Accessed October 17, 2008.

99 Nuclear Threat Initiative. Pakistan Profile. "Biological Overview." Available online. URL: http://www.nti.org/e_research/profiles/Pakistan/Biological/index.html. Accessed October 17, 2008.

100 Economist.com. "The Spider's Stratagem" (1/03/08). Available online. URL: http://www.economist.com/books/displaystory.cfm?story_id=10424283. Accessed November 29, 2008.

101 Thadeusz Strulak. "The Nuclear Suppliers Group." *The Nonproliferation Review* (Fall 1993), pp. 2–3. The NSG had 15 members by 1978 and has since grown to 45 members; Gordon Corega. *Shopping for Bombs: Nuclear Proliferation, Global Insecurity, and the Rise and Fall of the A. Q. Khan Network.* New York: Oxford University Press, 2008, pp. 11–14.

102 Cirincione, Wolfsthal, and Rajkumar. *Deadly Arsenals,* pp. 243–244.

103 Cirincione, Wolfsthal, and Rajkumar. *Deadly Arsenals,* pp. 247–249; Nuclear Threat Initiative. North Korea Profile. "Nuclear Overview." Available online. URL: http://www.nit.org/e_research/profiles/NK/Nuclear/index.html. Accessed December 2, 2008.

104 Federation of American Scientists. "Pakistan Nuclear Weapons." Available online. URL: http://www.fas.org/nuke/guide/pakistan/nuke/. Accessed October 17, 2008.

105 Cirincione, Wolfsthal, and Rajkumar. *Deadly Arsenals,* pp. 244–245; Federation of American Scientists. WMD Around the World. "Pakistan Nuclear Weapons." Available online. URL: http://www.fas.org/nuke/guide/pakistan/nuke/. Accessed October 17, 2008.

[106] Robert S. Norris and Hans M. Kristensen. "Pakistan's Nuclear Forces, 2007." *Bulletin of the Atomic Scientists* (May/June 2007), pp. 71–74; Cirincione, Wolfsthal, and Rajkumar. *Deadly Arsenals,* pp. 239, 250–251; Federation of American Scientists. "Pakistan Nuclear Weapons." Available online. URL: http://www.fas.org/nuke/guide/pakistan/nuke/. Accessed October 17, 2008.

[107] Robert Windrem. "Pakistan Expanding Its Nuclear Capability." MSNBC.com (5/12/09). Available online. URL: http://www.msnbc.msn.com/id/30648446/. Accessed May 12, 2009; David Albright and Paul Brannan. "Pakistan Appears to Be Building a Third Plutonium Production Reactor at Kushab Nuclear Site" (6/21/07). Available online. URL: www.isis-online.org/publications/southasia/Thirdkushabreactor.pdf. Accessed May 12, 2009. The Albright quote is from the Windrem article.

[108] Windrem. "Pakistan Expanding Its Nuclear Capability"; Rowan Scarborough. "U.S. Has Plan to Secure Pakistan Nukes if Country Falls to Taliban." FOXnews.com (5/14/09). Available online. URL: http://www.foxnews.com/politics/2009/05/14/plan-pakistan-teeters-falling-taliban/. Accessed May 14, 2009.

[109] "India's Spy Satellite Goes into Orbit." Indiaedunews.com (4/20/09). Available online. URL: http://indiaedunews.net/Science/India's_spy_satellite_goes_into_orbit_7959/. Accessed May 15, 2009; DEBKA.com. "Israeli Elite Unit Officers In Big Indian Anti-Terror Exercise" (5/6/09). Available online. URL: http://www.debka.com/headline.php?hid=6059. Accessed May 6, 2009.

[110] GlobalSecurity.org. "Chemical Weapons—India Nuclear Forces." Available online. URL: http://www.globalsecurity.org/wmd/world/india/cw.htm. Accessed May 14, 2009. GlobalSecurity.org. "Biological Warfare—India." Available online. URL: http://www.globalsecurity.org/wmd/world/bw.htm. Accessed May 15, 2009.

[111] Animesh Roul. "India Missile Defense Dreams." International Relations and Security Network (3/27/08). Available online. URL: http://www.isn.ethz.ch/isn/Current-Affairs/Security-Watch/Detail/?ots591=4888CA A0-B3DB-1461-98B9-E20E7B9C13D4&lng=en&id=52022. Accessed May 15, 2009; "India on Way to Joining Exclusive BMD Club." *The Times of India* (11/26/07). Available online. URL: http://www.articlearchives.com/international-relations/weapons-arms-military-weapons/1697 127-1.html. Accessed May 14, 2009.

[112] Nuclear Threat Initiative. North Korea Profile. "Chemical Overview." Available online. URL: http://www.nti.org/e_research/profiles/NK/Chemical/index.html. Accessed December 2, 2008.

[113] Nuclear Threat Initiative. North Korea Profile. "Chemical Overview."

[114] Nuclear Threat Initiative. North Korea Profile. "Biological Overview." Available online. URL: http://www.nti.org/e_research/profiles/NK/Biological/index.html. Accessed December 2, 2008.

[115] Cirincione, Wolfsthal, and Rajkumar. *Deadly Arsenals,* p. 280; William J. Broad. "The Hidden Travels of the Bomb." *New York Times* (12/09/08), pp. D1–4.

[116] Nuclear Threat Initiative. North Korea Profile. "Nuclear Facilities: IRT-2000 Nuclear Research Reactor." Available online. URL: http://www.nti.org/e_research/profiles/NK/45_552.html. Accessed December 10, 2008; Nuclear Threat Initiative. North Korea Profile. "Nuclear Facilities: 5MW(e) Experimental Reactor." Available online. URL: http://www.nti.org/e_research/profiles/NK/45_551.html. Accessed December 10, 2008; Cirincione, Wolfsthal, and Rajkumar. *Deadly Arsenals,* pp. 284–286.

[117] Nuclear Weapons Archive. "North Korea's Nuclear Weapons Program." Available online. URL: http://nuclearweaponsarchive.org/DPRK/index.html. Accessed November 27,

2008; Nuclear Threat Initiative. North Korea Profile. "Nuclear Overview." Available online. URL: http://www.nti.org/e_research/profiles/NK/Nuclear/index.html. Accessed December 2, 2008.

118 David C. Wright. "An Analysis of the North Korean Missile Program." (November 2000). Available online. URL: http://www.fas.org/irp/threat/missile/rumsfeld/pt2_wright.htm. Accessed December 10, 2008; Cirincione, Wolfsthal, and Rajkumar. *Deadly Arsenals,* p. 290.

119 Center for Defense Information. "Fact Sheet: North Korea's Nuclear Weapons Program." Updated January 23, 2003. Available online. URL: http://www.cde.org/nuclear/nk-fact-sheet-pr.cfm. Accessed June 16, 2008; Cirincione, Wolfsthal, and Rajkumar. *Deadly Arsenals,* pp. 289–290; Nuclear Threat Initiative. North Korea Profile. "Nuclear Overview." Available online. URL: http://www.nti.org/e_research/profiles/NK/Nuclear/index.html. Accessed December 2, 2008; Nuclear Threat Initiative. North Korea Profile. "Missile Overview." Available online. URL: http://www.nti.org/e_research/profiles/NK/Missile/index.html. Accessed December 2, 2008; Institute for Science and International Security. "North Korea." Available online. URL: http://www.isis-online.org/mapproject/country_pages/northkorea.html. Accessed December 12, 2008; BBC News. "Q&A: N. Korea Nuclear Stand-Off" (11/11/08). Available online. URL: http://news.bbc.co.uk/2/hi/asia-pacific2340405.stm. Accessed December 12, 2008; "North Korea is Fully Fledged Nuclear Power, Experts Agree." *Times* online (4/24/09). Available online. URL: http://www.timesonline.co.uk/tol/news/world/asia/article6155956.ece. Accessed April 24, 2009.

120 Choe Sang-hun. "North Korea Claims to Conduct 2nd Nuclear Test." *New York Times* (5/25/09). Available online. URL: http://www.nytimes.com/2009/05/25/world/asia/25nuke.html. Accessed May 25, 2009.

PART II

Primary Sources

4

United States Documents

The documents in this section are of three basic types. Two documents deal with the American use of biological or chemical weapons: the Lieber Code of 1863, which dates from an era before modern WMD existed, and President Nixon's 1969 announcement on chemical and biological weapons. Eight documents, beginning with Albert Einstein's 1939 letter and ending with President Truman's 1950 announcement, deal with the American development of nuclear weapons and cover the earliest discussions about building an atomic bomb to the decision to develop a thermonuclear bomb. The remaining documents, which cover the period from 2002 to the present, focus primarily on how the United States has dealt with the problem of WMD in the hands of other countries or terrorist organizations and the American program to destroy its chemical weapons. The shorter documents are produced in their entirety; longer documents, as noted, are excerpted.

The Lieber Code of 1863 / General Orders No. 100 (April 24, 1863) (excerpt)

The Lieber Code was an attempt by the government of the United States to codify the laws of war and, in fact, was the first such attempt. The original version of the code was drawn up by Francis Lieber, a professor at Columbia University. Lieber's version was then revised by a board of military officers and formally issued by President Lincoln as General Orders No. 100. Lieber's main concern was to distinguish between combatants and civilians and to ensure that civilian life and property be spared whenever possible. He also was concerned that prisoners of war be treated humanely. General Orders No. 100 contains 157 articles, divided into 10 sections. The ban on using poison "in any manner" is article #70; it appears in section three, which deals with "Deserters, Prisoners of war, Hostages, and Booty on the battle-field." This except from General Orders No. 100 includes a dozen articles from section three.

WAR DEPT., *ADJT. GENERAL'S OFFICE, Washington,* April 24, 1863

The following "Instructions for the Government of Armies of the United States in the Field," prepared by Francis Lieber, LL.D., and revised by a board of officers, of which Maj. Gen. E. A. Hitchcock is president, having been approved by the President of the United States, he commands that they be published for the information of all concerned.

By order of the Secretary of War:

E. D. TOWNSEND,

Assistant Adjutant-General.

INSTRUCTIONS FOR THE GOVERNMENT OF ARMIES OF THE UNITED STATES IN THE FIELD.

. . .

60. It is against the usage of modern war to resolve, in hatred and revenge, to give no quarter. No body of troops has the right to declare that it will not give, and therefore will not expect, quarter; but a commander is permitted to direct his troops to give no quarter, in great straits, when his own salvation makes it impossible to cumber himself with prisoners.

61. Troops that give no quarter have no right to kill enemies already disabled on the ground, or prisoners captured by other troops.

62. All troops of the enemy known or discovered to give no quarter in general, or to any portion of the Army, receive none.

63. Troops who fight in the uniform of their enemies, without any plain, striking, and uniform mark of distinction of their own, can expect no quarter.

64. If American troops capture a train containing uniforms of the enemy, and the commander considers it advisable to distribute them for use among his men, some striking mark or sign must be adopted to distinguish the American soldier from the enemy.

65. The use of the enemy's national standard, flag, or other emblem of nationality, for the purpose of deceiving the enemy in battle, is an act of perfidy by which they lose all claim to the protection of the laws of war.

66. Quarter having been given to an enemy by American troops, under a misapprehension of his true character, he may, nevertheless, be ordered to suffer death if, within three days after the battle, it be discovered that he belongs to a corps which gives no quarter.

67. The law of nations allows every sovereign government to make war upon another sovereign State, and, therefore, admits of no rules or laws different from those of regular warfare, regarding the treatment of prisoners of war, although they may belong to the army of a government which the captor may consider as a wanton and unjust assailant.

68. Modern wars are not internecine wars, in which the killing of the enemy is the object. The destruction of the enemy in modern war, and, indeed, modern war itself, are means to obtain that object of the belligerent which lies beyond the war.

Unnecessary or revengeful destruction of life is not lawful.

69. Outposts, sentinels, or pickets are not to be fired upon, except to drive them in, or when a positive order, special or general, has been issued to that effect.

70. The use of poison in any manner, be it to poison wells, or food, or arms, is wholly excluded from modern warfare. He that uses it puts himself out of the pale of the law and usages of war.

71. Whoever intentionally inflicts additional wounds on an enemy already wholly disabled, or kills such an enemy, or who orders or encourages soldiers to do so, shall suffer death, if duly convicted, whether he belongs to the Army of the United States, or is an enemy captured after having committed his misdeed.

. . .

Source: WarHistorian.org. Available online. URL: http://www.warhistorian.org/lieber.php#sec1.

Albert Einstein's Letter to President Franklin D. Roosevelt (August 2, 1939)

In experiments with uranium conducted in fall 1938, the German chemists Otto Hahn and Fritz Strassmann became the first scientists to achieve nuclear fission. News of their accomplishment swept the world of physics like a firestorm, in part because physicists understood, at least theoretically, that it was now possible to build an atomic bomb, a weapon exponentially more powerful than anything then in existence. Since Hahn and Strassman lived and worked in Nazi Germany, there was justifiable fear in scientific circles of what would happen if the Nazis succeeded in building an atomic bomb. No country in the world would be safe from Nazi aggression. It was against this background that Albert Einstein decided he had to make America's leaders aware of these potential dangers. Einstein was the world's most famous physicist; he also was one of hundreds of thousands of Jews who had been forced to flee Nazi Germany during the 1930s because of violent anti-Semitism and discrimination. At the urging and with the help of Leo Szilard, another prominent physicist who, like Einstein, had fled Germany and come to the United States, Einstein wrote a letter to President Roosevelt in August 1939. He warned that advances in physics had made an atomic bomb possible and that Nazi Germany was likely to build such a bomb. By the time Roosevelt saw the letter in mid-October, Germany had attacked Poland and plunged Europe into World War II. Roosevelt was convinced that Nazi Germany was not only a threat to Europe but also a direct threat to America's security. He responded to Einstein's letter by setting up a committee to investigate whether it was possible to build an atomic bomb. Although at first the investigative process moved very slowly, Roosevelt had set in motion events that eventually led to the Manhattan Project and the building of the atomic bomb.

Albert Einstein
Old Grove Rd.
Nassau Point
Peconic, Long Island

August 2nd, 1939
F. D. Roosevelt,
President of the United States,
White House
Washington, D.C.

Sir:

Some recent work by E. Fermi and L. Szilard, which has been communicated to me in manuscript, leads me to expect that the element uranium may be turned into a new and important source of energy in the immediate future. Certain aspects of the situation which has arisen seem to call for watchfulness and, if necessary, quick action on the part of the Administration. I believe therefore that it is my duty to bring to your attention the following facts and recommendations:

In the course of the last four months it has been made probable—through the work of Joliot in France as well as Fermi and Szilard in America—that it may become possible to set up a nuclear chain reaction in a large mass of uranium by which vast amounts of power and large quantities of new radium-like elements would be generated. Now it appears almost certain, that this could be achieved in the immediate future.

This new phenomenon would also lead to the construction of bombs, and it is conceivable—though much less certain—that extremely powerful bombs of a new type may thus be constructed. A single bomb of this type, carried by boat and exploded in a port, might very well destroy the whole port together with some of the surrounding territory. However, such bombs might very well prove to be too heavy for transportation by air.

The United States has only very poor ores of uranium in moderate quantities. There is some good ore in Canada and the former Czechoslovakia, while the most important source of uranium is Belgian Congo.

In view of this situation you may think it desirable to have some permanent contact maintained between the Administration and the group of physicists working on chain reactions in America. One possible way of achieving this might be for you to entrust with this task a person who has your confidence and who could perhaps serve in an inofficial capacity. His task might comprise the following:

a) to approach Government Departments, keep them informed of the further development, and put forward recommendations for Government action, giving particular attention to the problem of securing a supply of uranium ore for the United States;

b) to speed up the experimental work, which is at present being carried on within the limits of the budgets of University laboratories, by providing funds, if such funds be required, through his contacts with private persons who are willing to make contributions for this cause, and perhaps also by obtaining the co-operation of industrial laboratories which have the necessary equipment.

I understand that Germany has actually stopped the sale of uranium from the Czechoslovakian mines which she has taken over. That she should have taken such early action might perhaps be understood on the ground that the son of the German Under-Secretary of State, von Weizäcker, is attached to the Kaiser-Wilhelm-Institut in Berlin, where some of the American work on uranium is now being repeated.

Yours very truly,

(Albert Einstein)

Source: Michael Stoff, Jonathan F. Fanton, and R. Hall Williams. *The Manhattan Project: A Documentary History to the Atomic Age*. New York: McGraw Hill, 1991, pp. 18–19.

Recommendations of the Interim Committee's Scientific Panel Regarding Whether to Use the Atomic Bomb against Japan (June 16, 1945)

Within days of his inauguration after the death of President Roosevelt, President Harry S. Truman ordered the formation of a committee, called the Interim Committee, to advise him on wartime and postwar nuclear policy. That committee of eight included several of the president's most trusted advisers, including his secretaries of state and war. The Interim Committee in turn established a Scientific Panel to advise it on atomic policy. That panel included Robert Oppenheimer, the head of the Los Alamos Laboratory; Enrico Fermi, a refugee from fascist Italy who had headed the team that built the first U.S. nuclear reactor and in December 1942 achieved the world's first controlled nuclear chain reaction; and E. O. Lawrence and Arthur H. Compton, both Nobel Prize–winning physicists who had been deeply involved in the development of the atomic bomb. In June 1945 the Scientific Panel was asked to comment on a petition by a group of Manhattan Project physicists—called the Franck Report—urging that Japanese leaders be allowed to see a demonstration of the atomic bomb before it was used in combat against their country. The Scientific Panel rejected the idea that a demonstration would have the desired effect on the Japanese leaders, arguing instead that its members could see "no acceptable alternative to military use." The panel's members added that despite their expertise in scientific matters related to nuclear energy and the atomic bomb, they as scientists did not believe they had "special competence" in solving military, political, or social problems.

RECOMMENDATIONS ON THE IMMEDIATE USE OF NUCLEAR WEAPONS

A. H. Compton
E. O. Lawrence
J. R. Oppenheimer
E. Fermi
J. R. Oppenheimer
For the Panel

June 16, 1945

You have asked us to comment on the initial use of the new weapon. This use, in our opinion, should be such as to promote a satisfactory adjustment of our international relations. At the same time, we recognize our obligation to our nation to use the weapons to help save American lives in the Japanese war.

(1) To accomplish these ends we recommend that before the weapons are used not only Britain, but also Russia, France, and China be advised that we have made considerable progress in our work on atomic weapons, that these may be ready to use during the present war, and that we would welcome suggestions as to how we can cooperate in making this development contribute to improved international relations.

(2) The opinions of our scientific colleagues on the initial use of these weapons are not unanimous: they range from the proposal of a purely technical demonstration to that of the military application best designed to induce surrender. Those who advocate a purely technical demonstration would wish to outlaw the use of atomic weapons, and have feared that if we use the weapons now our position in future negotiations will be prejudiced. Others emphasize the opportunity of saving American lives by immediate military use, and believe that such use will improve the international prospects, in that they are more concerned with the prevention of war than with the elimination of this specific weapon. We find ourselves closer to these latter views; we can propose no technical demonstration likely to bring an end to the war; we see no acceptable alternative to direct military use.

With regard to these general aspects of the use of atomic energy, it is clear that we, as scientific men, have no proprietary rights. It is true that we are among the few citizens who have had occasion to give thoughtful consideration to these problems during the past few years. We have, however, no claim to special competence in solving the political, social, and military problems which are presented by the advent of atomic power.

Source: Michael Stoff, Jonathan F. Fanton, and R. Hall Williams. *The Manhattan Project: A Documentary History to the Atomic Age.* New York: McGraw Hill, 1991, pp. 149–150.

The First Atomic Explosion: Eyewitness Account by General Leslie Groves (July 18, 1945) (excerpt)

The first test of an atomic bomb, called Trinity, took place in a desert region of New Mexico on July 16, 1945. The bomb exploded with a force of 20,000 tons of TNT, shocking everyone who witnessed the test with its terrifying destructive power. Those witnesses included General Leslie Groves, the army general who was the head of the Manhattan Project. Groves forwarded his account of the Trinity test to Secretary of War Henry L. Stimson. Stimson at the time was in Germany with President Truman attending the Potsdam Conference, the last wartime conference of World War II between the leaders of the United States, Great Britain, and the Soviet Union. Those three powers had cooperated in bringing about Germany's defeat in May 1945, and their leaders were in Potsdam to plan the final defeat of Japan and establish a basis for a peaceful world once Japan surrendered and World War II finally came to an end. Having already been informed in short reports that the Trinity test had been successful, Truman received Groves's detailed report on July 21. It reinforced his hope, although nothing was certain, that the United States had a weapon that could force Japan to surrender and avoid an American invasion of Japan's home islands, which would have produced enormous casualties. On July 26, in what is known as the Potsdam Declaration, the United States, Britain, and China (the Soviet Union was not yet at war with Japan) warned Japan to surrender or face devastating consequences. When Japan ignored the warning, the stage was set for the use of atomic bombs.

Commanding General, Manhattan District Project (Groves) to the Secretary of War (Stimson)

TOP SECRET — WASHINGTON, 18 July 1945

MEMORANDUM FOR THE SECRETARY OF WAR

Subject: The Test.

1. This is not a concise, formal military report but an attempt to recite what I would have told you if you had been here on my return from New Mexico.

2. At 0530, 16 July 1945, in a remote section of the Alamogordo Air Base, New Mexico, the first full scale test was made of the implosion type atomic fission bomb. For the first time in history there was a nuclear explosion. And what an explosion! . . . The bomb was not dropped from an airplane but was exploded on a platform on top of a 100-foot high steel tower.

3. The test was successful beyond the most optimistic expectations of anyone. Based on the data which it has been possible to work up to date, I estimate the energy generated to be in excess of the equivalent of 15,000 to 20,000 tons of TNT; and this is a conservative estimate. Data based on measurements which we have not yet been able to reconcile would make the energy release several times the conservative figure. There were tremendous blast effects. For a brief period there was a lighting effect within a radius of 20 miles equal to several suns in midday; a huge ball of fire was formed which lasted for several seconds. This ball mushroomed and rose

to a height of over ten thousand feet before it dimmed. The light from the explosion was seen clearly at Albuquerque, Santa Fe, Silver City, El Paso and other points generally to about 180 miles away. The sound was heard to the same distance in a few instances but generally to about 100 miles. Only a few windows were broken although one was some 125 miles away. A massive cloud was formed which surged and billowed upward with tremendous power, reaching the substratosphere at an elevation of 41,000 feet, 36,000 feet above the ground, in about five minutes, breaking without interruption through a temperature inversion at 17,000 feet which most of the scientists thought would stop it. Two supplementary explosions occurred in the cloud shortly after the main explosion. The cloud contained several thousand tons of dust picked up from the ground and a considerable amount of iron in the gaseous form. Our present thought is that this iron ignited when it mixed with the oxygen in the air to cause these supplementary explosions. Huge concentrations of highly radioactive materials resulted from the fission and were contained in this cloud.

4. A crater from which all vegetation had vanished, with a diameter of 1200 feet and a slight slope toward the center, was formed. In the center was a shallow bowl 130 feet in diameter and 6 feet in depth. The material within the crater was deeply pulverized dirt. The material within the outer circle is greenish and can be distinctly seen from as much as 5 miles away. The steel from the tower was evaporated. 1500 feet away there was a four-inch iron pipe 16 feet high set in concrete and strongly guyed. It disappeared completely.

5. One-half mile from the explosion there was a massive steel test cylinder weighing 220 tons. The base of the cylinder was solidly encased in concrete. Surrounding the cylinder was a strong steel tower 70 feet high, firmly anchored to concrete foundations. This tower is comparable to a steel building bay that would be found in typical 15 or 20 story skyscraper or in warehouse construction. Forty tons of steel were used to fabricate the tower which was 70 feet high, the height of a six story building. The cross bracing was much stronger than that normally used in ordinary steel construction. The absence of the solid walls of a building gave the blast a much less effective surface to push against. The blast tore the tower from its foundations, twisted it, ripped it apart and left it flat on the ground. The effects on the tower indicate that, at that distance, unshielded permanent steel and masonry buildings would have been destroyed. I no longer consider the Pentagon a safe shelter from such a bomb. Enclosed are a sketch showing the tower before the explosion and a telephotograph showing what it looked like afterwards. None of us had expected it to be damaged.

6. The cloud traveled to a great height first in the form of a ball, then mushroomed, then changed into a long trailing chimney-shaped column and finally was sent in several directions by the variable winds at the different elevations. It deposited its dust and radioactive materials over a wide area. It was followed and monitored by medical doctors and scientists with instruments to check its radioactive effects. While here and there the activity on the ground was fairly high, at no place did it reach a concentration which required evacuation of the population. Radioactive material in small quantities was located as much as 120 miles away. The measurements are being continued in order to have adequate data with which to protect the Government's interests in case of future claims. For a few hours I was none too comfortable about the situation.

7. For distances as much as 200 miles away, observers were stationed to check on blast effects, property damage, radioactivity and reactions of the population. While complete reports have not yet been received, I now know that no persons were injured nor was there any real property damage outside our Government area. As soon as all the voluminous data can be checked and correlated, full technical studies will be possible.

. . .

Source: Michael Stoff, Jonathan F. Fanton, and R. Hall Williams. *The Manhattan Project: A Documentary History to the Atomic Age*. New York: McGraw Hill, 1991, pp. 188–193.

Eyewitness Report on the Bombing of Nagasaki (August 9, 1945) (excerpt)

Before going to work for the Manhattan Project, the journalist William L. Laurence was the science writer for the New York Times *and a Pulitzer Prize winner. He flew on one of the two observer planes that accompanied the B-29 that dropped an atomic bomb on the Japanese city of Nagasaki on August 9, 1945. Laurence's description of what he and others saw is in the form of a press release written for the U.S. War Department on August 9; however, it was not released to the public for a full month, after Japan had surrendered. Japan offered to surrender a day after Nagasaki was bombed, although with conditions that would have left its political system unchanged and which the United States therefore found unacceptable. An exchange of messages followed. It bridged the differences between the two sides, and on August 14 Japan accepted Allied terms specified in the Potsdam Declaration. Japan's formal surrender took place onboard the U.S. battleship* Missouri, *which was moored in Tokyo Bay, on September 2.*

WAR DEPARTMENT
Bureau of Public Relations
PRESS BRANCH

. . .

FOR RELEASE SUNDAY, SEPTEMBER 9, 1945

EYE WITNESS ACCOUNT
ATOMIC BOMB MISSION OVER NAGASAKI

. . .

WITH THE ATOMIC BOMB MISSION TO JAPAN, AUGUST 9 (DELAYED)—We are on our way to bomb the mainland of Japan. Our flying contingent consists of three specially designed B-29 Superforts, and two of these carry no bombs. But our lead plane is on its way with another atomic bomb, the second in three days.

. . .

We heard pre-arranged signal on our radio, put on our ARC welder's glasses and watched tensely the maneuverings of the strike ship about half a mile in front of us.

"There she goes!" someone said. Out of the belly of the Artiste what looked like a black object came downward.

Captain Bock swung around to get out of range, but even though we were turning away in the opposite direction, and despite the fact that it was broad daylight in our cabin, all of us became aware of a giant flash that broke through the dark barrier of our ARC welder's lenses and flooded our cabin with an intense light.

We removed our glasses after the first flash but the light still lingered on, a bluish-green light, that illuminated the entire sky all around. A tremendous blast wave struck our ship and made it tremble from nose to tail. This was followed by four more blasts in rapid succession, each resounding like the boom of cannon fire hitting our plane from all directions.

Observers in the tail of our ship saw a giant ball of fire rise as though from the bowels of the earth, belching forth enormous white smoke rings. Next they saw a giant pillar of purple fire, 10,000 feet high, shooting skyward with enormous speed.

By the time our ship had made another turn in the direction of the atomic explosion the pillar of purple fire had reached the level of our altitude. Only about 45 seconds had passed. Awestruck, we watched it shoot upward like a meteor coming from the earth instead of from outer space, becoming ever more alive as it climbed skyward through the white clouds. It was no longer smoke, or dust, or even a cloud of fire. It was a living thing, a new species of being, born right before our incredulous eyes.

At one stage of its evolution, covering missions of years in terms of seconds, the entity assumed the form of a giant square totem pole, with its base about three miles long, tapering off to about a mile at the top. Its bottom was brown, its center was amber, its top white. But it was a living totem pole, carved with many grotesque masks grimacing at the earth.

Then, just when it appeared as though the thing has settled down into a state of permanence, there came shooting out of the top a giant mushroom that increased the height of the pillar to a total of 45,000 feet. The mushroom top was even more alive than the pillar, seething and boiling in a white fury of creamy foam, sizzling upwards and then descending earthward, a thousand old faithful geysers rolled into one.

It kept struggling in an elemental fury, like a creature in the act of breaking the bonds that held it down. In a few seconds it had freed itself from its gigantic stem and floated upward with tremendous speed, its momentum carrying into the stratosphere to a height of about 60,000 feet.

But no sooner did this happen when another mushroom, smaller in size than the first one, began emerging out of the pillar. It was as though the decapitated monster was growing a new head.

As the first mushroom floated off into the blue it changed its shape into a flower-like form, its giant petal curving downward, creamy white outside, rose-colored inside. It still retained that shape when we last gazed at it from a distance of about 200 miles.

Source: Atomicarchive.com. Available online. URL: http://www.atomicarchive.com/Docs/Hiroshima/Nagasaki.shtml. Accessed December 21, 2008.

Central Intelligence Agency Estimate of the Status of the Soviet Atomic Bomb Project (July 25, 1948)

After World War II, the United States was the world's only atomic power, but no one expected that situation to last as it was known that the Soviet Union was urgently working to develop the bomb. However, the United States did not expect the Soviets to succeed as quickly as they did. This is clear from the July 1948 memorandum to President Truman from the head of the Central Intelligence Agency. The CIA, consistent with its estimate of seven months earlier, informed the president that there is a "remote" possibility that the Soviets might have a bomb by mid-1950 but that a more probable date is 1953. That assessment, as noted in the last paragraph, was shared by other U.S. intelligence agencies. It turns out that all of them had underestimated the progress the Soviets, helped by a spy network that during World War II had penetrated the Manhattan Project, were making. Barely a year after this CIA memorandum, on August 29, 1949, the Soviet Union successfully tested an atomic bomb.

MEMORANDUM TO THE PRESIDENT

Subject: Estimate of the Status of the Russian Atomic Energy Project

In the interval since the 15 December 1947 report on the Status of the Soviet Atomic Energy Program was issued, no information has been received that necessitates changes in the argument of that report. It has remained necessary to rely on knowledge of the United States, British, and Canadian experience in order to project present information into the future. Information received since December adds somewhat to our knowledge of the scope and details of the USSR's project, but it continues to be impossible to determine its exact status or to determine the data scheduled by the Soviets for the completion of their first atomic bomb. It has been learned, however, that in the summer of 1947 the highest Soviet authority was seriously disturbed by the lack of progress.

On the basis of the evidence now in our possession, it is estimated that the earliest date by which it is remotely possible that the USSR may have completed its first atomic bomb is mid-1950, but the most probable date is believed to be mid-1953. Further discussions with geological consultants, further literature studies, and such information as has been received from the field lead to the conclusion that previous estimates of the total reserves of uranium available to the USSR were low. As a result, the estimated production of bombs has been increased. It is now believed that the maximum number of bombs in the Soviet stockpile in 1955 will be not more than 20 if the first bomb is completed in 1953, or not more than 50 if it is completed in 1950.

The above report was delivered to the Joint Congressional Atomic Energy Committee of which Senator Hickenlooper is the chairman and in addition has also been disseminated to the Armed Services and the Department of State. This report, although prepared by the Central Intelligence Agency, was examined and concurred in by the intelligence agencies of the State, Army and Air Force Departments as well as by the Atomic Energy Commission.

R. H. Hillenhoeffer
Rear Admiral, USN
Director of Central Intelligence

Source: Atomicarhive.com Available online. URL: http://www.atomicarchive.com/Docs/Hydrogen/Soviet.shtml. Accessed December 21, 2008.

President Truman's Announcement of the Soviet Union's Successful Test of an Atomic Bomb (September 23, 1949)

The Soviet test of an atomic bomb took place on August 29, 1949. On September 3, an American weather plane equipped with special instruments flying off the coast of Siberia collected air samples that showed abnormal amounts of radioactivity. Additional samples soon confirmed that the source of the radiation had to be a Soviet nuclear test. A somber President Truman informed the American people of the Soviet test on September 23. Truman tried to minimize the factor of surprise by pointing out he had stated four years earlier that no nation could maintain a nuclear monopoly. He also called for an "effective enforceable" international control of atomic energy.

I believe the American people, to the fullest extent consistent with national security, are entitled to be informed of all developments in the field of atomic energy. That is my reason for making public the following information.

We have evidence that within recent weeks an atomic explosion occurred in the USSR.

Ever since atomic energy was first released by man, the eventual development of this new force by other nations was to be expected. This probability has always been taken into account by us.

Nearly 4 years ago I pointed out that "scientific opinion appears to be practically unanimous that the essential theoretical knowledge upon which the discovery is based is already widely known. There is also substantial agreement that foreign research can come abreast of our present theoretical knowledge in time." And, in the Three-Nation Declaration of the President of the United States and the Prime Ministers of United Kingdom and of Canada, dated November 15, 1945, it was emphasized that no single nation could in fact have a monopoly of atomic weapons.

This recent development emphasizes once again, if indeed such emphasis were needed, the necessity for that truly effective enforceable international control of atomic energy which this Government and the large majority of the members of the United Nations support.

Source: Atomicarchive.com. Available online. URL: http://www.atomicarchive.com/Docs/Hydrogen/SovietAB.shtml. Accessed December 21, 2008.

Lewis L. Strauss Recommends the United States Develop a Thermonuclear Bomb (November 25, 1949)

In 1949, Strauss was one of five commissioners in charge of running the Atomic Energy Commission (AEC), the civilian agency created by the 1946 Atomic Energy Act to control and advance U.S. peacetime development of atomic energy. On January 1, 1947, the AEC took over from the Manhattan Project the facilities that had been used to develop the atomic bomb. The question of whether to develop the hydrogen bomb became an urgent issue after the August 1949 Soviet test of an atomic bomb. America's leading nuclear scientists and its high-level political figures were deeply divided, a fact that Strauss refers to in his letter to Truman. In fact, three of the five AEC commissioners opposed the development of the hydrogen bomb (Strauss mentions Gordon Dean, the other commissioner who supported development), while a Special Committee Truman appointed in mid-November supported the project by a vote of two to one. As noted in chapter 2, none of the Americans debating the development of the hydrogen bomb during fall 1949 knew that the Soviets had been working on that bomb for several years.

Dear Mr. President,

As you know, the thermonuclear (super) bomb was suggested by scientists working at Los Alamos during the war. The current consideration of the super bomb was precipitated, I believe, by a memorandum which I addressed to my fellow Commissioners following your announcement on September 23rd of an atomic explosion in Russia. I participated in the discussions which were antecedent to the letter to you from the Commission on November 9th, but did not join in the preparation of the letter as I was then on the Pacific Coast, It was my belief that a comprehensive recommendation should be provided for you, embodying the judgement of the Commission (in the areas where it is competent), together with the views of the Departments of State and Defense. My colleagues, however, felt that you would prefer to obtain these views separately.

Difference on the broad question of policy between my associates as individuals were included in the Commission's letter to you, and it was correctly stated that the views of Commissioner Dean and mine were in substantial accord on the main issue. It is proper, I believe, that I should state them on my own responsibility, and in my own words.

I believe that the United States must be as completely armed as any possible enemy. From this, it follows that I believe it unwise to renounce, unilaterally, any weapon which an anemy can reasonably be expected to possess, I recommend that the President direct the Atomic Energy Commission to proceed with the development of the thermonuclear bomb, at highest priority subject only to the judgement of the Department of Defense as to its value as a weapon, and of the advice of the Department of State as to the diplomatic consequences of its unilateral renunciation or its possession. In the event that you may be interested, my reasoning is appended in a memorandum.

Lewis L. Strauss

25 November 1949

This is a memorandum to accompany a letter of even date to the President to supply the reasoning for my recommendation that he should direct the Atomic Energy Commission to proceed at highest priority with the development of the thermonuclear weapon.

PREMISES

(1) The production of such a weapon appears to be feasible (i.e., better than a 50-50 chance).

(2) Recent accomplishments by the Russians indicate that the production of a thermonuclear weapon is within their technical competence.

(3) A government of atheists is not likely to be dissuaded from producing the weapon on "moral" grounds. ("Reason and experience both forbid us to expect that national morality can prevail in exclusion of religious principle" G. Washington, September 17, 1796).

(4) The possibility of producing the thermonuclear weapon was suggested more than six years ago, and considerable theoretical work which may be known to the Soviets—the principle has certainly been known to them.

(5) The time in which the development of this weapon can be perfected is perhaps of the order of two years, so that a Russian enterprise started some years ago may be well along to completion.

(6) It is the historic policy of the United States not to have its forces less well armed than those of any other country (viz., the 5:3:3 naval ratio, etc., etc.)

(7) Unlike the atomic bomb which has certain limitations, the proposed weapon may be tactically employed against a mobilized army over an area of the size ordinarily occupied by such a force.

(8) The Commission's letter of November 9th to the President mentioned the "possibility that the radioactivity released by a small number (perhaps ten) of these bombs would pollute the earth's atmosphere to a dangerous extent." Studies requested by the Commission have since indicated that the number of such weapons necessary to pollute the earth's atmosphere would run into many hundreds. Atmospheric pollution is a consequence of present atomic bombs if used in quantity.

CONCLUSIONS

(1) The danger in the weapon does not reside in its physical nature but in human behavior. Its unilateral renunciation by the United States could very easily result in its unilateral possession by the Soviet Government. I am unable to see any satisfaction in that prospect.

(2) The Atomic Energy Commission is competent to advise the President with respect to the feasibility of making the weapon; its economy in fissionable material as compared with atomic bombs; the possible time factor involved; and a description of its characteristics as compared with atomic bombs. Judgment, however, as to its strategic or tactical effect on friendly nations or or unilateral renunciation of the weapon is a subject for the Department of State. My opinion as an individual, however, based upon

discussion with military experts is to the effect that the weapon may be critically useful against a large enemy force both as a weapon of offense and as a defensive measure to prevent landings on our own shores.

(3) I am impressed with the arguments which have been made to the effect that this is a weapon of mass destruction on an unprecedented scale. So, however, was the atomic bomb when it was first envisaged and when the National Academy of sciences in its report of November 6, 1941, referred to it as "of superlatively destructive power." Also, on June 16, 1945, the Scientific Panel of the Interim Committee on Nuclear Power, comprising some of the present members of the General Advisory Committee, reported to the Secretary of War, "We believe that the subject of thermonuclear reactions among light nuclei is one of the most important that needs study. There is a reasonable presumption that with skillful research and development, fission bombs can be used to initiate the reactions of deuterium, tritium, and possibly other light nuclei. If this can be accomplished, the energy release of explosive units can be increased by a factor of 1000 or more over that of presently contemplated fission bombs." This statement was preceded by the recommendation, "Certainly we would wish to see work carried out on the problems mentioned below."

(4) Obviously the current atomic bomb as well as the proposed thermonuclear weapon are horrible to contemplate. All war is horrible. Until, however, some means is found of eliminating war, I cannot agree with those of my colleagues who feel that an announcement should be made by the President to the effect that the development of the thermonuclear weapon will not be undertaken by the United States at this time. This is because: (a) I do not think the statement will be credited in the Kremlin; (b) that when and if it should be decided subsequent to such a statement to proceed with the production of the thermonuclear bomb, it might in a delicate situation, be regarded as an affirmative statement of hostile intent; and (c) because primarily until disarmament is universal, our arsenal must not be less well equipped than with the most potent weapons that our technology can devise.

RECOMMENDATION

In sum, I believe that the President should direct the Atomic Energy Commission to proceed with all possible expedition to develop the thermonuclear weapon.

Source: Atomicarchive.com. Available online. URL: http://www.atomicarchive.com/Docs/Hydrogen/Strauss.shtml. Accessed December 21, 2008.

President Truman Announces the United States Will Develop the Hydrogen Bomb (January 31, 1950)

In mid-January 1950, President Truman received a memorandum from the Joint Chiefs of Staff, the advisory body that includes the heads of each of the country's armed services, supporting development of the hydrogen bomb. On January 31, the president met with the Special Committee he had appointed in November 1949 to advise him about whether to build the bomb. David Lilienthal, the AEC chairman and the member of the committee who opposed the project, was prepared to argue against going forward. Truman cut him off with the simple question, "Can the Russians do it?" When all agreed that the Soviets could build a hydrogen bomb, the president stated his support for the project. The entire meeting had taken only seven minutes. Truman made a public announcement to the nation later that day.

> It is part of my responsibility as Commander in Chief of the Armed Forces to see to it that our country is able to defend itself against any possible aggressor. Accordingly, I have directed the Atomic Energy Commission to continue work on all forms of atomic weapons, including the so-called hydrogen or super bomb. Like all other work in the field of atomic weapons, it is being and will be carried forward on a basis consistent with the over all objectives of our program for peace and security.
>
> This we shall continue to do until a satisfactory plan for international control of atomic energy is achieved. We shall also continue to examine all those factors that affect our program for peace and this country's security.

Source: Atomicarchive.com. Available online. URL: http://www.atomicarchive.com/Docs/Hydrogen/HBomb.shtml. Accessed December 21, 2008.

President Nixon Reaffirms the U.S. Policy of No First Use of Chemical Weapons and Renounces the Use of Biological Weapons (November 25, 1969)

By the late 1960s, the military value of chemical and biological weapons was being questioned. There also was considerable public concern about the dangers involved in the storage and testing of these weapons. As a result, several months after taking office in 1969, President Richard M. Nixon ordered a review of these weapons by the National Security Council under Henry Kissinger. The review was completed in November. The result was a presidential announcement reaffirming the U.S. policy of no first use of chemical weapons, extending that policy to cover agents that incapacitated but did not kill, and renouncing biological weapons. The president also called for the United States to ratify the 1925 Geneva Protocol, which banned both chemical and biological weapons. Nixon actually made his announcement twice on November 25: once at Fort Detrick, Maryland, where the U.S. Army's main facilities for biological warfare were located, and later that day, with a few minor changes, at the White House.

Statement on Chemical and Biological Defense Politics and Programs.

November 25, 1969

SOON AFTER taking office I directed a comprehensive study of our chemical and biological defense policies and programs. There had been no such review in over 15 years. As a result, objectives and policies in this field were unclear and programs lacked definition and direction.

Under the auspices of the National Security Council, the Departments of State and Defense, the Arms Control and Disarmament Agency, the Office of Science and Technology, the intelligence community, and other agencies worked closely together on this study for over 6 months. These Government efforts were aided by contributions from the scientific community through the President's Science Advisory Committee.

This study has now been completed and its findings carefully considered by the National Security Council. I am now reporting the decisions taken on the basis of this review.

Chemical Warfare Program

As to our chemical warfare program, the United States:

—Reaffirms its oft-repeated renunciation of the first use of lethal chemical weapons.

—Extends this renunciation to the first use of incapacitating chemicals.

Consonant with these decisions, the administration will submit to the Senate, for its advice and consent to ratification, the Geneva Protocol of 1925 which prohibits the first use in war of "asphyxiating, poisonous or other Gases and of Bacteriological Methods of Warfare." The United States has long supported the principles and objectives of this Protocol. We take this step toward formal ratification to reinforce our continuing advocacy of international constraints on the use of these weapons.

Biological Research Program

Biological weapons have massive, unpredictable and potentially uncontrollable consequences. They may produce global epidemics and impair the health of future generations. I have therefore decided that:

—The United States shall renounce the use of lethal biological agents and weapons, and all other methods of biological warfare.

—The United States will confine its biological research to defensive measures such as immunization and safety measures.

—The Department of Defense has been asked to make recommendations as to the disposal of existing stocks of bacteriological weapons.

In the spirit of these decisions, the United States associates itself with the principles and objectives of the United Kingdom Draft Convention which would ban the use of biological methods of warfare. We will seek, however, to clarify specific provisions of the draft to assure that necessary safeguards are included.

Neither our association with the Convention nor the limiting of our program to research will leave us vulnerable to surprise by an enemy who does not observe these rational restraints. Our intelligence community will continue to watch carefully the nature and extent of the biological programs of others.

These important decisions, which have been announced today, have been taken as an initiative toward peace. Mankind already carries in its own hands too many of the seeds of its own destruction. By the examples we set today, we hope to contribute to an atmosphere of peace and understanding between nations and among men.

Source: U.S. Department of State. *Foreign Relations, 1969–1976, vol. E-2, Documents on Arms Control, 1969–1972.* Available online. URL: http://www.state.gov/documents/organization/90920.pdf. Accessed December 21, 2008.

The National Security Strategy of the United States of America (September 17, 2002)

The executive branch of the U.S. government has periodically issued a document known as The National Security Strategy of the United States of America. In the past, these documents were classified, meaning they were not released to the public. The best-known of these documents, NSC-68, *was issued in 1950. It provided the justification for the U.S. policy of containment during the cold war, a policy directed at keeping in check the expansionist policies of the Soviet Union.* NSC-68 *was not declassified until 1975. More recently, national security strategy documents have been made public when they are completed and approved.* The National Security Strategy of the United States *of 2002 reflected the reality of the September 11, 2001, attack by Islamic terrorists on the United States that demolished New York's World Trade Center, badly damaged the Pentagon, and killed almost 3,000 people. It is divided into nine parts. Part five is entitled "Preventing Our Enemies from Threatening Us, Our Allies, and Our Friends with Weapons of Mass Destruction." This section stresses the emergence during the 1990s of so-called rogue states that have no regard for international law and support terrorism worldwide. It points out the need to prevent these states and their terrorist clients from using weapons of mass destruction against the United States and its allies. Among the countermeasures discussed as being necessary to protect the United States is "preemption," which means not waiting for an attack to take place but, when faced with an imminent threat, taking action that if necessary would involve the use of force. The document argues that "the greater the threat, the greater the threat of inaction." In other words, it is not only actions that pose risks to a country; sometimes doing nothing carries serious risks as well.*

v. Prevent Our Enemies from Threatening Us, Our Allies, and Our Friends with Weapons of Mass Destruction

"The gravest danger to freedom lies at the crossroads of radicalism and technology. When the spread of chemical and biological and nuclear weapons, along with ballistic missile technology—when that occurs, even weak states and small groups could attain a catastrophic power to strike great nations. Our enemies have declared this very intention, and have been caught seeking these terrible weapons. They want the capability to blackmail us, or to harm us, or to harm our friends—and we will oppose them with all our power."

President Bush
West Point, New York
June 1, 2002

The nature of the Cold War threat required the United States—with our allies and friends—to emphasize deterrence of the enemy's use of force, producing a grim strategy of mutual assured destruction. With the collapse of the Soviet Union and the end of the Cold War, our security environment has undergone profound transformation.

Having moved from confrontation to cooperation as the hallmark of our relationship with Russia, the dividends are evident: an end to the balance of terror that divided us; an historic reduction in the nuclear arsenals on both sides; and cooperation in areas such as counterterrorism and missile defense that until recently were inconceivable.

But new deadly challenges have emerged from rogue states and terrorists. None of these contemporary threats rival the sheer destructive power that was arrayed against us by the Soviet Union. However, the nature and motivations of these new adversaries, their determination to obtain destructive powers hitherto available only to the world's strongest states, and the greater likelihood that they will use weapons of mass destruction against us, make today's security environment more complex and dangerous.

In the 1990s we witnessed the emergence of a small number of rogue states that, while different in important ways, share a number of attributes. These states:

- brutalize their own people and squander their national resources for the personal gain of the rulers;
- display no regard for international law, threaten their neighbors, and callously violate international treaties to which they are party;
- are determined to acquire weapons of mass destruction, along with other advanced military technology, to be used as threats or offensively to achieve the aggressive designs of these regimes;
- sponsor terrorism around the globe; and
- reject basic human values and hate the United States and everything for which it stands.

At the time of the Gulf War, we acquired irrefutable proof that Iraq's designs were not limited to the chemical weapons it had used against Iran and its own people, but also extended to the acquisition of nuclear weapons and biological agents. In the past decade North Korea has become the world's principal purveyor of ballistic missiles, and has tested increasingly capable missiles while developing its own WMD arsenal. Other rogue regimes seek nuclear, biological, and chemical weapons as well. These states' pursuit of, and global trade in, such weapons has become a looming threat to all nations.

We must be prepared to stop rogue states and their terrorist clients before they are able to threaten or use weapons of mass destruction against the United States and our allies and friends. Our response must take full advantage of strengthened alliances, the establishment of new partnerships with former adversaries, innovation in the use of military forces, modern technologies, including the development of an effective missile defense system, and increased emphasis on intelligence collection and analysis.

Our comprehensive strategy to combat WMD includes:

- *Proactive counterproliferation efforts.* We must deter and defend against the threat before it is unleashed. We must ensure that key capabilities—detection, active and passive defenses, and counterforce capabilities—are integrated into our defense transformation and our homeland security systems. Counterproliferation must also be integrated into the doctrine, training, and equipping of our forces and those of our allies to ensure that we can prevail in any conflict with WMD-armed adversaries.
- *Strengthened nonproliferation efforts to prevent rogue states and terrorists from acquiring the materials, technologies, and expertise necessary for weapons of mass destruction.* We will enhance diplomacy, arms control, multilateral export controls, and threat reduction assistance that impede states and terrorists seeking WMD, and when necessary, interdict enabling technologies and materials. We will continue to build coalitions to support these efforts, encouraging their increased political and financial support for nonproliferation and threat reduction programs. The recent G-8 agreement to commit up to $20 billion to a global partnership against proliferation marks a major step forward.
- *Effective consequence management to respond to the effects of WMD use, whether by terrorists or hostile states.* Minimizing the effects of WMD use against our people will help deter those who possess such weapons and dissuade those who seek to acquire them by persuading enemies that they cannot attain their desired ends. The United States must also be prepared to respond to the effects of WMD use against our forces abroad, and to help friends and allies if they are attacked.

It has taken almost a decade for us to comprehend the true nature of this new threat. Given the goals of rogue states and terrorists, the United States can no longer solely rely on a reactive posture as we have in the past. The inability to deter a potential attacker, the immediacy of today's threats, and the magnitude of potential harm that could be caused by our adversaries' choice of weapons, do not permit that option. We cannot let our enemies strike first.

- In the Cold War, especially following the Cuban missile crisis, we faced a generally status quo, risk-averse adversary. Deterrence was an effective defense. But deterrence based only upon the threat of retaliation is less likely to work against leaders of rogue states more willing to take risks, gambling with the lives of their people, and the wealth of their nations.

- In the Cold War, weapons of mass destruction were considered weapons of last resort whose use risked the destruction of those who used them. Today, our enemies see weapons of mass destruction as weapons of choice. For rogue states these weapons are tools of intimidation and military aggression against their neighbors. These weapons may also allow these states to attempt to blackmail the United States and our allies to prevent us from deterring or repelling the aggressive behavior of rogue states. Such states also see these weapons as their best means of overcoming the conventional superiority of the United States.
- Traditional concepts of deterrence will not work against a terrorist enemy whose avowed tactics are wanton destruction and the targeting of innocents; whose so-called soldiers seek martyrdom in death and whose most potent protection is statelessness. The overlap between states that sponsor terror and those that pursue WMD compels us to action.

For centuries, international law recognized that nations need not suffer an attack before they can lawfully take action to defend themselves against forces that present an imminent danger of attack. Legal scholars and international jurists often conditioned the legitimacy of preemption on the existence of an imminent threat—most often a visible mobilization of armies, navies, and air forces preparing to attack.

We must adapt the concept of imminent threat to the capabilities and objectives of today's adversaries. Rogue states and terrorists do not seek to attack us using conventional means. They know such attacks would fail. Instead, they rely on acts of terror and, potentially, the use of weapons of mass destruction—weapons that can be easily concealed, delivered covertly, and used without warning.

The targets of these attacks are our military forces and our civilian population, in direct violation of one of the principal norms of the law of warfare. As was demonstrated by the losses on September 11, 2001, mass civilian casualties is the specific objective of terrorists and these losses would be exponentially more severe if terrorists acquired and used weapons of mass destruction.

The United States has long maintained the option of preemptive actions to counter a sufficient threat to our national security. The greater the threat, the greater is the risk of inaction—and the more compelling the case for taking anticipatory action to defend ourselves, even if uncertainty remains as to the time and place of the enemy's attack. To forestall or prevent such hostile acts by our adversaries, the United States will, if necessary, act preemptively.

The United States will not use force in all cases to preempt emerging threats, nor should nations use preemption as a pretext for aggression. Yet in an age where the enemies of civilization openly and actively seek the world's most destructive technologies, the United States cannot remain idle while dangers gather.

We will always proceed deliberately, weighing the consequences of our actions. To support preemptive options, we will:

- build better, more integrated intelligence capabilities to provide timely, accurate information on threats, wherever they may emerge;
- coordinate closely with allies to form a common assessment of the most dangerous threats; and
- continue to transform our military forces to ensure our ability to conduct rapid and precise operations to achieve decisive results.

The purpose of our actions will always be to eliminate a specific threat to the United States or our allies and friends. The reasons for our actions will be clear, the force measured, and the cause just.

Source: The White House. Available online. URL: http://www.thewhitehouse.gov/nsc/nss/2002/index.html. Accessed December 20, 2008.

National Strategy to Combat Weapons of Mass Destruction (December 11, 2002)

President George W. Bush officially issued the National Strategy to Combat Weapons of Mass Destruction on December 11, 2002. It is based on three complementary strategies, or pillars: counterproliferation, to deter and defend against the use of WMD; nonproliferation, to prevent states and terrorists from acquiring WMD; and preparation, what the document calls "consequence management," to respond to any use of WMD against the United States and its allies.

National Strategy to Combat Weapons of Mass Destruction

"The gravest danger our Nation faces lies at the crossroads of radicalism and technology, Our enemies have openly declared that they are seeking weapons of mass destruction, and evidence indicates that they are doing so with determination. The United States will not allow these efforts to succeed. . . . History will judge harshly those who saw this coming danger but failed to act. In the new world we have entered, the only path to peace and security is the path of action."

President Bush
The National Security Strategy of the United States of America
September 17, 2002

Introduction

Weapons of mass destruction (WMD)—nuclear, biological, and chemical—in the possession of hostile states and terrorists represent one of the greatest security challenges facing the United States. We must pursue a comprehensive strategy to counter this threat in all of its dimensions.

An effective strategy for countering WMD, including their use and further proliferation, is an integral component of the National Security Strategy of the United States of America. As with the war on terrorism, our strategy for homeland security, and our new concept of deterrence, the U.S. approach to combat WMD represents a fundamental change from the past. To succeed, we must take full advantage of today's opportunities, including the application of new technologies, increased emphasis on intelligence collection and analysis, the strengthening of alliance relationships, and the establishment of new partnerships with former adversaries.

Weapons of mass destruction could enable adversaries to inflict massive harm on the United States, our military forces at home and abroad, and our friends and allies. Some states, including several that have supported and continue to support terrorism, already possess WMD and are seeking even greater capabilities, as tools of coercion and intimidation. For them, these are not weapons of last resort, but militarily useful weapons of choice intended to overcome our nation's advantages in conventional forces and to deter us from responding to aggression against our friends and allies in regions of vital interest. In addition, terrorist groups are seeking to acquire WMD with the stated purpose of killing large numbers of our people and those of friends and allies—without compunction and without warning.

We will not permit the world's most dangerous regimes and terrorists to threaten us with the world's most destructive weapons. We must accord the highest priority to the protection of the United States, our forces, and our friends and allies from the existing and growing WMD threat.

Pillars of Our National Strategy

Our National Strategy to Combat Weapons of Mass Destruction has three principal pillars:

Counterproliferation to Combat WMD Use

The possession and increased likelihood of use of WMD by hostile states and terrorists are realities of the contemporary security environment. It is therefore critical that the U.S. military and appropriate civilian agencies be prepared to deter and defend against the full range of possible WMD employment scenarios. We will ensure that all needed capabilities to combat WMD are fully integrated into the emerging defense transformation plan and into our homeland security posture. Counterproliferation will also be fully integrated into the basic doctrine, training, and equipping of all forces, in order to ensure that they can sustain operations to decisively defeat WMD-armed adversaries.

Strengthened Nonproliferation to Combat WMD Proliferation

The United States, our friends and allies, and the broader international community must undertake every effort to prevent states and terrorists from acquiring WMD and missiles. We must enhance traditional measures—diplomacy, arms control, multilateral agreements, threat reduction assistance, and export controls—that seek to dissuade or impede proliferant states and terrorist networks, as well as to slow and make more costly their access to sensitive technologies, material, and expertise. We must ensure compliance with relevant international agreements, including the Nuclear Nonproliferation Treaty (NPT), the Chemical Weapons Convention (CWC), and the Biological Weapons Convention (BWC). The United States will continue to work with other states to improve their capability to prevent unauthorized transfers of WMD and missile technology, expertise, and material. We will identify and pursue new methods of prevention, such as national criminalization of proliferation activities and expanded safety and security measures.

Consequence Management to Respond to WMD Use

Finally, the United States must be prepared to respond to the use of WMD against our citizens, our military forces, and those of friends and allies. We will develop and maintain the capability to reduce to the extent possible the potentially horrific consequences of WMD attacks at home and abroad.

The three pillars of the U.S. national strategy to combat WMD are seamless elements of a comprehensive approach. Serving to integrate the pillars are four cross-cutting enabling functions that need to be pursued on a priority basis: intelligence collection and analysis on WMD, delivery systems, and related technologies; research and development to improve our ability to respond to evolving threats; bilateral and multilateral cooperation; and targeted strategies against hostile states and terrorists.

Counterproliferation

We know from experience that we cannot always be successful in preventing and containing the proliferation of WMD to hostile states and terrorists. Therefore, U.S. military and appropriate civilian agencies must possess the full range of operational capabilities to counter the threat and use of WMD by states and terrorists against the United States, our military forces, and friends and allies.

Interdiction

Effective interdiction is a critical part of the U.S. strategy to combat WMD and their delivery means. We must enhance the capabilities of our military, intelligence, technical, and law enforcement communities to prevent the movement of WMD materials, technology, and expertise to hostile states and terrorist organizations.

Deterrence

Today's threats are far more diverse and less predictable than those of the past. States hostile to the United States and to our friends and allies have demonstrated their willingness to take high risks to achieve their goals, and are aggressively pursuing WMD and their means of delivery as critical tools in this effort. As a consequence, we require new methods of deterrence. A strong declaratory policy and effective military forces are essential elements of our contemporary deterrent posture, along with the full range of political tools to persuade potential adversaries not to seek or use WMD. The United States will continue to make clear that it reserves the right to respond with overwhelming force—including through resort to all of our options—to the use of WMD against the United States, our forces abroad, and friends and allies.

In addition to our conventional and nuclear response and defense capabilities, our overall deterrent posture against WMD threats is reinforced by effective intelligence, surveillance, interdiction, and domestic law enforcement capabilities, Such combined capabilities enhance deterrence both by devaluing an adversary's WMD and missiles, and by posing the prospect of an overwhelming response to any use of such weapons.

Defense and Mitigation

Because deterrence may not succeed, and because of the potentially devastating consequences of WMD use against our forces and civilian population,

U.S. military forces and appropriate civilian agencies must have the capability to defend against WMD-armed adversaries, including in appropriate cases through preemptive measures. This requires capabilities to detect and destroy an adversary's WMD assets before these weapons are used. In addition, robust active and passive defenses and mitigation measures must be in place to enable U.S. military forces and appropriate civilian agencies to accomplish their missions, and to assist friends and allies when WMD are used.

Active defenses disrupt, disable, or destroy WMD en route to their targets. Active defenses include vigorous air defense and effective missile defenses against today's threats. Passive defenses must be tailored to the unique characteristics of the various forms of WMD. The United States must also have the ability rapidly and effectively to mitigate the effects of a WMD attack against our deployed forces.

Our approach to defend against biological threats has long been based on our approach to chemical threats, despite the fundamental differences between these weapons. The United States is developing a new approach to provide us and our friends and allies with an effective defense against biological weapons.

Finally, U.S. military forces and domestic law enforcement agencies as appropriate must stand ready to respond against the source of any WMD attack. The primary objective of a response is to disrupt an imminent attack or an attack in progress, and eliminate the threat of future attacks. As with deterrence and prevention, an effective response requires rapid attribution and robust strike capability. We must accelerate efforts to field new capabilities to defeat WMD-related assets. The United States needs to be prepared to conduct post-conflict operations to destroy or dismantle any residual WMD capabilities of the hostile state or terrorist network. An effective U.S. response not only will eliminate the source of a WMD attack but will also have a powerful deterrent effect upon other adversaries that possess or seek WMD or missiles.

Nonproliferation

Active Nonproliferation Diplomacy

The United States will actively employ diplomatic approaches in bilateral and multilateral settings in pursuit of our nonproliferation goals. We must dissuade supplier states from cooperating with proliferant states and induce proliferant states to end their WMD and missile programs. We will hold countries responsible for complying with their commitments. In addition, we will continue to build coalitions to support our efforts, as well as to seek their increased support for nonproliferation and threat reduction cooperation programs. However, should our wide-ranging nonproliferation efforts fail, we must have available the full range of operational capabilities necessary to defend against the possible employment of WMD.

Multilateral Regimes

Existing nonproliferation and arms control regimes play an important role in our overall strategy. The United States will support those regimes that are currently in force, and work to improve the effectiveness of, and compliance with, those regimes. Consistent with other policy priorities, we will also promote new agreements and arrangements that serve our nonproliferation goals. Overall, we seek to cultivate an international environment that is more conducive to nonproliferation. Our efforts will include:

- Nuclear
    - Strengthening of the Nuclear Nonproliferation Treaty and International Atomic Energy Agency (IAEA), including through ratification of an IAEA Additional Protocol by all NPT states parties, assurances that all states put in place full-scope IAEA safeguards agreements, and appropriate increases in funding for the Agency;
    - Negotiating a Fissile Material Cut-Off Treaty that advances U.S. security interests; and
    - Strengthening the Nuclear Suppliers Group and Zangger Committee.
    - Chemical and Biological
    - Effective functioning of the Organization for the Prohibition of Chemical Weapons;
    - Identification and promotion of constructive and realistic measures to strengthen the BWC and thereby to help meet the biological weapons threat; and
    - Strengthening of the Australia Group.
    - Missile
    - Strengthening the Missile Technology Control Regime (MTCR), including through support for universal adherence to the International Code of Conduct Against Ballistic Missile Proliferation.

Nonproliferation and Threat Reduction Cooperation

The United States pursues a wide range of programs, including the Nunn-Lugar program, designed to address the proliferation threat stemming from the large quantities of Soviet-legacy WMD and missile-related expertise and materials. Maintaining an extensive and efficient set of nonproliferation and threat reduction assistance programs to Russia and other former Soviet states is a high priority. We will also continue to encourage friends and allies to increase their contributions to these programs, particularly through the G-8 Global Partnership Against the Spread of Weapons and Materials of Mass Destruction. In addition, we will work with other states to improve the security of their WMD-related materials.

Controls on Nuclear Materials

In addition to programs with former Soviet states to reduce fissile material and improve the security of that which remains, the United States will continue to discourage the worldwide accumulation of separated plutonium and to minimize the use of highly-enriched uranium. As outlined in the National Energy Policy, the United States will work in collaboration with international partners to develop recycle and fuel treatment technologies that are cleaner, more efficient, less waste-intensive, and more proliferation-resistant.

U.S. Export Controls

We must ensure that the implementation of U.S. export controls furthers our nonproliferation and other national security goals, while recognizing the realities that American businesses face in the increasingly globalized marketplace.

We will work to update and strengthen export controls using existing authorities. We also seek new legislation to improve the ability of our export control system to give full weight to both nonproliferation objectives and commercial interests. Our overall goal is to focus our resources on truly sensitive exports to hostile states or those that engage in onward proliferation, while removing unnecessary barriers in the global marketplace.

Nonproliferation Sanctions

Sanctions can be a valuable component of our overall strategy against WMD proliferation. At times, however, sanctions have proven inflexible and ineffective. We will develop a comprehensive sanctions policy to better integrate sanctions into our overall strategy and work with Congress to consolidate and modify existing sanctions legislation.

WMD Consequence Management

Defending the American homeland is the most basic responsibility of our government. As part of our defense, the United States must be fully prepared to respond to the consequences of WMD use on our soil, whether by hostile states or by terrorists. We must also be prepared to respond to the effects of WMD use against our forces deployed abroad, and to assist friends and allies.

The National Strategy for Homeland Security discusses U.S. Government programs to deal with the consequences of the use of a chemical, biological, radiological, or nuclear weapon in the United States. A number of these programs offer training, planning, and assistance to state and local governments. To maximize their effectiveness, these efforts need to be integrated and comprehensive. Our first responders must have the full range of protective, medical, and remediation tools to identify, assess, and respond rapidly to a WMD event on our territory.

The White House Office of Homeland Security will coordinate all federal efforts to prepare for and mitigate the consequences of terrorist attacks within the United States, including those involving WMD. The Office of Homeland Security will also work closely with state and local governments to ensure their planning, training, and equipment requirements are addressed. These issues, including the roles of the Department of Homeland Security, are addressed in detail in the National Strategy for Homeland Security.

The National Security Council's Office of Combating Terrorism coordinates and helps improve U.S. efforts to respond to and manage the recovery from terrorist attacks outside the United States. In cooperation with the Office of Combating Terrorism, the Department of State coordinates interagency efforts to work with our friends and allies to develop their own emergency preparedness and consequence management capabilities.

Integrating the Pillars

Several critical enabling functions serve to integrate the three pillars—counterproliferation, nonproliferation, and consequence management—of the U.S. National Strategy to Combat WMD.

Improved Intelligence Collection and Analysis

A more accurate and complete understanding of the full range of WMD threats is, and will remain, among the highest U.S. intelligence priorities, to enable us to prevent proliferation, and to deter or defend against those who would use those capabilities against us. Improving our ability to obtain timely and accurate knowledge of adversaries' offensive and defensive capabilities, plans, and intentions is key to developing effective counter- and nonproliferation policies and capabilities. Particular emphasis must be accorded to improving: intelligence regarding WMD-related facilities and activities; interaction among U.S. intelligence, law enforcement, and military agencies; and intelligence cooperation with friends and allies.

Research and Development

The United States has a critical need for cutting-edge technology that can quickly and effectively detect, analyze, facilitate interdiction of, defend against, defeat, and mitigate the consequences of WMD. Numerous U.S. Government departments and agencies are currently engaged in the essential research and development to support our overall strategy against WMD proliferation.

The new Counterproliferation Technology Coordination Committee, consisting of senior representatives from all concerned agencies, will act to improve interagency coordination of U.S. Government counterproliferation research and development efforts. The Committee will assist in identifying priorities, gaps, and overlaps in existing programs and in examining options for future investment strategies.

Strengthened International Cooperation

WMD represent a threat not just to the United States, but also to our friends and allies and the broader international community. For this reason, it is vital that we work closely with like-minded countries on all elements of our comprehensive proliferation strategy.

Targeted Strategies Against Proliferants

All elements of the overall U.S. strategy to combat WMD must be brought to bear in targeted strategies against supplier and recipient states of WMD proliferation concern, as well as against terrorist groups which seek to acquire WMD.

A few states are dedicated proliferators, whose leaders are determined to develop, maintain, and improve their WMD and delivery capabilities, which directly threaten the United States, U.S. forces overseas, and/or our friends and allies. Because each of these regimes is different, we will pursue country-specific strategies that best enable us and our friends and allies to prevent, deter, and defend against WMD and missile threats from each of them. These strategies must also take into account the growing cooperation among proliferant states—so-called secondary proliferation—which challenges us to think in new ways about specific country strategies.

One of the most difficult challenges we face is to prevent, deter, and defend against the acquisition and use of WMD by terrorist groups. The current and potential future linkages between terrorist groups and state sponsors of terrorism are particularly dangerous and require priority attention. The full range of counterproliferation, nonproliferation, and consequence management measures must be brought to bear against the WMD terrorist threat, just as they are against states of greatest proliferation concern.

End Note

Our National Strategy to Combat WMD requires much of all of us—the Executive Branch, the Congress, state and local governments, the American people, and our friends and allies. The requirements to prevent, deter, defend against, and respond to today's WMD threats are complex and challenging. But they are not daunting. We can and will succeed in the tasks laid out in this strategy; we have no other choice.

Source: The White House. Available online. URL: http://www.whitehouse.gov/news/releases/200212/WMD Strategy.pdf. Accessed June 15, 2008.

White House Statement on Progress in Missile Defense Capabilities (December 17, 2002)

The United States officially withdrew from the 1972 ABM treaty in June 2002. On December 17, President George W. Bush, who had made the decision to withdraw from the treaty, announced plans to make certain parts of a new American missile defense system operational beginning in 2004 and 2005.

Statement by the President

When I came to office, I made a commitment to transform America's national security strategy and defense capabilities to meet the threats of the 21st century. Today, I am pleased to announce that we will take another important step in countering these threats by beginning to field missile defense capabilities to protect the United States, as well as our friends and allies. These initial capabilities emerge from our research and development program and build on the test bed that we have been constructing. While modest, these capabilities will add to America's security and serve as a starting point for improved and expanded capabilities later, as further progress is made in researching and developing missile defense technologies and in light of changes in the threat.

September 11, 2001, underscored that our Nation faces unprecedented threats, in a world that has changed greatly since the Cold War. To better protect our country against the threats of today and tomorrow, my Administration has developed a new national security strategy, and new supporting strategies for making our homeland more secure and for combating weapons of mass destruction. Throughout my Administration, I have made clear that the United States will take every necessary measure to protect our citizen's against what is perhaps the gravest danger of all:

the catastrophic harm that may result from hostile states or terrorist groups armed with weapons of mass destruction and the means to deliver them.

Missile defenses have an important role to play in this effort. The United States has moved beyond the doctrine of Cold War deterrence reflected in the 1972 ABM Treaty. At the same time we have established a positive relationship with Russia that includes partnership in counterterrorism and in other key areas of mutual concern. We have adopted a new concept of deterrence that recognizes that missile defenses will add to our ability to deter those who may contemplate attacking us with missiles. Our withdrawal from the ABM Treaty has made it possible to develop and test the full range of missile defense technologies, and to deploy defenses capable of protecting our territory and our cities.

I have directed the Secretary of Defense to proceed with fielding an initial set of missile defense capabilities. We plan to begin operating these initial capabilities in 2004 and 2005, and they will include ground-based interceptors, sea-based interceptors, additional Patriot (PAC-3) units, and sensors based on land, at sea, and in space.

Because the threats of the 21st century also endanger our friends and allies around the world, it is essential that we work together to defend against them. The Defense Department will develop and deploy missile defenses capable of protecting not only the United States and our deployed forces, but also our friends and allies. The United States will also structure our missile defense program in a manner that encourages industrial participation by other nations. Demonstrating the important role played by our friends and allies, as part of our initial missile defense capabilities, the United States will seek agreement from the United Kingdom and Denmark to upgrade early-warning radars on their territory.

The new strategic challenges of the 21st century require us to think differently, but they also require us to act. The deployment of missile defenses is an essential element of our broader efforts to transform our defense and deterrence policies and capabilities to meet the new threats we face. Defending the American people against these new threats is my highest priority as Commander-in-Chief, and the highest priority of my Administration.

Source: Atomicarchive.com. Available online. URL: http://www.atomicarchive.com/Docs/Missile/MissileDefense.shtml. Accessed June 29, 2008.

National Security Presidential Directive/NSPD-23 (December 16, 2002)

During the administration of George W. Bush (2001–09), presidential decisions regarding national security decisions were summarized in what were called National Security Presidential Directives (NSPDs). Each NSPD was numbered; NSPD-23 dealt with the Bush administration's policy regarding missile defense. NSPD-23 pointed out the new threat from hostile states, including states that sponsor international terrorism, that are developing long-range ballistic missiles which some day could threaten the United States and its allies. The directive pointed out that it is far more difficult to deter states such as North Korea than it was to deter the Soviet Union during the cold war, which is why the United States needed a long-range missile defense system. The directive also supplies details about the proposed system and notes that parts of it will become operational in 2004 and 2005.

THE WHITE HOUSE
WASHINGTON
December 16, 2002

NATIONAL SECURITY PRESIDENTIAL DIRECTIVE/ NSPD-23

MEMORANDUM FOR
THE VICE PRESIDENT
THE SECRETARY OF STATE
THE SECRETARY OF THE TREASURY
THE SECRETARY OF DEFENSE
THE SECRETARY OF ENERGY
DIRECTOR OF THE OFFICE OF MANAGEMENT AND BUDGET
CHIEF OF STAFF TO THE PRESIDENT
ASSISTANT TO THE PRESIDENT FOR NATIONAL SECURITY AFFAIRS
DIRECTOR, OFFICE OF SCIENCE AND TECHNOLOGY POLICY
DIRECTOR OF CENTRAL INTELLIGENCE
CHAIRMAN OF THE JOINT CHIEFS OF STAFF

SUBJECT: National Policy on Ballistic Missile Defense

Restructuring our defense and deterrence capabilities to correspond to emerging threats remains one of the Administration's highest priorities, and the deployment of missile defenses is an essential component of this broader effort.

WEAPONS OF MASS DESTRUCTION

Changed Security Environment

As the events of September 11 demonstrated, the security environment is more complex and less predictable than in the past. We face growing threats from weapons of mass destruction (WMD) in the hands of states or non-state actors, threats that range from terrorism to ballistic missiles intended to intimidate and coerce us by holding the U.S. and our friends and allies hostage to WMD attack.

Hostile states, including those that sponsor terrorism, are investing large resources to develop and acquire ballistic missiles of increasing range and sophistication that could be used against the United States and our friends and allies. These same states have chemical, biological, and/or nuclear weapons programs. In fact, one of the factors that make long-range ballistic missiles attractive as a delivery vehicle for weapons of mass destruction is that the United States and our allies lack effective defenses against this threat.

The contemporary and emerging missile threat from hostile states is fundamentally different from that of the Cold War and requires a different approach to deterrence and new tools for defense. The strategic logic of the past may not apply to these new threats, and we cannot be wholly dependent on our capability to deter them. Compared to the Soviet Union, their leaderships often are more risk prone. These are leaders that also see WMD as weapons of choice, not of last resort. Weapons of mass destruction are their most lethal means to compensate for our conventional strength and to allow them to pursue their objectives through force, coercion, and intimidation.

Deterring these threats will be difficult. There are no mutual understandings or reliable lines of communication with these states. **Moreover, the dynamics of deterrence are different than in the Cold War when we sought to keep the Soviet Union from expanding outward.** What our new adversaries seek is to keep us out of their region, leaving them free to support terrorism and to pursue aggression against their neighbors. By their own calculations, these leaders may believe they can do this by holding a few of our cities hostage. Our adversaries seek enough destructive capability to blackmail us from coming to the assistance of our friends who would then become the victims of aggression. **In recognition of these new threats, I have directed that the United States must make progress in fielding a new triad composed of long-range conventional and nuclear strike capabilities, missile defenses, and a robust industrial and research development infrastructure.**

Some states, **such as North Korea,** are aggressively pursuing the development of weapons of mass destruction and long-range missiles as a means of coercing the United States and our allies. To deter such threats, we must devalue missiles as tools of extortion and aggression, undermining the confidence of our adversaries that threatening a missile attack would succeed in blackmailing us. In this way, although missile defenses are not a replacement for an offensive response capability, they are an added and critical dimension of contemporary deterrence. Missile defenses will also help to assure allies and friends, and to dissuade countries from pursuing ballistic missiles in the first instance by undermining their military utility.

Finally, history teaches that, despite our best efforts, there will be military surprises, failures of diplomacy, intelligence, and deterrence. Missile defenses help provide protection against such events.

National Missile Defense Act of 1999

On July 22, 1999, the National Missile Defense Act of 1999 (Public Law 106-38) was signed into law. This law states, "It is the policy of the United States to deploy as soon as is technologically possible an effective National Missile Defense system capable of defending the territory of the United States against limited ballistic missile attack (whether accidental, unauthorized, or deliberate) with funding subject to the annual authorization of appropriations and the annual appropriation of funds for National Missile Defense." The Administration's program on missile defense is fully consistent with this policy.

Missile Defense Program

Upon taking office, I directed the Secretary of Defense to examine the full range of available technologies and basing modes for missile defenses that could protect the United States, our deployed forces, and our friends and allies. **As I have previously directed,** our policy is to develop and deploy, at the earliest possible date, ballistic missile defenses drawing on the best technologies available.

The Administration has also eliminated the artificial distinction between "national" and "theater" missile defenses.

- The defenses we will develop and deploy must be capable of not only defending the United States and our deployed forces, but also friends and allies;

- The distinction between theater and national defenses was largely a product of the ABM Treaty and is outmoded. For example, some of the systems we are pursuing, such as boost-phase defenses, are **intended to be** capable of intercepting missiles of all ranges, blurring the distinction between theater and national defenses; and
- The terms "theater" and "national" are interchangeable depending on the circumstances, and thus are not a meaningful means of categorizing missile defenses. For example, some of the systems being pursued by the United States to protect deployed forces are capable of defending the entire national territory of some friends and allies, thereby meeting the definition of a "national" missile defense system.

Building on previous missile defense work, over the past year and a half, the Defense Department has pursued a robust research, development, testing, and evaluation program designed to develop layered defenses capable of intercepting missiles of varying ranges in all phases of flight. The testing regimen employed has become increasingly stressing, and the results of recent tests have been impressive.

Fielding Missile Defenses

In light of the changed security environment and progress made to date in our development efforts, the United States plans to begin deployment of a set of missile defense capabilities in 2004. These capabilities will serve as a starting point for fielding improved and expanded missile defense capabilities later.

The Defense Department plans to employ an evolutionary approach to the development and deployment of missile defenses to improve our defenses over time. The United States will not have a final, fixed missile defense architecture. Rather, we will deploy an initial set of capabilities that will evolve to meet the changing threat and to take advantage of technological developments. The composition of missile defenses, to include the number and location of systems deployed, will change over time.

In August 2002, the **Secretary of Defense** proposed an evolutionary way ahead for the deployment of missile defenses. The capabilities planned for operational use in 2004 and 2005 will include ground-based interceptors, sea-based interceptors, additional Patriot (PAC-3) units, and sensors based on land, at sea, and in space. In addition, the United States will **seek permission respectively from the U.K. and Denmark** to upgrade early-warning radars **in Fylingdales and Thule, Greenland** as part of our capability.

Under the approach **presented by the Secretary of Defense,** these capabilities may be improved through additional measures such as:

- Deployment of additional ground- and sea-based interceptors, and Patriot (PAC-3) units;
- Initial deployment of the THAAD and Airborne Laser systems;
- Development of a family of boost-phase and midcourse hit-to-kill interceptors based on sea-, air-, and ground-based platforms;
- Enhanced sensor capabilities; and
- Development and testing of space-based defenses.

The Defense Department **shall** begin to **execute** the approach **proposed by the Secretary of Defense** and **shall proceed** with plans to deploy a set of initial missile defense capabilities beginning in 2004. **Recognizing the evolutionary nature of our missile defense program, the Secretary of Defense, as appropriate, shall update me and propose changes.**

Cooperation with Friends and Allies

Because the threats of the 21st century also endanger our friends and allies around the world, it is essential that we work together to defend against these threats. Missile defense cooperation will be a feature of U.S. relations with close, long-standing allies, and an important means to build new relationships with new friends like Russia.

- **The Department of Defense shall** develop and deploy missile defenses capable of protecting not only the United States and our deployed forces, but also friends and allies;
- **The Secretary of Defense shall** also structure the missile defense program in a manner that encourages industrial participation by friends and allies, consistent with overall U.S. national security; and
- **The Secretaries of Defense and State shall** promote international missile defense cooperation, including within bilateral and alliance structures such as NATO, **and shall negotiate appropriate arrangements for this purpose.**

As part of our efforts to deepen missile defense cooperation with friends and allies, the United States **shall** seek to eliminate **unnecessary** impediments to such cooperation. **The Secretaries of Defense and State shall** review existing policies and practices governing technology sharing and cooperation on missile defense, including U.S. export control regulations and statutes, with this aim in mind. **They shall issue a report with**

recommendations for improvements including, if appropriate, proposals for statutory changes within 6 months. This review will be a related, but distinct part of the broader effort to update and strengthen all U.S. export controls, as called for in the National Strategy to Combat Weapons of Mass Destruction.

The goal of the Missile Technology Control Regime (MTCR) is to help reduce the global missile threat by curbing the flow of missiles and related technology to proliferators. The MTCR and missile defenses play complementary roles in countering the global missile threat. The United States intends to implement the MTCR in a manner that does not impede missile defense cooperation with friends and allies. **In support of these objectives, the Secretaries of Defense and State shall review U.S. policy concerning the impact of U.S. commitments under the MTCR on cooperation and transfers of missile defense systems and technology to other countries and issue a joint report in 6 months on the results of that review. The report should include any recommendations for improvements to existing policies and practices.**

Conclusion

The new strategic challenges of the 21st century require us to think differently, but they also require us to act. The deployment of effective missile defenses is an essential element of the United States' broader efforts to transform our defense and deterrence policies and capabilities to meet the new threats we face. Defending the American people against these new threats is **my highest priority as Commander in Chief, and** the highest priority **of my Administration.**

[signed:] GEORGE W. BUSH

Source: Federation of American Scientists. Available online. URL: http://www.fasorg.irp/offdoes/nspd/nspd-23.htm. Accessed December 24, 2008.

U.S. Request to Extend Chemical Weapons Convention (CWC) Deadline for Complete Destruction of Chemical Weapons Stocks (April 20, 2006)

This fact sheet issued by the U.S. Department of State notes that the United States is requesting a extension of the deadline to destroy its chemical weapons stocks from 2007 to 2012. The fact sheet outlines the U.S. record in destroying its chemical weapons, the reasons the extension is needed, the plan for destroying the remaining chemical weapons stockpile, and the status of each facility engaged in carrying out the task.

Fact Sheet
Bureau of International Security and Nonproliferation (ISN)
Washington, DC
April 20, 2006

U.S. Request to Extend Chemical Weapons Convention (CWC) Deadline for Complete Destruction of Chemical Weapons Stocks

- The United States is requesting an extension of the Chemical Weapons Convention (CWC) deadline for destroying 100% of CW stocks from April 29, 2007 to April 29, 2012. (The CWC requires such a request be submitted by April 29, 2006.)
- The U.S. remains deeply committed to the CWC and eliminating its entire stockpile of chemical weapons by the earliest possible date, in a safe and secure manner.

The U.S. Record to Date on CW Destruction

- As of March 31, 2006 the U.S. has destroyed 10,103 metric tons of chemical agent since Entry-into-Force of the CWC, or 36.4% of its declared inventory of 27,768 metric tons, far more than all other declared CW possessors combined.
- The U.S. has completed operations at two chemical weapons destruction facilities (CWDFs) at Johnston Island and Aberdeen, Maryland. Six other major facilities are currently operating. Site preparations are underway for construction of the final two CWDFs.
- The U.S. met its 1% and 20% destruction deadlines early, and is working towards its 45% destruction milestone date of December 31, 2007, as extended by the OPCW.
- The U.S. has devoted enormous resources to the effort to safely and expeditiously destroy its CW stocks, including over $1.5 billion in 2005, and a projected $32–34 billion over the lifetime of the project (for comparison—total 2005 budget for OPCW was $91.6 million).
- Have concentrated on destroying our most lethal weapons first, specifically VX and sarin nerve agent, with over 86% of the latter already destroyed. Will finish destruction of binary agents—our most modern stocks—by the end of 2007.

Reasons for the Proposed Extension

- Destroying the world's 2nd largest stockpile safely is extraordinarily difficult and complex.
- The U.S. has encountered delays in initiating operations and lower-than-planned destruction rates for reasons listed below:
- Delays in obtaining environmental permits necessary to start operations;
- Start-up delays due to additional community emergency preparedness requirements;
- Longer than projected downtime for maintenance and changeover to other agents;
- Work stoppages to investigate and resolve problems, along with reductions in throughout;
- Development of protocols to improve operational safety; and
- Deteriorating munitions more challenging to handle and safely destroy than anticipated.
- The U.S. continues to improve as the program progresses, incorporating lessons learned at the start of each new facility.

Plan for Destruction During the Proposed Extension

- The U.S. plans to incorporate lessons learned and risk mitigation measures that may accelerate the schedule of chemical agent destruction, but at this time, we do not expect to be able to meet the April 29, 2012 deadline for destruction of the U.S. declared CW stockpile.
- Current projections indicate that four facilities will be operating past 2012 (Tooele. Anniston, Umatilla, and Pine Bluff), and two facilities that have not yet been constructed (in Pueblo and Bluegrass) are expected to commence destruction operations no earlier than 2011.
- The U.S. has evaluated a number of alternatives to improve our CW destruction progress in order to meet the existing timelines, but has not identified at this time an option or combination of options that would result in the U.S. meeting the 2012 extended deadline.
- The U.S. continues to seek opportunities to improve our CW destruction progress in order to complete destruction with the goal of reaching the 2012 deadline or if that is not possible completing destruction as soon as feasible thereafter.

Status of Each Main CWDF

- Johnston Atoll Chemical Agent Disposal System has completed operations, destroying 640 metric tons of agents by November 2000.
- Hawthorne (NV) has completed destruction of 458 metric tons of binary precursor chemicals contained in canisters in projectiles in July 1999.
- Aberdeen (MD) Chemical Agent Disposal Facility (ABCDF) has completed operations, destroying 1472 metric tons of agent by February 2006. This facility used neutralization followed by bio-treatment to destroy mustard agent (HD) drained from ton containers.
- Anniston (AL) Chemical Agent Disposal Facility (ANCDF) began operations in August 2003, and has destroyed by incineration all 397 metric tons of GB, with 1,648 metric tons of other agents remaining. Start-up was delayed 7 months to implement additional community emergency preparedness. Currently inactive while preparing for destruction of VX.
- Blue Grass (KY) Chemical Agent Disposal Pilot Plant (BGCAPP) is currently in the design phase, with 475 metric tons to be destroyed. Will use neutralization, followed by supercritical water oxidation, to destroy GB, VX, and HD. Projected to start in 2011.
- Newport (IN) Chemical Agent Disposal Facility (NECDF) began operations in May 2005 to neutralize bulk nerve agent (VX) totaling 1,152 metric tons. Resulting hydrolysate is currently stored in intermodal containers awaiting a decision on off-site treatment/disposal.
- Pine Bluff (AR) Binary Destruction Facility (PBBDF) began operations in December 2005 to destroy DF and QL stocks totaling 161 metric tons. Using neutralization, followed by wet air oxidation, will destroy binary stocks by the end of 2007.
- Pine Bluff (AR) Chemical Agent Disposal Facility (PBCDF) began operations in March 2005, and has destroyed 166 metric tons of GB using incineration, with 3,327 metric tons remaining. Currently inactive undergoing maintenance, expected to resume by 15 May.
- Pueblo (CO) Chemical Agent Disposal Pilot Plant (PCAPP) is currently in the design phase, with 2,371 metric tons to be destroyed. Will use neutralization followed by biotreatment to destroy mustard agent. Projected to start in 2011.
- Tooele (UT) Chemical Agent Disposal Facility (TOCDF) began operations in August 1996, and has destroyed 6,489 metric tons of CW since EIF using incineration, including all GB and VX, with 5.632 metric tons remaining. Facility was shut down 8 months to implement a

new safety plan following an incident of worker exposure to a minute amount of agent. Currently inactive preparing for destruction of mustard agent. Contamination of some mustard stocks with mercury raises complications.

- Umatilla (OR) Chemical Agent Disposal Facility (UMCDF) began operations in September 2004, and has destroyed 478 metric tons of GB stocks using incineration, with 2,896 metric tons remaining. Encountering delays as a result of repeated fires in the explosive containment rooms during the rocket shearing process. Steps were taken to mitigate any safety issues.

Source: U.S. Department of State. Available online. URL: http://www.state.gov/t/isn/rls/fs/64874.htm. Accessed July 15, 2008.

U.S. Army Chemical Materials Agency Announcement on Destruction of Half of the Chemical Munitions in the National Stockpile (August 30, 2006)

This news release by the agency responsible for the destruction of the U.S. chemical weapons arsenal announces that as of August 2006 half of the chemical weapons in the U.S. arsenal have been destroyed. Those weapons contained 39 percent (by weight) of the chemical agents in the stockpile.

For Immediate Release
August 30, 2006

U.S. Army Chemical Materials Agency destroys half of total number of munitions in national stockpile

ABERDEEN PROVING GROUND, Md.—The U.S. Army announced today the destruction of 50 percent of the number of munitions in its declared chemical stockpile.

This achievement demonstrates the United States' commitment to its international obligations as a signatory to the Chemical Weapons Convention (CWC). When the United States ratified the CWC in 1997, they agreed to stop producing, stockpiling or transferring chemical weapons.

Since beginning chemical weapons destruction, the U.S. Army Chemical Materials Agency (CMA) has destroyed more than 1.7 million munitions of the total original stockpile. The stockpile includes bombs, rockets, mortars, projectiles, land mines and spray tanks filled with nerve agents GB (sarin) and VX, plus blister agents H, HD and HT (mustard).

CMA has been disposing of chemical munitions since 1990 when it began munitions destruction at Johnston Atoll Chemical Agent Disposal System (JACADS), located 825 miles southwest of Honolulu, Hawaii. The JACADS disposal mission was completed in 2000, and the site remains a wildlife refuge. Aberdeen, Md. was the first facility within the continental United States to destroy its stockpile; an important milestone achieved in 2006. Other disposal missions began at each site as follows: Utah in 1996, Alabama in 2003, Oregon in 2004, and Indiana plus Arkansas in 2005. The munitions destroyed to date contained more than 39 percent of the total amount of agent, by weight, in the original stockpile.

CMA maintains high safety standards for its workers, the public and the environment. In achieving this 50 percent milestone, CMA successfully overcame operational challenges in the chemical weapons disposal project, including permitting delays and facility work stoppages. In particular, delays resulted from the challenges associated with obtaining, modifying and/or closing environmental permits. In addition, unexpected facility work stoppages were necessary to evaluate and correct problems.

CMA will safely lower the public risk associated with these aging munitions by ultimately eliminating all of the United States' stockpile of chemical weapons.

. . .

Source: U.S. Army Chemical Weapons Agency. Available online. URL: http://www.cma.army.mil/fndocumentviewer.aspx?docid=003675943. Accessed July 16, 2008.

Homeland Security Presidential Directive 18: Medical Countermeasures against Weapons of Mass Destruction (January 31, 2007)

Homeland Security Presidential Directives (HSPDs) were issued during the administration of George W. Bush (2001–09) to communicate information regarding issues of homeland security. HSPD-18 focuses on preparations against an attack by terrorists using weapons of mass destruction. It admits that it is not possible to have medical resources stockpiled to counter every possible threat. HSPD-18 outlines three principles to most effectively meet the challenges ahead: focus on the threat agents most likely to be used by hostile states or terrorist organizations to cause catastrophic damage; invest in the medical countermeasures with the best potential to prevent, treat, or mitigate that damage; link medical countermeasures to deployment strategies that federal, state, and local authorities are likely to be able to carry out. HSPD-18 was issued on January 31, 2007, and released to the public by the White House on February 7, 2007.

Homeland Security Presidential Directive/HSPD-18

January 31, 2007

Subject: Medical Countermeasures against Weapons of Mass Destruction

Background

(1) Weapons of Mass Destruction (WMD)—chemical, biological, radiological, and nuclear agents (CBRN)—in the possession of hostile states or terrorists represent one of the greatest security challenges facing the United States. An attack utilizing WMD potentially could cause mass casualties, compromise critical infrastructure, adversely affect our economy, and inflict social and psychological damage that could negatively affect the American way of life.

(2) Our *National Strategy to Combat Weapons of Mass Destruction* (December 2002) and *Biodefense for the 21st Century* (April 2004) identify response and recovery as key components of our Nation's ability to manage the consequences of a WMD attack. Our primary goal is to prevent such an attack, but we must be fully prepared to respond to and recover from an attack if one occurs. Accordingly, we have made significant investments in our WMD consequence management capabilities in order to mitigate impacts to the public's health, the economy, and our critical infrastructure. The development and acquisition of effective medical countermeasures to mitigate illness, suffering, and death resulting from CBRN agents is central to our consequence management efforts.

(3) It is not presently feasible to develop and stockpile medical countermeasures against every possible threat. The development of vaccines and drugs to prevent or mitigate adverse health effects caused by exposure to biological agents, chemicals, or radiation is a time-consuming and costly process. This directive builds upon the vision and objectives articulated in our

National Strategy to Combat Weapons of Mass Destruction and *Biodefense for the 21st Century* to ensure that our Nation's medical countermeasure research, development, and acquisition efforts:

(a) Target threats that have potential for catastrophic impact on our public health and are subject to medical mitigation;

(b) Yield a rapidly deployable and flexible capability to address both existing and evolving threats;

(c) Are part of an integrated WMD consequence management approach informed by current risk assessments of threats, vulnerabilities, and capabilities; and

(d) Include the development of effective, feasible, and pragmatic concepts of operation for responding to and recovering from an attack.

(4) In order to address the challenges presented by the diverse CBRN threat spectrum, optimize the investments necessary for medical countermeasures development, and ensure that our activities significantly enhance our domestic and international response and recovery capabilities, our decisions as to the research, development, and acquisition of medical countermeasures will be guided by three overarching principles:

(a) Our preparations will focus on countering current and anticipated threat agents that have the greatest potential for use by state and non-state actors to cause catastrophic public health consequences to the American people.

(b) We will invest in medical countermeasures and public health interventions that have the greatest potential to prevent, treat, and mitigate the consequences of WMD threats.

(c) We will link acquisition of medical countermeasures to the existence of effective deployment strategies that are supportable by the present and foreseeable operational and logistic capabilities of Federal, State, and local assets following a WMD attack or other event that presents a catastrophic public health impact.

(5) Mitigating illness and preventing death are the principal goals of our medical countermeasure efforts. As a class, biological agents offer the greatest opportunity for such medical mitigation, and this directive prioritizes our countermeasure efforts accordingly. This directive also provides for

tailoring our Nation's ongoing research and acquisition efforts to continue to yield new countermeasures against CBRN agents and for incorporating such new discoveries into our domestic and international response and recovery planning efforts.

Biological Threats

(6) The biological threat spectrum can be framed in four distinct categories, each of which presents unique challenges and significant opportunities for developing medical countermeasures:

(a)2 Traditional Agents: Traditional agents are naturally occurring microorganisms or toxin products with the potential to be disseminated to cause mass casualties. Examples of traditional agents include *Bacillus anthracis* (anthrax) and *Yersinia pestis* (plague).

(b) Enhanced Agents: Enhanced agents are traditional agents that have been modified or selected to enhance their ability to harm human populations or circumvent current countermeasures, such as a bacterium that has been modified to resist antibiotic treatment.

(c) Emerging Agents: Emerging agents are previously unrecognized pathogens that might be naturally occurring and present a serious risk to human populations, such as the virus responsible for Severe Acute Respiratory Syndrome (SARS). Tools to detect and treat these agents might not exist or might not be widely available.

(d) Advanced Agents: Advanced agents are novel pathogens or other materials of biological nature that have been artificially engineered in the laboratory to bypass traditional countermeasures or produce a more severe or otherwise enhanced spectrum of disease.

Nuclear and Radiological Threats

(7) Threats posed by fissile and other radiological material will persist. Our Nation must improve its biodosimetry capabilities and continue to develop medical countermeasures as appropriate to mitigate the health effects of radiation exposure from the following threats:

(a) Improvised Nuclear Devices: Improvised nuclear devices incorporate radioactive materials designed to result in the formation of a nuclear-yield reaction. Such devices can be wholly fabricated or can be created by modifying a nuclear weapon.

(b) Radiological Dispersal Devices: Radiological Dispersal Devices (RDDs) are devices, other than a nuclear explosive device, designed to disseminate radioactive material to cause destruction, damage, or injury.

(c) Intentional Damage or Destruction of a Nuclear Power Plant: Deliberate acts that cause damage to a reactor core and destruction of the containment facility of a nuclear reactor could contaminate a wide geographic area with radioactive material.

Chemical Threats

(8) Existing and new types of chemicals present a range of threats. Development of targeted medical countermeasures might be warranted for materials in the following categories:

(a) Toxic Industrial Materials and Chemicals: Toxic Industrial Materials and Chemicals are toxic substances in solid, liquid, or gaseous form that are used or stored for use for military or commercial purposes.

(b) Traditional Chemical Warfare Agents: Traditional chemical warfare agents encompass the range of blood, blister, choking, and nerve agents historically developed for warfighter use.

(c) Non-traditional Agents: Non-traditional agents (NTAs) are novel chemical threat or toxicants requiring adapted countermeasures.

(9) Creating defenses against a finite number of known or anticipated agents is a sound approach for mitigating the most catastrophic CBRN threats; however, we also must simultaneously employ a broad-spectrum "flexible" approach to address other current and future threats. We must be capable of responding to a wide variety of potential challenges, including a novel biological agent that is highly communicable, associated with a high rate of morbidity or mortality, and without known countermeasure at the time of its discovery. Although significant technological, organizational, and procedural challenges will have to be overcome, such a balanced strategic approach would mitigate current and future CBRN threats and benefit public health.

Policy

(10) It is the policy of the United States to draw upon the considerable potential of the scientific community in the public and private sectors to address our medical countermeasure requirements relating to CBRN

threats. Our Nation will use a two-tiered approach for development and acquisition of medical countermeasures, which will balance the immediate need to provide a capability to mitigate the most catastrophic of the current CBRN threats with long-term requirements to develop more flexible, broader spectrum countermeasures to address future threats. Our approach also will support regulatory decisions and will permit us to address the broadest range of current and future CBRN threats.

Tier I: Focused Development of Agent-Specific Medical Countermeasures

(11) The first tier uses existing, proven approaches for developing medical countermeasures to address challenges posed by select current and anticipated threats, such as traditional CBRN agents. Recognizing that as threats change our countermeasures might become less effective, we will invest in an integrated and multi-layered defense. Department-level strategies and implementation plans will reflect the following three guiding principles and objectives:

(a) Evaluate and clearly define investments in near- and mid-term defenses: We will develop and use risk assessment processes that integrate data and threat assessments from the life science, consequence management, public health, law enforcement, and intelligence communities to guide investment priorities for current and anticipated threats. We will openly identify the high-risk threats that hold potential for catastrophic consequences to civilian populations and warrant development of targeted countermeasures.

(b) Target medical countermeasure strategies to satisfy practical operational requirements: We will model the potential impact of high-risk threats and develop scenario-based concepts of operations for medical consequence management and public health mitigation and treatment of a large-scale attack on our population. These concepts of operations will guide complementary decisions regarding medical countermeasure development and acquisition.

(c) Take advantage of opportunities to buttress U.S. defenses: We will coordinate interagency efforts to identify and evaluate vulnerabilities in our current arsenal of countermeasures to protect the U.S. population. Where appropriate, we will target the development of alternate or supplementary medical countermeasures to ensure that a multi-layered defense against the most significant high-impact CBRN threats is established.

Tier II: Development of a Flexible Capability for New Medical Countermeasures

(12) Second tier activities will emphasize the need to capitalize upon the development of emerging and future technologies that will enhance our ability to respond flexibly to anticipated, emerging, and future CBRN threats. Importantly, this end-state will foster innovations in medical technologies that will provide broad public health benefit. Department-level strategic and implementation plans will reflect the following guiding principles and objectives:

(a) Integrate fundamental discovery and medical development to realize novel medical countermeasure capabilities: We will target some investments to support the development of broad spectrum approaches to surveillance, diagnostics, prophylactics, and therapeutics that utilize platform technologies. This will require targeted, balanced, and sustained investments between fundamental research to discover new technologies and applied research for technology development to deliver new medical capabilities and countermeasures. Although by no means all-inclusive, our goals could include identification and use of early markers for exposure, greater understanding of host responses to target therapeutics, and development of integrated technologies for rapid production of new countermeasures.

(b) Establish a favorable environment for evaluating new approaches: We must ensure that our investments lead to products that expand the scientific data base, increase the efficiency with which safety and efficacy can be evaluated, and improve the rate at which products under Investigational New Drug or Investigational Device Exemption status progress through the regulatory or approval process. In addition, we must continue to use new tools to evaluate and utilize promising candidates in a time of crisis. Examples of such tools include the "Animal Rule" for testing the efficacy of medical countermeasures against threat agents when human trials are not ethically feasible and the Emergency Use Authorization. Although by no means all-inclusive, our desired end-state could include the use of novel approaches for improved evaluation tools, streamlined clinical trials that meet safety and regulatory needs, and the development and use of novel approaches to manufacturing.

(c) Integrate the products of new and traditional approaches: We must address the challenges that will arise from integrating these new approaches with existing processes. We must incorporate the use of non-pharmacological interventions in our response planning. This integration will forge a flexible biodefense capability that aligns our national requirements for medical countermeasures with the concepts of operation that are used in conjunction with other strategies for mitigating the public health impacts of WMD attacks.

(13) In order to achieve our Tier I and II objectives, it will be necessary to facilitate the development of products and technologies that show promise but are not yet eligible for procurement through BioShield or the Strategic National Stockpile.

We will support the advanced development of these products through targeted investments across a broad portfolio, with the understanding that some of these products may be deemed unsuitable for further investment as additional data becomes available, but the expectation that others will become candidates for procurement.

Policy Actions

(14) We will employ an integrated approach to WMD medical countermeasure development that draws upon the expertise of the public health, life science, defense, homeland security, intelligence, first responder, and law enforcement communities, as well as the private sector, to promote a seamless integration throughout the product development life cycle.

(a) The Secretary of Health and Human Services (Secretary) will lead Federal Government efforts to research, develop, evaluate, and acquire public health emergency medical countermeasures to prevent or mitigate the health effects of CBRN threats facing the U.S. civilian population. The Department of Health and Human Services (HHS) will lead the interagency process and strategic planning and will manage programs supporting medical countermeasures development and acquisition for domestic preparedness.

(i) Stewardship. Not later than 60 days after the date of this directive, the Secretary shall establish an interagency committee to provide advice in setting medical countermeasure requirements and coordinate HHS research, development, and procurement activities. The committee will include representatives designated by the Secretaries of Defense and Homeland Security and the heads of other appropriate executive departments and agencies. This committee will serve as the primary conduit for communication among entities involved in medical countermeasure development.

The chair of the committee shall keep the joint Homeland Security Council/National Security Council Biodefense Policy Coordination Committee apprised of HHS efforts to integrate investment strategies and the Federal Government's progress in the development and acquisition of medical countermeasures.

(ii) Strategic Planning. Not later than 60 days after the date of this directive, the Secretary shall establish a dedicated strategic planning activity to integrate risk-based requirements across the threat spectrum and over the full range of research, early-, mid-, and late-stage development, acquisition, deployment, and life-cycle management of medical countermeasures. The Secretary shall align all relevant HHS programs and functions to support this strategic planning.

(iii) Execution. The Secretary shall ensure that the efforts of component agencies, centers and institutes are coordinated and targeted to facilitate both development of near-term medical countermeasures and transformation of our capability to address future challenges. The Secretary shall also establish an advanced development portfolio that targets investments in promising countermeasures and technologies that are beyond early development, but not yet ready for acquisition consideration. In order to realize the full potential for broad partnership with academia and industry, the Secretary shall ensure that HHS coordinates strategies and implementation plans in a manner that conveys integrated priorities, activities, and objectives across the spectrum of relevant Federal participants.

(iv) Engaging the Private Sector and Nongovernmental Entities. The Secretary shall develop and implement a strategy to engage the unique expertise and capabilities of the private sector in developing medical countermeasures to combat WMD, and shall provide clear and timely communication of HHS priorities and objectives. The Secretary shall consider creating an advisory committee composed of leading experts from academia and the biotech and pharmaceutical industries to provide insight on barriers to progress and help identify promising innovations and solutions to problems such as life-cycle management of medical countermeasures. The Secretary shall designate one office within HHS as the principal liaison for nongovernmental entities who wish to bring new technologies, approaches, or potential medical countermeasures to the attention of the Federal Government.

(b) The Secretary of Defense shall retain exclusive responsibility for research, development, acquisition, and deployment of medical countermeasures to prevent or mitigate the health effects of WMD threats and naturally occurring threats to the Armed Forces and shall continue to direct strategic planning for and oversight of programs to support medical countermeasures development and acquisition for our Armed Forces personnel. The Secretaries of Health and Human Services and Defense shall ensure that the efforts of the Department of Defense (DOD) and HHS are coordinated to promote synergy, minimize redundancy, and, to the extent feasible, use common requirements for medical countermeasure development. The Secretary of Defense shall ensure that DOD continues to draw upon its longstanding investment and experience in WMD medical countermeasure research, development, acquisition, and deployment to ensure protection of the Armed Forces, but also to accelerate and improve the overall national effort, consistent with Departmental authorities and responsibilities, and shall ensure that DOD continues to place a special focus on medical countermeasure development for CBRN threat agents because of the unique facilities, testing capabilities, and trained and experienced personnel within the Department. These efforts will constitute the basis for interagency partnership and combined investment to safeguard the American people.

(c) The Secretary of Homeland Security shall develop a strategic, integrated all-CBRN risk assessment that integrates the findings of the intelligence and law enforcement communities with input from the scientific, medical, and public health communities. Not later than June 1, 2008, the Secretary of Homeland Security shall submit a report to the President through the Assistant to the President for Homeland Security and Counterterrorism, which shall summarize the key findings of this assessment, and shall update those findings when appropriate, but not less frequently than every 2 years. The Department of Homeland Security shall continue to issue Material Threat.

Determinations for those CBRN agents that pose a material threat to national security.

(d) The Secretaries of Health and Human Services, Defense, and Homeland Security shall ensure the availability of the infrastructure required to test and evaluate medical countermeasures for CBRN threat agents.

(i) The Secretaries of Health and Human Services, Defense, and Veterans Affairs shall leverage their partnership to identify and accelerate research, development, testing, and evaluation programs for the acquisition of medical countermeasures for CBRN threats.

(ii) The Secretary of Health and Human Services and the Secretary of Homeland Security shall develop effective and streamlined processes, including mutually agreed-upon timelines, to assist the respective Secretaries in jointly recommending that the Special Reserve Fund (SRF) be used for the acquisition of specified security countermeasures.

(iii) The Director of National Intelligence shall facilitate coordination across the intelligence community and, in coordination with the Attorney General, engage the law enforcement community to provide all relevant and appropriate WMD-related intelligence information to DHS for the development of the integrated CBRN risk assessment that is used in prioritizing the development, acquisition, and maintenance of medical countermeasures.

General

(15) This directive:

(a) shall be implemented consistent with applicable law and the authorities of executive departments and agencies, or heads of such departments and agencies, vested by law, and subject to the availability of appropriations;

(b) shall not be construed to impair or otherwise affect the functions of the Director of the Office of Management and Budget relating to budget, administrative, and legislative proposals; and

(c) is not intended to, and does not, create any rights or benefits, substantive or procedural, enforceable at law or in equity by a party against the United States, its agencies, instrumentalities, or entities, its officers, employees, or agents, or any other person.

GEORGE W. BUSH

. . .

Source: The White House. Available online. URL: http://www.whitehouse.gov/news/releases/2007/02/20070207-2.html. Accessed July 28, 2008.

President Obama's Statement on North Korean Nuclear Test (May 25, 2009)

Immediately after North Korea announced its second nuclear test in May 2009, the White House issued a statement by the president condemning the test as a violation of international law and a threat to international stability. However, the statement did not mention specific actions the United States would take to counter further North Korean nuclear weapons activities.

FOR IMMEDIATE RELEASE May 25, 2009
STATEMENT BY THE PRESIDENT

Today, North Korea said that it has conducted a nuclear test in violation of international law. It appears to also have attempted a short range missile launch. These actions, while not a surprise given its statements and actions to date, are a matter of grave concern to all nations. North Korea's attempts to develop nuclear weapons, as well as its ballistic missile program, constitute a threat to international peace and security.

By acting in blatant defiance of the United Nations Security Council, North Korea is directly and recklessly challenging the international community. North Korea's behavior increases tensions and undermines stability in Northeast Asia. Such provocations will only serve to deepen North Korea's isolation. It will not find international acceptance unless it abandons its pursuit of weapons of mass destruction and their means of delivery.

The danger posed by North Korea's threatening activities warrants action by the international community. We have been and will continue working with our allies and partners in the Six-Party Talks as well as other members of the U.N. Security Council in the days ahead.

Source: The White House. Available online. URL: http://www.whitehouse.gov/the_press_office/STATEMENT-FROM-THE-PRESIDENT-RE GARDING-NORTH-KOREA/. Accessed June 2, 2009.

5

International Documents

The documents in this chapter fall into five categories. There are four international treaties signed by many countries, dating from 1925 to 1993. Three of them deal with chemical or biological weapons while one, the NPT, deals with nuclear weapons. There are six documents that deal with nuclear weapons agreements between the United States and the Soviet Union or, after 1991, Russia. Five are treaties, and one is a U.S. State Department fact sheet. The documents in the next three categories deal with Israel, India/Pakistan, and North Korea, respectively. The shorter documents are reprinted here in their entirety while the longer ones are excerpted.

INTERNATIONAL TREATIES

Protocol for the Prohibition of the Use in War of Asphyxiating, Poisonous, or Other Gasses, and of Bacteriological Methods of Warfare (June 17, 1925)

The Geneva Protocol, as it is commonly known since it was signed in the city of Geneva, was a response to the use of poison gas by all major combatants during World War I. However, like the prewar Hague conventions of 1899 and 1907, the Geneva Protocol had no enforcement mechanisms. Spain and Italy, countries that signed the protocol, respectively used chemical weapons in the 1920s and 1930s, while Japan, which did not sign, used WMD extensively against Chinese soldiers and civilians between 1937 and 1945. It is generally agreed that the reason Germany did not use its arsenal of advanced chemical weapons during World War II was that its leaders feared retaliation by the Allies. In short, the Geneva Protocol was a failure.

Protocol for the Prohibition of the Use in War of Asphyxiating, Poisonous or Other Gases, and of Bacteriological Methods of Warfare

Signed at Geneva June 17, 1925
Entered into force February 8, 1928
Ratification advised by the U.S. Senate December 16, 1974
Ratified by U.S. President January 22, 1975
U.S. ratification deposited with the Government of France April 10, 1975

Proclaimed by U.S. President April 29, 1975

The Undersigned Plenipotentiaries, in the name of their respective Governments:

Whereas the use in war of asphyxiating, poisonous or other gases, and of all analogous liquids, materials or devices, has been justly condemned by the general opinion of the civilized world; and

Whereas the prohibition of such use has been declared in Treaties to which the majority of Powers of the World are Parties; and

To the end that this prohibition shall be universally accepted as a part of International Law, binding alike the conscience and the practice of nations:

Declare:

That the High Contracting Parties, so far as they are not already Parties to Treaties prohibiting such use, accept this prohibition, agree to extend this prohibition to the use of bacteriological methods of warfare and agree to be bound as between themselves according to the terms of this declaration.

The High Contracting Parties will exert every effort to induce other States to accede to the present Protocol. Such accession will be notified to the Government of the French Republic, and by the latter to all signatory and acceding Powers, and will take effect on the date of the notification by the Government of the French Republic.

The present Protocol, of which the French and English texts are both authentic, shall be ratified as soon as possible. It shall bear today's date.

The ratifications of the present Protocol shall be addressed to the Government of the French Republic, which will at once notify the deposit of such ratification to each of the signatory and acceding Powers.

The instruments of ratification of and accession to the present Protocol will remain deposited in the archives of the Government of the French Republic.

The present Protocol will come into force for each signatory Power as from the date of deposit of its ratification, and, from that moment, each Power will be bound as regards other powers which have already deposited their ratifications.

IN WITNESS WHEREOF the Plenipotentiaries have signed the present Protocol.

DONE at Geneva in a single copy, this seventeenth day of June, One Thousand Nine Hundred and Twenty-Five.

Source: United States Arms Control and Disarmament Agency. *Arms Control and Disarmament Agreements: Texts and Histories of the Negotiations*. Washington, D.C.: United States Arms Control and Disarmament Agency, 1990, p. 15.

Treaty on the Non-Proliferation of Nuclear Weapons (NPT) (July 1, 1968)

In the immediate aftermath of World War II, efforts to achieve an agreement that would lead to nuclear disarmament failed. Between 1945 and the mid-1960s, the Soviet Union (in 1949), Great Britain (in 1952), France (in 1960), and the People's Republic of China (in 1964) all became nuclear powers. Meanwhile, in 1961, the UN General Assembly unanimously voted for a resolution calling on all states to negotiate an international agreement to stop the spread of nuclear weapons. These negotiations took place under the auspices of the Eighteen-Nation Disarmament Committee, which was established by the UN in 1962 and met in Geneva. The committee included five Western nations, five nations from the Soviet bloc, and eight countries that were considered neutral in the cold war. The NPT distinguishes between "non-nuclear-weapon" states, accepting the NPT pledge not to develop or acquire nuclear weapons, and "nuclear-weapon" states. It thereby recognizes as nuclear powers five countries that had nuclear weapons as of 1968: the United States, the Soviet Union (its treaty obligations were assumed after 1991 by Russia), Great Britain, France, and the People's Republic of China. According to vague provisions filled with loopholes that were included in the treaty's preamble and Article VI, the nuclear-weapons states pledge to work toward ending the nuclear arms race and overall nuclear disarmament.

Treaty on the Non-Proliferation of Nuclear Weapons

Signed at Washington, London, and Moscow July 1, 1968
Ratification advised by U.S. Senate March 13, 1969
Ratified by U.S. President November 24, 1969

U.S. ratification deposited at Washington, London, and Moscow March 5. 1970

Proclaimed by U.S. President March 5, 1970
Entered into force March 5, 1970

The States concluding this Treaty, hereinafter referred to as the "Parties to the Treaty",

Considering the devastation that would be visited upon all mankind by a nuclear war and the consequent need to make every effort to avert the danger of such a war and to take measures to safeguard the security of peoples,

Believing that the proliferation of nuclear weapons would seriously enhance the danger of nuclear war,

In conformity with resolutions of the United Nations General Assembly calling for the conclusion of an agreement on the prevention of wider dissemination of nuclear weapons,

Undertaking to cooperate in facilitating the application of International Atomic Energy Agency safeguards on peaceful nuclear activities.

Expressing their support for research, development and other efforts to further the application, within the framework of the International Atomic Energy Agency safeguards system, of the principle of safeguarding effectively the flow of source and special fissionable materials by use of instruments and other techniques at certain strategic points,

Affirming the principle that the benefits of peaceful applications of nuclear technology, including any technological by-products which may be derived by nuclear-weapon States from the development of nuclear explosive devices, should be available for peaceful purposes to all Parties of the Treaty, whether nuclear-weapon or non-nuclear weapon States,

Convinced that, in furtherance of this principle, all Parties to the Treaty are entitled to participate in the fullest possible exchange of scientific information for, and to contribute alone or in cooperation with other States to, the further development of the applications of atomic energy for peaceful purposes,

Declaring their intention to achieve at the earliest possible date the cessation of the nuclear arms race and to undertake effective measures in the direction of nuclear disarmament,

Urging the cooperation of all States in the attainment of this objective,

Recalling the determination expressed by the Parties to the 1963 Treaty banning nuclear weapon tests in the atmosphere, in outer space and under water in its Preamble to seek to achieve the discontinuance of all test explosions of nuclear weapons for all time and to continue negotiations to this end,

Desiring to further the easing of international tension and the strengthening of trust between States in order to facilitate the cessation of the manufacture of nuclear weapons, the liquidation of all their existing stockpiles, and the elimination from national arsenals of nuclear weapons and the means of their delivery pursuant to a treaty on general and complete disarmament under strict and effective international control,

Recalling that, in accordance with the Charter of the United Nations, States must refrain in their international relations from the threat or use of force against the territorial integrity or political independence of any State, or in any other manner inconsistent with the Purposes of the United Nations, and that the establishment and maintenance of international peace and security are to be promoted with the least diversion for armaments of the world's human and economic resources,

Have agreed as follows:

Article I

Each nuclear-weapon State Party to the Treaty undertakes not to transfer to any recipient whatsoever nuclear weapons or other nuclear explosive devices or control over such weapons or explosive devices directly, or indirectly; and not in any way to otherwise acquire nuclear weapons or other nuclear explosive devices, or control over such weapons or explosive devices.

Article II

Each non-nuclear-weapon State Party to the Treaty undertakes not to receive the transfer from any transfer or whatsoever of nuclear weapons or other nuclear explosive devices or of control over such weapons or explosive devices directly, or indirectly; not to manufacture or otherwise acquire nuclear weapons or other nuclear explosive devices; and not to seek or receive any assistance in the manufacture of nuclear weapons or other nuclear explosive devices.

Article III

1. Each non-nuclear-weapon State Party to the Treaty undertakes to accept safeguards, as set forth in an agreement to be negotiated and concluded with the International Atomic Energy Agency in accordance with the Statute of the International Atomic Energy Agency and the Agency's safeguards system, for the exclusive purpose of verification of the fulfill-

ment of its obligations assumed under this Treaty with a view to preventing diversion of nuclear energy from peaceful uses to nuclear weapons or other nuclear explosive devices. Procedures for the safeguards required by this article shall be followed with respect to source or special fissionable material whether it is being produced, processed or used in any principal nuclear facility or is outside any such facility. The safeguards required by this article shall be applied to all source or special fissionable material in all peaceful nuclear activities within the territory of such State, under its jurisdiction, or carried out under its control anywhere.

2. Each State Party to the Treaty undertakes not to provide: (a) source or special fissionable material, or (b) equipment or material especially designed or prepared for the processing, use or production of special fissionable material, to any non-nuclear-weapon State for peaceful purposes, unless the source or special fissionable material shall be subject to the safeguards required by this article.

3. The safeguards required by this article shall be implemented in a manner designed to comply with article IV of this Treaty, and to avoid hampering the economic or technological development of the Parties or international cooperation in the field of peaceful nuclear activities, including the international exchange of nuclear material and equipment for the processing, use or production of nuclear material for peaceful purposes in accordance with the provisions of this article and the principle of safeguarding set forth in the Preamble of the Treaty.

4. Non-nuclear-weapon States Party to the Treaty shall conclude agreements with the International Atomic Energy Agency to meet the requirements of this article either individually or together with other States in accordance with the Statute of the International Atomic Energy Agency. Negotiation of such agreements shall commence within 180 days from the original entry into force of this Treaty. For States depositing their instruments of ratification or accession after the 180-day period, negotiation of such agreements shall commence not later than the date of such deposit. Such agreements shall enter into force not later than eighteen months after the date of initiation of negotiations.

Article IV

1. Nothing in this Treaty shall be interpreted as affecting the inalienable right of all the Parties to the Treaty to develop research, production and use of nuclear energy for peaceful purposes without discrimination and in conformity with articles I and II of this Treaty.

2. All the Parties to the Treaty undertake to facilitate, and have the right to participate in, the fullest possible exchange of equipment, materials and scientific and technological information for the peaceful uses of nuclear energy. Parties to the Treaty in a position to do so shall also cooperate in contributing alone or together with other States or international organizations to the further development of the applications of nuclear energy for peaceful purposes, especially in the territories of non-nuclear-weapon States Party to the Treaty, with due consideration for the needs of the developing areas of the world.

Article V

Each party to the Treaty undertakes to take appropriate measures to ensure that, in accordance with this Treaty, under appropriate international observation and through appropriate international procedures, potential benefits from any peaceful applications of nuclear explosions will be made available to non-nuclear-weapon States Party to the Treaty on a nondiscriminatory basis and that the charge to such Parties for the explosive devices used will be as low as possible and exclude any charge for research and development. Non-nuclear-weapon States Party to the Treaty shall be able to obtain such benefits, pursuant to a special international agreement or agreements, through an appropriate international body with adequate representation of non-nuclear-weapon States. Negotiations on this subject shall commence as soon as possible after the Treaty enters into force. Non-nuclear-weapon States Party to the Treaty so desiring may also obtain such benefits pursuant to bilateral agreements.

Article VI

Each of the Parties to the Treaty undertakes to pursue negotiations in good faith on effective measures relating to cessation of the nuclear arms race at an early date and to nuclear disarmament, and on a treaty on general and complete disarmament under strict and effective international control.

Article VII

Nothing in this Treaty affects the right of any group of States to conclude regional treaties in order to assure the total absence of nuclear weapons in their respective territories.

Article VIII

1. Any Party to the Treaty may propose amendments to this Treaty. The text of any proposed amendment shall be submitted to the

Depositary Governments which shall circulate it to all Parties to the Treaty. Thereupon, if requested to do so by one-third or more of the Parties to the Treaty, the Depositary Governments shall convene a conference, to which they shall invite all the Parties to the Treaty, to consider such an amendment.

2. Any amendment to this Treaty must be approved by a majority of the votes of all the Parties to the Treaty, including the votes of all nuclear-weapon States Party to the Treaty and all other Parties which, on the date the amendment is circulated, are members of the Board of Governors of the International Atomic Energy Agency. The amendment shall enter into force for each Party that deposits its instrument of ratification of the amendment upon the deposit of such instruments of ratification by a majority of all the Parties, including the instruments of ratification of all nuclear-weapon States Party to the Treaty and all other Parties which, on the date the amendment is circulated, are members of the Board of Governors of the International Atomic Energy Agency. Thereafter, it shall enter into force for any other Party upon the deposit of its instrument of ratification of the amendment.

3. Five years after the entry into force of this Treaty, a conference of Parties to the Treaty shall be held in Geneva, Switzerland, in order to review the operation of this Treaty with a view to assuring that the purposes of the Preamble and the provisions of the Treaty are being realized. At intervals of five years thereafter, a majority of the Parties to the Treaty may obtain, by submitting a proposal to this effect to the Depositary Governments, the convening of further conferences with the same objective of reviewing the operation of the Treaty.

Article IX

1. This Treaty shall be open to all States for signature. Any State which does not sign the Treaty before its entry into force in accordance with paragraph 3 of this article may accede to it at any time.

2. This Treaty shall be subject to ratification by signatory States. Instruments of ratification and instruments of accession shall be deposited with the Governments of the United States of America, the United Kingdom of Great Britain and Northern Ireland and the Union of Soviet Socialist Republics, which are hereby designated the Depositary Governments.

3. This Treaty shall enter into force after its ratification by the State, the Governments of which are designated Depositaries of the Treaty, and forty other States signatory to this Treaty and the deposit of their instruments of ratification. For the purposes of this Treaty, a nuclear-weapon State is one

which has manufactured and exploded a nuclear weapon or other nuclear explosive device prior to January 1, 1967.

4. For States whose instruments of ratification or accession are deposited subsequent to the entry into force of this Treaty, it shall enter into force on the date of the deposit of their instruments of ratification or accession.

5. The Depositary Governments shall promptly inform all signatory and acceding States of the date of each signature, the date of deposit of each instrument of ratification or of accession, the date of the entry into force of this Treaty, and the date of receipt of any requests for convening a conference or other notices.

6. This Treaty shall be registered by the Depositary Governments pursuant to article 102 of the Charter of the United Nations.

Article X

1. Each Party shall in exercising its national sovereignty have the right to withdraw from the Treaty if it decides that extraordinary events, related to the subject matter of this Treaty, have jeopardized the supreme interests of its country. It shall give notice of such withdrawal to all other Parties to the Treaty and to the United Nations Security Council three months in advance. Such notice shall include a statement of the extraordinary events it regards as having jeopardized its supreme interests.

2. Twenty-five years after the entry into force of the Treaty, a conference shall be convened to decide whether the Treaty shall continue in force indefinitely, or shall be extended for an additional fixed period or periods. This decision shall be taken by a majority of the Parties to the Treaty

Article XI

This Treaty, the English, Russian, French, Spanish and Chinese texts of which are equally authentic, shall be deposited in the archives of the Depositary Governments. Duly certified copies of this Treaty shall be transmitted by the Depositary Governments to the Governments of the signatory and acceding States.

IN WITNESS WHEREOF the undersigned, duty authorized, have signed this Treaty.

DONE in triplicate, at the cities of Washington, London, and Moscow, this first day of July one thousand nine hundred sixty-eight.

Source: United States Arms Control and Disarmament Agency. *Arms Control and Disarmament Agreements: Texts and Histories of the Negotiations.* Washington, D.C.: United States Arms Control and Disarmament Agency, 1990, pp. 98–102.

Convention on the Prohibition of the Development, Production, and Stockpiling of Bacteriological (Biological) and Toxin Weapons and on Their Destruction (Biological Weapons Convention) (April 10, 1972)

The negotiations that eventually led to the Biological Weapons Convention began in 1970 and initially included chemical weapons as well. Many of the discussions took place under the auspices of the Conference of the Committee on Disarmament (CCD), the new name for the Eighteen-Nation Disarmament Committee after it was enlarged to 26 countries in 1969. However, the negotiations stalled until chemical weapons were dropped from the agenda and all efforts focused on biological weapons. The BWC that emerged from these negotiations in 1972 was toothless, as it had no inspection or enforcement mechanisms. The Soviet Union signed the agreement in 1972, ratified it in 1975, and then proceeded to operate the world's largest biological weapons program into the 1990s. Not until 1992, by which time the Soviet Union had collapsed, did Russia admit its existence. The BWC has not been ratified by several countries known to have offensive biological weapons programs.

Convention on the Prohibition of the Development, Production and Stockpiling of Bacteriological (Biological) and Toxin Weapons and on Their Destruction

Signed at Washington, London, and Moscow April 10, 1972
Ratification advised by U.S. Senate December 16, 1974
Ratified by U.S. President January 22, 1975
U.S. ratification deposited at Washington, London, and Moscow March 26, 1975

Proclaimed by U.S. President March 26, 1975
Entered into force March 26, 1975

The States Parties to this Convention,

Determined to act with a view to achieving effective progress towards general and complete disarmament, including the prohibition and elimination of all types of weapons of mass destruction, and convinced that the prohibition of the development, production and stockpiling of chemical and bacteriological (biological) weapons and their elimination, through effective measures, will facilitate the achievement of general and complete disarmament under strict and effective international control,

Recognizing the important significance of the Protocol for the Prohibition of the Use in War of Asphyxiating, Poisonous or Other Gases, and of Bacteriological Methods of Warfare, signed at Geneva on June 17, 1925, and conscious also of the contribution which the said Protocol has already made, and continues to make, to mitigating the horrors of war,

Reaffirming their adherence to the principles and objectives of that Protocol and calling upon all States to comply strictly with them,

Recalling that the General Assembly of the United Nations has repeatedly condemned all actions contrary to the principles and objectives of the Geneva Protocol of June 17, 1925,

Desiring to contribute to the strengthening of confidence between peoples and the general improvement of the international atmosphere,

Desiring also to contribute to the realization of the purposes and principles of the Charter of the United Nations,

Convinced of the importance and urgency of eliminating from the arsenals of States, through effective measures, such dangerous weapons of mass destruction as those using chemical or bacteriological (biological) agents,

Recognizing that an agreement on the prohibition of bacteriological (biological) and toxin weapons represents a first possible step towards the achievement of agreement on effective measures also for the prohibition of the development, production and stockpiling of chemical weapons, and determined to continue negotiations to that end,

Determined, for the sake of all mankind, to exclude completely the possibility of bacteriological (biological) agents and toxins being used as weapons,

Convinced that such use would be repugnant to the conscience of mankind and that no effort should be spared to minimize this risk,

Have agreed as follows:

Article I

Each State Party to this Convention undertakes never in any circumstances to develop, produce, stockpile or otherwise acquire or retain:

(1) Microbial or other biological agents, or toxins whatever their origin or method of production, of types and in quantities that have no justification for prophylactic, protective or other peaceful purposes;

(2) Weapons, equipment or means of delivery designed to use such agents or toxins for hostile purposes or in armed conflict.

Article II

Each State Party to this Convention undertakes to destroy, or to divert to peaceful purposes, as soon as possible but not later than nine months after the entry into force of the Convention, all agents, toxins, weapons, equipment and means of delivery specified in article I of the Convention, which are in its possession or under its jurisdiction or control. In implementing the provisions of this article all necessary safety precautions shall be observed to protect populations and the environment.

Article III

Each State Party to this Convention undertakes not to transfer to any recipient whatsoever, directly or indirectly, and not in any way to assist, encourage, or induce any State, group of States or international organizations to manufacture or otherwise acquire any of the agents, toxins, weapons, equipment or means of delivery specified in article I of the Convention.

Article IV

Each State Party to this Convention shall, in accordance with its constitutional processes, take any necessary measures to prohibit and prevent the development, production, stockpiling, acquisition, or retention of the agents, toxins, weapons, equipment and means of delivery specified in article I of the Convention, within the territory of such State, under its jurisdiction or under its control anywhere.

Article V

The States Parties to this Convention undertake to consult one another and to cooperate in solving any problems which may arise in relation to the objective of, or in the application of the provisions of, the Convention. Consultation and cooperation pursuant to this article may also be undertaken through appropriate international procedures within the framework of the United Nations and in accordance with its Charter.

Article VI

(1) Any State Party to this Convention which finds that any other State Party is acting in breach of obligations deriving from the provisions of the Convention may lodge a complaint with the Security Council of the United Nations. Such a complaint should include all possible evidence confirming its validity, as well as a request for its consideration by the Security Council.

(2) Each State Party to this Convention undertakes to cooperate in carrying out any investigation which the Security Council may initiate, in accordance with the provisions of the Charter of the United Nations, on the basis of the complaint received by the Council. The Security Council shall inform the States Parties to the Convention of the results of the investigation.

Article VII

Each State Party to this Convention undertakes to provide or support assistance, in accordance with the United Nations Charter, to any Party to the Convention which so requests, if the Security Council decides that such Party has been exposed to danger as a result of violation of the Convention.

Article VIII

Nothing in this Convention shall be interpreted as in any way limiting or detracting from the obligations assumed by any State under the Protocol for the Prohibition of the Use in War of Asphyxiating, Poisonous or Other Gases, and of Bacteriological Methods of Warfare, signed at Geneva on June 17, 1925.

Article IX

Each State Party to this Convention affirms the recognized objective of effective prohibition of chemical weapons and, to this end, undertakes to continue negotiations in good faith with a view to reaching early agreement on effective measures for the prohibition of their development, production and stockpiling and for their destruction, and on appropriate measures concerning equipment and means of delivery specifically designed for the production or use of chemical agents for weapons purposes.

Article X

(1) The States Parties to this Convention undertake to facilitate, and have the right to participate in, the fullest possible exchange of equipment, materials and scientific and technological information for the use of bacteriological (biological) agents and toxins for peaceful purposes. Parties to the Convention in a position to do so shall also cooperate in contributing individually or together with other States or international organizations to the further development and application of scientific discoveries in the field of bacteriology (biology) for prevention of disease, or for other peaceful purposes.

(2) This Convention shall be implemented in a manner designed to avoid hampering the economic or technological development of States Parties to the Convention or international cooperation in the field of peaceful bacteriological (biological) activities, including the international exchange of bacteriological (biological) agents and toxins and equipment for the processing, use or production of bacteriological (biological) agents and toxins for peaceful purposes in accordance with the provisions of the Convention.

Article XI

Any State Party may propose amendments to this Convention. Amendments shall enter into force for each State Party accepting the amendments upon their acceptance by a majority of the States Parties to the Convention and thereafter for each remaining State Party on the date of acceptance by it.

Article XII

Five years after the entry into force of this Convention, or earlier if it is requested by a majority of Parties to the Convention by submitting a proposal to this effect to the Depositary Governments, a conference of States Parties to the Convention shall be held at Geneva, Switzerland, to review the operation of the Convention, with a view to assuring that the purposes of the preamble and the provisions of the Convention, including the provisions concerning negotiations on chemical weapons, are being realized. Such review shall take into account any new scientific and technological developments relevant to the Convention.

Article XIII

(1) This Convention shall be of unlimited duration.

(2) Each State Party to this Convention shall in exercising its national sovereignty have the right to withdraw from the Convention if it decides that

extraordinary events, related to the subject matter of the Convention, have jeopardized the supreme interests of its country. It shall give notice of such withdrawal to all other States Parties to the Convention and to the United Nations Security Council three months in advance. Such notice shall include a statement of the extraordinary events it regards as having jeopardized its supreme interests.

Article XIV

(1) This Convention shall be open to all States for signature. Any State which does not sign the Convention before its entry into force in accordance with paragraph (3) of this Article may accede to it at any time.

(2) This Convention shall be subject to ratification by signatory States. Instruments of ratification and instruments of accession shall be deposited with the Governments of the United States of America, the United Kingdom of Great Britain and Northern Ireland and the Union of Soviet Socialist Republics, which are hereby designated the Depositary Governments.

(3) This Convention shall enter into force after the deposit of instruments of ratification by twenty-two Governments, including the Governments designated as Depositaries of the Convention.

(4) For States whose instruments of ratification or accession are deposited subsequent to the entry into force of this Convention, it shall enter into force on the date of the deposit of their instruments of ratification or accession.

(5) The Depositary Governments shall promptly inform all signatory and acceding States of the date of each signature, the date of deposit of each instrument of ratification or of accession and the date of the entry into force of this Convention, and of the receipt of other notices.

(6) This Convention shall be registered by the Depositary Governments pursuant to Article 102 of the Charter of the United Nations.

Article XV

This Convention, the English, Russian, French, Spanish and Chinese texts of which are equally authentic, shall be deposited in the archives of the Depositary Governments. Duly certified copies of the Convention shall be transmitted by the Depositary Governments to the Governments of the signatory and acceding states.

IN WITNESS WHEREOF the undersigned, duly authorized, have signed this Convention.

DONE in triplicate, at the cities of Washington, London and Moscow, this tenth day of April, one thousand nine hundred and seventy-two.

Source: Federation of American Scientists. Available online. URL: http://www.fas.org/nuke/control/bwc/text/bwc.htm. Accessed July 19, 2008.

Convention on Prohibition of the Development, Production, Stockpiling, and Use of Chemical Weapons and Their Destruction. (Chemical Weapons Convention) (January 13, 1993) (excerpt)

The Chemical Weapons Convention was the product of a decade of negotiations. It was adopted by the UN General Assembly on November 30, 1992, opened for signature in Paris on January 13, 1993, and officially entered into force on April 29, 1997. The convention bans all development, production, stockpiling, transfer, and use of chemical weapons. It also requires each nation that is a party to the agreement to destroy all its chemical weapons and facilities that can produce them. The CWC includes lengthy verification provisions that involve reporting and on-site inspections. It also contains provisions to provide help if a country that is party to the agreement is attacked or threatened with attack by chemical weapons. The Organization for the Prohibition of Chemical Weapons (OPCW), which is based in the Hague in the Netherlands, is responsible for enforcing the CWC. The Preamble and Article I, which summarizes the obligations of each country that is party to the agreement, are reproduced below.

Convention on the Prohibition of the Development, Production, Stockpiling and Use of Chemical Weapons and Their Destruction

PREAMBLE

The States Parties to this Convention.

Determined to act with a view to achieving effective progress towards general and complete disarmament under strict and effective international control, including the prohibition and elimination of all types of weapons of mass destruction,

Desiring to contribute to the realization of the purposes and principles of the Charter of the United Nations,

Recalling that the General Assembly of the United Nations has repeatedly condemned all actions contrary to the principles and objectives of the Protocol for the Prohibition of the Use in War of Asphyxiation, Poisonous or Other Gases, and of Bacteriological Methods of Warfare, signed at Geneva on 17 June 1925 (the Geneva Protocol of 1925),

Recognizing that this Convention reaffirms principles and objectives of and obligation assumed under the Geneva Protocol of 1925, and the Convention on the Prohibition of the Development, Production and Stockpiling of Bacteriological (Biological) and Toxin Weapons and on their Destruction signed at London, Moscow and Washington on 10 April 1972,

Bearing in mind the objective contained in Article IX of the Convention on the Prohibition of the Development, Production and Stockpiling of Bacteriological (Biological) and Toxin Weapons and their Destruction,

Determined for the sake of all mankind, to exclude completely the possibility of the use of chemical weapons, through the implementation of the provisions of this Convention, thereby complementing the obligations assumed under the Geneva Protocol of 1925,

Recognizing the prohibition, embodied in the pertinent agreements and relevant principles of international law, of the use of herbicides as a method of warfare,

Considering that achievements in the field of chemistry should be used exclusively for the benefit of mankind,

Desiring to promote free trade in chemicals as well as international cooperation and exchange of scientific and technical information in the field of chemical activities for purposes not prohibited under this Convention in order to enhance the economic and technological development of all States Parties,

Convinced that the complete and effective prohibition of the development, production, acquisition, stockpiling, retention, transfer and use of chemical weapons, and their destruction, represent a necessary step towards the achievement of these common objectives,

Have Agreed as follows:

Article I

GENERAL OBLIGATIONS

1. Each State Party to this Convention undertakes never under any circumstances:

(a) To develop, produce, otherwise acquire, stockpile or retain chemical weapons, or transfer, directly or indirectly, chemical weapons to anyone;

(b) To use chemical weapons;

(c) To engage in any military preparations to use chemical weapons;

(d) To assist, encourage or induce, in any way, anyone to engage in any activity prohibited to a State Party under this Convention.

2. Each State Party undertakes to destroy chemical weapons it owns or possesses, or that are located in any place under its jurisdiction or control, in accordance with the provisions of this Convention.

3. Each State Party undertakes to destroy all chemical weapons it abandoned on the territory of another State Party, in accordance with the provisions of this Convention.

4. Each State Party undertakes to destroy any chemical weapons production facilities it owns or possesses, or that are located in any place under its jurisdiction or control, in accordance with the provisions of this Convention.

5. Each State Party undertakes not to use riot control agents as a method of warfare.

Source: United States Chemical Weapons Convention Web Site. Available online. URLs: http://www.cwc.gov/cwc_treaty_preamble.html; http://www.cwc.gov/cwc_treaty_article_01.html. Accessed December 26, 2008.

TREATIES BETWEEN THE UNITED STATES AND THE SOVIET UNION

SALT I: Treaty between the United States of America and the Union of Soviet Socialist Republics on the Limitation of Anti-Ballistic Missile Systems (May 26, 1972)

The ABM treaty is one of the two treaties that made up the 1972 SALT I agreement between the Soviet Union and the United States. SALT I was the first agreement to put some limits on the cold war nuclear arms race between the two superpowers. The logic underpinning the ABM treaty was that the best way to avoid a nuclear war between the United States and the Soviet Union was to guarantee that neither country could fight such a war without suffering intolerable losses. This idea was called "mutually assured destruction," or MAD. As long as MAD was operative, the reasoning went, neither side would attack the other with nuclear weapons. This in turn required that each superpower had to protect its nuclear arsenal so it could retaliate with devastating force—called a "second strike"—if attacked. The inevitability of a "second strike" would deter a first strike. In order to guarantee the ability to launch a second strike, both the Soviet Union and the United States built nuclear arsenals that included land-based missiles, submarine-based missiles, and aircraft capable of delivering nuclear weapons. This so-called triad was designed to guarantee that in any nuclear attack enough nuclear weapons would survive for a deadly second strike. Still, there was the possibility that one side might attack the other if it believed it could defend itself against a second strike. The ABM treaty, by strictly limiting defensive missiles, was designed to avoid that destabilizing possibility. Its other virtue, according to supporters of the ABM treaty, was that it avoided an enormously expensive race to build defensive missiles at a time when building such missiles might well prove to be technologically impossible. The ABM treaty never was without its critics. After the cold war ended, some critics argued that the ABM treaty was preventing the United States from responding to new dangers not anticipated in 1972. Thus in December 2001, President George W. Bush, citing the need to defend against so-called rogue states like Iran and North Korea and terrorist groups, declared the United States was withdrawing from the ABM treaty. The declaration took effect after six months, in June 2002.

Treaty Between the United States of America and the Union of Soviet Socialist Republics on the Limitation of Anti-Ballistic Missile Systems

Signed at Moscow May 26, 1972
Ratification advised by U.S. Senate August 3, 1972
Ratified by U.S. President September 30, 1972
Proclaimed by U.S. President October 3, 1972
Instruments of ratification exchanged October 3, 1972
Entered into forces October 3, 1972

The United States of America and the Union of Soviet Socialist Republics, hereinafter referred to as the Parties,

Proceeding from the premise that nuclear war would have devastating consequences for all mankind,

Considering that effective measures to limit anti-ballistic missile systems would be a substantial factor in curbing the race in strategic offensive arms and would lead to a decrease in the risk of outbreak of war involving nuclear weapons,

Proceeding from the premise that the limitation of anti-ballistic missile systems, as well as certain agreed measures with respect to the limitation of strategic offensive arms, would contribute to the creation of more favorable conditions for further negotiations on limiting strategic arms,

Mindful of their obligations under Article VI of the Treaty on the Non-Proliferation of Nuclear Weapons,

Declaring their intention to achieve at the earliest possible date the cessation of the nuclear arms race and to take effective measures toward reductions in strategic arms, nuclear disarmament, and general and complete disarmament,

Desiring to contribute to the relaxation of international tension and the strengthening of trust between States,

Have agreed as follows:

Article I

1. Each party undertakes to limit anti-ballistic missile (ABM) systems and to adopt other measures in accordance with the provisions of this Treaty.

2. Each Party undertakes not to deploy ABM systems for a defense of the territory of its country and not to provide a base for such a defense, and not to deploy ABM systems for defense of an individual region except as provided for in Article III of this Treaty.

Article II

1. For the purpose of this Treaty an ABM system is a system to counter strategic ballistic missiles or their elements in flight trajectory, currently consisting of:

(a) ABM interceptor missiles, which are interceptor missiles constructed and deployed for an ABM role, or of a type tested in an ABM mode;

(b) ABM launchers, which are launchers constructed and deployed for launching ABM interceptor missiles; and

(c) ABM radars, which are radars constructed and deployed for an ABM role, or of a type tested in an ABM mode.

2. The ABM system components listed in paragraph 1 of this Article include those which are:

(a) operational;

(b) under construction;

(c) undergoing testing;

(d) undergoing overhaul, repair or conversion; or

(e) mothballed.

Article III

Each Party undertakes not to deploy ABM systems or their components except that:

(a) within one ABM system deployment area having a radius of one hundred and fifty kilometers and centered on the Party's national capital, a Party may deploy: (1) no more than one hundred ABM launchers and no more than one hundred ABM interceptor missiles at launch sites, and (2) ABM radars within no more than six ABM radar complexes, the area of each complex being circular and having a diameter of no more than three kilometers; and

(b) within one ABM system deployment area having a radius of one hundred and fifty kilometers and containing ICBM silo launchers, a Party may deploy: (1) no more than one hundred ABM launchers and no more than one hundred ABM interceptor missiles at launch sites, (2) two large phased-array ABM radars comparable in potential to corresponding ABM radars operational or under construction on the date of signature of the Treaty in an ABM system deployment area containing ICBM silo launchers, and (3) no more than eighteen ABM radars each having a potential less than the potential of the smaller of the above-mentioned two large phased-array ABM radars.

Article IV

The limitations provided for in Article III shall not apply to ABM systems or their components used for development or testing, and located within current or additionally agreed test ranges. Each Party may have no more than a total of fifteen ABM launchers at test ranges.

Article V

1. Each Party undertakes not to develop, test, or deploy ABM systems or components which are sea-based, air-based, space-based, or mobile land-based.

2. Each Party undertakes not to develop, test, or deploy ABM launchers for launching more than one ABM interceptor missile at a time from each launcher, not to modify deployed launchers to provide them with such a capacity, not to develop, test, or deploy automatic or semi-automatic or other similar systems for rapid reload of ABM launchers.

Article VI

To enhance assurance of the effectiveness of the limitations on ABM systems and their components provided by the Treaty, each Party undertakes:

(a) not to give missiles, launchers, or radars, other than ABM interceptor missiles, ABM launchers, or ABM radars, capabilities to counter strategic ballistic missiles or their elements in flight trajectory, and not to test them in an ABM mode; and

(b) not to deploy in the future radars for early warning of strategic ballistic missile attack except at locations along the periphery of its national territory and oriented outward.

Article VII

Subject to the provisions of this Treaty, modernization and replacement of ABM systems or their components may be carried out.

Article VIII

ABM systems or their components in excess of the numbers or outside the areas specified in this Treaty, as well as ABM systems or their components prohibited by this Treaty, shall be destroyed or dismantled under agreed procedures within the shortest possible agreed period of time.

Article IX

To assure the viability and effectiveness of this Treaty, each Party undertakes not to transfer to other States, and not to deploy outside its national territory. ABM systems or their components limited by this Treaty.

Article X

Each Party undertakes not to assure any international obligations which would conflict with this Treaty.

Article XI

This Parties undertake to continue active negotiations for limitations on strategic offensive arms.

Article XII

1. For the purpose of providing assurance of compliance with the provisions of this Treaty, each Party shall use national technical means of verification at its disposal in a manner consistent with generally recognized principles of international law.

2. Each Party undertakes not to interfere with the national technical means of verification of the other Party operating in accordance with paragraph 1 of this Article.

3. Each Party undertakes not to use deliberate concealment measures which impede verification by national technical means of compliance with the provisions of this Treaty. This obligation shall not require changes in current construction, assembly, conversion or overhaul practices.

Article XIII

1. To promote the objectives and implementation of the provisions of this Treaty, the Parties shall establish promptly a Standing Consultative Commission, within the framework of which they will:

(a) consider questions concerning compliance with the obligations assumed and related situations which may be considered ambiguous;

(b) provide on a voluntary basis such information as either Party considers necessary to assure confidence in compliance with the obligations assumed;

(c) consider questions involving unintended interference with national technical means of verification;

(d) consider possible changes in the strategic situation which have a bearing on the provisions of this Treaty;

(e) agree upon procedures and dates for destruction or dismantling of ABM systems or their components in cases provided for by the provisions of this Treaty;

(f) consider, as appropriate, possible proposals for further increasing the viability of this Treaty; including proposals for amendments in accordance with the provisions of this Treaty;

(g) consider, as appropriate, proposals for further measures aimed at limiting strategic arms.

2. The Parties through consultation shall establish, and may amend as appropriate, Regulations for the Standing Consultative Commission governing procedures, composition and other relevant matters.

Article XIV

1. Each Party may propose amendments to this Treaty. Agreed amendments shall enter into force in accordance with the procedures governing the entry into force of this Treaty.

2. Five years after entry into force of this Treaty, and at five-year intervals thereafter, the Parties shall together conduct a review of this Treaty.

Article XV

1. This Treaty shall be of unlimited duration.

2. Each Party shall, in exercising its national sovereignty, have the right to withdraw from this Treaty if it decides that extraordinary events related to the subject matter of this Treaty have jeopardized its supreme interests. It shall give notice of its decision to the other Party six months prior to withdrawal from the Treaty. Such notice shall include a statement of the extraordinary events the notifying Party regards as having jeopardized its supreme interests.

Article XVI

1. This Treaty shall be subject to ratification in accordance with the constitutional procedures of each Party. The Treaty shall enter into force on the day of the exchange of instruments of ratification.

2. This Treaty shall be registered pursuant to Article 102 of the Charter of the United Nations.

DONE at Moscow on May 26, 1972, in two copies, each in the English and Russian languages, both texts being equally authentic.

FOR THE UNITED STATES OF AMERICA

RICHARD NIXON
President of the United States of America

FOR THE UNION OF SOVIET SOCIALIST REPUBLICS

L.I. BREZHNEV
General Secretary of the Central Committee of the CPSU

Source: United States Arms Control and Disarmament Agency. *Arms Control and Disarmament Agreements: Texts and Histories of the Negotiations.* Washington, D.C.: United States Arms Control and Disarmament Agency, 1990, pp. 157–161.

SALT I: Interim Agreement between the United States of America and the Union of Soviet Socialist Republics on Certain Measures with Respect to the Limitation of Strategic Arms (May 26, 1972)

The SALT I Interim Agreement put limits on the Soviet and American arsenals of ICBMs and SLBMs for five years. During that time, the two sides were committed to negotiate a more comprehensive agreement, which was known as SALT II. SALT I allowed the Soviet Union a larger number of both types of strategic missiles than the United States: 1,618 versus 1,054 ICBMS and 740 versus 656 SLBMs. Significantly, the agreement did not cover MIRVs, or multiple independently targeted reentry vehicles. Since MIRV technology made it possible to put more than one nuclear warhead on a ballistic missile, SALT I did not limit the number of warheads the Soviet Union or the United States could field. The United States had a lead in MIRV technology, which is one reason it agreed to be limited to a lower total number of ICBMs and SLBMs than the Soviet Union. In fact, because hundreds of U.S. missiles already were equipped with multiple warheads, the 1972 limits left the United States with more warheads than the Soviet Union. In addition, the United States had an advantage in strategic bombers, another weapon not covered by SALT I. Although SALT I was the first agreement to put some limits on the nuclear arms race, it did not stop it. Both sides increased their nuclear warhead arsenals by developing MIRVs and by modernizing their arsenal in other ways. Other agreements would be required to shrink the size of the superpowers' nuclear arsenals.

Interim Agreement between the United States of America and the Union of Soviet Socialist Republics on Certain Measures with Respect to the Limitation of Strategic Offensive Arms

Signed at Moscow May 26, 1972
Approval authorized by U.S. Congress September 30, 1972
Approved by U.S. President September 30, 1972
Notices of acceptance exchanged October 3, 1972
Entered into force October 3, 1972

The United Stales of America and the Union of Soviet Socialist Republics, hereinafter referred to as the Parties,

Convinced that the Treaty on the Limitation of Anti-Ballistic Missile Systems and this Interim Agreement on Certain Measures with Respect to the Limitation of Strategic Offensive Arms will contribute to the creation of more favorable conditions for active negotiations on limiting strategic arms as well as to the relaxation of international tension and the strengthening of trust between States,

Taking into account the relationship between strategic offensive and defensive arms,

Mindful of their obligations under Article VI of the Treaty on the Non-Proliferation of Nuclear Weapons,

Have agreed as follows:

Article I

The Parties undertake not to start construction of additional fixed land-based intercontinental ballistic missile (ICBM) launchers after July 1, 1972.

Article II

The Parties undertake not to convert land-based launchers for fight ICBMs, or for ICBMs of older types deployed prior to 1964, into land-based launchers for heavy ICBMs of types deployed after that time.

Article III

The Parties undertake to limit submarine-launched ballistic missile (SLBM) launchers and modern ballistic missile submarines to the numbers operational and under construction on the date of signature of this Interim Agreement, and in addition to launchers and submarines constructed under procedures established by the Parties as replacements for an equal number of ICBM launchers of older types deployed prior to 1964 or for launchers on older submarines.

Article IV

Subject to the provisions of this Interim Agreement, modernization and replacement of strategic offensive ballistic missiles and launchers covered by this Interim Agreement may be undertaken.

Article V

1. For the purpose of providing assurance of compliance with the provisions of this Interim Agreement, each Party shall use national technical means of verification at its disposal in a manner consistent with generally recognized principles of international law.

2. Each Party undertakes not to interfere with the national technical means of verification of the other Party operating in accordance with paragraph 1 of this Article.

3. Each Party undertakes not to use deliberate concealment measures which impede verification by national technical means of compliance with the provisions of this Interim Agreement. This obligation shall not require changes in current construction, assembly, conversion, or overhaul practices.

Article VI

To promote the objectives and implementation of the provisions of this Interim Agreement, the Parties shall use the Standing Consultative Commission established under Article XIII of the Treaty on the Limitation of Anti-Ballistic Missile Systems in accordance with the provisions of that Article.

Article VII

The Parties undertake to continue active negotiations for limitations on strategic offensive arms. The obligations provided for in this Interim Agreement shall not prejudice the scope or terms of the limitations on strategic offensive arms which may be worked out in the course of further negotiations.

Article VIII

1. This Interim Agreement shall enter into force upon exchange of written notices of acceptance by each Party, which exchange shall take place simultaneously with the exchange of instruments of ratification of the Treaty on the Limitation of Anti-Ballistic Missile Systems.

2. This Interim Agreement shall remain in force for a period of five years unless replaced earlier by an agreement on more complete measures limiting strategic offensive arms. It is the objective of the Parties to conduct active follow-on negotiations with the aim of concluding such an agreement as soon as possible.

3. Each Party shall, in exercising its national sovereignty, have the right to withdraw from this Interim Agreement if it decides that extraordinary events related to the subject matter of this Interim Agreement have jeopardized its supreme interests. It shall give notice of its decision to the other Party six months prior to withdrawal from this Interim Agreement. Such notice shall include a statement of the extraordinary events the notifying Party regards as having jeopardized its supreme interests.

DONE at Moscow on May 26, 1972, in two copies, each in the English and Russian languages, both texts being equally authentic.

FOR THE UNITED STATES OF AMERICA	**FOR THE UNION OF SOVIET SOCIALIST REPUBLICS**
RICHARD NIXON	**L. I. BREZHNEV**
President of the United States of America	*General Secretary of the Central Committee of the CPSU*

Source: United States Arms Control and Disarmament Agency. *Arms Control and Disarmament Agreements: Texts and Histories of the Negotiations*. Washington, D.C., 1990, pp. 169–171.

Intermediate-Range Nuclear Forces Treaty (INF): Treaty between the United States of America and the Union of Soviet Socialist Republics on the Elimination of Their Intermediate-Range and Shorter-Range Missiles (December 8, 1987)

The INF treaty of 1987 required the Soviet Union and the United States to eliminate all their ground-launched nuclear missiles with ranges between 300 and 3,300 miles. It was the first treaty to produce an actual reduction in the Soviet and American nuclear arsenals. Just as significant, it was and remains the only nuclear weapons treaty to eliminate an entire class of weapons. Both sides had to destroy all of their ground-launched ballistic and cruise missiles with ranges between 300 and 3,400 miles (500 and 5,500 km). The INF treaty included the most comprehensive inspection system yet established, although four years later the START I inspection system would be even more extensive. Both sides—with

Russia replacing the Soviet Union as the responsible partner after 1991—conducted hundreds of inspections from the time the treaty entered into force in 1988 through 2001. The INF treaty eliminated 846 U.S. missiles and, 1,846 Soviet missiles, for a total of 2,692 missiles.

Treaty Between the United States of America and the Union of Soviet Socialist Republics on the Elimination of Their Intermediate-Range and Shorter-Range Missiles

Signed at Washington December 8, 1987
Ratification advised by U.S. Senate May 27, 1988
Instruments of ratification exchanged June 1, 1988
Entered into force June 1, 1988
Proclaimed by U.S. President December 27, 1988

The United States of America and the Union of Soviet Socialist Republics, hereinafter referred to as the Parties,

Conscious that nuclear war would have devastating consequences for all mankind,

Guided by the objective of strengthening strategic stability,

Convinced that the measures set forth in this Treaty will help to reduce the risk of outbreak of war and strengthen international peace and security, and

Mindful of their obligations under Article VI of the Treaty on the Non-Proliferation of Nuclear Weapons,

Have agreed as follows:

Article I

In accordance with the provisions of this Treaty which includes the Memorandum of Understanding and Protocols which form an integral part thereof, each Party shall eliminate its intermediate-range and shorter-range missiles, not have such systems thereafter, and carry out the other obligations set forth in this Treaty.

Article II

For the purposes of this Treaty:

1. The term "ballistic missile" means a missile that has a ballistic trajectory over most of its flight path. The term "ground-launched ballistic missile (GLBM)" means a ground-launched ballistic missile that is a weapon-delivery vehicle.

2. The term "cruise missile" means an unmanned, self-propelled vehicle that sustains flight through the use of aerodynamic lift over most of its flight path. The term "ground-launched cruise missile (GLCM)" means a ground-launched cruise missile that is a weapon-delivery vehicle.

3. The term "GLBM launcher" means a fixed launcher or a mobile land-based transporter-erector-launcher mechanism for launching a GLBM.

4. The term "GLCM launcher" means a fixed launcher or a mobile land-based transporter-erector-launcher mechanism for launching a GLCM.

5. The term "intermediate-range missile" means a GLBM or a GLCM having a range capability in excess of 1000 kilometers but not in excess of 5500 kilometers.

6. The term "shorter-range missile" means a GLBM or a GLCM having a range capability equal to or in excess of 500 kilometers but not in excess of 1000 kilometers.

7. The term "deployment area" means a designated area within which intermediate-range missiles and launchers of such missiles may operate and within which one or more missile operating bases are located.

8. The term "missile operating base" means:

(a) in case of intermediate-range missiles, a complex of facilities, located within a deployment area, at which intermediate-range missiles and launchers of such missiles normally operate, in which support structures associated with such missiles and launchers are also located and in which support equipment associated with such missiles and launchers is normally located; and

(b) in the case of shorter-range missiles, a complex of facilities, located any place, at which shorter-range missiles and launchers of such missiles normally operate and in which support equipment associated with such missiles and launchers is normally located.

9. The term "missile support facility," as regards intermediate-range or shorter-range missiles and launchers of such missiles, means a missile production facility or a launcher production facility, a missile repair facility or a launcher repair facility, a training facility, a missile storage facility or a launcher storage facility, a test range, or an elimination facility as those terms are defined in the Memorandum of Understanding.

10. The term "transit" means movement, notified in accordance with paragraph 5(f) of Article IX of this Treaty, of an intermediate-range missile or a launcher of such a missile between missile support facilities, between such a facility and a deployment area or between deployment areas, or of a shorter-range missile or a launcher of such a missile from a missile support facility or a missile operating base to an elimination facility.

11. The term "deployed missile" means an intermediate-range missile located within a deployment area or a shorter-range missile located at a missile operating base.

12. The term "non-deployed missile" means an intermediate-range missile located outside a deployment area or a shorter-range missile located outside a missile operating base.

13. The term "deployed launcher" means a launcher of an intermediate-range missile located within a deployment area or a launcher of a shorter-range missile located at a missile operating base.

14. The term "non-deployed launcher" means a launcher of an intermediate-range missile located outside a deployment area or a launcher of a shorter-range missile located outside a missile operating base.

15. The term "basing country" means a country other than the United States of America or the Union of Soviet Socialist Republics on whose territory intermediate-range or shorter-range missiles of the Parties, launchers of such missiles or support structures associated with such missiles and launchers were located at any time after November 1, 1987. Missiles or launchers in transit are not considered to be "located."

Article III

1. For the purpose of this Treaty, existing types of intermediate-range missiles are:

(a) for the United States of America, missiles of the types designated by the United States of America as the Pershing II and the BGM-109G, which are known to the Union of Soviet Socialist Republics by the same designations; and

(b) for the Union of Soviet Socialist Republics, missiles of the types designated by the Union of Soviet Socialist Republics as the RSD-10, the R-12 and the R-14, which are known to the United States of America as the SS-20, the SS-4 and the SS-5, respectively.

2. For the purposes of this Treaty, existing types of shorter-range missiles are:

(a) for the United States of America, missiles of the type designated by the United States of America as the Pershing IA, which is known to the Union of Soviet Socialist Republics by the same designation; and

(b) for the Union of Soviet Socialist Republics, missiles of the types designated by the Union of Soviet Socialist Republics as the OTR-22 and the OTR-23, which are known to the United States of America as the SS-12 and the SS-23, respectively.

Article IV

1. Each Party shall eliminate all its intermediate-range missiles and launchers of such missiles, and all support structures and support equipment of the categories listed in the Memorandum of Understanding associated with such missiles and launchers, so that no later than three years after entry into force of this Treaty and thereafter no such missiles, launchers, support structures or support equipment shall be possessed by either Party.

2. To implement paragraph 1 of this Article, upon entry into force of this Treaty, both Parties shall begin and continue throughout the duration of each phase, the reduction of all types of their deployed and non-deployed intermediate-range missiles and deployed and non-deployed launchers of such missiles and support structures and support equipment associated with such missiles and launchers in accordance with the provisions of this Treaty. These reductions shall be implemented in two phases so that:

(a) by the end of the first phase, that is, no later than 29 months after entry into force of this Treaty:

(i) the number of deployed launchers of intermediate-range missiles for each Party shall not exceed the number of launchers that are capable of carrying or containing at one time missiles considered by the Parties to carry 171 warheads;

(ii) the number of deployed intermediate-range missiles for each Party shall not exceed the number of such missiles considered by the Parties to carry 180 warheads;

(iii) the aggregate number of deployed and non-deployed launchers of intermediate-range missiles for each Party shall not exceed the number of launchers that are capable of carrying or containing at one time missiles considered by the Parties to carry 200 warheads;

(iv) the aggregate number of deployed and non-deployed intermediate-range missiles for each Party shall not exceed the number of such missiles considered by the Parties to carry 200 warheads; and

(v) the ratio of the aggregate number of deployed and non-deployed intermediate-range GLBMs of existing types for each Party to the aggregate number of deployed and non-deployed intermediate-range missiles of existing types possessed by that Party shall not exceed the ratio of such intermediate-range GLBMs to such intermediate-range missiles for that Party as of November 1, 1987, as set forth in the Memorandum of Understanding; and

(b) by the end of the second phase, that is, no later than three years after entry into force of this Treaty, all intermediate-range missiles of each Party, launchers of such missiles and all support structures and support equipment of the categories listed in the Memorandum of Understanding associated with such missiles and launchers, shall be eliminated.

. . .

Source: United States Arms Control and Disarmament Agency. *Arms Control and Disarmament Agreements: Texts and Histories of the Negotiations.* Washington, D.C., 1990, pp. 350–362.

START I: Treaty between the United States of America and the Union of Soviet Socialist Republics on the Reduction and Limitation of Strategic Offensive Arms (July 31, 1991) (excerpt)

The START I treaty was the product of proposals and discussions that began with an arms reduction proposal by U.S. president Ronald Reagan in 1982. The negotiations that followed lasted through both of Reagan's terms and three years into the presidency of his vice president and successor, George H. W. Bush. When Bush and Soviet president Mikhail Gorbachev signed the treaty, the Soviet Union itself was within five months of its final collapse. At that point, the Russian Federation, as the legal successor to the Soviet Union, took on the responsibilities of the treaty.

Implementation of the treaty was delayed by the Soviet Union's collapse and by the fact that its collapse left three new countries other than Russia—Ukraine, Belarus, and Kazakhstan—with nuclear weapons. Those three countries had to ratify START I and agree to become nonnuclear members of the NPT, a process that took until the end of 1994. START I, the most complex arms control agreement ever negotiated, contained a detailed system of reporting and verification, provided for continuous monitoring, and included 12 different types of on-site inspections. It required each side to reduce its total strategic ballistic missiles (ICBMs and SLBMs) to 1,600 and total warheads to 6,000. Articles I and II of the treaty's 19 articles appear below. These articles are followed by hundreds of pages of annexes, protocols, and other documents.

Treaty Between the United States of America and the Union of Soviet Socialist Republics on the Reduction and Limitation of Strategic Offensive Arms

The United States of America and the Union of Soviet Socialist Republics, hereinafter referred to as the Parties,

Conscious that nuclear war would have devastating consequences for all humanity, that it cannot be won and must never be fought,

Convinced that the measures for the reduction and limitation of strategic offensive arms and the other obligations set forth in this Treaty will help to reduce the risk of outbreak of nuclear war and strengthen international peace and security,

Recognizing that the interests of the Parties and the interests of international security require the strengthening of strategic stability,

Mindful of their undertakings with regard to strategic offensive arms in Article VI of the Treaty on the Non-Proliferation of Nuclear Weapons of July 1, 1968; Article XI of the Treaty on the Limitation of Anti-Ballistic Missile Systems of May 26, 1972; and the Washington Summit Joint Statement of June 1, 1990,

Have agreed as follows:

Article I

Each Party shall reduce and limit its strategic offensive arms in accordance with the provisions of this Treaty, and shall carry out the other obligations set forth in this Treaty and its Annexes, Protocols, and Memorandum of Understanding.

Article II

1. Each Party shall reduce and limit its ICBMs and ICBM launchers, SLBMs and SLBM launchers, heavy bombers, ICBM warheads, SLBM warheads, and heavy bomber armaments, so that seven years after entry into force of this Treaty and thereafter, the aggregate numbers, as counted in accordance with Article III of this Treaty, do not exceed:

(a) 1600, for deployed ICBMs and their associated launchers, deployed SLBMs and their associated launchers, and deployed heavy bombers, including 154 for deployed heavy ICBMs and their associated launchers;

(b) 6000, for warheads attributed to deployed ICBMs, deployed SLBMs, and deployed heavy bombers, including:

(i) 4900, for warheads attributed to deployed ICBMs and deployed SLBMs;

(ii) 1100, for warheads attributed to deployed ICBMs on mobile launchers of ICBMs;

(iii) 1540, for warheads attributed to deployed heavy ICBMs.

2. Each Party shall implement the reductions pursuant to paragraph 1 of this Article in three phases, so that its strategic offensive arms do not exceed:

(a) by the end of the first phase, that is, no later than 36 months after entry into force of this Treaty, and thereafter, the following aggregate numbers:

(i) 2100, for deployed ICBMs and their associated launchers, deployed SLBMs and their associated launchers, and deployed heavy bombers;

(ii) 9150, for warheads attributed to deployed ICBMs, deployed SLBMs, and deployed heavy bombers;

(iii) 8050, for warheads attributed to deployed ICBMs and deployed SLBMs;

(b) by the end of the second phase, that is, no later than 60 months after entry into force of this Treaty, and thereafter, the following aggregate numbers:

(i) 1900, for deployed ICBMs and their associated launchers, deployed SLBMs and their associated launchers, and deployed heavy bombers;

(ii) 7950, for warheads attributed to deployed ICBMs, deployed SLBMs, and deployed heavy bombers;

(iii) 6750, for warheads attributed to deployed ICBMs and deployed SLBMs;

(c) by the end of the third phase, that is, no later than 84 months after entry into force of this Treaty: the aggregate numbers provided for in paragraph 1 of this Article.

3. Each Party shall limit the aggregate throw-weight of its deployed ICBMs and deployed SLBMs so that seven years after entry into force of this Treaty and thereafter such aggregate throw-weight does not exceed 3600 metric tons.

. . .

Source: United States Arms Control and Disarmament Agency. *Arms Control and Disarmament Agreements. START: Treaty between the United States of America and the Union of Soviet Socialist Republics on the Reduction of Strategic Offensive Arms.* Washington, D.C., 1991.

START I Treaty Final Reductions. U.S. Department of State Fact Sheet (December 5, 2001)

The final reductions in the Soviet and American strategic nuclear arsenals under START I were completed at the end of 2001. Each side was below the mandated limits of 1,600 strategic delivery vehicles and 6,000 warheads. The State Department fact sheet includes a chart detailing those reductions. START I was followed by START II, which was completed and signed by the Soviet Union and the United States in 1993. It called for each side to reduce its arsenal to 3,000–3,500 warheads. However, the treaty never entered into force. The United States ratified the treaty in 1996, but when Russia finally did so in 2000, it included the stipulation that the United States must continue to remain a party to the 1972 ABM treaty. When the United States pulled out of that treaty in 2002 in order to build a missile defense against rogue states and international terrorists, Russia withdrew from START. Shortly thereafter, START was replaced by the SORT treaty (see next entry).

Fact Sheet
Bureau of Arms Control
Washington, DC
December 5, 2001

START Treaty Final Reductions

December 5, 2001, marks the successful completion of the third and final phase of reductions in strategic offensive arms required by the Strategic Arms Reduction Treaty (START Treaty). The United States and Russia each now maintain fewer than the Treaty's mandated limits of 1,600 deployed strategic delivery vehicles and 6,000 accountable warheads, a reduction of some 30 to 40 percent of aggregate levels since 1994, when the Treaty entered into force. In addition, all nuclear warheads and strategic offensive arms have been removed from Belarus, Kazakhstan, and Ukraine.

The START Treaty reductions, inspection regime, notifications and telemetry exchanges have produced stabilizing changes that have contributed to international security and strategic stability.

The START Treaty was signed in Moscow on July 31, 1991, by President George H. W. Bush, for the United States, and President Mikhail Gorbachev, for the Soviet Union. The instruments of ratification of the START Treaty were exchanged in Budapest, Hungary, in December 1994, after several years of sustained effort to adapt the Treaty's original bilateral implementation regime to a new multilateral context that established Belarus, Kazakhstan, Russia, and Ukraine as the legal successors to the Soviet Union for the purposes of the START Treaty.

Although the START Treaty's required reductions have been met within the required seven years, the Treaty, including its inspection and verification provisions, remains in force. The Treaty's fifteen-year duration may be extended by agreement among the Parties for successive five-year periods.

A significant aspect of the START Treaty's regime lies in its use of rigorous, equitable and verifiable methods to monitor its implementation. The right to perform on-site inspections and other verification measures will continue for the duration of the Treaty, in order to verity compliance. In addition, data exchanges and notifications on each side's strategic systems and facilities as well as exchanges of telemetry data from missile flight tests will help to maintain confidence in the status and level of the Parties' strategic forces. The Parties will also continue to meet as necessary within the framework of the Treaty's implementing body, the Joint Compliance and Inspection Commission, which the Treaty established to ensure continued effective implementation of the Treaty and to seek resolution of compliance and implementation issues.

START has achieved significant reductions from Cold War nuclear force levels. President George W. Bush is committed to achieve significant additional cuts in offensive nuclear forces to the lowest possible number of nuclear weapons consistent with our national security needs and our obligations to friends and allies. The United States seeks to create a new strategic framework with Russia based on a broad array of cooperation on political, economic, and security issues, including substantial reductions in the number of operationally deployed nuclear forces and measures to promote confidence and transparency. Thus, during the November 2001 Washington/Crawford Summit, President Bush announced that the United States will further reduce the number of operationally deployed warheads to between 1,700 and 2,200 over the next ten years, a level consistent with American security.

FINAL START I TREATY STRATEGIC OFFENSIVE ARMS LEVELS DECEMBER 5, 2001

UNITED STATES		CATEGORY OF DATA AND CENTRAL LIMIT	FORMER SOVIET UNION	
Dec 5, 1994	Dec 5, 2001		Dec 5, 1994	*Projected Dec 5, 2001
1,838	1,238	Deployed ICBMs and Their Associated Launchers, Deployed SLBMs and Their Associated Launchers, and Deployed Heavy Bombers: 1,600	1,956	~1,140
8,824	5,949	Warheads Attributed to Deployed ICBMs, Deployed SLBMs, and Deployed Heavy Bombers: 6,000	9,568	~5,520
6,793	4,821	Warheads Attributed to Deployed ICBMs and Deployed SLBMs: 4,900	8,638	~4,900
2,176.5	1,732.5	Throw-weight of Deployed ICBMs and Deployed SLBMs: 3,600 metric tons	5,930.4	~3,320

* The Parties will exchange formal force data in January 2002. The START I Treaty prohibits the U.S. Government from releasing the other Parties' final Phase III data until April 2002.

Source: U.S. Department of State. Available online. URL: http://www.fas.org/nuke/control/start1/news/startfinalnum.htm. Accessed June 1, 2009.

SORT: Treaty between the United States of America and the Russian Federation on Strategic Offensive Reductions (May 24, 2002)

Also known as the Moscow Treaty, this agreement states that the United States and the Soviet Union will reduce their operational nuclear warheads to between 1,700 and 2,200 within the next 10 years. It is to remain in force until December 31, 2012. This short treaty lacks a timetable or specific benchmarks that the two powers have to meet during that period. It does provide for a Bilateral Implementation Commission to meet twice a year to review how the treaty is being observed. According to documents that accompanied the treaty, the two parties will use the verification system established by START I to assure that each side is meeting its obligations. However, unlike START I, the SORT agreement does not specify what is to be done with warheads that have been removed from their delivery systems. The U.S. Senate unanimously ratified SORT on March 6, 2003; the Russian Duma did the same on May 14, 2003.

Bureau of Verification, Compliance, and Implementation

May 24, 2002

. . .

Text of Treaty

The United States of America and the Russian Federation, hereinafter referred to as the Parties,

Embarking upon the path of new relations for a new century and committed to the goal of strengthening their relationship through cooperation and friendship,

Believing that new global challenges and threats require the building of a qualitatively new foundation for strategic relations between the Parties,

Desiring to establish a genuine partnership based on the principles of mutual security, cooperation, trust, openness, and predictability,

Committed to implementing significant reductions in strategic offensive arms,

Proceeding from the Joint Statements by the President of the United States of America and the President of the Russian Federation on Strategic Issues of July 22, 2001 in Genoa and on a New Relationship between the United States and Russia of November 13, 2001 in Washington,

Mindful of their obligations under the Treaty Between the United States of America and the Union of Soviet Socialists Republics on the Reduction and Limitation of Strategic Offensive Arms of July 31, 1991, hereinafter referred to as the START Treaty,

Mindful of their obligations under Article VI of the Treaty on the Non-Proliferation of Nuclear Weapons of July 1, 1968, and

Convinced that this Treaty will help to establish more favorable conditions for actively promoting security and cooperation, and enhancing international stability,

Have agreed as follows:

Article I

Each Party shall reduce and limit strategic nuclear warheads, as stated by the President of the United States of America on November 13, 2001 and as stated by the President of the Russian Federation on November 13, 2001 and December 13, 2001 respectively, so that by December 31, 2012 the aggregate number of such warheads does not exceed 1700–2200 for each Party. Each Party shall determine for itself the composition and structure of its strategic offensive arms, based on the established aggregate limit for the number of such warheads.

Article II

The Parties agree that the START Treaty remains in force in accordance with its terms.

Article III

For purposes of implementing this Treaty, the Parties shall hold meetings at least twice a year of a Bilateral Implementation Commission.

Article IV

1. This Treaty shall be subject to ratification in accordance with the constitutional procedures of each Party. This Treaty shall enter into force on the date of the exchange of instruments of ratification.

2. This Treaty shall remain in force until December 31, 2012 and may be extended by agreement of the Parties or superseded earlier by a subsequent agreement.

3. Each Party, in exercising its national sovereignty, may withdraw from this Treaty upon three months written notice to the other Party.

Article V

This Treaty shall be registered pursuant to Article 102 of the Charter of the United Nations.

Done at Moscow on May 24, 2002, in two copies, each in the English and Russian languages, both texts being equally authentic.

FOR THE UNITED STATES OF AMERICA
George W. Bush

FOR THE RUSSIAN FEDERATION
Vladimir V. Putin

Source: U.S. Department of State. Available online. URL: http://www.armscontrol.org/documents/sort. Accessed June 1, 2009.

ISRAEL

National Intelligence Estimate 4-66: The Likelihood of Further Nuclear Proliferation (January 20, 1966)

This evaluation by the Central Intelligence Agency discussed a dozen countries but found only Israel and India to be serious candidates to develop nuclear weapons in the near future. It concluded that Israel would develop nuclear weapons if it believed that it could no longer fend off the Arab threat by conventional means. Some of the information in this NIE is still classified.

National Intelligence Estimate Number 4-66
The Likelihood of Further Nuclear Proliferation

The Problem
To estimate the capabilities of additional countries to acquire nuclear weapons, and the likelihood that such countries will do so.

Conclusions

A. Beyond the present five nuclear powers, only India is likely to undertake a nuclear weapons program in the next several years. Israel and Sweden might do so. (*Paras. 19–25, 34*)

. . .

B. Israel

. . .

24. A variety of incentives and restraints are at work on Israel, but we believe that in the final analysis Israel's decision on developing nuclear weapons will depend primarily on its judgment concerning trends in relative military strength between it and its Arab neighbors. For the next few years, at least, Israel will probably judge that it can maintain its security through acquisition of conventional weapons from the US and other Western sources. However, Israel probably would develop nuclear weapons if it came to believe that the threat from the Arab states could no longer be contained by conventional means. In this situation even a combination of international agreements, pressure from the US, and explicit US security guarantees might not restrain the Israelis.

. . .

Source: The National Security Archive: National Security Archive Electronic Briefing Book No. 155. Available online. URL: http://www.gwu.edu/~nsarchiv/NSAEBB/NSAEBB155/index.htm. Accessed June 1, 2009.

Light Flash Produced by an Atmospheric Nuclear Explosion (November 1979)

This report is one of numerous studies done for the U.S. government as part of its effort to determine exactly what a VELA spy satellite detected in the southern Indian Ocean on September 22, 1979. There is still disagreement in the intelligence and scientific communities about whether what occurred was an unusual natural phenomenon or an Israeli nuclear test. The weight of the evidence seems to indicate the latter. Guy E. Barasch, a scientist at the Los Alamos Scientific Laboratory, was one of the experts who studied the evidence. He concluded that the nature of the light flash that the VEGA satellite detected makes it "unmistakable" that the event in question was an "atmospheric nuclear event."

Light Flash Produced by an Atmospheric Nuclear Explosion

Current concern regarding nuclear-weapon proliferation has re-emphasized the interest in detecting nuclear tests conducted anywhere in the world.

Such tests could be conducted underground or in the atmosphere. One means of detecting atmospheric nuclear explosions utilizes a "bhangmeter," an optical sensor developed during the years of US atmospheric nuclear tests. It detects and records the extremely bright and characteristic flash of light from an atmospheric explosion. The high intensity of the light flash makes this a sensitive technique, and the distinctive signature of the light signal reduces the likelihood of errors in identifying the detected signal as a nuclear event. In addition, timing information in the light signature can be used to infer the energy released by the nuclear explosion, i.e., the yield.

This review describes the light flash that would be detected by a bhangmeter from an atmospheric nuclear explosion and the method by which the yield of the explosion is obtained. It presents the physical processes that produce the light flash and determine its characteristics, and incorporates an analysis showing that naturally occurring signals would not be mistaken for that of a nuclear explosion.

Characteristic Signature

Figure 1 shows the light-flash signature of a 19-kiloton atmospheric nuclear test conducted in Nevada on May 1, 1952. The two distinct light peaks, with a dimmer but still luminous minimum between them, are characteristic of the optical signature of all atmospheric nuclear explosions below about 30 km altitude. A nonlinear (logarithmic) time scale is used to display this

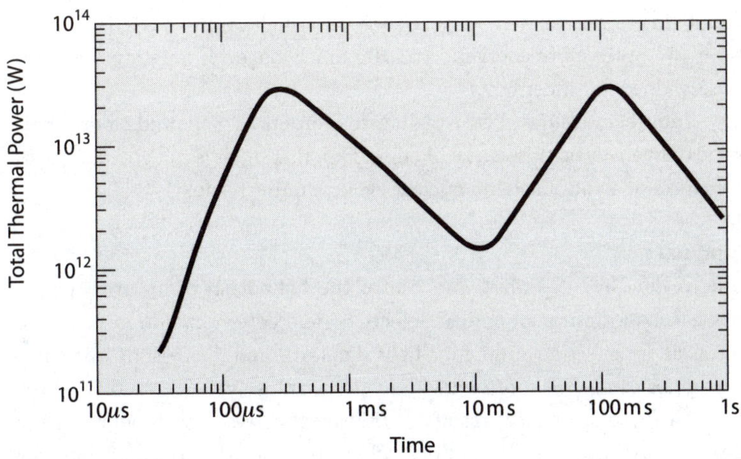

curve so that details can be shown of the very fast first-peak and minimum-signal regions.

. . .

Uniqueness

The two-peaked character of the light pulse, together with the very large energy radiated during the second maximum, make it unmistakable that this light signature originated in a nuclear explosion. For a one-kiloton explosion the thermal pulse radiates one-fourth kiloton (about 10^{12} joules) in a half second. The peak radiated power during that time, about 4×10^{12} watts, is more than ten times larger than the total electrical generating capacity of the United States. Pulsed light sources do occur in nature, or can be built, that match either this power level or the pulse duration. However, no other source is known that matches both.

In particular, natural lightning has been suggested as a source that could produce the pulse shape and intensity required to simulate a nuclear-explosion light flash. Lightning pulses are not energetic enough for this, even the rare "super bolts," which emit 10^9 joules of visible-light energy in a single short-lived intense stroke. The closest lightning simulation to the timing and intensity characteristics would require an ordinary stroke followed by a long-lived "super-bolt" stroke, producing 10^9 joules of visible light in ~100 ms. This assumption is conservative because although long-lived ordinary strokes have been observed, long-lived super strokes have not. The postulated lightning signal would have a peak radiated power of approximately 10^{10} watts, which is about 400 times smaller than that of a one-kiloton explosion. To achieve the pulse shape and peak-radiated power simulating a one-kiloton nuclear explosion, lightning would have to be both 400 times more energetic and 100 times longer in duration than ever observed for the super bolts.

Thus, because the nuclear signature is orders of magnitude more energetic than any other terrestrial phenomenon that might simulate it, the light signature of an atmospheric nuclear event is unmistakable.

Summary

This review has described: the use of the light flash of an atmospheric nuclear explosion as an optical detection/yield determination method; the physical processes governing the light signature; and the reasons why natural signals cannot be confused with nuclear explosions.

All these are typical results of the weapons-research program at the Los Alamos Scientific Laboratory, which has included research into the effects of nuclear explosions in the atmosphere. Techniques developed in this program are being used in continued atmospheric research and in research addressing the physical processes associated with nuclear weapon development.

Source: The National Security Archive: National Security Archive Electronic Briefing Book No. 190. Available online. URL: http://www.gwu.edu/~nsarchiv/NSAEBB/NSAEBB190/index.htm. Accessed June 1, 2009.

INDIA AND PAKISTAN

Indian Government Statement Announcing Nuclear Tests (May 11, 1998)

This announcement refers to India's three nuclear tests on May 11, 1998. (Two others followed on May 13.) The announcement included the claim that one of the tests was of a thermonuclear device, although it is likely that the thermonuclear test was not entirely successful. The announcement included a statement that India supports the global elimination of nuclear weapons, offering as proof India's adherence to both the Chemical Weapons Convention and the Biological Weapons Convention. A similar statement followed the two May 13 tests.

Indian government statement on nuclear tests

May 11, 1998

As announced by the Prime Minister this afternoon today India conducted three underground nuclear tests in the Pokhran range. The tests conducted today were with a fission device, a low yield device and a thermonuclear device. The measured yields are in line with expected values. Measurements have also confirmed that there was no release of radioactivity into the atmosphere. These were contained explosions like the experiment conducted in May 1974.

These tests have established that India has a proven capability for a weaponised nuclear programme. They also provide a valuable database which is useful in the design of nuclear weapons of different yields for different applications and for different delivery systems. Further they are expected to carry Indian scientists towards a sound computer simulation capability which may be supported by sub-critical experiments if considered necessary.

WEAPONS OF MASS DESTRUCTION

The Government is deeply concerned as were previous Governments, about the nuclear environment in India's neighbourhood. These tests provide reassurance to the people of India that their national security interests are paramount and will be promoted and protected. Succeeding generations of Indians would also rest assured that contemporary technologies associated with nuclear option have been passed on to them in this the 50th year of our Independence.

It is necessary to highlight today that India was in the vanguard of nations which ushered in the Partial Test Ban Treaty in 1963 due to environmental concerns. Indian representatives have worked in various international forums, including the Conference on Disarmament, for universal, non-discriminatory and verifiable arrangements for the elimination of weapons of mass destruction. The Government would like to reiterate its support to efforts to realise the goal of a truly comprehensive international arrangement which would prohibit underground nuclear testing of all weapons as well as related experiments described as sub-critical or "hydronuclear."

India would be prepared to consider being an adherent to some of the undertakings in the Comprehensive Test Ban Treaty. But this cannot obviously be done in a vacuum. If would necessarily be an evolutionary process from concept to commitment and would depend on a number of reciprocal activities.

We would like to reaffirm categorically that we will continue to exercise the most stringent control on the export of sensitive technologies, equipment and commodities especially those related to weapons of mass destruction. Our track record has been impeccable in this regard. Therefore we expect recognition of our responsible policy by the international community.

India remains committed to a speedy process of nuclear disarmament leading to total and global elimination of nuclear weapons. Our adherence to the Chemical Weapons Convention and the Biological Weapons Convention is evidence of our commitment to any global disarmament regime which is non-discriminatory and verifiable. We shall also be happy to participate in the negotiations for the conclusion of a fissile material cut-off treaty in the Geneva based conference on Disarmament.

In our neighbourhood we have many friends with whom relations of fruitful cooperation for mutual benefit have existed and deepened over a long period. We assure them that it will be our sincere endeavour to intensify and diversify those relations further for the benefit of all our peoples. For India, as for others, the prime need is for peaceful cooperation and economic development.

Source: Atomicarchive.com Available online. URL: http://www.atomicarchive.com/Docs/Deterrence//IndiaStatement2.shtml. Accessed December 24, 2008.

Announcement of Pakistan's Five Nuclear Tests by Prime Minister Mohammad Nawaz Sharif (May 28, 1998)

Pakistan successfully conducted five nuclear tests in a single day, May 28, 1998, just weeks after India conducted a series of nuclear tests. In announcing Pakistan's tests in a televised address to the nation, Sharif said they were necessary in light of India's tests to protect Pakistan's security. Toward the end of his announcement, Sharif stated that Pakistan had not and would not transfer nuclear technology to other states. This, of course, was totally untrue, as Abdul Qadeer Khan's network was deeply involved in nuclear proliferation, something it could not have done without the help of Pakistani government agencies, including the military.

Pakistani government statement on nuclear tests

Islamabad, Pakistan May 29, 1998

Pakistan today successfully conducted five nuclear tests. The results were as expected. There was no release of radio- activity. I congratulate all Pakistani scientists, engineers and technicians for their dedicated team work and expertise in mastering complex and advanced technologies. The entire nation takes justifiable pride in the accomplishments of the Pakistan Atomic Energy Commission, Dr. A. Q. Khan Research Laboratories and all affiliated Organizations. They have demonstrated Pakistan's ability to deter aggression. Pakistan has been obliged to exercise the nuclear option due to weaponization of India's nuclear programme. This had led to the collapse of the "existential deterrence" and had radically altered the strategic balance in our region. Immediately after its nuclear tests, India had brazenly raised the demand that "Islamabad should realize the change in the geo-strategic situation in the region" and threatened that "India will deal firmly and strongly with Pakistan".

Our security, and peace and stability of the entire region was thus gravely threatened. As a self-respecting nation we had no choice left to us. Our hand was forced by the present Indian leadership's reckless actions. After due deliberation and a careful review of all options we took the decision to restore the strategic balance. The nation would not have expected anything less from its leadership. For the past three decades Pakistan repeatedly drew attention of the international community to India's incremental steps on the nuclear and ballistic ladder. Our warnings remained unheeded. Despite the continuing deterioration in Pakistan's security environment, we exercised utmost restraint. We pursued in all earnest the goal of non-proliferation in South Asia. Our initiatives to keep South Asia free of nuclear and ballistic weapon systems were spurned. The international response to the Indian nuclear tests did not factor the security situation in our region. While asking us to exercise restraint, powerful voices urged acceptance of the Indian weaponization as a fait-accompli. Pakistan's legitimate security concerns were not addressed, even after the threat of use of nuclear weapons and nuclear blackmail. We could not have remained complacent about threats to our security. We could not have ignored the magnitude of the threat.

Under no circumstances would the Pakistani nation compromise on matters pertaining to its life and existence. Our decision to exercise the nuclear option has been taken in the interest of national self-defence. These weapons are to deter aggression, whether nuclear or conventional. Pakistan will continue to support the goals of nuclear disarmament and non-proliferation, especially in the Conference on Disarmament, bearing in mind the new realities. We are undertaking a re-evaluation of the applicability and relevance of the global non-proliferation regimes to nuclearized South Asia. We are ready to engage in a constructive dialogue with other countries, especially major powers, on ways and means to promoting these goals, in the new circumstances. Pakistan has always acted with utmost restraint and responsibility. We will continue to do so in the future. We are prepared to resume Pakistan-India dialogue to address all outstanding issues including the core issue of Jammu and Kashmir, as well as peace and security. These should include urgent steps for mutual restraint and equitable measures for nuclear stabilization. Pakistan has already offered a non-aggression pact to India on the basis of a just settlement of the Jammu and Kashmir dispute. I would like to reiterate this offer. We have instituted effective command and control structures. We are fully conscious of the need to handle these weapon systems with the highest sense of responsibility. We have not and will not transfer sensitive technologies to other states or entities.

At the same time, Pakistan will oppose all unjust embargoes aimed at preventing it from exercising its right to develop various technologies for self-defence or peaceful purposes. I would like to again assure all countries that our nuclear weapon systems are meant only for self-defence and there should be no apprehension or concern in this regard. The Pakistani people are united in their resolve to safeguard, at all costs, Pakistan's independence, sovereignty and territorial integrity. I would like to congratulate the nation on the achievements of our scientists and engineers. They have made it possible for the people of Pakistan to enter the next century, with confidence in themselves and faith in their destiny.

Source: Atomicarchive.com. Available online. URL: http://www.atomicarchive.com/Docs/Deterrence/Pakistan Statement2.shtml. Accessed December 24, 2008.

India's Nuclear Doctrine: Draft Report of the National Advisory Board on Indian Nuclear Doctrine (August 17, 1999)

The publication of this draft report four months after its five nuclear tests in May 1994 in effect was India's official announcement that it was a nuclear power. However, this statement remained a draft until January 2003, when it was formally adopted. The document affirms that India built and retains nuclear weapons to deter enemies and will use nuclear weapons only in retaliation for a nuclear attack. That in turn means that India must have a nuclear arsenal that can survive any type of attack. The report states that "extraordinary precautions" have been taken to assure that its nuclear arsenal and everything associated with it are safe from theft, sabotage, or unauthorized access. India probably is the only country that has adopted a nuclear doctrine after lengthy discussions and debate not only at home but also abroad.

Draft Report of National Security Advisory Board on Indian Nuclear Doctrine

August 17, 1999

Preamble

1.1. The use of nuclear weapons in particular as well as other weapons of mass destruction constitutes the gravest threat to humanity and to peace and stability in the international system. Unlike the other two categories of weapons of mass destruction, biological and chemical weapons which have been outlawed by international treaties, nuclear weapons remain instruments for national and collective security, the possession of which on a selective basis has been sought to be legitimised through permanent extension of the Nuclear Non-proliferation Treaty (NPT) in May 1995. Nuclear weapon states have asserted that they will continue to rely on nuclear weapons with some of them adopting policies to use them even in a non-nuclear context. These developments amount to virtual abandonment of nuclear disarmament. This is a serious setback to the struggle of the international community to abolish weapons of mass destruction.

1.2. India's primary objective is to achieve economic, political, social, scientific and technological development within a peaceful and democratic framework. This requires an environment of durable peace and insurance against potential risks to peace and stability. It will be India's endeavour to proceed towards this overall objective in cooperation with the global democratic trends and to play a constructive role in advancing the international system toward a just, peaceful and equitable order.

1.3. Autonomy of decision making in the developmental process and in strategic matters is an inalienable democratic right of the Indian people. India will strenuously guard this right in a world where nuclear weapons for a select few are sought to be legitimised for an indefinite future, and where there is growing complexity and frequency in the use of force for political purposes.

1.4. India's security is an integral component of its development process. India continuously aims at promoting an ever-expanding area of peace and stability around it so that developmental priorities can be pursued without disruption.

1.5. However, the very existence of offensive doctrine pertaining to the first use of nuclear weapons and the insistence of some nuclear weapons states on the legitimacy of their use even against non-nuclear weapon countries constitute a threat to peace, stability and sovereignty of states.

1.6. This document outlines the broad principles for the development, deployment and employment of India's nuclear forces. Details of policy and strategy concerning force structures, deployment and employment of nuclear forces will flow from this framework and will be laid down separately and kept under constant review.

2. Objectives

2.1. In the absence of global nuclear disarmament India's strategic interests require effective, credible nuclear deterrence and adequate retaliatory capability should deterrence fail. This is consistent with the UN Charter, which sanctions the right of self-defence.

2.2. The requirements of deterrence should be carefully weighed in the design of Indian nuclear forces and in the strategy to provide for a level of capability consistent with maximum credibility, survivability, effectiveness, safety and security.

2.3. India shall pursue a doctrine of credible minimum nuclear deterrence. In this policy of "retaliation only", the survivability of our arsenal is critical. This is a dynamic concept related to the strategic environment, technological imperatives and the needs of national security. The actual size components, deployment and employment of nuclear forces will be decided in the light of these factors. India's peacetime posture aims at convincing any potential aggressor that:

(a) any threat of use of nuclear weapons against India shall invoke measures to counter the threat: and (b) any nuclear attack on India and its forces shall result in punitive retaliation with nuclear weapons to inflict damage unacceptable to the aggressor.

2.4. The fundamental purpose of Indian nuclear weapons is to deter the use and threat of use of nuclear weapons by any State or entity against India and its forces. India will not be the first to initiate a nuclear strike, but will respond with punitive retaliation should deterrence fail.

2.5. India will not resort to the use or threat of use of nuclear weapons against States which do not possess nuclear weapons, or are not aligned with nuclear weapon powers.

2.6. Deterrence requires that India maintain:

(a) Sufficient, survivable and operationally prepared nuclear forces,

(b) a robust command and control system,

(c) effective intelligence and early warning capabilities, and

(d) comprehensive planning and training for operations in line with the strategy, and

(e) the will to employ nuclear forces and weapons

2.7. Highly effective conventional military capabilities shall be maintained to raise the threshold of outbreak both of conventional military conflict as well as that of threat or use of nuclear weapons.

3. Nuclear Forces

3.1. India's nuclear forces will be effective, enduring, diverse, flexible, and responsive to the requirements in accordance with the concept of credible minimum deterrence. These forces will be based on a triad of aircraft, mobile land-based missiles and sea-based assets in keeping with the objectives outlined above. Survivability of the forces will be enhanced by a combination of multiple redundant systems, mobility, dispersion and deception.

3.2. The doctrine envisages assured capability to shift from peacetime deployment to fully employable forces in the shortest possible time, and the ability to retaliate effectively even in a case of significant degradation by hostile strikes.

4. Credibility and Survivability

The following principles are central to India's nuclear deterrent:

4.1. Credibility: Any adversary must know that India can and will retaliate with sufficient nuclear weapons to inflict destruction and punishment that the aggressor will find unacceptable if nuclear weapons are used against India and its forces.

4.2. Effectiveness: The efficacy of India's nuclear deterrent be maximised through synergy among all elements involving reliability, timeliness, accuracy and weight of the attack.

4.3 Survivability:

(i) India's nuclear forces and their command and control shall be organised for very high survivability against surprise attacks and for rapid punitive response. They shall be designed and deployed to ensure survival against a first strike and to endure repetitive attrition attempts with adequate retaliatory capabilities for a punishing strike which would be unacceptable to the aggressor.

(ii) Procedures for the continuity of nuclear command and control shall ensure a continuing capability to effectively employ nuclear weapons.

5. Command and Control

5.1. Nuclear weapons shall be tightly controlled and released for use at the highest political level. The authority to release nuclear weapons for use resides in the person of the Prime Minister of India, or the designated successor(s).

5.2. An effective and survivable command and control system with requisite flexibility and responsiveness shall be in place. An integrated operational plan, or a series of sequential plans, predicated on strategic objectives and a targeting policy shall form part of the system.

5.3. For effective employment the unity of command and control of nuclear forces including dual capable delivery systems shall be ensured.

5.4. The survivability of the nuclear arsenal and effective command, control, communications, computing, intelligence and information (C_1J_2) systems shall be assured.

5.5. The Indian defence forces shall be in a position to, execute operations in an NBC environment with minimal degradation.

5.6. Space based and other assets shall be created to provide early warning, communications, damage/detonation assessment.

6. Security and Safety

6.1. Security: Extraordinary precautions shall be taken to ensure that nuclear weapons, their manufacture, transportation and storage are fully guarded against possible theft, loss, sabotage, damage or unauthorised access or use.

6.2. Safety is an absolute requirement and tamper proof procedures and systems shall be instituted to ensure that unauthorised or inadvertent activation/use of nuclear weapons does not take place and risks of accident are avoided.

6.3. Disaster control: India shall develop an appropriate disaster control system capable of handling the unique requirements of potential incidents involving nuclear weapons and materials.

7. Research and Development

7.1. India should step up efforts in research and development to keep up with technological advances in this field.

7.2. While India is committed to maintain the deployment of a deterrent which is both minimum and credible, it will not accept any restraints on building its R&D capability.

8. Disarmament and Arms Control

8.1. Global, verifiable and non-discriminatory nuclear disarmament is a national security objective. India shall continue its efforts to achieve the goal of a nuclear weapon-free world at an early date.

8.2. Since no-first use of nuclear weapons is India's basic commitment, every effort shall be made to persuade other States possessing nuclear weapons to join an international treaty banning first use.

8.3. Having provided unqualified negative security assurances, India shall work for internationally binding unconditional negative security assurances by nuclear weapon states to non-nuclear weapon states.

8.4. Nuclear arms control measures shall be sought as part of national security policy to reduce potential threats and to protect our own capability and its effectiveness.

8.5. In view of the very high destructive potential of nuclear weapons, appropriate nuclear risk reduction and confidence building measures shall be sought, negotiated and instituted.

Source: Embassy of India, Washington D.C. Available online. URL: http://www.indianembassy.org/policy/CTBT/nuclear_doctrine_Aug_17_1999.html. Accessed December 24, 2008. See also Harsh V. Pant. "India's Nuclear Doctrine and Command Structure: Implications for India and the World." Paper for delivery at the 2004 Annual Meeting of the American Political Science Association, September 2–September 5, 2004.

NORTH KOREA

North Korean Statement on Its Withdrawal from the NPT (January 10, 2003)

According to the Agreed Framework signed by North Korea and the United States in 1994, North Korea was required to freeze its nuclear weapons program and dismantle its facilities for producing and processing plutonium. That agreement followed an 18-month-long crisis and intense diplomatic negotiations. However, North Korea violated that agreement, actually expanding the scope of its nuclear weapons program by acquiring technology to produce highly enriched uranium. As evidence of that particular violation came to light, North Korea admitted to American representatives in October 2002 that it had equipment to enrich uranium. In response, the Korean Peninsula Energy Development Organization (KEDO), the organization formed under the Agreed Framework to provide aid to North Korea, suspended oil shipments to North Korea. North Korea responded on January 10 by announcing that it was withdrawing from the Nuclear Nonproliferation Treaty (NPT), effective January 11. That withdrawal itself violated the NPT, which requires three months' notice of withdrawal. However, North Korea claimed this was not the case because almost 10 years earlier, in March 1993, it had announced its withdrawal from the treaty but then suspended that withdrawal.

Pyongyang, 10 January: The government of the Democratic People's Republic of Korea issued a statement today as regards the grave situation where the national sovereignty and the supreme interests of the state are most seriously threatened by the US vicious hostile policy towards the DPRK.

The full text of the statement reads: A dangerous situation where our nation's sovereignty and our state's security are being seriously violated is prevailing on the Korean Peninsula due to the US vicious hostile policy towards the DPRK.

The United States instigated the International Atomic Energy Agency (IAEA) to adopt another "resolution" against the DPRK on 6 January in the wake of a similar "resolution" made on 29 November, 2002.

Under its manipulation, the IAEA in those "resolutions" termed the DPRK "a criminal" and demanded it scrap what the US called a "nuclear programme" at once by a verifiable way in disregard of the nature of the nuclear issue, a product of the US hostile policy towards the DPRK, and its unique status in which it declared suspension of the effectuation of its withdrawal from the Nuclear Non-Proliferation Treaty (NPT).

Following the adoption of the latest "resolution", the IAEA director general issued an ultimatum that the agency would bring the matter to the UN Security Council to apply sanctions against the DPRK unless it implements the "resolution" in a few weeks.

This clearly proves that the IAEA still remains a servant and a spokesman for the US and the NPT is being used as a tool for implementing the US hostile policy towards the DPRK aimed to disarm it and destroy its system by force.

A particular mention should be made of the fact that the IAEA in the recent "resolution" kept mum about the US which has grossly violated the NPT and the DPRK-US agreed framework, but urged the DPRK, the victim, to unconditionally accept the US demand for disarmament and forfeit its right to self-defence, and the agency was praised by the US for "saying all what the US wanted to do." This glaringly reveals the falsehood and hypocrisy of the signboard of impartiality the IAEA put up.

The DPRK government vehemently rejects and denounces this "resolution" of the IAEA, considering it as a grave encroachment upon our country's sovereignty and the dignity of the nation.

It is none other than the US which wrecks peace and security on the Korean Peninsula and drives the situation there to an extremely dangerous phase.

After the appearance of the Bush administration, the United States listed the DPRK as part of an "axis of evil", adopting it as a national policy to oppose its system, and singled it out as a target of pre-emptive nuclear attack, openly declaring a nuclear war.

Systematically violating the DPRK-US Agreed Framework, the US brought up another "nuclear suspicion" and stopped the supply of heavy oil, reducing the AF to a dead document. It also answered the DPRK's sincere proposal for the conclusion of the DPRK-US non-aggression treaty and its patient efforts for negotiations with such threats as "blockade" and "military punishment" and with such an arrogant attitude as blustering that it may talk but negotiations are impossible.

The US went so far to instigate the IAEA to internationalize its moves to stifle the DPRK, putting its declaration of a war into practice. This has eliminated the last possibility of solving the nuclear issue of the Korean Peninsula in a peaceful and fair way.

It was due to such nuclear war moves of the US against the DPRK and the partiality of the IAEA that the DPRK was compelled to declare its withdrawal from the NPT in March 1993 when a touch-and-go situation was created on the Korean Peninsula.

As it has become clear once again that the US persistently seeks to stifle the DPRK at any cost and the IAEA is used as a tool for executing the US hostile policy towards the DPRK, we can no longer remain bound to the NPT, allowing the country's security and the dignity of our nation to be infringed upon.

Under the grave situation where our state's supreme interests are most seriously threatened, the DPRK government adopts the following decisions to protect the sovereignty of the country and the nation and their right to existence and dignity: firstly, the DPRK government declares an automatic and immediate effectuation of its withdrawal from the NPT, on which "it unilaterally announced a moratorium as long as it deemed necessary" according to the 11 June, 1993, DPRK-US joint statement, now that the US has unilaterally abandoned its commitments to stop nuclear threat and renounce hostility towards the DPRK in line with the same statement.

Secondly, it declares that the DPRK withdrawing from the NPT is totally free from the binding force of the safeguards accord with the IAEA under its Article 3.

The withdrawal from the NPT is a legitimate self-defensive measure taken against the US moves to stifle the DPRK and the unreasonable behaviour of the IAEA following the US though we pull out of the NPT, we have no intention to produce nuclear weapons and our nuclear activities at this stage will be confined only to peaceful purposes such as the production of electricity.

If the US drops its hostile policy to stifle the DPRK and stops its nuclear threat to the DPRK, the DPRK may prove through a separate verification between the DPRK and the US that it does not make any nuclear weapon.

The United States and the IAEA will never evade their responsibilities for compelling the DPRK to withdraw from the NPT, by ignoring the DPRK's last efforts to seek a peaceful settlement of the nuclear issue through negotiations.

Source: Atomicarchive.com. Available online. URL: http://www.atomicarchive.com/Docs/Deterrence/DPRKNPT statement.shtml. Accessed December 24, 2008.

North Korean Announcements of Nuclear Tests in 2006 and 2009 (October 9, 2006, and May 25, 2009)

Three years and nine months after withdrawing from the NPT, North Korea announced its first nuclear test. The North Koreans announced a second test in 2009. In both cases the tests were widely condemned by nations around the world, but nothing was done to restrain the North Korean nuclear weapons program.

DPRK Successfully Conducts Underground Nuclear Test

Pyongyang, October 9, 2006 (KCNA)—The Korean Central News Agency released the following report: The field of scientific research in the DPRK successfully conducted an underground nuclear test under secure conditions on October 9, Juche 95 (2006) at a stirring time when all the people of the country are making a great leap forward in the building of a great prosperous powerful socialist nation:

It has been confirmed that there was no such danger as radioactive emission in the course of the nuclear test as it was carried out under a scientific consideration and careful calculation.

The nuclear test was conducted with indigenous wisdom and technology 100 percent. It marks a historic event as it greatly encouraged and pleased the KPA and people that have wished to have powerful self-reliant defence capability.

It will contribute to defending the peace and stability on the Korean Peninsula and in the area around it.

KCNA Report on One More Successful Underground Nuclear Test

Pyongyang, May 25, 2009 (KCNA)—The Korean Central News Agency released the following report on Monday in connection with one more successful underground nuclear test in the DPRK.

Democratic People's Republic of Korea successfully conducted one more underground nuclear test on May 25 as part of the measures to bolster up its nuclear deterrent for self-defence in every way as requested by its scientists and technicians.

The current nuclear test was safely conducted on a new higher level in terms of its explosive power and technology of its control and the results of the test helped satisfactorily settle the scientific and technological problems arising in further increasing the power of nuclear weapons and steadily developing nuclear technology.

The successful nuclear test is greatly inspiring the army and people of the DPRK all out in the 150-day campaign, intensifying the drive for effecting a new revolutionary surge to open the gate to a thriving nation.

The test will contribute to defending the sovereignty of the country and the nation and socialism and ensuring peace and security on the Korean Peninsula and the region around it with the might of Songun.

Source: Korean Central News Agency of the DPRK. Available online. URLs: http://www.kcna.co.jp/item/2006/200610/news10/10.htm; http://www.kcna.co.jp/item/2009/200905/news25/20090525-12ee.html. Accessed June 1, 2009.

PART III

Research Tools

6

How to Research Weapons of Mass Destruction

Anyone who regularly keeps up with current events can hardly avoid learning something about weapons of mass destruction. The nuclear weapons programs of Iran, North Korea, and Pakistan and the threats they pose both to their neighbors and to the United States are constantly in the news. Another regular news story is the overall instability in the Middle East, which inevitably is tied to weapons of mass destruction known to be in the hands of several countries in the region. It may no longer be front-page news, but the issue of Russian-American arms control is widely discussed in the media as well as by academics, independent scholars, Congress, and government officials. How to defend against WMD—whether nuclear, biological, or chemical—is another issue that generates a huge amount of discussion in the media. Nor is it difficult to find technical information on WMD, from how they are made to the dangers posed simply by storing them or moving them around.

The information on WMD comes from many sources: books, magazine articles, articles in scholarly journals, television and radio programs, and, of course, the Internet. The problem is not finding the information. Any researcher starting out will soon be overwhelmed by what is available. The problem is sorting through it all to separate fact from opinion and figure out what is reliable and what is not. That requires finding material produced by people with two fairly rare qualities: expertise in the subject they are discussing and a commitment to present information and make arguments in a balanced way.

GETTING STARTED

If you are preparing a research project or a written report, nothing is more important than defining your topic. The overall issue of weapons of mass destruction is a vast subject with dozens of branches and subtopics. Is your project or report going to be about what these weapons are and how they work? Are you going to discuss the three different types of WMD or, for example, only nuclear or biological or chemical weapons? Do you want to focus on how to defend against WMD, on attempts to stop the spread of those weapons, or on how terrorists might try to use these weapons? Will your project or report be about the United States or Russia, or perhaps some other country or a particular region of the world? Will your project or report include some combination of these topics? Since the subject of WMD probably is new to you, if you are doing a project or report it will take some research before you can define your topic so that it is manageable. This often is the most difficult part of a research project, but it is something you want to do as quickly as possible so that you can move forward in an effective and orderly fashion.

Today, the most popular way for students to start a research project is to turn on their computers and Google the subject in which they are interested. This is not necessarily the best way, even though a computer search almost immediately will turn up hundreds or even thousands of sources. The problem is that with the Internet it is very difficult to know the quality of the information you are getting. Some Web sites belonging to government agencies, private research institutes, colleges or universities, or even groups that exist to promote certain causes are excellent sources of information. However, the Internet is littered with Web sites put up by people or organizations with a variety of agendas. Often these agendas are unstated, and the information the Web sites in question provide, although it looks impressive and may in fact be helpful if it is used carefully, is biased and one-sided. Just as often it may be completely inaccurate. As a result, even people who already know something about the subject they are researching can be misled. Almost anyone can set up a Web site or a blog, claim expertise and balance, and then say whatever they want. Some sites, as anyone who uses the Internet ought to know, are not simply uninformative or misleading but quite literally dangerous, as they are put up by people who know how to infect your computer with malicious viruses.

It may be tempting to begin researching by accessing the Wikipedia online encyclopedia, whose articles often look expert and impressive and, in fact, sometimes are quite good. The problem is that you never know. Reputable publications such as the *Encyclopedia Britannica,* the *Columbia Encyclopedia,* or the *World Book Encyclopedia* hire recognized experts to write their articles and entries, and then often identify the author so you know whose work you are reading. There is a consistent quality to the articles they contain, no matter what the subject. In contrast, anyone can write for

Wikipedia. Students who turn to Wikipedia may find themselves reading an article by a reliable expert, but the author of what looks like a scholarly article may be someone else entirely.

Perhaps your Wikipedia author is a recognized professional, although that is doubtful, or someone else who knows a great deal about your subject. But perhaps it is someone else. It could easily be another student or someone with an axe to grind. It could even be someone who knows less about your subject than you do but feels like showing off. The more controversial a subject is—and WMD are controversial—the more likely that a Wikipedia article will be seriously flawed. So it is vital that you begin, and continue, your research somewhere other than Wikipedia.

BREADTH BEFORE DEPTH

When beginning the study of a complex subject such as weapons of mass destruction, an excellent approach is to look at several sources that provide a broad overview of your subject. Consulting several sources—books, articles, or Web site entries—has a number of advantages. Because WMD are such an enormous subject, different authors inevitably stress different aspects of them. Consulting several sources normally will give you a fuller view of the overall subject than just looking at one source. It will help direct your research to the specific topics you are most interested in learning about. Consulting several sources also will make you more aware of how different authors and experts on a topic can approach it differently, focus on different questions, and use the same information to reach different conclusions. This in turn will make you aware that you will have to look critically at every source you consult and rely on your own educated judgment in balancing conflicting information and conclusions others have drawn from their data.

CREDENTIALS AND CREDIBILITY

It takes someone who is well informed to give a student a useful overview of a subject. That is why it is so important to know the credentials of the person or persons who wrote what you are reading, produced the news or information program you are watching, or manages the Web site you are accessing. Doctors, lawyers, accountants, and other professionals often post their academic degrees on their office walls to assure prospective clients they have the expertise those clients seek. A journalist with a scientific background is better prepared to understand and explain the dangers posed by Level 4 laboratories than one with similar overall experience but with an educational background in politics or history. A specialist on current Russian politics is likely to do a better job of interpreting the available information about Russian WMD programs than someone who is not familiar with the Russian government and its objectives. Expertise also comes from being on the job for a while. A journalist who has spent years covering military affairs in Washington is more likely to have better credentials for discussing weapons of mass destruction than a colleague with the same college or university degree who has focused on local politics in New York or California. A person who has worked for years as a national security specialist for a government agency or a respected private institution can draw on a wealth of background information that a newcomer to that field does not have.

In other words, credentials are extremely important. But so are reasoned judgment and balance, qualities that do not get a line on a person's résumé. The fact that someone has a Ph.D. in a particular subject or has spent years working in a given field is no guarantee of objectivity. It does not guarantee that bias or a particular point of view will not distort how that person looks at a problem and ultimately reports on it to you. Every person has his or her point of view, and every source therefore must be examined with a critical eye. Sources must be checked against other sources. This is particularly true with a subject such as weapons of mass destruction, where experts strongly disagree about issues such as the usefulness of certain treaties, the potential effectiveness of defensive systems against ballistic missiles, and the best way to deal with countries such as Iran and North Korea. In short, students beginning a research project must not only ask questions about their subject but about where their source material on that subject is coming from.

SOURCES OF INFORMATION

Print Resources

BOOKS

As with putting information on the Internet, anyone can write a book. But then a vetting process begins. An author must find someone to publish his or her book. Publishers vary in quality. They can be every bit as biased or malicious as Web sites, so just because a book has been published does not mean it is objective or reliable. To be sure, a lot of terrible books get published every year. But, in most cases, it is easier for students to find out about authors and publishers than about Internet Web sites. Authors and book publishers over time develop reputations, and careful checking—perhaps with a teacher, librarian, or even on the Internet—can help you learn about whose work you are reading and the company that published the book. In addition, books that reach the shelves of school libraries must make it past librarians who are trained to find materials that are helpful to students. Many books have a short blurb that identifies their authors. This information normally includes their professional credentials, other works they have written, and similar material. Often this can be checked. This system is far from foolproof, but leaves a lot less to chance than when you simply Google a phrase, go to a Web site you or anyone else has never heard of, and start reading without, quite literally, knowing where you are.

Books have other advantages. No matter what the subject, any author can give a reader more background, context, analysis, and information in a book than is possible in a shorter work. Because of their size, books have more depth and/or breadth than a typical Internet entry. At the same time, to the extent a book stresses depth it must sacrifice breadth, and vice versa. Take, for example, two books on weapons of mass destruction you can find in the bibliography of this volume. *Commonsense on Weapons of Mass Destruction,* by Thomas Graham, Jr., which runs 200 pages, gives readers a helpful general overview of WMD, including information on biological and chemical weapons as well as nuclear weapons. *Bomb Scare: The History and Future of Nuclear Weapons,* by Joseph Cirincione, is about the same length, but as its title tells us it focuses exclusively on nuclear weapons. The former introduces the reader to all three kinds of WMD—although mainly to nuclear weapons—but the latter covers nuclear weapons more thoroughly. In their coverage of nuclear weapons, both books introduce their readers to the development of the hydrogen bomb, but by necessity only for a few pages. If one needs a truly comprehensive description of how the hydrogen bomb was developed, the place to go is a book like *Dark Sun: The Making of the Hydrogen Bomb,* by Richard Rhodes, who devotes about 700 pages to that subject alone. Both *Commonsense on Weapons of Mass Destruction* and *Bomb Scare* touch on Israel's nuclear program. But if you really want to know how Israel succeeded in developing nuclear weapons you are better advised to check out *The Bomb in the Basement* by Michael Karpin, who takes almost 400 pages just to tell the story of that small episode in the history of nuclear weapons. The same applies to India's nuclear program. Both *Commonsense on Weapons of Mass Destruction* and *Bomb Scare* provide brief introductions to that subject, but you must go elsewhere for a thorough discussion. That is what George Perkovich will give you in his 600-page volume *India's Bomb: The Impact on Global Proliferation.*

If you are interested in all of these countries, and others as well, and also in all types of weapons of mass destruction, a good book to turn to is *Deadly Arsenals: Nuclear Biological and Chemical Threats,* by Joseph Cirincione, Jon B. Wolfstahl, and Miriam Rajkuman. While focusing on the situation as it exists today, *Deadly Arsenals* also provides some historical background on the WMD programs of different countries. In *War of Nerves: Chemical Warfare from World War I to Al-Qaeda,* Jonathan B. Tucker provides an outstanding overview of the history of modern chemical warfare. Jeanne

Guillemin focuses on biological weapons in *Biological Weapons: From the Invention of State-Sponsored Programs to Contemporary Bioterrorism.* An excellent survey of both biological and chemical warfare is *Chemical and Biological Warfare: A Comprehensive Survey for the Concerned Citizen,* by Eric Croddy.

SCHOLARLY JOURNALS

Scholarly journals are very valuable sources of information. They also generally are more up to date than books, as books take a longer time to write and publish. However, scholarly journals are not for everyone. Most of the articles in scholarly journals are written by experts in a particular field for other experts, and so they often are dense and quite technical and can be tough going for students and other nonspecialists. One advantage of scholarly journals is a process known as peer review. Most scholarly journals have articles that are sent to them for publication read by several experts in the field. Depending on what those experts say, the article is accepted or rejected. Sometimes the editors of the journal or members of its editorial board review the article themselves. Either way, articles submitted to scholarly journals go through a careful vetting process. This by no means eliminates bias, but it still is a useful method of quality control.

Scholarly journals are specialized, and some of the fields they cover are quite narrow. However, often those fields are broader, and journals concerned with history, science, international relations, or even medicine therefore will publish articles dealing with weapons of mass destruction. For example, in this book's annotated bibliography you will find an article called "Biological Warfare in Eighteenth-Century North America: Beyond Jeffrey Amherst." It was published in the *Journal of American History,* most of whose contributors are college professors whose interests range across the full spectrum of American history. Another article on the history of WMD, "History of Chemical and Biological Warfare Agents," appeared in the journal *Toxicology,* a highly specialized scientific journal that publishes articles on biological poisons dangerous to humans and animals. *Toxicology* is the official journal of the British Toxicology Society and the German Toxicology Society. In 2007, the *Journal of the American Medical Association,* the leading American medical journal, carried a short article on concerns about the rapid expansion in the number of Level 4 biosafety laboratories in the United States. Other articles on WMD in the bibliography come from *Science,* the highly respected journal of the American Association for the Advancement of Science; the *Nonproliferation Review,* a peer-reviewed journal published by the James Martin Center for Nonproliferation Studies; and *Emerging Infectious Diseases,* which is published by the Centers for Disease Control, a branch of the U.S. Department of Health and Human Services.

Occasionally a scholarly journal will dedicate all or part of an issue to a single topic. For example, in 2008 *Joint Force Quarterly,* a publication of the U.S. government's National Defense University, printed a group of articles on weapons of mass destruction. Several of those articles are listed in this book's bibliography. A journal that regularly publishes some of the most up-to-date information on nuclear weapons and arsenals is the *Bulletin of the Atomic Scientists,* which is available online.

Scholarly journals are published by a variety of organizations, from academic groups to private think tanks to government agencies. There is, unfortunately, no single journal devoted exclusively to weapons of mass destruction, so students or researchers interested in WMD must cast their nets widely when studying this subject.

MAGAZINES AND NEWSPAPERS

Magazines and newspapers can provide up-to-date information on issues such as weapons of mass destruction. Some of the better publications also provide very useful background articles or even commentary by experts in the field. These articles can be very helpful to students because they are aimed at the general reader. However, it is important to remember that journalists who write these articles rarely have the expertise of authors of scholarly articles or books. The three leading circulation newsmagazines in the United States are *U.S. News and World Report, Newsweek,* and *Time.* The *Wall Street Journal* and the *New York Times* are two daily newspapers with the resources to cover issues such as weapons of mass destruction in depth. There are many other magazines and newspapers that can be helpful as well. A good idea is to speak with a librarian about the publications available at your school or public library.

Sources on the Internet

There is not much that cannot be found on the Internet. You can access scholarly journals, visit the online sites of newspapers and television networks, and even find entire books posted at an assortment of Web sites. Collections of documents that once required trips to specialized libraries to use are now available on the Internet. This section will briefly survey some of the different types of Web sites on the Internet that are helpful in learning about weapons of mass destruction.

PRIVATE ORGANIZATIONS

Some of the Web sites with the best information on WMD belong to private organizations that engage in research but also are working to limit or reverse the spread of WMD. The Nuclear Threat Initiative (NTI), which was founded in 2001 by former Georgia senator Sam Nunn and businessman Ted

Turner, is one such organization. While it is fair to say that the NTI favors certain policies, such as providing money and expertise to Russia to help it secure dangerous materials, the reports it compiles nonetheless are remarkably objective and informative. Another organization with a similar point of view that provides reliable information and produces excellent reports is the James Martin Center for Nonproliferation Studies (CNS). GlobalSecurity.org also produces and posts well-researched reports. However, the news reports posted on its Web site come from a variety of organizations, some of which are more reliable than others. NTI, CNS, and GlobalSecurity.org are all based in the United States. The Stockholm International Peace Research Institute is based in Sweden, but thanks to the Internet many of the reports of this respected international organization are now easily within reach of all of us.

U.S. GOVERNMENT AGENCIES AND INTERNATIONAL ORGANIZATIONS

Agencies of the U.S. government also can be excellent sources for reports and up-to-date news. These include the Central Intelligence Agency, whose *CIA World Factbook* contains an up-to-date overview, including key statistics, of every country in the world. Similar information is available at the Web site of the U.S. State Department. The Web sites of the Defense Threat Reduction Agency, a branch of the Department of Defense, and the Department of Homeland Security, have very helpful information on weapons of mass destruction. So does the Web site of the National Nuclear Security Administration, a branch of the Department of Energy. The Congressional Research Service publishes reports for members of Congress on a wide variety of issues, including WMD.

The International Atomic Energy Agency (IAEA), the organization charged with verifying compliance with the Nuclear Nonproliferation Treaty, provides reports regarding its mission on its Web site. That is also true of the Organization for the Prohibition of Chemical Weapons, whose mission is to assure compliance with the Chemical Weapons Convention. Both of these organizations, while independent, have special working relationships with the United Nations. Both also have what may be called an institutional bias toward international diplomacy, even in cases where lengthy diplomatic efforts have not been successful. The United Nations itself presents another problem for researchers. Not all of its agencies are equally reliable as sources of information. Several of them are dominated by officials from undemocratic nations and justifiably have been accused of bias against certain countries.

7

Facts and Figures

INTERNATIONAL

1.1 Nuclear Testing Chronology, 1945–2009

COUNTRY	1945 –49	1950 –59	1960 –69	1970 –79	1980 –89	1990 –99	2006 –09	TOTAL
United States[1]	6	188	428	232	155	21		1,030
USSR/Russia	1	82	232	227	172	1		715
Great Britain[2]	0	21	5	5	12	2		45
France	0	0	31	69	92	18		210
China	0	0	10	16	7	10		43
India	0	0	0	1	0	5		6
Pakistan	0	0	0	0	0	6		6
North Korea	0	0	0	0	0	0	2	2
Totals	**7**	**291**	**706**	**550**	**438**	**64**		**2,057**

[1] This total excludes 24 joint U.S./British nuclear tests.
[2] This total includes the 24 US/British nuclear tests.

This table includes only known nuclear tests. Many experts believe that Israel has conducted at least one nuclear test, in 1979 in cooperation with South Africa, and perhaps two more. The United States conducted its first nuclear test in 1945, its last in 1992. Russia (at the time the Soviet Union) conducted its first nuclear test in 1949, its last in 1990. Great Britain's first and last nuclear tests were, respectively, in 1952 and 1991; France's in 1960 and 1996; and China's in 1964 and 1996. India conducted a nuclear test in 1974 and then five more in May 1998. Pakistan conducted six nuclear tests in May 1998.

Source: Atomicarchive.com. Atomicarchive.com only lists tests up to 1999. Also, it lists seven Indian tests rather than six.

1.2 U.S. and Soviet Nuclear Tests by Year, 1945–1992

YEAR	U.S. TESTS/ +U.S.-UK	SOVIET TESTS	YEAR	U.S. TESTS/ +U.S.-UK	SOVIET TESTS
1945	1	n/a	1969	46	19
1946	2	n/a	1970	39	16
1947	0	n/a	1971	24	23
1948	3	n/a	1972	27	24
1949	0	1	1973	24	17
1950	0	0	1974	22/+1	21
1951	16	2	1975	22	19
1952	10	0	1976	20/+1	21
1953	11	5	1977	20	24
1954	6	10	1978	19/+2	31
1955	18	6	1979	15/+1	31
1956	18	9	1980	14/+3	24
1957	32	16	1981	16/+1	21
1958	77	34	1982	18/+1	19
1959	0	0	1983	18/+1	25
1960	0	0	1984	18/+2	27
1961	10	59	1985	17/+1	10
1962	96/+2	79	1986	14/+1	0
1963	47	0	1987	14/+1	23
1964	45/+2	9	1988	15	16
1965	38/+1	14	1989	11/+1	7
1966	48	18	1990	8/+1	1
1967	42	17	1991	7/+1	n/a
1968	56	17	1992	6	n/a
			total	**1,054**	**715**

The U.S. numbers include 24 tests conducted jointly with Great Britain. The number of exclusive U.S. tests is 1,030. Of the 1,054 tests, 210 were in the atmosphere, 839 were underground, and five were underwater. Of the 715 Soviet nuclear tests, 219 were in the atmosphere, underwater, or in space, and 496 were underground.

Sources: Department of Energy. *United States Nuclear Tests: July 1945 through September 1992* (December 2000). Ministry of the Russian Federation for Atomic Energy. *USSR Nuclear Tests and Peaceful Nuclear Explosions,* edited by V. N. Mikailov, 1996; *Catalogue of Worldwide Nuclear Testing*. V. N Mikahilov, editor in chief; National Defense Resource Council.

1.3 Defense Threat Reduction Agency Inspections under Four WMD Treaties

Treaty/Agreement	Date Signed	Signatories to Date	Entry into Force	Expiration Date	Number of Inspections to Date	Comments
Chemical Weapons Convention (CWC)	January 13, 1993	183 countries, including the U.S. and Russia	April 29, 1997	None	865 inspections of DoD[1] sites; 84 inspections of U.S. commercial industry facilities	The Technical Secretariat of the OPCW[2] conducts inspections.
Comprehensive Test Ban Treaty (CTBT)	Sept. 24, 1996	177 countries, including all NPT-recognized nuclear weapons states; 140 countries have ratified.	Not in force	None	None	U.S. Senate rejected the CTBT on October 13, 1999, by a vote of 51-48. However, the U.S. continues a moratorium on nuclear tests.
Intermediate Range Nuclear Forces (INF) Treaty	Dec. 8, 1997	U.S., U.S.S.R/Russia, Belarus, Kazakhstan, Ukraine	June 1, 1988	Inspections ceased May 31, 2001, after 13 years.	U.S. conducted 511 inspections in Russia; Russia conducted 275 inspections in U.S. and Europe.	All INF missile systems were eliminated as of May 30, 1991; continuous on-site portal[3] monitoring occurred at Votkinsk, Russia, and Magna, Utah, from July 1988 through May 31, 2001.
Strategic Arms Reduction Treaty (START)	July 1, 1991	U.S., Russia, Ukraine, Belarus, Kazakhstan	Dec. 5, 1994	15 years with possible extensions	Through Treaty Year 10, December 2004, U.S. conducted 569 inspections and Russia conducted 389.	

[1] Department of Defense

[2] Organization for the Prohibition of Chemical Weapons

[3] Monitoring by equipment installed at the facility in question

The Defense Threat Reduction Agency is the agency of the Department of Defense that is responsible for carrying out arms control inspections and monitoring under the verification provisions to arms control treaties signed by the United States. This chart shows the status of four of the treaties discussed in this volume.

Source: Defense Threat Reduction Agency. "DTRA Arms Control Inspections at a Glance." January 2008.

1.4 Countries with Weapons of Mass Destruction

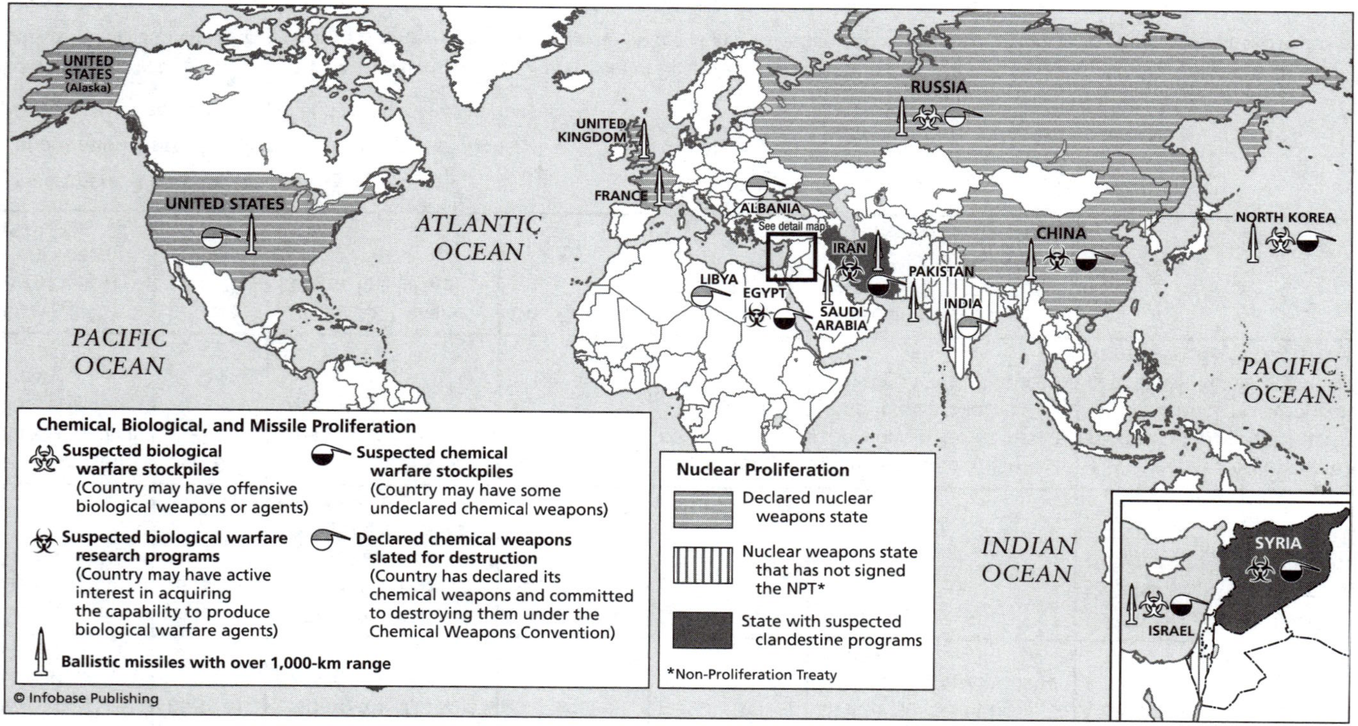

In addition to the countries that are known to have nuclear weapons or are suspected of having nuclear weapons programs, a number of countries are suspected of having chemical and/or biological weapons or programs to develop those weapons. Several countries are in the process of destroying their declared chemical weapons stockpiles. Every country with nuclear weapons also has ballistic missiles with a range of more than 1,000 km (600 miles).

Source: Carnegie Endowment for International Peace

U.S. AND SOVIET/RUSSIAN ARSENALS

2.1 U.S. and Russian Strategic Nuclear Forces under START I, START II, and the Treaty of Moscow

	START I		START II		TREATY OF MOSCOW	
	Launchers[1]	Warheads	Launchers	Warheads	Launchers	Warheads
ICBMS: United States	550	1,700	550	500	450	500–600
ICBMs: Russia	542	2,168	805	805	300	900
SLBMs: United States	432	3,168	336	1,680	264	1,056–1,152
SLBMs: Russia	292	1,592	228	1,512	96	384
Bombers: United States	206	1,098	97	1,276	77	500–850
Bombers: Russia	78	624	78	936	65	780
Total: United States	1,188	5,966	933	3,456	791	2,200
Total: Russia	912	4,383	1,111	3,253	461	2,064
Total:	**2,100**	**10,349**	**2,044**	**6,709**	**1,252**	**4,264**

[1] Launchers are called "delivery vehicles" in the text.

This table shows the declining size of the U.S. and Russian nuclear arsenals permitted by START I, START II, and the Treaty of Moscow. START II never entered into force.

Source: Congressional Research Service. CRS Report for Congress. Amy F. Woolf. "Nuclear Arms Control: The Strategic Offensive Reductions Treaty." Updated January 8, 2008. (Order Code RL31448)

2.2 Nuclear Warheads and Bombs in the U.S. Arsenal in 2009

WEAPON	TYPE	DELIVERY SYSTEM	PRIMARY USE	SERVICE	ENTERED STOCKPILE
W62	ICBM	Minuteman III	Surface to Surface	Air Force	1970
W78	ICBM	Minuteman III	Surface to Surface	Air Force	1979
W87	ICBM	Minuteman III	Surface to Surface	Air Force	1986
W76	SLBM	Trident I (C4)	Underwater to Surface	Navy	1978
W88	SLBM	Trident II (C5)	Underwater to Surface	Navy	1989
B61-3/4/10	Bomb	F-15, F-16	Air to Surface	Air Force	1979/1990
B61-7/11	Bomb	B-52H, B-2A	Air to Surface	Air Force	1985/1996
B83	Bomb	B-52H, B-2A	Air to Surface	Air Force	1983
W80-0/1	Missile	SSN Submarine B-52-H	Underwater to Surface Air to Surface	Navy Air Force	1984/1982

The total number of weapons in the U.S. nuclear arsenal and the quantity of each type is kept secret for national security purposes. The Minuteman and Trident are ballistic missiles. The F-15, F-16, F-52H, and B-2A are airplanes. The W80-0 and W80-1 are warheads. The W80-0 is designed to be delivered by a Tomahawk cruise missile launched from a submarine. The W80-1 is designed to be carried by a cruise missile launched from a B52-H bomber.

Source: National Nuclear Security Administration. Available online. URL: http://nnsa.energy.gov/defense_programs/weapons.htm. Accessed June 2, 2009.

2.3 Strategic Nuclear Weapons in Non-Russian Former Soviet Republics

STATE	STRATEGIC NUCLEAR WEAPONS IN 1991	STRATEGIC NUCLEAR WEAPONS AS OF 2002
Belarus	81 SS-25 single-warhead mobile ICBSs	All SS-25 single-warhead mobile ICBMs, with warheads and launchers, removed in November 1996.
Kazakhstan	104 SS-18 10-warhead silo-based ICBMs (1,040 warheads) 40 Bear H bombers	All SS-18s removed from silos and silos destroyed; all warheads, bombers, and cruise missiles returned to Russia.
Ukraine	130 SS-19 6-warhead silo-based ICBMs 46 SS-24 10-warhead silo-based ICBMs About 40 strategic bombers More than 500 air-launched cruise missiles	All SS-19 silos and SS-24 silos have been destroyed. Ukraine has completed dismantling of bombers, after transferring 11 to Russia; and transferred or dismantled all cruise missiles.

This report documents the elimination of all Soviet-era nuclear weapons from Belarus, Kazakhstan, and Ukraine. These countries contained 20 percent of the Soviet Union's strategic nuclear weapons. All of the Soviet nuclear warheads were returned to Russia by the end of 1996. Only Ukraine had missiles (without warheads) and silos after that date. By 2002, all silos had been destroyed and all ICBMs and had either been eliminated or disassembled.

Sources: U.S. Department of Defense; CRS Issue Brief for Congress. Amy F. Woolf. "Nuclear Weapons in Russia: Safety, Security and Control Issues." Updated April 12, 2002. (Order Code IB98038)

2.4 Nunn-Lugar Fiscal Year Funding

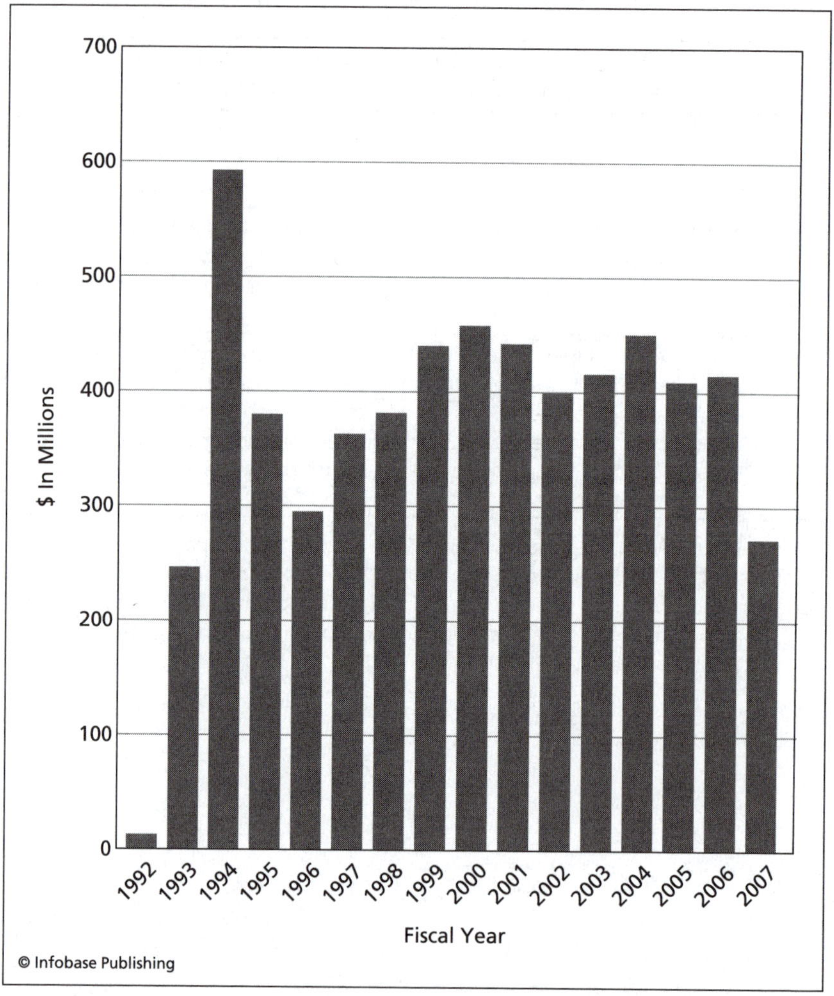

Along with eliminating nuclear weapons and materials, the Nunn-Lugar program works to secure and destroy chemical and biological weapons. It has also participated in two projects—the International Science and Technology Centers and the International Proliferation Program—that reemploy scientists and/or facilities formerly involved in weapons research in peaceful research initiatives.

Source: Office of Senator Richard G. Lugar. "The Nunn-Lugar Scorecard" (December 2008). Available online. URL: http://lugar.senate.gov/nunnlugar/scorecard.html. Accessed June 2, 2009.

2.5 Nunn-Lugar Scorecard for Russia and Other States of the Former Soviet Union (as of December 2008)

WEAPON OR ACTIVITY	REDUCTIONS TO DATE	PERCENT OF 2012 TARGETS	2012 TARGETS
Warheads deactivated	7,298	79%	9,222
ICBMs destroyed	728	67%	1,078
ICBM silos eliminated	496	77%	645
ICBM mobile launchers destroyed	137	51%	267
Nuclear weapons carrying submarines destroyed	31	88%	35
SLBMs eliminated	631	91%	691
SLBM launchers eliminated	456	81%	564
Nuclear air-to-surface missiles destroyed	906	100%	906
Bombers eliminated	155	100%	155
Nuclear test tunnels/holes sealed	194	100%	194
	Established or carried out to date	**Percent of 2012 Targets**	**2012 Targets**
Nuclear weapon storage site upgrades	18	75%	24
Biological monitoring stations built and equipped	16	29%	55

The Nunn-Lugar Scorecard is issued by the office of Senator Richard Lugar of Indiana. It mentions that Ukraine, Kazakhstan, and Belarus are free of nuclear weapons.

Source: Office of Senator Richard G. Lugar. "The Nunn-Lugar Scorecard" (December 2008). Available online. URL: http://lugar.senate.gov/nunnlugar/scorecard.html. Accessed June 2, 2009.

3.1 Locations of Select WMD Sites in Israel

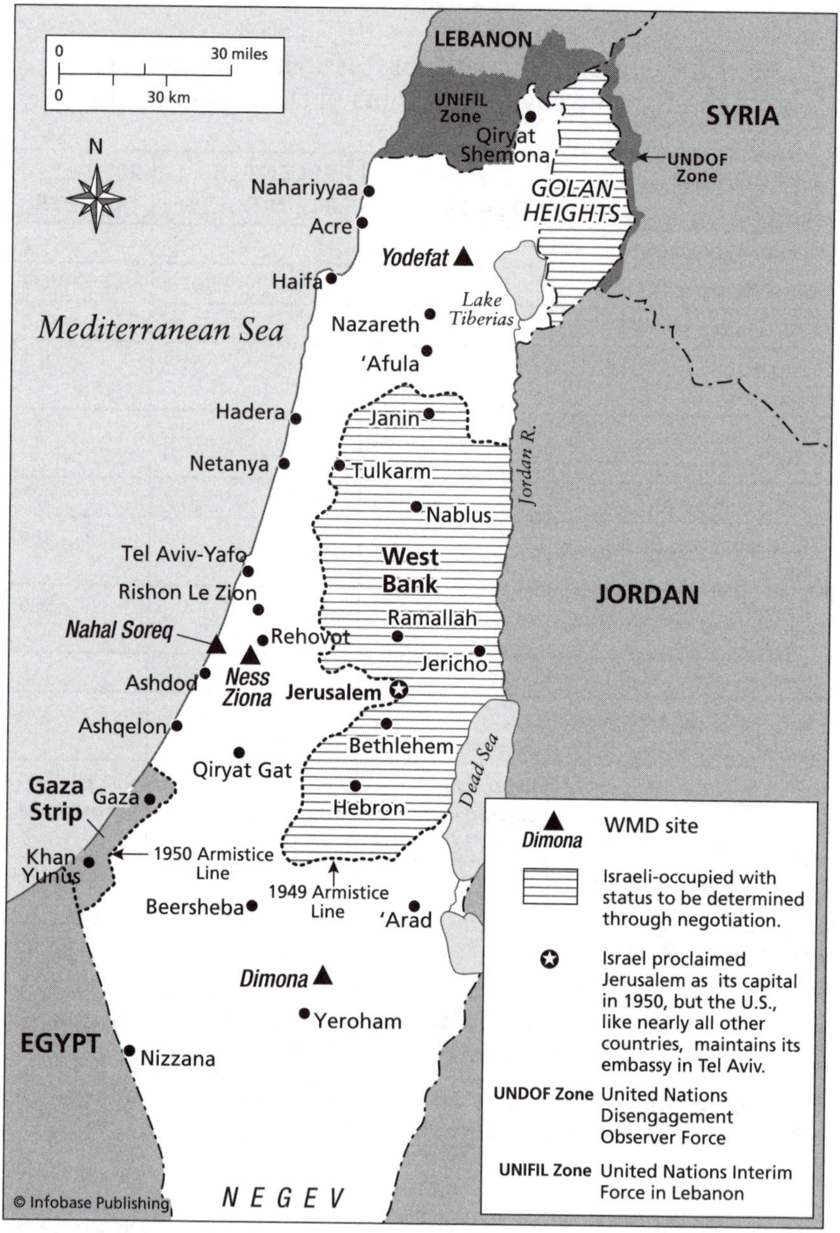

Dimona: Site of the Negev Nuclear Research Center. Includes a nuclear reactor, a plant to reprocess plutonium, facilities for enriching uranium, and other facilities related to Israel's nuclear weapons program.

Nahal Soreq: Probably Israel's laboratory for weapons design and research. It has a small research reactor that Israel purchased from the United States in the mid-1950s.

Yodefat: Possibly the location of a facility that assembles nuclear weapons.

Ness Ziona: Location of the Israel Institute of Biological Research (IIBR), Israel's center for defense-related biological and chemical research.

3.2 Locations of Select WMD Sites in India

Trombay: Site of the Bhabha Atomic Research Center (BARC), India's most important nuclear weapons program institution. The center has a range of nuclear research programs, two research reactors that produce plutonium, and a plant for reprocessing plutonium for nuclear weapons. BARC also builds nuclear weapons.

Tarapur: Site of nuclear power station and a plant that extracts plutonium from spent fuel for use in nuclear weapons.

Kalpakkam: Site of the Indira Gandhi Center for Atomic Research and a plant for reprocessing plutonium for use in nuclear weapons.

Pokhran: Location of the nuclear test range where India's nuclear tests of 1974 and 1998 were conducted.

3.3 Locations of Select WMD Sites in Pakistan

Kahuta: Location of the Khan Research Laboratory, Pakistan's most important nuclear weapons facility. It includes a plant that uses centrifuges to produce weapons-grade uranium.

Kushab: Center for Pakistan's plutonium program, which uses a nuclear reactor not open to IAEC inspections.

Multan: Site of a facility producing heavy water for nuclear reactors.

Rawalpindi: Laboratory and facilities for plutonium reprocessing.

Ras Koh and Wazir Khan Kosa: The two sites used for Pakistan's 1998 nuclear tests. The first five tests, on May 28, were done at a mountainous area called Ras Koh; the sixth test, on May 30, was done about 60 miles (100 km) to the west in a desert location called Wazir Khan Kosa.

3.4 Locations of Select WMD Sites in North Korea

Yongbyon: The most important of the estimated 18 locations in North Korea that have facilities related to the production of nuclear weapons. Yongbyon includes the original research reactor supplied by the Soviet Union, North Korea's 5MW(e) nuclear reactor, a facility for reprocessing plutonium, and other facilities. The complex also includes an unfinished 50MW reactor whose design would have made it a major source of plutonium. Construction was suspended under the 1994 Agreed Framework. An estimated 3,000 scientists and researchers work at Yongbyon.

Pyongyang: North Korea's capital houses various nuclear-related laboratories and facilities. Recent intelligence has revealed a secret underground nuclear power plant in the city.

Taechon: Site of an unfinished 200MW(e) nuclear power reactor whose design would have made it a major source of plutonium. Construction was suspended under the 1994 Agreed Framework.

Sunchon: Site of facility for processing uranium ore, some of which comes from nearby mines.

Sinpo: Site of two light-water nuclear power plants that were to have been built under the 1994 Agreed Framework. Construction was suspended when that agreement collapsed.

8

Key Players A to Z

MAHMOUD AHMADINEJAD (1956–)
President of Iran since 2005. Ahmadinejad is a bitter foe of the United States and a virulent anti-Semite who has repeatedly called for the destruction of Israel. His views are shared by many of Iran's leaders, a country ruled by an Islamic theocracy. For these and many other reasons, Iran's nuclear program is of grave concern to the United States and other democratic nations. Not only Israel, but several of Iran's neighbors that are Muslim and Arab, consider Iran's nuclear program to be a threat to their security.

IRA BALDWIN (1895–1999) Head of scientific research for the U.S. biological weapons program during World War II. Baldwin was the chairman of the bacteriology department at the University of Wisconsin before taking his wartime position in the Special Operations Division, a unit within the Chemical Warfare Service. Baldwin enforced the strictest safety precautions in his facilities at Camp Detrick (now Fort Detrick). After the war he returned to the University of Wisconsin but also continued to advise the U.S. government on biological weapons and the threat posed by the Soviet Union. Baldwin supported tests in which harmless bacteriological agents were sprayed into the air in public urban places like subways to test the potential effectiveness of pathogens dispersed in that manner. The tests were conducted from the mid-1940s through the mid-1960s and became controversial when they became public knowledge in 1977.

DAVID BEN-GURION (1886–1973) Founding prime minister of Israel. Ben-Gurion served as Israel's prime minister from the country's founding in 1948 until 1953 and again from 1955 until 1963. He was convinced that Israel had to have nuclear weapons to guarantee its security in the face of the refusal of Arab states to accept Israel's right to exist. Since Israel in 1948 was incapable of undertaking a nuclear program, Ben-Gurion promoted the development of chemical and biological weapons as interim measures. But he remained convinced that nuclear weapons were vital, and Israel began its nuclear program in the early 1950s.

ERNST DAVID BERGMANN (1903–1975) Israeli scientist. Bergmann was born in Germany and earned a doctorate in chemistry at the University of Berlin. With the founding of Israel in 1948, Bergmann became a close adviser to Prime Minister DAVID BEN-GURION, who appointed him head of the Scientific Corps of the Israeli Defense Forces. In 1952, Bergmann founded both the Israel Institute for Biological Research (IIBR) and the country's Atomic Energy Commission. He played a central role in the development of Israel's chemical and biological warfare programs on the one hand and its nuclear weapons program on the other.

LAVRENTY BERIA (1899–1953) One of Soviet dictator JOSEPH STALIN's most brutal and sadistic henchmen, and also one of the most competent and efficient, Beria headed the Soviet secret police from 1938 until the end of World War II. In 1941, he became deputy chairman of the Soviet government and played a key role in organizing the economy for the war effort. In 1945, Stalin put Beria in charge of the Soviet program to build an atomic bomb, the postwar project Stalin considered the country's single most important priority. As always, Beria was utterly ruthless and grimly efficient in rushing the project to a successful conclusion. Most of the construction and mining was done under appalling conditions by hundreds of thousands of slave laborers from the Soviet network of labor camps known as the Gulag. Even many of the scientists who worked on the project were Gulag prisoners, although they were housed and worked in special facilities under tolerable conditions. Beria was present at the first Soviet atomic bomb test on August 29, 1949. By the time of the first hydrogen bomb test in August 1953, Stalin was dead and Beria, who was feared and hated by most of Stalin's other top lieutenants, was under arrest. He was executed in December 1953.

HOMI JEHANGIR BHABHA (1909–1966) Indian physicist, considered the father of India's nuclear program. Bhabha had an outstanding academic career as a physicist before World War II, which included studying with ENRICO FERMI in Rome. He established India's Atomic Energy Commission in 1948 and consistently argued that India should develop nuclear weapons. India's most important nuclear research center, located in the Mumbai suburb of Trombay, is named in his honor. Bhabha died in a plane crash in 1966.

ZULFIKAR ALI BHUTTO (1928–1979) Prime minister of Pakistan, 1973 to 1977. Well before he became prime minister, Bhutto strongly advocated that Pakistan develop nuclear weapons. He strongly supported that program while serving as his country's leader. Bhutto was overthrown by a military coup in 1977 and eventually executed.

GEORGE HERBERT WALKER BUSH (1924–) President of the United States, 1989 to 1993. Bush was president when the cold war finally ended. After Iraq invaded neighboring Kuwait in 1990, Bush organized a broad coalition of nations that drove Iraq from Kuwait. In the aftermath of that war, Iraq had to agree to UN inspections that eliminated its programs of mass destruction, including a nuclear program that was far more advanced than anyone had expected. In July 1991, Bush concluded the START I nuclear arms treaty with Soviet president MIKHAIL GORBACHEV.

GEORGE W. BUSH (1946–) President of the United States, 2001 to 2009. Bush was in office less than a year when Islamic terrorists destroyed the World Trade Center in New York City and badly damaged the Pentagon in Washington, D.C., killing nearly 3,000 people. In 2002, he withdrew the United States from the 1972 ABM treaty so that the United States could build a missile defense system to defend itself against rogue states such as Iran or North Korea. In 2003, concerned that Iraq was still hiding weapons of mass destruction and might pass them on to terrorists, Bush ordered the invasion of Iraq to depose SADDAM HUSSEIN.

JAMES EARL CARTER (1924–) President of the United States, 1977 to 1981. As president, Carter signed the SALT II treaty with Soviet leader Leonid Brezhnev. However, because of growing tensions between the United States and the Soviet Union that treaty was never ratified and did not enter into force. In 1994, Carter brokered the Agreed Framework between North Korea and the United States that was supposed to end North Korea's nuclear weapons program. However, North Korea violated that agreement, secretly continuing its program and eventually conducting a nuclear test in 2006.

WILLIAM JEFFERSON CLINTON (1946–) President of the United States, 1993 to 2001. The Clinton administration signed the Agreed Framework with North Korea, which North Korea ultimately violated. During the 1990s, the Clinton administration successfully arranged for Ukraine, Belarus, and Kazakhstan to give up the nuclear weapons they had inherited when the Soviet Union collapsed and transfer them to Russia. It also implemented the Nunn-Lugar Cooperative Threat Reduction Program, which had been enacted into law in 1991. In 1993, the Clinton administration cancelled the Strategic Defense Initiative antiballistic missile project begun during the REAGAN administration.

ALBERT EINSTEIN (1879–1955) Author of the theories of special and general relativity and 1921 Nobel Prize laureate in physics. Einstein is recognized as one of the greatest minds in the history of science. His theories literally revolutionized modern physics and our understanding of the universe. Forced to flee Germany in 1933 because of Nazi anti-Semitism, Einstein immigrated to the United States. In 1939, he wrote a letter to President Roosevelt warning that Nazi Germany might attempt to develop the atomic bomb. That letter helped to set in motion events that led to the Manhattan Project and the successful U.S. effort to build an atomic bomb. The transuranic element einsteinium (atomic number 99) is named in his honor.

DWIGHT D. EISENHOWER (1890–1969) President of the United States, 1953 to 1961. As part of an effort to reduce the cost of maintaining a military strong enough to deter the Soviet Union, Eisenhower supported the buildup of the U.S. nuclear arsenal. A large nuclear arsenal permitted a reduction in U.S. conventional forces, which in turn allowed Eisenhower to limit the overall military budget.

ENRICO FERMI (1901–1954) Head of the team that achieved the world's first controlled chain reaction and 1938 Nobel Prize laureate in physics. Fermi was one of the greatest physicists of the 20th century. He fled his native Italy to escape fascism in 1938 and immigrated to the United States. Fermi joined the Manhattan Project and headed the team that built the world's first nuclear reactor and, on December 2, 1942, achieved the world's first controlled nuclear chain reaction. After World War II, Fermi took a position at the University of Chicago. The transuranic element fermium (atomic number 100) is named in his honor.

PAUL FILDES (1882–1971) Head of the biology department at Porton Down, the facility that housed Great Britain's chemical and biological warfare programs during World War II. Fildes was in charge of Britain's anthrax experiments on Guinard Island during 1942 and 1943. With Prime Minister Winston Churchill's support, Fildes drew plans for a massive anthrax bombing of Germany, although the war ended before these plans could be carried out. After the war, in the late 1940s, Fildes was in charge of open-sea testing of biological weapons.

KLAUS FUCHS (1911–1988) Physicist and Soviet spy. A member of Germany's Communist Party, Fuchs fled his native country in 1933 and went to Britain, where he earned his doctorate in physics. In 1943, he was one of the British scientists sent to the United States to work on the atomic bomb. He was assigned to work at Los Alamos, from where he passed on crucial information about the plutonium implosion bomb to the Soviet Union. After the war, he also passed on information about the hydrogen bomb, although that information was not particularly useful since U.S. scientists themselves still had not yet mastered the key methods for building such a bomb. Fuchs was tried and convicted in Britain of espionage in 1950 and sentenced to 14 years in prison. Upon release after serving only nine years, Fuchs lived in East Germany for the rest of his life.

INDIRA GANDHI (1917–1984) Prime Minister of India from 1966 to 1977 and again from 1980 until 1984. Gandhi strongly supported India's nuclear weapons program, and India's first test of a nuclear device in 1974 took place during her first term in office. During that term, India and Pakistan fought the war that resulted in Pakistan being split into two parts, Pakistan and Bangladesh. Gandhi was assassinated while in office in 1984.

MIKHAIL GORBACHEV (1931–) Leader of the Soviet Union from 1985 to 1991. As Soviet leader, Gorbachev introduced both dramatic domestic reforms and major changes in Soviet foreign policy. Under his leadership, the Soviet Union entered two major nuclear arms control agreements with the United States: the INF treaty in 1987 and the START I treaty in 1991. Gorbachev deserves a major share of the credit for ending the cold war. However, Gorbachev never admitted the existence of the Biopreparat biological weapons program, which the Soviet Union maintained in violation of the Biological Weapons Convention.

LESLIE R. GROVES (1896–1970) Head of the Manhattan Project. A West Point graduate, Groves compiled a distinguished record in the Army Corps of Engineers, which included overseeing the construction of the Pentagon. He was placed in charge of the Manhattan Project in September 1942. One of his most important decisions was choosing J. ROBERT OPPENHEIMER to head the laboratory within the Manhattan Project that designed and built the atomic bomb. Groves chose Oppenheimer despite the latter's close ties to known communists but also had Oppenheimer watched very carefully throughout the Manhattan Project years. Groves retired from the army in 1948 and worked for the Sperry Rand Corporation until 1961.

OTTO HAHN (1879–1968) Codiscoverer of nuclear fission and 1944 Nobel Prize laureate in chemistry. Working in Berlin in 1938, Hahn and radiochemist Fritz Strassmann conducted experiments by bombarding uranium with neutrons. Their objective was to produce transuranic elements, but the experiments yielded unexpected results. It turned out that the experiment had caused the uranium to fission. This discovery opened the possibility that it was possible to build an atomic bomb and that Nazi Germany would attempt to do so. These conclusions caused the United States to begin the Manhattan Project.

SADDAM HUSSEIN (1937–2006) Dictator of Iraq from 1979 to 2003. Saddam Hussein was a murderous tyrant who admired both Adolf Hitler and JOSEPH STALIN. He promoted extensive programs to develop biological, chemical, and nuclear weapons. During Iraq's war with Iran (1980–88), which began when Hussein ordered an attack on Iran, Iraq used chemical weapons against Iranian soldiers and against Kurdish citizens of Iraq. Iraq may have been within six months of developing an atomic bomb when Hussein invaded and occupied neighboring Kuwait. The occupation of Kuwait led to a multinational assault against Iraq led by the United States and a short conflict known as the Gulf War of 1991. Iraq's defeat in that war was followed by the dismantling of its WMD programs by UN inspectors. In 2003, Hussein's refusal to permit UN inspectors to continue their work led to an American invasion and Hussein's overthrow. He was tried for crimes against humanity and executed in 2006.

SHIRO ISHII (1892–1959) Head of Japan's biological weapons program during World War II. As the head of a special unit within the Japanese army called Unit 731, Ishii was responsible for horrific experiments involving biological pathogens on thousands of prisoners that have justifiably been compared to the experiments carried out by the Nazi at the same time. Unit 731 also released fleas infected with bubonic plague, contaminated Chinese water sources, and committed many other similar acts that undoubtedly were war crimes. However, Ishii escaped prosecution for his crimes because the United States hoped he could provide valuable information on biological warfare. It turned out that his information had little value.

BRUCE E. IVINS (1946–2008) Anthrax mailing suspect. Ivins was a microbiologist for 28 years at the U.S. government's biodefense laboratory at Fort Detrick. He committed suicide when he was informed he was about to be indicted for murder in the 2001 anthrax mailing attacks that killed five U.S. postal workers.

JOHN F. KENNEDY (1917–1963) President of the United States, 1961 to 1963. Upon taking office, Kennedy began a major buildup of U.S. nuclear forces, which he believed was necessary in light of the Soviet military threat. However, after the Cuban missile crisis of 1962, Kennedy attempted to reduce tensions with the Soviet Union. One result was the signing of the Limited Nuclear Test Ban Treaty of 1963 by the United States, the Soviet Union, and Great Britain. President Kennedy was assassinated less than four months after that treaty was signed.

ABDUL QADEER KHAN (1939–) Pakistani nuclear scientist whose secret network provided nuclear weapons equipment and technology to Iran, Libya, North Korea, and possibly other countries. Khan is considered the father of Pakistan's nuclear bomb, whose development he assisted in part with technology he stole while working in Europe. His international black market network helped make him a rich man while also helping to advance Pakistan's program.

YULI B. KHARITON (1904–1996) Physicist who was the first scientific director of the Soviet Union's Arzamas-16 nuclear weapons facility, a post he held from its founding in 1946 until 1992. Most of Khariton's work remains shrouded in secrecy, although some details finally became public during the 1990s. In an interview in 1993, Khariton confirmed that as a result of Soviet spying on the Manhattan Project the first Soviet atomic bomb, which was tested in 1949, was a copy of the first American plutonium bomb developed at Los Alamos in 1945. Khariton remained an important adviser to the Soviet government on nuclear weapons issues throughout his career. It is believed that he was the last surviving physicist who helped develop the first Soviet atomic bomb.

NIKITA KHRUSHCHEV (1894–1971) Leader of the Soviet Union, 1953 to 1964. As Soviet leader, Khrushchev strongly supported the Soviet nuclear weapons program and the development of ballistic missiles, especially ICBMs, to deliver them to their targets. At the same time, he undertook reforms at home to lessen the harshness of the Soviet system and improve the country's standard of living. In 1961, Khrushchev ended the moratorium the Soviet Union had been observing on nuclear tests, beginning a series of tests that included the detonation of Tsar Bomba, the 57-megaton bomb. In October of 1962, he blundered into the Cuban missile crisis, which brought the United States and the Soviet Union to the brink of nuclear war.

KIM IL SUNG (1912–1994) North Korean dictator. Kim was the founding dictator of North Korea and the architect of its totalitarian communist dictatorship. Kim caused the Korean War by invading South Korea in 1950 and established the priorities that deprived the Korean people of basic necessities while diverting most of the country's resources to its military and nuclear program.

KIM JONG IL (1941–) Dictator of North Korea. Kim Jong Il succeeded his father KIM IL SUNG as dictator of North Korea, although it appears that it took him three years to fully establish his power. He continued his father's policies. Under Kim Jong Il's leadership, North Korea violated the Agreed Framework signed with the United States in 1994, renounced the NPT in 2003, and conducted a nuclear test in 2006.

RICHARD KUHN (1900–1967) Developer of soman and 1938 Nobel Prize laureate in chemistry. Kuhn was born in Vienna, Austria, and studied chemistry at Vienna University and Munich University, where he received his Ph.D when he was only 22 years old. He won the Nobel Prize in chemistry for his work on carotenoids and vitamins, but because Hitler objected to the award he was unable to accept the award until after World War II. During the war, Kuhn worked for the German army on tabun and sarin; it was while doing that work that he discovered soman in 1944. After the war Kuhn was professor of chemistry, and then biochemistry, at the University of Heidelberg.

IGOR KURCHATOV (1903–1960) Physicist and the father of the Soviet atomic bomb. During the 1930s, Kurchatov headed a laboratory in Leningrad that did groundbreaking work in nuclear physics. His first job during World War II was working on ways to protect ships from magnetic mines. Kurchatov was appointed scientific director of the Soviet Union's atomic bomb project at its inception in 1943 and served in that post until his death in 1960. Aided by information provided by Soviet spies, Kurchatov's team successfully tested the Soviet Union's first atomic bomb on August 29, 1949. It appears that Kurchatov, who worked directly under LAVRENTY BERIA, feared he would be shot if the test failed. Kurchatov also worked on the development of a thermonuclear bomb. However, after the U.S. test of a 15-megaton bomb in 1954 and the Soviet test of a fully thermonuclear bomb of 1.5 megatons in 1955, Kurchatov became seriously worried of the dangers posed to civilization and even life on Earth by hydrogen bombs. He spoke out against further nuclear testing and refused to take charge of any more nuclear weapons tests.

RICHARD M. NIXON (1913–1994) President of the United States, 1969 to 1974. Nixon dealt with all three categories of WMD during his presidency. In 1969, he announced that the United States was renouncing the use of biological weapons and would destroy its stock of those weapons. He reaffirmed a no-first-use policy regarding chemical weapons and extended that policy to include chemical weapons that incapacitate rather than kill. Most notably, as part of the policy of improving relations with the Soviet Union, the Nixon administration negotiated and in 1972 signed the SALT I nuclear arms control treaties—the ABM treaty and the interim agreement on offensive nuclear missiles—with the Soviet Union.

J. ROBERT OPPENHEIMER (1904–1966) Oppenheimer was a brilliant physicist but also a remarkable manager, which is why he was chosen by General LESLIE GROVES to head the Los Alamos laboratory, the unit of the Manhattan Project charged with designing and actually building an atomic bomb. Under Oppenheimer's direction, the staff at Los Alamos grew from a few dozen to several thousand. It solved a vast array of theoretical and practical problems and by the summer of 1945 produced two types of fission bombs: a uranium gun-fired bomb and a plutonium implosion bomb. After the war, Oppenheimer was an adviser to the U.S. Atomic Energy Commission from 1947 to 1952 and also headed Princeton University's Institute of Advanced Studies. As an adviser to the AEC, he opposed the development of the hydrogen bomb. In 1953, Oppenheimer was accused of being a security risk because of his political beliefs. Although several of his friends and family members were communists, and while there is considerable evidence that in the 1930s Oppenheimer himself was a secret member of the Communist Party, there was no evidence that he ever betrayed any nuclear secrets. Still, the Atomic Energy Commission took away his security clearance, which was necessary to have access to state secrets involving nuclear research, in a case that bitterly divided the country's scientific community. In 1963, Oppenheimer was awarded the prestigious Enrico Fermi Award of the Atomic Energy Commission by President Lyndon Johnson. Oppenheimer died three years later of throat cancer.

VLADIMIR PASECHNIK (1937–2001) Soviet defector who exposed Biopreparat. Pasechnik was an outstanding microbiologist who headed an elite biological warfare laboratory in Leningrad before he defected from the Soviet Union. By the 1980s, he had become very distressed about the nature of his work. When he was allowed to travel abroad for the first time in 1989, he defected by going to the British embassy in Paris. His information led the United States and Great Britain to pressure Soviet leader Mikhail Gorbachev to reveal more about Biopreparat, which clearly violated the Biological Weapons Convention, but the Soviets were uncooperative. Pasechnik's information was confirmed when Ken Alibek defected from Russia in 1992.

SHIMON PERES (1923–) President of Israel and architect of Israel's nuclear weapons program. In his long career, Peres has held most of the key leadership positions in Israel, including that of prime minister, foreign minister, and minister of defense. In 1953, when he was only 29 years old, Peres was appointed director general of the Ministry of Defense, a post he held until 1959. In that position, and as deputy defense minister from 1959 until 1965, Peres oversaw the establishment of Israel's nuclear program and the building of the Dimona nuclear reactor. Peres was the key person in establishing Israel's cooperative relationship with France that included cooperation in nuclear weapons research and France selling Israel a nuclear reactor.

RONALD REAGAN (1911–2004) President of the United States, 1981 to 1989. Reagan was a staunch anticommunist who during his first term took a hard line in dealings with the Soviet Union but during his second term worked successfully with Soviet leader Mikhail Gorbachev to reverse the Soviet-American nuclear arms race. In 1983, Reagan proposed the development of an antiballistic missile system called the Strategic Defense Initiative (SDI). In 1987, during Reagan's second term, the United States and Soviet Union signed the INF treaty, which eliminated the two countries' intermediate- and short-range land-based ballistic missiles. In 1991, the two countries signed the START I treaty, which significantly reduced Soviet and U.S. arsenals of strategic missiles. Although Reagan and his successor, George H. W. Bush, funded SDI, the program was cancelled by the Clinton administration.

FRANKLIN D. ROOSEVELT (1882–1945) President of the United States, 1933 to 1945. Roosevelt led the United States through most of World War II, dying a month before Germany's surrender and four months before Japan's surrender and the end of the war. Deeply concerned that Germany might develop an atomic bomb, Roosevelt authorized the establishment of the Manhattan Project. In order to keep the project secret—including from most members of Congress—its huge budget was hidden inside the overall military budget. Roosevelt did not live to see the final development of the bomb. The United States tested its first atomic bomb on July 16, 1945, two months after he died from a stroke.

ANDREI SAKHAROV (1921–1989) Designer of the first Soviet hydrogen bomb and 1975 Nobel Peace Prize laureate. Sakharov was working at the Physics Institute of the Soviet Union's Academy of Science when he was recruited to work for Igor Kurchatov in the Soviet nuclear weapons program. Sakharov produced his layer cake design that year, and it was successfully tested in August 1953. After that test, Sakharov continued to work with other leading Soviet physicists on a fully thermonuclear bomb. That work produced a successful test in November 1955. Sakharov also worked on the 57-megaton Tsar Bomba, which was detonated in October 1961. But by then he was having misgivings about the danger of thermonuclear weapons and spoke against nuclear testing. From there, Sakharov moved on to become an advocate of human rights and, increasingly, a critic of the dictatorial nature of the Soviet Union. In 1968, he warned that the Soviet Union would decline if it did not undertake democratic reforms, and in 1975 he was awarded the Nobel Peace Prize. The Soviet regime kept Sakharov in internal exile from 1980 to 1986 in the city of Gorky—a city closed to foreigners—until he was released by Mikhail Gorbachev. Sakharov continued to be a prominent supporter of democratic reform in the Soviet Union until felled by a heart attack in 1989.

GERHARD SCHRADER (1903–1990) Discoverer of tabun and sarin. Schrader was a chemist working on developing insecticides for the German chemical giant I. G. Farbin when he accidentally discovered sarin in December 1936. In 1938, he developed an even more deadly nerve agent, initially called substance 146, that eventually was called sarin. Schrader was arrested by the British after World War II but released in 1946 and allowed to continue his career as a chemist.

JOSEPH STALIN (1878–1953) Soviet dictator from the 1920s until 1953. Stalin was one of the most brutal and murderous dictators of all time. Between 1929 and his death in 1953, he was responsible for the deaths of tens of millions of Soviet citizens. After the United States used an atomic bomb to attack Hiroshima in August 1945, Stalin made the development of a Soviet nuclear bomb a top priority, putting Lavrenty Beria in charge of the project. The first Soviet fission bomb was tested almost exactly four years later. The first Soviet hydrogen bomb was tested in August 1953, five months after Stalin's death.

HENRY L. STIMSON (1867–1950) U.S. secretary of war during World War II. Stimson had a long and distinguished career in government service, including serving as secretary of state from 1929 to 1933, before becoming Franklin D. Roosevelt's secretary of war in 1940. In that position, Stimson played a key role in the decision-making that led to the bomb's use against Japan. He chaired the Interim Committee appointed by Harry S. Truman to advise him on both wartime and postwar matters related to the bomb. It was at Stimson's insistence that the bomb not be used against the city of Kyoto, Japan's ancient capital and the site of many of its historical national treasures. Stimson retired from government service in 1945, shortly after Japan's surrender brought World War II to an end.

EDWARD TELLER (1908–2003) Considered the father of the hydrogen bomb. Teller was one of many Jewish scientists who were forced to flee Germany because of Nazi persecution. In 1935, he came to the United States and was appointed professor of physics at George Washington University. Teller had made several important contributions in both physics and chemistry when he was invited to work on the Manhattan Project. He worked at Los Alamos until 1946. After the war, Teller strongly urged the United States to develop a hydrogen bomb. His initial design for a thermonuclear bomb turned out to be faulty, but soon thereafter he and the mathematician Stanislaw Ulam came up with a design that did in fact work. Teller was associate director of the newly established Lawrence Livermore National Laboratory from 1954 to 1958 and its director from 1958 to 1960. During his tenure there the laboratory developed the first nuclear warhead for a submarine-launched ballistic missile. Teller believed it was both necessary and possible for the

United States to build an antimissile defense system. He helped to convince Ronald Reagan to begin the SDI program and vigorously defended the program in the debates that took place after it was announced.

PAUL TIBBETS, JR. (1915–2007) Pilot of the mission that bombed Hiroshima. Tibbets was one of the outstanding U.S. bomber pilots when he was chosen to command and train a newly established unit whose task it would be to drop an atomic bomb on Japan. The unit, the 509th Composite Group, began intensive training in December 1944. Tibbets elected to fly the crucial mission against Hiroshima himself, naming the B-29 that carried the first atomic bomb the *Enola Gay* after his mother. In order to prevent a catastrophic accident in case the plane crashed on takeoff—not an uncommon occurrence with the complex aircraft that had been rushed into combat—the atomic bomb on board was not armed until after *Enola Gay* was safely airborne. That task, under freezing conditions in the bomb bay, was performed by naval gunnery expert William S. Parsons. The bombing of Hiroshima set in motion events that finally forced Japan to surrender, ending World War II.

HARRY S. TRUMAN (1884–1972) President of the United States, 1945 to 1953. Shortly after becoming president after the death of Franklin D. Roosevelt, Truman made the final decision to use the atomic bomb against Japan. Two bombs were dropped, the first on Hiroshima on August 6, 1945, and the second on Nagasaki three days later. In 1950, Truman authorized the development of the hydrogen bomb.

9

Organizations and Agencies

Many organizations provide information on weapons of mass destruction. Some of the most informative are U.S. government agencies, especially those attached to the Department of Defense, Department of Energy, and the State Department. International organizations such as the Organization for the Prohibition of Chemical Weapons (OPCW) or the International Atomic Energy Agency (IAEA) are valuable sources in their areas of responsibility and expertise. There also are many private organizations of varying points of view with the expertise to gather and publish useful material on matters ranging from technical information about weapons of mass destruction to issues such as arms control and WMD nonproliferation. It is important to understand that many private groups and think tanks, while claiming to be nonpartisan, are in fact advocacy groups with an agenda. They have excellent information on WMD, but at the same time they support policies they believe will promote the national interest or some other desirable goal. The following is a selection of private and government organizations and agencies that can help you learn about weapons of mass destruction.

Aerospaceweb.org
URL:// http:www.aerospaceweb.org

This is an educational Web site operated by engineers and scientists in the aerospace field. It was created in 2000 and in April 2006 was selected by the Voice of America, a U.S. government-funded news service, as the "Website of the Week." The Aerospace.org Web site provides information on subjects ranging from military aircraft and strategic and tactical missiles to space travel and careers in the industry. It is a good place to learn about a career in the aerospace industry. The site contains a virtual museum and an "Ask a Rocket Scientist" feature. The latter feature receives about 100 questions per week. The eight aerospace professionals responsible for the site cannot answer all the questions they receive; instead each week they respond to one or two they believe will be of interest to their readership as a whole.

American Association for the Advancement of Science
1200 New York Avenue NW
Washington, D.C. 20005
Phone: (202) 326-6400
E-mail: webmaster@aaas.org
URL: http://www.aaas.orgg/

The AAAS, founded in 1848, is affiliated with 272 societies and academies of sciences worldwide. It publishes the highly respected journal *Science.* Its Web site provides links to an enormous variety of reports and papers on topics such as nuclear weapons policy, U.S. national security, and other subjects related to weapons of mass destruction. Its many activities range from hosting high-level scientific conferences to promoting the teaching and learning of science in our schools.

American Enterprise Institute for Public Policy Research
1150 Seventeenth Avenue NW
Washington, D.C. 20036
Phone: (202) 862-5800
URL: http://www.aei.org

The American Enterprise Institute is a private foundation that focuses its research and education efforts on issues of government, politics, economics, and social welfare. It has a staff of resident and visiting scholars and fellows and also works with about 100 adjunct scholars and fellows, most of whom are academics at universities in the United States. A keyword search at the AEI Web site for "nuclear weapons," "weapons of mass destruction," "chemical weapons," and "biological weapons" yields a vast array of sources, including many articles the AEI calls "short publications." The AEI's approach tends to be conservative and supportive of a strong national defense.

The Brookings Institution
1775 Massachusetts Avenue
Washington, D.C. 20036
Phone (202) 797-6000
URL: http://www.brook.edu

The Brookings Institution was established in 1927. Its staff includes more than 200 resident and nonresident scholars who produce a vast variety of books, articles, papers, studies, and other material on a wide array of contemporary issues. The Brookings Institution tends to have a reformist, liberal approach to these issues. A keyword search at the Brookings Web site on either "weapons of mass destruction" or "nuclear weapons" yields more than 1,000 sources on each subject, while a keyword search on "chemical weapons" or "biological weapons" yields several hundred sources on each subject.

Bulletin of the Atomic Scientists
77 West Washington Street
Suite 2120
Chicago, IL 60602
Phone (312) 364-9710
URL: http://www.thebulletin.org

The *Bulletin of the Atomic Scientists* is a magazine founded in 1945 by scientists who had worked on the Manhattan Project, were concerned about the threat nuclear weapons posed to all nations, and wanted to see international control of those weapons. It is published by a foundation with the same name. Today, the magazine's interests have broadened beyond nuclear weapons. Its Web site states that its purpose is to inform the public about the "threats to the survival and development of humanity posed by nuclear weapons, climate change, and emerging technologies in the life sciences." Among the many useful articles are overviews of the nuclear forces of various nuclear powers, such as "U.S. nuclear forces, 2008" and "Russian nuclear forces, 2008." The *Bulletin of the Atomic Scientists* has tended to be critical of the U.S. government's nuclear weapons policy. It its view, the United States has relied too much on nuclear weapons for its security and not enough on international agreements to control those weapons. Although the *Bulletin of the Atomic Scientists* and the Federation of American Scientists have ties with each other, they are separate organizations.

Center for Defense Information
1779 Massachusetts Avenue NW
Washington, D.C. 20036-2109
Phone: (202) 332-0600
URL: http://www.cdi.org

The Center for Defense Information, a private foundation, is a division of the World Security Institute. The CDI publishes a bimonthly newsletter, the *Defense Monitor,* which is widely read in Washington by members of Congress and other government officials. Its goal is to provide expert analysis on national security issues. The CDI Web site includes a "Chemical and Biological Weapons Site," which provides an overview of countries that possess or are seeking these weapons.

Center for Nonproliferation Studies

See entry for James Martin Center for Nonproliferation Studies. Best known as the CNS, this organization was renamed the James Martin Center for Nonproliferation Studies in 2007.

Center for Strategic and International Studies
1800 K. Street
Washington, D.C. 20006
Phone: (202) 775-3199
URL: http://www.csis.org

The Center for Strategic and International Studies was founded in 1962 to meet the challenges of survival posed by the cold war. Since then, it has grown into a leading private institution dealing with issues of international security. The CSIS has more than 220 full-time staff and works with a large network of affiliated scholars. It does research and sponsors programs in a wide range of subjects including defense policy, terrorism, homeland security, and the prevention of WMD proliferation. In December 2008 it published *Nuclear Weapons in the 21st Century, U.S. National Security,* which is a report by a joint working group of the AAAS, the American Physical Society, and the CSIS. The chairman of the CSIS is former Georgia senator Sam Nunn, who is also the CEO and cochair of the Nuclear Threat Initiative.

Central Intelligence Agency
Office of Public Affairs
Washington, D.C. 20505
Phone: (703) 482-0623
URL: http://www.cia.gov

The Central Intelligence Agency is an agency of the U.S. government. It was established by the National Security Act of 1947. While its primary job is to provide national security intelligence for this country's leaders that normally is classified, the CIA also has a Web site that is an excellent source of information on a variety of subjects. Probably the most useful feature for students on the CIA Web site is the *CIA World Factbook,* which contains up-to-date information on every country in the world. Another useful feature is the site's "World Leaders" link, which provides the names of the chiefs of state and cabinet members of every country, from Afghanistan to Zimbabwe.

Congressional Research Service
The Library of Congress
101 Independence Avenue
Washington, D.C. 20540-7500
Phone: (202) 707-5627
URL: http://www.loc.gov/crsinfo

The Congressional Research Service is a government think tank that provides reports to members of Congress on a wide variety of issues. It is divided into five divisions, one of which is Foreign Affairs, Defense, and Trade. That division in turn is divided into seven sections, one of which, Defense Policy and Arms Control, provides reports on weapons of mass destruction. A CRS report must be released by a member of Congress before it becomes available to the public. The best way to access CRS reports, however, is not on the CRS Web site. Instead, go to the Web site of Open CRS (http://opencrs.org) and type in keywords where it says "Search Open CRS." Often CRS reports are available on other Web sites, such as that of the Federation of American Scientists.

Defense Threat Reduction Agency
8725 John J. Kingman Road, Stop 6021
Fort Belvoir, VA 22060-6201
Phone: (703) 767-5870
URL: http://www.dtra.mil

The Defense Threat Reduction Agency, established in October 1998, is a branch of the U.S. Department of Defense. Its mission is to safeguard the United States and its allies from weapons of mass destruction. That assignment includes developing the capabilities to reduce or eliminate the threat itself and to develop measures to minimize the effects of a WMD attack. The DTRA Web site has information about how the organization carries out its mission. In addition, by clicking on "News Media Resources" it is possible to access a helpful series of fact sheets. They cover topics such as "Arms Control Conventions at a Glance," "Glossary of Chemical Weapons Agreement Terms," and "Strategic Arms Reduction Treaty (START)."

Defense Treaty Inspection Readiness Program
8275 John J. Kingman Road, Stop 6201

Fort Belvior, VA 22060-6201
Phone: (800) 419-2899
URL: http://http://dtrip.dtra.milo

The Defense Treaty Inspection Readiness Program is a U.S. Department of Defense outreach program established in 1990. Its job is to assist U.S. facilities that are subject to arms control inspections to fulfill their obligations without compromising national secrets. It uses a team of experts in fields such as counterintelligence, security expertise, and treaty inspection to accomplish that goal. This assistance is provided both to facilities belonging to the Department of Defense and to private defense contractors. The DTIRP Web site contains helpful information on WMD in its "Treaty Information Center." That feature contains three sections: "Treaty Texts and Fact Sheets," "Treaty Synopses," and "Implementation Status."

Department of Homeland Security
U.S. Department of Homeland Security
Washington, D.C. 20528
Phone: (202) 202-8000
URL: http://www.dhs.gov

The Department of Homeland Security was established in 2002, after the September 11, 2001, terrorist attacks that killed almost 3,000 Americans. The head of the agency is a member of the president's cabinet whose appointment must be approved by the Senate. The department's primary mission is to protect the United States against acts of terrorism, but as its *2008 Strategic Plan* points out, the DHS charter also charges the department with "preparation for and response to all hazards and disasters." That plan, "One Team, One Mission, Securing Our Homeland," covers the years 2008–13 and is available on the DHS Web site.

Department of State
U.S. Department of State
2201 C. Street NW
Washington, D.C. 20520
Phone: (202) 647-4000
URL: http://www.state.gov

The State Department is charged with carrying out the foreign policy of the United States. Its head is a member of the president's cabinet. The department's Web site contains an enormous range of information. For students studying WMD, an informative feature is the "A-Z List of Countries and Other

Areas," which contains extensive background information on every country in the world. Access the Office of the Coordinator for Counterterrorism for the *Country Reports on Terrorism* and related materials.

Environmental Foundation Bellona
Boks 2141 Grüerløkka
0505 Oslo, Norway
Phone: (47-2) 323-4600
URL: http://www.bellona.org

The Environmental Foundation Bellona, usually just called Bellona, was founded in Norway in 1986. Its U.S. office, which only has a post office address (P.O. Box 42090, Washington, D.C., 20015) was opened in 1996. Bellona is an advocacy group for environmental protection. There also are two offices in Russia and one in Belgium. Bellona's most urgent concern outside of Norway is nuclear contamination in Russia. The Web site contains information on Soviet nuclear testing, the security of nuclear materials in Russia and in several other former Soviet republics, Russian assistance to Iran's nuclear program, and related matters involving Russian nuclear policy. Senator Richard Lugar, cosponsor of the bill that established the Cooperative Threat Reduction Program, has praised Bellona's work in combating nuclear proliferation.

Federation of American Scientists
1725 DeSales Street NW
6th Floor
Washington, D.C. 20006
Phone: (202) 546-3300
URL: http://www.fas.org

The Federation of American Scientists was founded after World War II by scientists who had worked on the Manhattan Project. Originally called the Federation of Atomic Scientists, the FAS brought together several groups that had been formed at a number of Manhattan Project facilities. These scientists believed that they had a responsibility to inform policy makers and the public of the potential dangers posed by nuclear weapons and related scientific advances and to promote public policy that would maximize the benefits of new scientific knowledge. The FAS posts a wide variety of reports on its Web site dealing with weapons of mass destruction. It has been an advocate of arms control and often has been critical of the U.S. government for allegedly not being sufficiently committed to that end. In recent years, the FAS expanded its mission to include issues such as housing, energy, and education. Although the

Federation of American Scientists and the *Bulletin of the Atomic Scientists* have ties with each other, they are separate organizations.

GlobalSecurity.org
300 N. Washington Street
Suite B-100
Alexandria, VA 22314
Phone: (703) 548-2700
URL: http://www.globalsecurity.org

GlobalSecurity.org, established in 2000, provides background information and current news stories in fields such as weapons of mass destruction, defense, and homeland security. It is often a source used by other news organizations covering these fields. The GlobalSecurity.org Web site is updated hourly. The Web site also features a "Defense Jobs Career Center" that lists thousands of jobs with leading employers in the defense industry that are available to "U.S. citizens with active federal clearance."

Henry L. Stimson Center
1111 19th Street NW
12th Floor
Washington, D.C. 20036
Phone: (202) 223-5956
URL: http://www.stimson.org

The Henry L. Stimson Center, named in honor of the former secretary of state and secretary of war, was founded in 1989 to promote international peace and security. Its priorities, as stated on its Web site, are to strengthen institutions for international peace and security, to build regional security, and to reduce weapons of mass destruction and other transnational threats. Reports, background papers, books, and other sources on WMD are available on the center's Web site. The easiest way to access them is to click on "topic" (upper righthand side of the home page) and then on topics such as "biological and chemical," "nonproliferation." "nuclear weapons," and "theater missile defense."

Institute for Energy and Environmental Research
6935 Laurel Avenue
Suite 201
Takoma Park, MD 20912
Phone: (301) 270-5500
URL: http://www.ieer.org

The Institute for Energy and Environmental Research (IEER) is a private nonprofit organization that provides technical assistance to the public in a form people without specialized scientific knowledge or training can understand. Especially helpful are a series of fact sheets on the IEER Web site that cover topics such as nuclear physics and fission, uranium, plutonium, fissile material, nuclear reactors, and reprocessing. The IEER staff includes an engineer with a specialty in nuclear fusion, two physicists, and a chemist, as well as people with other areas of expertise.

Institute for Science and International Security
236 Massachusetts Avenue NE
Suite 500
Washington, D.C. 20002
Phone: (202) 547-3633
URL: http://http://isis-online.org

The Institute for Science and International Security is a nonprofit organization established to inform the public about science and policy issues related to international security. Its concerns include stopping the proliferation of nuclear weapons and the reduction of world nuclear arsenals. The ISIS Web site contains a variety of reports, including updates on developments in Iran, Pakistan, Iran, and North Korea. Many are written or cowritten by David Albright, a physicist and president of ISIS. The organization has a staff of eight.

International Atomic Energy Agency
Wagramer Strasse 5
1220 Vienna, Austria
Phone: (43-1) 2600-0
URL: http://www.iaea.or.at

The International Atomic Energy Agency was established in 1957 to deal with the dangers posed by the discovery of nuclear energy. Since then a key part of its mission has been to prevent the proliferation of nuclear weapons. As part of that effort, the IAEA inspects the nuclear facilities of 145 countries around the world. It is the verification authority for the Treaty on the Nonproliferation of Nuclear Weapons (NPT), which dates from 1968. The IAEA is an independent organization that is related to the United Nations by a special agreement. Its Web site contains a wide spectrum of resources related to WMD. Click on "Related Resources" to find sections on "Treaties and Agreements" and "Topical Booklets." The "Issues and Focus" button takes you to updates such as "IAEA and Iran," "IAEA and NPT," and "IAEA and DRNK" (Democratic Republic of North Korea).

James Martin Center for Nonproliferation Studies
460 Pierce Street
Monterey, CA 93940
Phone: (831) 647-4154
URL: http://http://cns.miis.edu

Known until 2007 as the Center for Nonproliferation Studies, this private organization is based at the Monterey Institute for International Studies, an affiliate of Middlebury College in Vermont. The CNS, as it is most often called, is the world's largest nongovernmental organization focusing on education and research in the field of nonproliferation studies. Aside from Monterey, the CNS has offices in Washington, D.C., and in Almaty, Kazakhstan, the capital of that Central Asian country. It considers its main task to "train the next generation of nonproliferation specialists."

Lexington Institute
1600 Wilson Boulevard
Suite 900
Arlington, VA 22209
Phone: (703) 522-5828
URL: http://lexingtonsintitute.org

The Lexington Institute is a public policy think tank established in 1998 to promote democratic capitalism and a strong national defense. It has a staff of 11. The Web site has relatively short reports on a wide variety of subjects, including issues such as homeland security and defense.

Missile Defense Agency
7100 Defense Pentagon
Washington, D.C. 20301-7100
Phone: (703) 882-6144
URL: http://www.mda.mil/mdalink/html/mdalink.html

The Missile Defense Agency is a unit of the U.S. Department of Defense. It was established in its current form in 2002, although its history dates back to the Strategic Defense Initiative program set up by the Reagan administration in 1984. The MDA is the agency charged with developing a missile defense system for the United States and its allies. The MDA Web site contains a "BMD BASICS" button that takes you to a series of "Quick

Links." These include topics such as "The Threat," "Boost Phase Defense," "Midcourse Phase Defense," and "Terminal Phase Defense." There is also a link to fact sheets.

Missilethreat.com
937 West Foothill Boulevard
Suite E
Claremont, CA 917711
Phone: (909) 626-6825
URL: http://www.missilethreat.com

Missilethreat.com is an advocacy group that believes the United States needs a missile defense system. It argues that the strategies dating from the cold war era are no longer applicable. Its Web site contains a wealth of information on ballistic missiles proliferation and missile defense. Features include a detailed database of ballistic missiles worldwide, an analysis of the threat posed by specific countries, a history of ballistic missiles and missile defense initiatives, a chronology of missile defense, a glossary of missile defense terms, and other resources. There also is an extensive bibliography of major books and articles by experts on security matters with varying points of view, including those on both sides of the missile defense debate.

National Nuclear Security Administration
100 Independence Avenue SW
Washington, D.C. 20585
Phone: (800) dial-DOE
URL: http://nnsz.energy.gov

The National Nuclear Security Administration was established in 2000 as a unit of the U.S. Department of Energy. The NNSA has several assignments, including the management and security of this country's nuclear stockpile. It also responds to nuclear emergencies both at home and abroad. The Web site has a wide range of information about the U.S. nuclear stockpile and related subjects. To learn about the U.S. nuclear stockpile, click on "Programs," "Defense Programs," and "the Stockpile." The last feature contains information on the NNSA's life-extension programs for nuclear warheads, the reliable replacement warhead program, and on the dismantlement of U.S. warheads. It also contains a chart on the warheads and bombs currently in the U.S. nuclear arsenal.

National Science Digital Library
UCAR/NDSL
P.O. Box 3000
Boulder, CO 80307
Phone: (303) 497-2933
URL: http://ndsl.org
www.atomicarchive.com

The National Science Digital Library is funded by the National Science Foundation. One of the NDSL collections on its Web site is atomicarchive.com, whose own Web site is listed here along with the NDSL Web site. (Atomicarchive.com can be accessed from the NSDL home page by clicking on "Collections" and scrolling down to Atomic Archive.) Atomicarchive.com is one of the very best Web sites on the Internet for learning about nuclear weapons. It presents materials on the development of the atomic bomb, the possible effects of nuclear warfare, key documents related to the atomic age, information on nuclear tests and test sites, and much more. There also are videos showing phenomena such as fission, fusion, and a chain reaction.

Natural Resources Defense Council
40 West 20th Street
New York, NY 10011
Phone: (212) 727-2700
URL: http://www.nrdc.org

The National Resources Defense Council is an advocacy group for environmental protection. Its antinuclear agenda includes being strongly opposed to using nuclear power as a replacement for coal and oil to generate electricity. The NRDC was founded in 1970 by law students and attorneys who helped to write some of America's most significant environmental laws. The organization has a staff of about 300 lawyers, scientists, and experts in other fields. On the Web site, click on "Issues" and then on "Nuclear Weapons, Waste, and Energy" for a variety of reports, including a summary and informative chart called "New Estimates of the U.S. Nuclear Weapons Stockpile, 2007 and 2012."

North Atlantic Treaty Organization
NATO Headquarters
B-110 Brussels
Belgium
Phone: (32.2) 707.41.11
URL: http://www.nato.int

NATO is the defensive alliance formed by the United States and its allies after World War II as a response to the security threat posed by the Soviet Union. Today, it is composed of 26 countries in North America and Europe. The NATO Web site contains a variety of sources helpful to the study of WMD. Some of the most helpful can be accessed by clicking on "NATO e-Documentation," including a glossary of nuclear terms and definitions. Documents on NATO's activities regarding WMD can be accessed by typing "weapons of mass destruction" in the "Search" box in the upper left-hand corner of the home page.

Nuclear Threat Initiative
1747 Pennsylvania Avenue NW
7th Floor
Washington, D.C. 20006
Phone: (202) 296-4810
URL: http://www.nti.org

The Nuclear Threat Initiative is a private organization founded in 2001 by former Georgia senator Sam Nunn and businessman Ted Turner, who serve as the organization's cochairs. Its mission, as stated on its Web site, is to "strengthen global security by reducing the risk of use and preventing the spread of nuclear, biological, and chemical weapons, and to work to build the trust, transparency and security which are preconditions to the ultimate fulfillment of the Non-Proliferation Treaty's goals and ambitions." Its Web site is one of the most informative, useful, and unbiased on the Internet for the study of WMD. The "Country Reports" are comprehensive and detailed, and the "Teacher's Toolkit" provides a wealth of information for understanding WMD.

Open CRS
1634 I Street NW, #1100
Washington, D.C. 20006
Phone: (202) 637-9800
URL: http://opencrs.cdt.org

Open CRS is a project of the Center for Democracy and Technology established to provide the public with access to Congressional Research Service (CRS) reports. The Open CRS Web site points out that there is no systematic way to gather all the CRS reports, which means that not all reports appear on that site. The address and phone number given above are those of the Center for Democracy and Technology, a private nonprofit organization dedicated to promoting openness on the Internet.

Organisation for the Prohibition of Chemical Weapons
Johan de Willaan 32
2517 JR—The Hague
The Netherlands
Phone: (31-70) 416-3300
URL: http://www.opcw.org

The Organisation for the Prohibition of Chemical Weapons was established in 1997 to implement the Chemical Weapons Convention and assure that member states comply with its provisions. The OPCW Web site contains reports and other information related to that mission, including lists of states that are parties to the CWC, states that have signed but not ratified the convention, and states that have not signed the convention.

Stockholm International Peace Research Institute
Signalistgarden 9
SE-169 70 Solna
Sweden
Phone: (46-8) 655-97-00
URL: http://www.sipri.org

The Stockholm International Peace Research Institute was founded in 1966. Most of its funding comes from a grant from the Swedish government. It publishes a wide variety of highly respected materials, some of which can be downloaded from the Web site but also others that must be bought. SIPRI probably is best known for an annual yearbook that deals with armaments, disarmament, and national security. Its Web site correctly points out that it is read worldwide by political figures, researchers, journalists, and others. Although the yearbooks, including the *SIPRI Yearbook 2008: Armaments, Disarmament, and International Security,* must be purchased, the Web site does have a link that provides summaries of each of the book's sections. Those summaries also can be assessed directly by going to http://yearbook2008.sipri.org. SIPRI also has published numerous books on chemical and biological warfare.

U.S. Army Chemical Materials Agency
CMA Headquarters
Public Affairs Office
AMSCM-PA
5183 Blackhawk Road
AEG-EA, MD 20210-5424
Phone: (800) 488-0648

The Army Chemical Materials Agency is charged with storing and destroying this country's aging chemical weapons. Its job includes developing technologies to safely store and eliminate these weapons. The agency's Web site includes information on the destruction process, the four sites where chemical agents are being incinerated, and news releases that provide up-to-date information on the full range of the agency's activities.

The White House
1600 Pennsylvania Avenue NW
Washington, D.C. 20500
Phone: (202) 456-1414
URL: http://www.whitehouse.gov

The White House is the residence and headquarters of the president of the United States. Its Web site makes available important documents regarding national policy such as the "National Strategy to Combat Weapons of Mass Destruction," issued in December 2002, and "National Strategy for Homeland Security," issued in October 2007.

Wisconsin Project on Nuclear Arms Control
1701 K Street
Suite 805
Washington, D.C. 20006
Phone: (202) 223-8299
URL: http://www.wisconsinproject.org

The Wisconsin Project on Nuclear Arms Control was established in 1986. It operates in Washington, D.C., under the auspices of the University of Wisconsin. The project attempts to stop the proliferation of WMD by uncovering and publicizing what it considers to be dangerous export transactions and works with various countries to improve their export control systems. One of the Wisconsin Project's services is the Web site Iran Watch, which tracks Iran's efforts to develop nuclear and chemical weapons and missiles capable of delivering those weapons.

World Nuclear Association
22a St. James Square
London, SW1Y 4JH
United Kingdom
Phone: (44-20) 7451-1520
URL: http://www.world-nuclear.org

The World Nuclear Association is a global private organization that promotes the peaceful use of nuclear energy, specifically the use of nuclear power to generate electricity. It is concerned with all aspects of producing nuclear energy, from mining and enrichment of uranium to plant manufacture and the safe disposal of spent nuclear fuel. The World Nuclear Association Web site includes a helpful description of what is known as the fuel cycle. The fuel cycle begins with the mining of uranium, continues through the building and operation of nuclear plants, and ends with the decommissioning of those plants and treatment and disposal of nuclear wastes. The Web site also has a glossary of terms used in the nuclear power industry, a country survey, and other material. There also is a lengthy section on safeguards to prevent nuclear weapons proliferation.

10

Annotated Bibliography

This bibliography is divided into topical sections, each of which contains books, articles, reports, and Web sites, as follows:

General Historical Overviews: background information dealing with the countries discussed in this volume or with the use of chemical and biological weapons before the 20th century

What Are Weapons of Mass Destruction?: technical information about weapons of mass destruction, whether biological, chemical, or nuclear

Modern Weapons of Mass Destruction: the history of the development of weapons of mass destruction since World War I, including international efforts to prevent their proliferation. This section includes works that span more than one of the topics listed in this bibliography. Examples are books or articles that discuss both Russia and the United States or that discuss subjects such as biological warfare, chemical warfare, the nuclear arms race, or missile defense.

U.S. Chemical and Biological Weapons Programs: information on the U.S. programs from their inception to the present, including strategies to counter these weapons

U.S. Nuclear Weapons Program: information on the U.S. program from its inception to the present, including strategies to counter these weapons and the current U.S. arsenal

Soviet/Russian Chemical and Biological Weapons Programs: information on the Soviet/Russian programs from their inception to the present

Soviet/Russian Nuclear Weapons Program: information on the Soviet/Russian program from its inception to the present, including the strategies to counter these weapons and the current Russian arsenal

The Unstable Middle East: information on the nuclear, biological, and chemical weapons programs and policies of various nations other than Israel in the Middle East

Israeli Chemical and Biological Weapons Programs: information on these programs from their inception to the present, including strategies to counter these weapons

Israeli Nuclear Weapons Program: information on Israel's nuclear program from its inception to the present, including strategies to counter these weapons

The Chemical and Biological Weapons Programs of India and Pakistan: information on these programs from their inception to the present

The Nuclear Weapons Programs of India and Pakistan: information on these programs from their inception to the present, including the current nuclear arsenals of these countries and their strategies to counter these weapons

North Korea's Chemical, Biological, and Nuclear Weapons Programs: information on these programs from their inception to the present, including the status of North Korea's current arsenals

GENERAL HISTORICAL OVERVIEWS

Eban, Abba. *My Country: The Story of Modern Israel.* New York: Random House, 1972. Eban served as Israel's ambassador to the United Nations, its ambassador to the United States, and its foreign minister. He chronicles the struggle to found Israel in the face of intense Arab opposition and the continued threats to its existence through the early 1970s. Eban also stresses how Israel became a modern democratic state while providing a home for Jewish refugees from all over the world.

Fenn, Elizabeth A. "Biological Warfare in Eighteenth-Century North America: Beyond Jeffrey Amherst." *The Journal of American History* (26 March 2000): 42–43. Available online. URL: http://www.historycooperative.org/journals/jah/86.4/fenn.html. Accessed June 6, 2008. Argues that the famous incident in 1763 in which the British used blankets contaminated with smallpox to infect Native Americans was not the only example of biological warfare in North America in the 18th century. In fact, Native Americans may have used biological warfare against the British decades earlier by contaminating the water supply of a British army.

Ferrell, Robert H. *Harry S. Truman and the Cold War Revisionists.* Columbia and London: University of Missouri Press, 2006. Includes a chapter on the American decision-making process that led to the bombing of Hiroshima and another that includes a discussion of American nuclear policy in the years immediately after

World War II. Ferrell is considered the leading scholar on the career of President Harry S. Truman.

Frank, Richard B. *Downfall: The Fall of the Imperial Japanese Empire.* New York: Random House, 1999. The definitive volume on the end of World War II in the Pacific and why the United States used atomic bombs against Japan to end the war. Frank argues persuasively that Japan was not prepared to surrender before the bombing of Hiroshima and that American leaders feared an invasion of Japan would cost U.S. casualties running into the hundreds of thousands.

Gaddis, John Lewis. *Now We Know: Rethinking Cold War History.* Oxford and New York: Clarendon Press, 1997. An extremely insightful discussion of the cold war by the dean of cold war historians that draws on documents from the Soviet archives made available during the 1990s.

Gilbert, Martin. *The Arab-Israeli Conflict: Its History in Maps.* London: Weidenfeld and Nicolson, 1974. Illustrates the history of the Arab-Israeli conflict with dozens of maps that cover both the historical and military aspects of the conflict.

Johnson, Thomas J. "A History of Biological Warfare from 300 B.C.E. to the Present." Available online. URL: http://www.aarc.org/resources/biological/history.asp. Accessed June 6, 2008. An overview of biological weapons by an associate professor of respiratory care and health sciences, School of Health Professions, Long Island University.

Kort, Michael. *The Columbia Guide to Hiroshima and the Bomb.* New York: Columbia University Press, 2007. An overview of the debate surrounding the American use of atomic bombs against Japan. Includes almost 200 documents.

———. *The Soviet Colossus: History and Aftermath.* Armonk, N.Y.: M. E. Sharpe, 2006. A history of the Soviet Union, with introductory background material on the Russian Empire and coverage of the post–Soviet Russian Federation.

Markels, Alex. "Will Terrorism Rewrite the Laws of War." Available online. URL: http://www.npr.org/templates/story/story.php?storyId=5011464. Accessed July 15, 2008. An overview of the U.S. policy of treating prisoners of war humanely dating from instructions given by President George Washington during the American Revolution. The article also discusses President Abraham Lincoln's ban on the use of poisons against the enemy during the Civil War.

Mayor, Adrienne. *Greek Fire, Poison Arrows, and Scorpion Bombs: Biological and Chemical Warfare in the Ancient World.* Woodstock, N.Y.: Overlook Duckworth, 2003. An overview of how ancient peoples developed and used chemical and biological weapons.

Reich, Bernard. *A Brief History of Israel.* New York: Checkmark Books, 2005. A concise but also comprehensive history of Israel by a leading scholar in the field.

Weinberg, Gerhard L. *A World at Arms: A Global History of World War II.* Cambridge and New York: Cambridge University Press, 1994. One of the standard works on World War II.

Werth, Nicholas. "A State against Its People: Violence, Repression, and Terror in the Soviet Union." In *The Black Book of Communism: Crimes, Terror, Repression.*

Edited by Stépnane Courtois, et al. Cambridge, Mass: Harvard University Press, 1999. A remarkable and disturbing survey of the violence the government of the Soviet Union committed against its people that draws on recently released documents from the Soviet archives.

WHAT ARE WEAPONS OF MASS DESTRUCTION?

Arms Control Association. "The Chemical Weapons Convention (CWC) at a Glance." October 2008. Available online. URL: http://www.armscontrol.org/factsheets/cwcglance. Accessed June 15, 2008. An overview of the CWC, including information on prohibitions, declaration requirements, destruction requirements, and penalties for noncompliance.

———. "Chemical and Biological Weapons Proliferation at a Glance" (September 2002). Available online. URL: http://www.armscontrol.org/print/2473. Accessed October 17, 2008. A chart with the biological and chemical weapons capabilities of 17 countries.

Atomic Archive. "The Energy of a Nuclear Weapon." Available online. URL: http://www.atomicarchive.com/Effects/effects1.shtml. Accessed June 18, 2008. Technical information on the effects of nuclear weapons.

———. "The Neutron Bomb." Available online. URL: http://www.atomicarchive.com/Fusion/Fusion5.shtml. Accessed June 27, 2008. Technical information on the neutron bomb.

Centers for Disease Control and Prevention, "Bioterrorism Agents/Diseases." Available online. URL: http://www.bt.cdc.gov/agent/agentlist-category.asp. Accessed June 21, 2008. Provides technical information on the three categories of threat into which the Centers for Disease Control divides biological pathogens.

Commission of the Prevention of WMD Proliferation and Terrorism. *World at Risk: Report of the Commission on the Prevention of WMD Proliferation and Terrorism.* Available online. URL: http://www.scribd.com/doc/8574914/World-at-Risk-The-Report-of-the-Commission-on-the- Prevention-of-WMD-Proliferation-and-Terrorism-Full-Report. Accessed December 15, 2008. The commission warned that unless steps are taken it is more likely than not that there will be a nuclear or biological attack somewhere in the world by 2013. It calculated that terrorists are more likely to obtain and use a biological weapon than a nuclear weapon. The commission further warned that despite steps that have been taken already terrorists are moving at a faster pace than authorities responsible for protecting the civilian population of the United States.

Cote, Jr., Owen T. "Appendix B: P Primer on Fissile Materials and Nuclear Weapons Design." In Graham T. Allison, Owen Cote, Jr., Richard A. Falkenrath, and Steven E. Miller. *Avoiding Nuclear Anarchy: Containing the Threat of Loose Russian Nuclear Weapons and Fissile Material.* Cambridge, Mass.: MIT Press, 1996. Available online. URL: http://www.pbs.org/wgbh/pages/frontline/shows/nukes/readings/appendixb.html. Accessed June 27, 2008. Technical information on the production of nuclear weapons.

Federation of American Scientists. *Special Weapons Primer.* "Nuclear Weapons Radiation Effects." Available online. URL: http://www.fas.org/nuke/intro/nuke/radiation.htm. Accessed June 27, 2008. Technical information on the radiation effects of nuclear weapons.

———. *Special Weapons Primer.* "Plutonium Production." Available online. URL: http://www.fas.org/nuke/intro/nuke/plutonium.htm. Accessed June 25, 2008. Technical information on the production of weapons-grade plutonium.

———. *Special Weapons Primer.* "Uranium Production." Available online. URL: http://www.fas.org/nuke/intro/nuke/uranium.htm. Accessed June 25, 2008. Technical information on the production of weapons-grade highly enriched uranium.

Global Security.org. Weapons of Mass Destruction. "Neutron Bomb/Enhanced Radiation Weapon." Available online. URL: http://www.globalsecurity.org/wmd/intro/neutron-bomb/htm. Accessed June 22, 2008. Technical information on the neutron bomb.

Graham, Bob. "Bioterrorism—a Preventable Catastrophe." *Boston Globe* (12/18/08). Available online. URL: http://www.boston.com/bostonglobe/editorial_opinion/oped/articles/2008/12/18/bioterrorism___a_preventable_catastrophe/. Accessed December 18, 2008. A warning by the chairman of the Commission on Weapons of Mass Destruction, Proliferation and Terrorism, which in December 2008 issued its report "World at Risk." Graham repeats the report's warning about the danger of a terrorist attack using a WMD by 2013. He is a former Florida governor and U.S. senator.

NATO Handbook on the Medical Aspects of NBC Operations AMedP-6(B). Washington, D.C.: Departments of the Army, Navy, and the Air Force, 1996. Available online. URL: http://www.fas.org/nuke/guide/usa/doctrine/dod/fm8-9/1toc.htm. Accessed June 16, 2008. A technical guide for military medical officers for dealing with WMD warfare under battle conditions. It is divided into three parts: nuclear, biological, and chemical. It is both a compilation of reference material and a source of information for training.

New York City Department of Health and Mental Hygiene: Public Health Emergency Preparedness. "Dirty Bombs." Available online. URL: http://www.nyc.gov/html/doh/html/bt/bt_fact_dirtybombs.shtml. Accessed June 23, 2008. Technical information on how to respond to an attack using a radiological bomb against an urban civilian target.

NuclearFiles.org: Project of the Nuclear Age Peace Foundation. "The Neutron Bomb." Available online. URL: http://www.nuclearfiles.org/menu/key-issues/nuclear-weapons/basics/neutron-bomb.htm. Accessed June 27, 2008. Historical and technical information on the neutron bomb.

Online News Hour. Tracking Nuclear Proliferation. "Types of Nuclear Bombs." Available online. URL: http://www.pbs.org/newshour/indepth_coverage/military/proliferation/types.html. Accessed June 27, 2008. Technical information on fission and thermonuclear weapons.

Union of Concerned Scientists. "Nuclear Weapons: How They Work." Available online. URL: www.ucsusa.org/global_security/nuclear_weapons/nuclear-weapons-how-they.html? Accessed June 26, 2008. Technical information on how nuclear weapons work.

United States Nuclear Regulatory Commission. "Uranium Enrichment." Available online. URL: http://www.nrc.gov/reading-rm/doc-collections/fact-sheets/enrichment.html. Accessed June 25, 2008. Technical information on uranium enrichment.

World Health Organization. "Nipah virus." Available online. URL: http://www.who.int/meciacentre/factsheet/fs262/en/. Accessed June 22, 2008. Technical information on the deadly Nipah virus.

World Nuclear Association. "Uranium Enrichment." Available online. URL: http://www.world-nuclear.org/info/inf28.html. Accessed June 25, 2008. Technical information on uranium enrichment.

MODERN WEAPONS OF MASS DESTRUCTION

Allison, Graham T. *Nuclear Terrorism: The Ultimate Preventable Catastrophe.* New York: Times Books, 2004. An overview of the threat posed by nuclear terrorism. The book includes a projection of what would happen if a 10-kiloton bomb was detonated in Times Square. The author estimates 500,000 people would be killed and all buildings within a third of a mile completely destroyed.

Arms Control Association. "Chemical and Biological Weapons Proliferation at a Glance." Available online. URL: http://www.armscontrol.org/factsheets/cbwprolif. Accessed September 14, 2008. A chart of 17 nations that either have stocks of biological or chemical weapons or have programs to develop them. Current as of September 2002.

Arora, D. R., and Vikas Guatam. "Bioterrorism: A Historical Perspective." *Tribune* (India) online edition (9/16/02). Available online. URL: http://www.tribuneindia.com/2002/20020916/edit.htm. Accessed May 15, 2008. Primarily a time line of events and programs related to biowarfare or bioterrorism.

Atomic Archive. "Limited Test Ban Treaty (1963)." Available online. URL: http://www.atomicarchive.com/Treaties/Treaty3.shtml. Accessed July 7, 2008. Short overview of the Limited Test Ban Treaty.

———. "New York City Example." Available online. URL: http://www.atomicarchive.com/Example/Example1.shtml. Accessed June 23, 2008. What would happen if terrorists detonated a 150-kiloton atomic bomb in mid-Manhattan.

"Bioterror in Context." Miller-McCune.com (June–July 2008), pp. 72–76. An interview with UCLA immunology professor William R. Clark, who suggests that the threat of a biological attack by terrorists has been exaggerated. Clark argues that the United States has more to fear from natural pandemic outbreaks involving viruses that cause diseases such as SARS or H5N1 avian flu.

Broad, William J. "The Hidden Travels of the Bomb." *New York Times* (12/9/08). A review of two upcoming books dealing with nuclear proliferation, both by authors who at one time were associated with top-secret U.S. weapons laboratories.

Bundy, McGeorge. *Danger and Survival: Choices about the Atomic Bomb in the First Fifty Years.* New York: Random House, 1988. A history of the development of atomic weapons and the nuclear arms race between the Soviet Union and the United States that followed World War II. Bundy also covers the development of nuclear weapons by Great Britain, France, China, and Israel. A longtime Washington insider, Bundy served as special assistant for national security under presidents Kennedy and Johnson.

Bunn, George. "The Nuclear Nonproliferation Treaty: History and Current Problems" (December 2003). Available online. Arms Control Association. URL: http://www.armscontrol.org/act/2003_12/Bunn.asp?print. Accessed July 7, 2008. Comprehensive overview of the problems involved with maintaining nuclear nonproliferation. Includes important information on countries that successfully hid their nuclear programs from international observers.

Carnegie Endowment for International Peace. "Summary of Syria's Chemical and Biological Weapons Programs." Available online. URL: http://www.carnegieendowment.org/publications/index.cfm?fa=print&id<0 x003D>13695. Accessed July 17, 2008. A short overview of these two programs.

Center for Defense Information. Chemical and Biological Weapons Site. "Biological Weapons Convention Overview." Available online. URL: http://www.cdi.org/issues/cbw/bwc.html. Accessed May 15, 2008. A historical overview of the establishment of the Biological Weapons Convention.

———. "Port and Maritime Security in the United States: Reactions to an Evolving Threat" (1/21/03). Available online. URL: http://www.cdi.org/terrorism/maritime security-pr.cfm. Accessed June 15, 2008. A report on efforts to improve security at U.S. ports. As of this report, only 2 percent of containers arriving in the U.S. by sea were inspected.

Cirincione, Joseph. *Bomb Scare: The History and Future of Nuclear Weapons.* New York: Columbia University Press, 2007. Cirincione traces the history of nuclear weapons from the atomic discoveries in the 1930s that made them possible to the effort at nonproliferation. The book includes a number of graphs and charts summarizing developments such as the rise and decline of the U.S. and Russian nuclear arsenals from 1945 to 2006, changes in the world's nuclear stockpiles over the same time period, and nuclear weapons eliminated by the Nunn-Lugar Cooperative Threat Reduction Program.

Cirincione, Joseph, Jon B. Wolfsthal, and Miriam Rajkumar. *Deadly Arsenals: Nuclear, Biological, and Chemical Threats.* 2nd ed., revised and expanded. Washington, D.C.: Carnegie Endowment for International Peace, 2005. A comprehensive overview of the problems and challenges posed by WMD today. The first part of the book includes a discussion of global trends regarding the problem of proliferation as well as technical information regarding chemical, biological, and nuclear weapons. Other sections of the book deal with the specific countries that currently have WMD and those countries that have given up their weapons. The book also has many useful tables and charts.

Committee for the Compilation of Materials on Damage Caused by the Atomic Bombs in Hiroshima and Nagasaki. *Hiroshima and Nagasaki: The Physical, Medical, and Social Effects of the Atomic Bombings.* Translated by Eisei Ishikawa and David L.

Swain. New York: Basic Books, 1981. This book, originally published in Japan, was compiled by 34 Japanese specialists. It probably is the most comprehensive scientific report on those two atomic bombings. It contains dozens of charts and graphs and some graphic and disturbing pictures.

Croddy, Eric. *Chemical and Biological Warfare: A Comprehensive Survey for the Concerned Citizen.* New York: Copernicus Books, 2002. A detailed survey of the key issues related to biological and chemical warfare. Croddy is a senior research associate at the Monterey Institute of International Studies who has written for the authoritative *Jane's Intelligence Review.*

DeGroot, Gerard J. *The Bomb: A Life.* Cambridge, Mass.: Harvard University Press, 2005. A history of nuclear weapons from the origin of nuclear physics at the turn of the 20th century to the turn of the 21st century.

Diakov, Anatoli, Eugene Miasnikov, and Mimur Kadyshev. *Non-Strategic Nuclear Weapons: Problems of Control and Reduction.* Moscow: Center for Arms Control, Energy, and Environmental Studies of the Moscow Institute of Physics and Technology, 2004. This study begins with an effort to classify nuclear weapons, pointing out the problem that there is no common view among nuclear arms control experts on the line between strategic and nonstrategic weapons. It then examines both Russian and U.S. nonstrategic nuclear weapons doctrine, analyzes NATO doctrine, and analyzes U.S. and Russian attitudes toward reductions of nonstrategic nuclear weapons. Among the conclusions is that the existence of nonstrategic weapons in the Soviet and American arsenals not subject to formal arms control agreements has negatively affected efforts to limit the proliferation of weapons of mass destruction.

Eubank, Keith. *The Bomb.* New York: Anvil, 1999. A history of the development of the atomic bomb, its use against Hiroshima and Nagasaki, and the development of the hydrogen bomb. The volume includes 24 documents.

Feakes, Daniel. "Getting Down to the Hard Cases." Available online. URL: http://www.armscontrol.org/act/2008_03/Feakes. Accessed July 6, 2008. Details the difficulties in getting certain countries to sign and ratify the Chemical Weapons Convention.

Federation of American Scientists. "Burundi Signs the Comprehensive Nuclear-Test-Ban Treaty." Available online. URL: http://www.fas.org/irp/news/2008/09/burundi.html. Accessed October 21, 2008. Update on the CTBT as of November 2008.

———. "Introduction to Chemical Weapons." Available online. URL: http://www.fas.org/programs/ssp/bio/chemweapons/introduction.html. Accessed July 15, 2008. A short article that focuses on the U.S. chemical stockpile. Includes a map and several charts.

———. Special Weapons Primer. "Cruise Missiles." Available online. URL: http://www.fas.org/nuke/intro/cm/index.html. Accessed July 22, 2008. An overview of cruise missiles, how they work, and the proliferation threat they pose.

Fox News. "Bush Signs U.S. Port Security Act: Contains Ban on Internet Gambling" (10/23/06). Available online. URL: http://www.foxnews.com/story/0,2933,220496,

00.html. Accessed August 2, 2008. A news report on the $400 million Security and Accountability for Every Port (SAFE) bill of 2006.

Gilmore, Gerry J. "Guard-Staffed WMD Civil Support Teams Slated for Increase." American Forces Press Service (1/20/04). Available online. URL: http://www.defenselink.mil/news/newsarticle.aspx?id=27474. Accessed July 29, 2008. A report issued by the Armed Forces Press Service on the National Guard's WMD civil support teams. It reports that there are 32 teams prepared to respond to biological, chemical, or nuclear attack and that Congress has approved funds for 11 more teams.

"Global Nuclear Stockpiles, 1945–2006." *Bulletin of the Atomic Scientists* (July/August 2006): 64–66. This article summarizes the growth and, in some cases, shrinkage of the nuclear stockpiles of all the nuclear weapons states. A chart indicates the numbers in the individual stockpiles of the United States, the Soviet Union/Russia, Britain, France, and China, as well as the total held by those powers.

Global Security.org. "Iran Expects Russia to Complete Bushehr power plant on schedule" (10/18/08). Available online. URL: http://www.globalsecurity.org/wmd/library/news/iran/2008/iran-081018-irna01.htm. Accessed October 31, 2008. A short report on the Iranian announcement concerning the completion of the Bushehr reactor.

———. "Weapons of Mass Destruction Civil Support Teams." Available online. URL: http://www.globalsecurity.org/military/agency/army/wmd-cst.htm. Accessed July 23, 2008. An overview of WMD Civil Support Teams, in particular what each team consists of and what its functions are. This report is current as of December 2007.

Goncharov, G. A. "American and Soviet H-Bomb development programmes: historical background." *History of Physics* 39, no. 10: 1,033–1,044. The author describes the historical background of the hydrogen bomb in the United States and the Soviet Union with emphasis on the crucial scientific ideas that made development of the bomb possible.

Graham, Jr., Thomas. *Commonsense on Weapons of Mass Destruction.* Seattle: University of Washington Press, 2004. A survey of a variety of topics including nuclear proliferation and nuclear terrorism, chemical and biological weapons, and international law and arms control. Graham has served as the acting head of the U.S. Arms Control and Disarmament Agency and as a special ambassador for nuclear disarmament issues.

Guillemin, Jeanne. *Biological Weapons: From the Invention of State-Sponsored Programs to Contemporary Bioterrorism.* New York: Columbia University Press, 2005. A survey of the development and use of biological weapons from the early 20th century to the present. Among other topics, this volume covers both the Soviet and American biological weapons programs and the current threat posed by bioterrorism.

Harris, Sheldon. "The Japanese Biological Warfare Programme: An Overview." In *Biological and Toxin Weapons: Research, Development and Use from the Middle Ages to 1945.* SIPRI Chemical and Biological Warfare Studies, no. 18. Edited by

Erhard Giessler and John Ellis van Courtland Moon. Oxford: Oxford University Press, 1999. An overview of Japan's use of biological weapons against China during World War II by one of the leading scholars in the field.

"Homeland Security Presidential Directive/HSPD-18." (1/31/07). The White House. Available online. URL: http://www.whitehouse.gov/news/releases/2007/02/20020207-2html. Accessed July 21, 2008. This directive mandates and explains the medical countermeasures to be taken against an attack by weapons of mass destruction.

Hutchinson, Robert. *Weapons of Mass Destruction: The No-Nonsense Guide to Nuclear, Chemical, and Biological Weapons Today.* London: Weidenfeld and Nicolson, 2003. Hutchinson is a journalist formerly associated with the highly respected magazine *Jane's Defense Weekly.* This volume surveys the history of modern WMD, how these weapons function, and who has them. It includes a discussion of the threat posed by terrorists who could acquire these weapons.

"Hyperphysics." Hosted by the Department of Physics and Astronomy, Georgia State University. Available online. URL: http://hyperphysics.phy-astr.gsu.edu/Hbase/NucEne/ligwat.html. Accessed August 4, 2009. Technical information on light water nuclear reactors.

James Martin Center for Nonproliferation Studies.* "Chemical and Biological Weapons: Possession and Programs Past and Present." Available online. URL: http://cns.miis.edu/research/cbw/possess.htm. Accessed May 23, 2008. An extremely comprehensive chart covering every country that has or may have had chemical and/or biological weapons. It covers up to 2002.

———. "Chronology of State Use and Biological and Chemical Weapons Control." Available online. URL: http://cns.miis.edu/research/cbw/pastuse.htm. Accessed June 30, 2008. Covers from ancient times through the end of the 20th century.

Kortepeter, Mark G., and Gerald W. Parker. "Potential Biological Weapons Threats." *Emerging Infectious Diseases* 5, no. 4 (July–August 1999). Available online. URL: http://www.cdc.gov/ncidod/EID/vol5no4/kortepeter.htm. Accessed June 15, 2008. A discussion of the most dangerous biological agents. The authors are associated with the U.S. Army Medical Research Institute of Infectious Diseases at Fort Detrick, Maryland. The journal is a publication of the U.S. government's Centers for Disease Control.

Kouri, Jim. "National Guard Teams Prepare for Terrorist WMD Attacks." Canada Free Press (7/27/08). Available online. URL: http://www.canadafreepress.com/index.php/article/4143. Accessed July 29, 2008. This article reports that as of mid-2008 the National Guard has 35 of its 55 approved Civil Support Teams fully certified to carry out their missions of assisting civilian authorities in the event of a WMD attack.

Lord, Alexandra. "A Brief History of Biowarfare." Available online. URL: http://lhncbc.nlm.nih.gov/apdb/phsHistory/resources/pdf/biowar_pics.pdf. Accessed December 10, 2008. The author, a staff historian at the Public Health Service, traces the use of biological weapons since the beginning of the 20th century. She suggests that the best preparation for a biological attack may be for the United States to invest in its public health system.

Lugar, Richard. "Speech at Conference on Defense against Weapons of Mass Destruction." Web site of Richard G. Lugar, United States Senator for Indiana. Available online. URL: http://lugar.senate.gov/press/record.cfm?id=291461. Accessed July 28, 2008. Senator Richard Lugar, cosponsor of the Nunn-Lugar Cooperative Threat Reduction Program, assesses the progress made and challenges remaining in preventing the proliferation of weapons of mass destruction.

———. "The Next Step in U.S. Nonproliferation Policy." *Arms Control Today* (December 2002). Available online. URL: http://www.armscontrol.org/act/2002_12/lugar_dec02. Accessed August 1, 2008. An article by Senator Lugar assessing the progress in arms control and the challenges that remain. Lugar stresses the cooperation between the United States and Russia in this area.

Macfarlane, Allison. "All Weapons of Mass Destruction Are Not Equal." *Audit of the Conventional Wisdom.* Edited by John Tirman. Available online. URL: http://web.mit.edu/cis/pdf/Audit_6_05Macfarlane.pdf. Accessed June 1, 2008. A comparison of the different types of WMD that demonstrates how nuclear weapons are far more powerful and dangerous than either chemical or biological weapons.

Medalia, Jonathan. "Comprehensive Nuclear Test-Ban Treaty: Background and Current Developments." Congressional Research Service. Updated May 28, 2008. Available online. URL: http://opencrs.cdt.org/document/RL33548. Accessed July 25, 2008. This report to Congress includes an overview of most recent developments, a history of the treaty, a report on North Korea's 2006 nuclear test, a section on the pros and cons of the CTBT, a chronology, and other information, including a table on U.S. nuclear tests by calendar year.

Miller, Judith, Stephen Engelberg, and William Broad. *Germs: Biological Weapons and America's Secret War.* New York: Simon and Schuster, 2001. An overview focusing on the growing danger posed by biological weapons and their potential use by terrorists. This volume includes a detailed profile of the Soviet Union's secret biological weapons program and how it finally was exposed.

Monterey Bay Aquarium Research Institute. "Dangerous Unknowns: MBARI Researcher Points Out the Lack of Information on Chemical Weapons Dumped at Sea." Available online. URL: http://www.mbari.org/news/homepage/2008/chem-weapons.html. Accessed July 2, 2008. Discussion of the environmental problems caused by the dumping of chemical weapons at sea after World War II.

"National Strategy for Homeland Security." (October 2007). The White House. Available online. URL: http://www.whitehouse.gov/infocus/homeland/nshs/2007/index.html. Accessed June 26, 2008. The official statement on the nation's strategy for protecting the civilian population from terrorist attacks and catastrophic natural disasters.

Nuclear Threat Initiative. "The Nunn-Lugar Cooperative Threat Reduction (CTR) Program." Available online. URL: http://www.nti.org/db/nisprofs/russia/forasst/nunn_lug/overview.htm. Accessed August 1, 2008. An overview of the history and achievements of the Lugar-Nunn Cooperative Threat Reduction Program.

———. "Proliferation and Use of Nuclear Weapons." Updated March 2008. Available online. URL: http://nti.org/f_wmd411/fla4_1a.html. Accessed June 5, 2008. Provides a list of the countries possessing nuclear weapons and some basic terminology regarding these weapons.

———. WMD411. "Missiles." Updated November 2008. Available online. URL: http://www.nti.org/f_wmd411/f1a5.html. Accessed November 6, 2008. A short introduction to ballistic and cruise missiles.

Organization for the Prohibition of Chemical Weapons. "The Chemical Weapons Ban: Facts and Figures." Available online. URL: http://www.opcw.org/factsandfigures/index.html. Accessed May 28, 2008. Information on the Chemical Weapons Convention from the Organization for the Prohibition of Chemical Weapons, the group charged with enforcing that convention.

Phillips, Michael B. "Bioterrorism: A Brief History." *Northeast Florida Medicine: Focus on Bioterrorism, 2005,* pp. 32–35. An overview of bioterrorism from ancient times to the present. The author, a medical doctor at the Mayo Clinic, urges a concerted effort to destroy all existing stockpiles of highly resistant bioengineered agents.

Podvig, Pavel. "Life after Start." *Bulletin of Atomic Scientists* (1/08/08). Available online. URL: http://www.thebulletin.org/web-edition/columnists/pavel-podvig/life-after-start. Accessed September 7, 2008. Podvig writes that the START system will expire in December 2009 and there is nothing in place that will replace it.

Rhodes, Richard. *The Making of the Atomic Bomb.* New York: Simon and Schuster, 1986. The best seller that tells the dramatic story of how the United States developed that atomic bomb during World War II. Contains many fascinating historical anecdotes as well as a wealth of technical information.

———. *Dark Sun: The Making of the Hydrogen Bomb.* New York: Simon and Schuster, 1995. Rhodes chronicles the race to develop a thermonuclear bomb between the Soviet Union and the United States after World War II and the postwar nuclear arms race between the two superpowers.

Roberts, Guy B. "Arms Control Without Arms Control: The Failure of the Biological Weapons Convention Protocol and a New Paradigm for Fighting the Threat of Biological Weapons." INSS Occasional Paper 49. United States Air Force Institute for National Security Studies, USAF Academy, Colorado (March 2003). Available online. URL: http://nti.org/e_reseach/officialdocs/other_us/INSSMarch.pdf. Accessed June 10, 2008. Writing in the wake of the October 2001 anthrax attacks that killed several people in the United States, the author maintains that the Biological Weapons Convention has been ineffective. The United States therefore advocated moving beyond that convention and finding new ways to combat the biological warfare and terrorist threats. These include new initiatives by NATO, INTERPOL, and EUROPOL, as well as international efforts to track and shut down financial networks run by terrorist organizations.

Sanger, David E. "The Khan Network." Available online. URL: http://iis-db.stanford.edu/evnts/3889/Khan_network-paper.pdf. Accessed June 16, 2008. Survey of the network established by the Pakistani scientist Abdul Qadeer Khan, which played a major role in promoting nuclear proliferation.

Siracusa, Joseph M. *Nuclear Weapons: A Very Short Introduction.* London: Oxford University Press, 2008. A brief history of the development of nuclear weapons. Includes a short chapter on technical aspects of building nuclear weapons.

Smithson, Amy E. "Prepared Statement before the Senate Committee on Foreign Relations" (3/19/03). Available online. URL: http://foreign.senate.gov/testimony/2003/SmithsonTestimony030319.pdf. Accessed June 10, 2008. An overview of chemical and biological weapons proliferation concerns. The director of the Chemical and Biological Weapons Nonproliferation Project at the Henry J. Stimson Center, Smithson includes recommendations to strengthen biosafety, biosecurity, and research oversight.

Strulak, Thadeusz. "The Nuclear Suppliers Group." *The Nonproliferation Review* (Fall 1993): pp. 2–10. A survey covering the founding and activities of the Nuclear Suppliers Group. Strulak, a Polish diplomat, served as chairman of the group in 1992.

Szinicz, L. "History of Chemical and Biological Warfare Agents." *Toxicology* 214 (2005): pp. 167–181. Available online. URL: http://www.sciencedirect.com. Accessed June 30, 2008. Discusses the development and use of the most prominent chemical and biological warfare agents.

"Text of the Treaty between the United States of America and the Russian Federation on Strategic Offensive Reductions." Arms Control Association (5/24/02). Available online. URL: http://www.armscontrol.org/docments/sort.asp. Accessed July 23, 2008. The treaty signed between the United States and the Russian Federation on May 24, 2002.

Tucker, Jonathan B. *War of Nerves: Chemical Warfare from World War I to Al-Qaeda.* New York: Pantheon Books, 2006. The most comprehensive source on the history of modern chemical weapons. Includes detailed coverage of how these weapons were developed and their impact when they have been used, both by nation-states on the battlefield and by terrorists against civilians.

U.S. Department of State. "Chapter 3—State Sponsors of Terrorism Overview." *Country Reports on Terrorism* (4/30/08). Available online. URL: http://www.state.gov/s/ct/rls/crt/2007/103711.htm. Accessed November 1, 2008. The U.S. government's official summary and statement regarding Iran's role as the world's leading sponsor of terrorism.

U.S. CHEMICAL AND BIOLOGICAL WEAPONS PROGRAMS

Avalon Project at Yale Law School. Available online. URL: http://www.yale.edu/lawweb/avalon/lieber.htm. Accessed July 15, 2008. A valuable resource for documents on a wide variety of subjects. As the URL indicates, it contains the Lieber Code, which was issued by the government during the Civil War as "General Orders No. 100: Instructions for the Government of Armies of the United States in the Field."

Center for Defense Information. Chemical and Biological Weapons Site. "Chemical Weapons Convention Overview." Available online. URL: http://cdi.org/issues/

cbw/chem.html. Accessed June 22, 2008. A detailed overview of the Chemical Weapons Convention, including sections on the objectives of the convention, how chemical agents are rated, and how the Organization for the Prohibition of Chemical Weapons (OPCW) is structured.

Cole, Leonard A. *Clouds of Secrecy: The Army's Germ Warfare Tests Over Populated Areas.* New York: Rowman and Littlefield, 1990. An overview of the U.S. Army's biological warfare tests after World War II that took place over populated areas. The author cites scientific opinion suggesting the bacteria used in the tests were not harmless and charges that the army did not monitor the health of the targeted population.

Federation of American Scientists. "Biosafety Levels Information." Available online. URL: http://www.fas.org/programs/ssp/bio/resource/biosafetylevels.html. Accessed July 30, 2008. Information on the nature of biological laboratories working with different types of biological agents, from Biosafety Level 1 to Biosafety Level 4. There is also a chart of all Biosafety Level 4 laboratories in the United States—operational, expanding, and planned—as of 2008.

Gurney, David H. "Executive Summary." *Joint Force Quarterly* (October 2008). A summary of the contents, which also serves as an overview of the destabilizing effects of Russian support of the Iranian nuclear program.

Kassenova, Toggzhan. "Biological Threat Reduction in Central Asia." *Bulletin of Atomic Scientists* (6/18/08). Available online. URL: http://thebulletin.org/web-edition/features/biological-threat-reduction-central-asia. Accessed September 14, 2008. The author reports that the U.S. government has invested $430 million in biological threat reduction programs since 1997. It has been very successful in working with scientists and governments in Central Asia to reduce threats posed by remains of the former Soviet biological weapons program in that region. The U.S. efforts are funded by the Cooperative Threat Reduction Program (CTRP), funded by the U.S. Department of Defense.

Leitenberg, Milton. "Assessing the Biological Weapons and Bioterrorism Threat" (December 2005). Available online. URL: http://www.strategicstudiesinstitute.army.mil/pdffiles/PUB639.pdf. Accessed July 20, 2008. Leitenberg argues that a thorough biological weapons threat assessment is necessary and that government officials should avoid exaggerating that threat. He has been associated with the Swedish International Peace Research Institute (SIPRI) and currently is senior research scholar at the University of Maryland's Center for International and Security Studies.

Lipton, Eric, and Scott Shane. "Anthrax Case Renews Questions on Bioterror Effort." *New York Times* (8/03/08). Available online. URL: http://www.nytimes.com/2008/08/03/us/03anthrax.html?hp#. Accessed August 3, 2008. Newspaper article that examines concerns that the boom in biodefense research may undermine national security by increasing the number of places and people with access to deadly germs.

Marburger, John. "Keynote Address on National Preparedness" (10/20/03). Office of Science and Technology Policy. Available online. URL: http://www.humanitarian.net/biodefense/ref/marburger_biosecurity2003.pdf. Accessed July 28, 2008.

Marburger was speaking as the director of the Office of Science and Technology Policy, which is attached to the Executive Office of the President. He includes summaries of Project BioWatch, Project Biosense, and Project BioShield.

Mauroni, Al. "The US Army Chemical Corps: Past, Present, Future." Army History Research Web site. Available online. URL: http://www.armyhistory.org/armyhistorical.aspx?pgID=868&id=133&exCompID=32. Accessed July 14, 2008. A concise history of the U.S. Army Chemical Corps. Mauroni argues that the discovery of nerve agents in Germany after World War II was an important factor in Congress's decision to maintain the wartime Chemical Warfare Service. Mauroni is a former member of the Army Chemical Corps and also has served as a consultant on chemical weapons to other branches of the U.S. government.

Miller, Judith, Stephen Engelberg, and William J. Broad. "U.S. Germ Warfare Research Pushes Treaty Limits." *New York Times* (9/4/01). Newspaper article that examines the question of whether certain biodefense research in the United States may violate the treaty banning biological weapons. The head of the U.S. delegation that negotiated the treaty is interviewed, and he states that the research is not illegal.

Mitka, Mike. "Congress Queries Need for and Safety of High-Containment Research Laboratories." *Journal of the American Medical Association* 298, no. 20 (11/28/07): 2,359–2,360. A short article in the country's leading medical journal on concerns about the rapid expansion in the number of BSL-4 laboratories in the United States.

Nuclear Theat Initiative. United States Profile. "Introduction." Updated May 2008. Available online. URL: http://www.nti.org/e_research/profiles/USA/index.html. Accessed July 14, 2008. Information on the U.S. nuclear, biological, chemical, and missile programs. Includes both historical information and data on the current arsenals.

Office of Weapons of Mass Destruction and Biodefense. "The Office of Weapons of Mass Destruction and Biodefense." Available online. URL: http://www.dhs.gov/xabout/structure/gc_1205180907841.shtm. Accessed July 29, 2008. A short but useful overview of the structure of this office, which is comprised of four divisions: National Biosurveillance Integration Center; Food, Agricultural and Veterinary Defense; Threats and Countermeasures; BioWatch.

Rambhia, Kunal. "Annual Report on Project BioShield Released to Congress" (7/11/08). Center for Biosecurity. Available online. URL: http://www.upmc-biosecurity.org/website/biosecurity_briefing/archive/countrmeasr_dev/2008/2008-07-11-annualrptbioshield.html. Accessed July 29, 2008. An overview of the report issued by the U.S. Department of Health and Human Services on July 9, 2008. The report includes information that 10 million doses of anthrax vaccine have been delivered to the Strategic National Stockpile and that another 10.4 million are going to be acquired.

Rosenberg, Barry. "Bolstering Bio-Defense." *Homeland Security* (June 2004). Available online. URL: http://www.mcgraw-hillhomelandsecurity.com/media/pdf/HSQ/HLS_Fourth_Article_issue_3 .pdf. Accessed July 28, 2008. Rosenberg reports that the U.S. government has presented a new national strategy and also increased the budgets of key programs to protect the country against biological attack. Most of the new funding is for Project Bioshield. Funds also have been provided for the Bio-Surveillance Program and to upgrade the BioWatch program.

"Scientist Suspected in 2001 Anthrax Attacks Dead in Apparent Suicide." Available online. URL: http://www.foxnews.com/story0.2933395723,00.html. Accessed August 1, 2008. News article on the suicide of Bruce E. Ivins, the scientist who was a suspect in the anthrax mailings that occurred after the September 11, 2001, terrorist attacks.

Smart, Jeffery K. "History of Chemical and Biological Warfare: An American Perspective." In *Medical Aspects of Chemical and Biological Warfare.* Bethesda: Office of the Surgeon General, Department of the United States Army, 1997, pp. 9–86. Available online. URL: http://www.bordeninstitute.army.mil/published_volumes/chemBio/chembio.html. Accessed July 17, 2008. Although this work covers biological and chemical warfare, its primary focus is on the history of the U.S. Army's chemical corps. It includes detailed information on chemical weapons and their production and numerous pictures of weapons, facilities for producing them, and defensive equipment. The author concludes that the United States has been very fortunate not to have experienced a chemical or biological Pearl Harbor.

"U.S. Army Chemical Materials Agency destroys half of total number of munitions in national stockpile." U.S. Army Chemical Materials Web site (8/30/06). Available online. URL: http://www.cma.army.mil/fndocumentviewer.aspx?docid=003675943. Accessed July 16, 2008. A press release on the progress regarding destruction of the U.S. arsenal of chemical weapons. This press release also includes some information on the overall composition of that arsenal.

U.S. Department of Defense. "Anthrax Vaccination Program Questions and Answers." Updated June 18, 1998. Available online. URL: http://www.defenselink.mil/other_info/qanda.html. Accessed October 17, 2008. Information about the U.S. program to protect U.S. military personnel from biological weapons using anthrax bacteria. The program will benefit from lessons learned in the 1991 Gulf War.

U.S. NUCLEAR WEAPONS PROGRAM

Arms Control Association. Fact Sheets: "Current U.S. Strategic Nuclear Forces" and "Changes in U.S. Strategic Forces Since 1990." Available online. URL: http://www.armscontrol.org/factsheets/usstrat.asp. Accessed July 22, 2008. These statistics are current as of January 1, 2008.

Boese, Wade. "More States Step Up Anti-Missile Work." *Arms Control Today* (January/February 2008). Available online. URL: http://www.armscontrol.org/act/2008_01-02/stepup.asp. Accessed July 28, 2008. A news article reporting on Japanese and Indian interest in missile defense. It also reports that Kuwait and the United Arab Emirates are interested in buying American Patriot Advanced Capability-3 short and medium-range defensive systems.

Brookings Institution. "50 Facts About U.S. Nuclear Weapons." Available online. URL: http://www.brookings.edu/projects/archive/nucweapons/50.aspx. Accessed July 21, 2008. Statistics about the number, cost, and other factors related to the U.S. nuclear weapons arsenal from the Manhattan Project through 1998.

Bureau of Arms Control, U.S. Department of State. "The Stockpile Stewardship Program" (10/08/99). A fact sheet on the Stockpile Stewardship Program, which was established in 1994, two years after the United States stopped nuclear testing, to ensure the safety and reliability of the U.S. nuclear weapons stockpile.

Federation of American Scientists. "Estimates of the US Nuclear Weapons Stockpile, 2007 and 2012" (5/02/07). Available online. URL: http://www.fas.org/blog/ssp/2007/05/estimates_of_us_nuclear_weapon.php.print. Accessed July 22, 2008. Overview of the growth and shrinkage of the U.S. nuclear stockpile, accompanied with one chart and two graphs.

———. "SSNB-726 Ohio-Class FBM Submarines." Available online. URL: http://www.fas.org/nuke/guide/usa/slbm/ssbn-726.htm. Accessed July 23, 2008. Contains a description of the Ohio-class ballistic missile submarines in terms of size and the weapons they carry as well as background information on the development of this class of ships.

"Fleet Ballistic Missile Submarines—SSBN." United States Navy Fact File. Available online. URL: http://www.navy.mil/navydata/fact_display.asp?cid=4100&tid=200&ct=4. Accessed June 15, 2008. Information on the U.S. Navy's ballistic missile submarines and the ballistic missiles they carry.

Garamone, Jim. "Iranian Threat Justifies Missile Defense, General Says." American Forces Press Services News Articles. Available online. URL: http://www.defenselink.mil/news/newsarticle.aspx?id=50511. Accessed July 28, 2008. News article reporting on the comments by Air Force Lt. General Henry A. Obering, chief of the U.S. Missile Defense Agency. The article discussed the American layered missile defense strategy, which combines boost-phase defense, mid-course defense, and terminal-stage defense.

GlobalSecurity.org "Arrow TMD." Available online. URL: http://www.globalsecurity.org/space/systems/arrow.htm. Accessed August 2, 2008. A concise history of Israel's program to build a theater missile defense, or TMD, that led to the development of the current Arrow 2 system.

Gordin, Michael D. *Five Days in August: How World War II Became a Nuclear War.* Princeton, N.J.: Princeton University Press, 2007. Gordon argues that the U.S. military did not fully understand the atomic bomb's revolutionary strategic potential prior to the bombing of Hiroshima and Nagasaki. He also provides intriguing details on the men stationed on Tinian Island in the Pacific who prepared and carried out the Hiroshima mission. Gordin adds that none of the scientists who built the bomb believed than one or two atomic bombs would end the war. As it turned out, Japan surrendered after the second bombing at Nagasaki.

Hewlett, Richard G., and Oscar E. Anderson, Jr. *The New World, 1939–1946,* vol. 1 of *A History of the United States Atomic Energy Commission.* University Park: Pennsylvania State University Press, 1962. A massive volume that is indispensable to the study of the development of nuclear weapons during World War II and U.S. policy for dealing with nuclear energy immediately after the war.

"History of Minuteman Missile Sites." National Park Service. Available online. URL: http://www.nps.gov/archive.mimi/history/srs/history.htm. Accessed July 23, 2008. A short overview of the deployment of the Minuteman missile and the eventual retirement of a large part of the Minuteman force, specifically the Minuteman II missiles. It also covers the establishment of the Minuteman Missile National Historic Site at the Ellsworth Air Force Base in South Dakota.

"Issues: Nuclear Weapons, Waste & Energy." National Resources Defense Council. Available online. URL: http://www.nrdc.org/nuclear/nudb/datab5.asp. Accessed July 23, 2008. A chart with information on the size and composition of the U.S. Navy's ballistic missile submarine forces from 1960 through 2007, with projections for 2012.

Jones, Vincent C. *Manhattan: The Army and the Atomic Bomb.* Washington, D.C.: Center of Military History, United States Army, 1985. The definitive study of the army's role in the building of the atomic bomb.

Kintisch, Eli. "Livermore Lab Dips into the Past to Win Weapons Design Contest." *Science* (3/09/07). Available online. URL http://www.sciencemag.org/cgi/content/full/315/5817/1348. Accessed July 30, 2008. A magazine article on the successful effort by the Lawrence Livermore National Laboratory in California to get the assignment to design a new hydrogen bomb that will not require testing. The Livermore lab won the competition over its archrival, the Los Alamos National Laboratory in New Mexico, with the help of engineers from the Sandia National Laboratories in Albuquerque, New Mexico. The assignment is part of the recently established Reliable Replacement Warhead program.

Medalia, Jonathan. "The Reliable Replacement Warhead Program: Background and Current Developments." Congressional Research Service. Updated May 19, 2008. Available online. URL: http://www.fas.org/sgp/crs/nuke/RL32929.pdf. Accessed July 24, 2008. An overview of the National Nuclear Security Administration's Life Extension Program (LEP) for U.S. nuclear warheads. It focuses on the debate whether the LEP is sufficient to maintain the U.S. arsenal or whether the United States must begin a Reliable Replacement Warhead program (RRP). It also notes that some exerts argue that even the RRP will not be sufficient and that the United States, which has not tested a nuclear weapon since 1992, should resume nuclear testing.

Missile Defense Agency, Department of Defense. *Missile Defense-Worldwide* (2008). A comprehensive overview of the ballistic missile defense system being developed by the United States. This report includes information on the overall system, the different types of defensive missiles under development, details on components, and what has been achieved as of the end of 2007. It also includes information on cooperation with other countries, such as Israel and Japan.

———. "Successful Missile Defense Intercept Test Takes Place Off Hawaii" (6/25/08). Available online. URL: http://www.mda.mil/mdaLink/pdf/08news/0071.pdf. Accessed August 1, 2008. A report on the successful test of the THAAD missile defense system.

National Nuclear Security Administration (NNSA). "Life Extension Programs." Available online. URL: http://nnsa.energy.gov/defense_programs/print/life_extension_programs.htm. Accessed July 25, 2008. A summary of the programs to extend the life of U.S. nuclear weapons, most of which were produced from 30 to 40 years ago. These programs are designed to extend the life of U.S. nuclear warheads and their components for an additional 20 to 30 years. The NNSA is responsible for the maintenance of U.S. nuclear weapons.

———. "NNSA Achieves Major Milestone in Project to Thwart Nuclear Terrorism in Kazakhstan" (7/02/08). Available online. URL: http://nnsa.energy.gov/print/2065.htm. Accessed July 24, 2008. The NNSA reports that Kazakhstan began operating eight new sites on its border equipped with radiation equipment.

———. "Nuclear and Radiological Material Removed from Japan, Germany, Sweden, and Denmark." Available online. URL: http://nnsa.energy.gov/print/2069.htm. Accessed August 4, 2008. The NNSA reports that almost 40 pounds of HEU and a quantity of PU-239 were returned from Japan, Germany, Sweden, and Denmark to the United States. This is the 42nd shipment of U.S.-origin nuclear fuel from 28 countries successfully returned to the United States.

———. "The Stockpile." Available online. URL: http://nnsa.energy.gov/defense_programs/print/The_Stockpile.htm. Accessed July 25, 2008. A short report that explains the changing mission of the NNSA over time, with the current emphasis being on enhancing the reliability and longevity of the current U.S. nuclear stockpile.

———. "Stockpile Stewardship Plan Overview, Fiscal Year 2007–2011" (11/13/06). Available online. URL: http://nnsa.energy.gov/defense_programs/documents/Stockplie_Overview_November_13_20 06pdf. Accessed December 15, 2008. This is the annual report of the NNSA, which is required by law according to the National Defense Authorization Act of 1998. This highly technical report covers all aspects of the program to ensure that the U.S. nuclear stockpile is safe and reliable.

———. "Working to Prevent Nuclear Terrorism." Available online. URL: http://nnsa.energy.gov/news/print/982.htm. Accessed July 24, 2008. Covers a wide range of activities, including facilities in Russia where nuclear warheads are stored, the reduction of weapons-grade plutonium at Russian reactors, and the removal of fissile materials from various locations around the world.

National Strategy to Combat Weapons of Mass Destruction (December 2002). Available online. URL: http://www.whitehouse.gov/news/releases/200212/WMDStrategy.pdf. Accessed June 15, 2008. Issued by the White House, this document surveys American efforts to protect the United States against chemical, biological, and nuclear weapons. It points out the urgency of countering the efforts of states that are engaged in proliferation of WMD and preventing these weapons from getting into the hand of terrorists.

Norris, Robert S., and Hans M. Kristensen. "U.S. Nuclear Forces, 2007." *Bulletin of the Atomic Scientists* (March/April 2007): 79–82. A detailed summary drawing on a wide selection of published, nonclassified sources. This report includes a chart of the U.S. nuclear arsenal listing ICBMs, SLBMs, bombers, and nonstrategic forces. Norris is associated with the Natural Resources Defense Council and Kristensen with the Federation of American Scientists.

———. "U.S. Nuclear Forces, 2008." *Bulletin of the Atomic Scientists* (March/April 2008): 50–53. A detailed summary drawing on a wide selection of published, nonclassified sources. This report includes a chart of the U.S. nuclear arsenal listing ICBMs, SLBMs, bombers, and nonstrategic forces. Norris is associated with the Natural Resources Defense Council and Kristensen with the Federation of American Scientists.

———. "U.S. Nuclear Forces, 2009." *Bulletin of the Atomic Scientists* (March/April 2009): 59–69. A detailed summary drawing on a wide selection of published, nonclassified sources. This report includes a chart of the U.S. nuclear arsenal listing ICBMs, SLBMs, bombers, and nonstrategic forces. Norris is associated with the Natural Resources Defense Council and Kristensen with the Federation of American Scientists.

Nuclear Weapon Archive. "Gallery of U.S. Nuclear Tests." Available online. URL: http://www.nuclearweaponarchive.org/Usa/Tests/index.html. Accessed July 22, 2008. An overview of U.S. nuclear tests. Includes a chart listing U.S. atmospheric tests and information on the location of U.S. nuclear test sites.

Office of the Deputy Assistant to the Secretary of Defense for Nuclear Matters. "U.S. Nuclear Stockpile: Nuclear Weapons Stockpile Management." Available online. URL: http://www.acq.osd.mil/ncbdp/nm/nuclearstockpile.html. Accessed July 21, 2008. A fact sheet covering the many aspects of managing the U.S. nuclear stockpile. Includes two charts: one lists and describes the different types of U.S. nuclear warheads; the other lists current warhead types and current delivery systems.

Richelson, Jeffrey T. *Spying on the Bomb: American Nuclear Intelligence from Nazi Germany to Iran and North Korea.* New York: Norton, 2006. A history of U.S. efforts to spy on other nations suspected of having nuclear programs. The author argues that the United States was concerned that nuclear proliferation would spur regional arms races. More recently, the concern has arisen that rogue nations such as Iran and North Korea would develop atomic weapons. Richelson is a senior fellow at the National Security Archive in Washington, D.C.

Thompson, Loren B. "Why Missile Defense Makes More Sense Today Than During the Cold War" (6/23/08). Available online. URL: http://lexingtoninstitute.org/printer_1285.shtml. Accessed July 21, 2008. Thompson, formerly deputy director of the Security Studies Program at Georgetown University, argues missile defense is necessary because of the diverse nature of adversaries who might get nuclear weapons. Some of those actors might not be deterred by the threat of retaliation.

"U.S. quits AMB treaty." CNN.com (12/14/01). Available online. URL: http://archives.cnn.com/2001/ALLPOLITICS/12/13/rec.bush.abm/. Accessed July 23, 2008. CNN report on the announcement by President George Bush that the United States notified Russia that it was withdrawing from the 1972 ABM treaty.

"US-Russian agreement repatriates highly enriched uranium from Poland." Bellona (6/9/07). Available online. URL: http://www.bellona.org/articles/articles_2007/

ebrd_grants?printerfriendly=yes. Accessed August 1, 2008. A report on the repatriation to Russia of 8.8 kilograms of HEU fuel under the Global Threat Reduction Initiative.

Walker, Stephen. *Shockwave: Countdown to Hiroshima.* New York: HarperCollins, 2005. A journalistic account of the three weeks leading up to the bombing of Hiroshima. Walker interviewed surviving Americans involved in the Hiroshima mission as well as Japanese who experienced the bombing. Walker reveals that American technicians and scientists on Tinian Island, from which the Hiroshima mission took off, feared that if a B-29 bomber carrying a nuclear weapon crashed on takeoff its bomb would detonate, killing thousands of American servicemen and destroying the entire island. This was more than a theoretical concern, as crashes of overloaded B-29s bound for Japan were a common occurrence on Tinian.

Williams, Robert C., and Philip L. Cantelon. *The American Atom: A Documentary History of Nuclear Policies from the Discovery of Fission to the Present, 1939–1984.* Philadelphia: University of Pennsylvania Press, 1984. A collection of 73 documents on topics ranging from the development of atomic bomb and the hydrogen bomb to arms control and nuclear power.

SOVIET/RUSSIAN CHEMICAL AND BIOLOGICAL WEAPONS PROGRAMS

"Agreement between the United States of America and the Union of Soviet Socialist Republics on Destruction and Non-Production of Chemical Weapons and on Measures to Facilitate the Multilateral Convention on Banning Chemical Weapons." Available online. URL: http://www.fas.org/nuke/control/bda/text/index.html. Accessed September 14, 2008. The Bilateral Destruction Agreement (BDA) signed by the Soviet Union and the United States on June 1, 1990.

Arms Control Association. "Building a Forward Line of Defense: Securing Former Soviet Biological Weapons." Available online. URL: http://www.armscontrol.org/act/2004_07-08/Luongo. Accessed April 22, 2009. A survey of the problems involved in securing former Soviet biological weapons, including continued Russian secrecy regarding important military facilities.

———. "Chemical Weapons Deadlines Extended" (January/February 2008). Available online. URL: http://www.armscontrol.org/act/2007_01-02/CWDeadlines. Accessed September 14, 2008. A report on the five-year extension to a 2007 deadline for the destruction of chemical weapons granted to both the United States and Russia.

Brand, David. "CU's Vogel: Russian biological warfare plans still pose global threat." *Cornell Chronicle* (2/22/01). Available online. URL: http://www.news.cornell.edu/chronicle/01/2.22.01/AAAS_Vogel.html. Accessed September 14, 2008. A news report on a speech by chemist Kathleen Vogel, who discussed the serious threat still posed by what remains in Russia of the former Soviet Union's biological weapons program.

Annotated Bibliography

CBCNews.ca. "Red Lies: Biological Warfare and the Soviet Union" (2/18/04). Available online. URL: www.cbc.ca/news/background/bioweapons/readlies.html. An in-depth investigative report on the 1979 anthrax outbreak in Sverdlovsk, the cover-up that followed, the defections by Russian scientists that finally exposed what had happened, and the questions that remain about the Soviet biological weapons program. The article points out that key facilities still remain secret and no one knows what agents are still stockpiled and whether any production lines are still in operation.

Davis, Christopher J. "Nuclear Blindness: An Overview of the Biological Weapons Programs of the Former Soviet Union and Iraq." *Emerging Infectious Diseases* 4, no. 4 (July–August 1999): 509–512. Available online. URL: http://www.cdc.gov/ncidod/EID/vol5no4/davis.htm. Accessed September 17, 2008. A survey of two WMD programs that the United States and its allies failed to detect for years.

Eisler, Peter. "Plan to Destroy Russian Weapons Nears Collapse." *USA Today* (10/01/02). Available online. URL: http://www.usatoday.com/news/world/2002-09-30-russian-weapons-1acover_x.htm. Accessed September 14, 2008. News article with information about the huge Russian chemical weapons storage facility in the town of Shchuch'ye in western Siberia.

Federation of American Scientists. "Ministry for Extraordinary Situations [EMERCOM]." Available online. URL: http://fas.org/nuke/guide/russia/agency/emercom.htm. Accessed April 22, 2009. An overview of the Russian Ministry of Civil Defense.

———. WMD Around the World. "Biopreparat." Available online. URL: http://www.fas.org/nuke/guide/russia/agency/bw.htm. Accessed September 21, 2008. A short introduction to Biopreparat.

———. WMD Around the World. "Chemical Weapons." Available online. URL: http://www.fas.org/nuke/guide/russia/cwb/cw/htm. Accessed July 15, 2008. An overview of the Soviet chemical weapons program that also surveys the destruction of Russia's chemical weapons stockpile. Includes pie charts on chemical agents in the Russian stockpile and the sites at which those agents are stored.

"Germany to Help Russia Destroy Chemical Weapons Stockpile" (6/10/08). Deutsche Welle. Available online. URL: http://www.dw-world.de/dw/article/0,2144,3401229,00.html. Accessed September 14, 2008; Nuclear Threat Initiative. Russia Profile. "Chemical Overview." Available online. URL: http://www.nti.org/e_research/profiles/Russia/Chemical/index.html. Accessed September 14, 2008. New report on Germany's contribution to the program to destroy Russian chemical weapons.

Global Security.org. "Obolensk NPO Biointez State Research Center for Applied Microbiology." Available online. URL: http://www.globalsecurity.org/wmd/world/russia/obolensk.htm. Accessed September 20, 2008. A short overview of the most important Soviet biological weapons facility, which is located about 48 miles (80 km) south of Moscow.

Miller, Judith. "Poison Island: A Special Report; At Bleak Asian Site, Killer Germs Survive." *New York Times* (6/2/99). Available online. URL: http://query.nytimes.com.

gts/fullpage.htm?res+9707E1D81030F931A35755C0A96 F9582. Accessed September 20, 2008. A newspaper article on the situation on Vozrozhdeniye Island in the Aral Sea before the United States decontaminated the anthrax bacteria buried there by Soviet authorities in 1988.

National Security Archive. *Volume V: Anthrax at Sverdlovsk, 1979.* Available online. URL: http://www.gwu.edu/~nsarchiv/NSAEBB/NSAEBB61/. Accessed September 20, 2008. A sourcebook on the deadliest modern outbreak of anthrax. Contains an introductory survey and 32 documents.

Nichol, Jim. CRS Report for Congress. "Central Asia: Regional Developments and Implications for U.S. Interests." Updated July 5, 2007. An overview of U.S. policy toward the various states of Central Asia that emerged from the collapse of the Soviet Union.

Nuclear Threat Initiative. Russia Profile. "Biological Overview." Available online. URL: www.nti.org/e_research/profiles/Russia/Biological/index.html. Accessed September 14, 2008. An overview of the Soviet biological weapons programs and what Russia has done with them since 1992.

———. Russia Profile. "Chemical Overview." Available online. URL: www.nti.org/e_research/profiles/Russia/Chemical/index.html. Accessed September 14, 2008. An overview of the Soviet chemical weapons programs and what Russia has done with them since 1992.

———. "Russia: Government and Selected Ministries." Available online. URL: http://www.nti.org/db/nisprofs/russia/govt/ministry.htm#mie. Accessed April 22, 2009. An overview of important Russian government ministries including the Ministry of Defense and the Ministry of Civil Defense, both of which are involved in protecting the country against WMD.

———. Russia Profile. "Biological Overview." Available online. URL: http://www.nti.org/e_research/profiles/russia/biological/index.html. Accessed September 14, 2008. An overview of the Soviet biological weapons program from its origins in the 1920s to Biopreparat.

———. Russia Profile. "Chemical Overview." Available online. URL: http://www.nti.org/e_research/profiles/Russia/Chemical/index.html. Accessed September 14, 2008. An overview of Russia's stock of chemical weapons. Includes a brief history of the Soviet program and a list of the locations of where these weapons are stored.

Renz, Bettina. "Crisis Response in War and Peace: Russia's Emergencies' Ministry and Security Sector Reform." *World Defense Systems,* 16. Available online. URL: http://www.sovereign-publications.com/wds-articles/Renz.pdf. Accessed July 23, 2009. An overview of the Russian Ministry of Civil Defense, whose responsibilities include protecting the country against WMD.

Roffey, Roger, Wilhelm Unge, Jenny Clevström, and Kristian S. Westerdahl. *Support to Threat Reduction of the Russian Biological Weapons Legacy—Conversion, Biodefence and the Role of Biopreparat.* Stockholm: Swedish Defense Research Agency, 2003. The authors describe the programs underway to reduce the biological weapons threat posed by the legacy of the Soviet program. They conclude that Russia still has considerable biological weapons and voice their concern that the programs currently in place have not reached the facilities of the Russia's Ministry of Defense.

"Russia Opens 4th Chemical Weapons Destruction Plant." *International Herald Tribune* (6/17/08). Available online. URL: http://www.int.com/articles/ap/2008/06/17/news/Russia-Chemical-Weapons.php. Accessed September 14, 2008. News story on the opening of a plant to destroy chemical weapons about 350 (550 km) southeast of Moscow.

Talkington, Adam S. "Chemical Weapons Production in Russia Is Closer to Being a 'Cold' Idea." *Combating WMD Journal* 2 (2008). Available online. URL: https://www.cbrniac.apgea.army.mil/Products/Documents/USANCA%20Journals%20and%2 0Reports/CWMD_Journal_No_2_Mar08.pdf. Accessed October 20, 2008. A report on the destruction of the Russian VX production plant in the city of Novocheboksarsk being carried out under the auspices of the Nuclear Threat Reduction Agency.

SOVIET/RUSSIAN NUCLEAR WEAPONS PROGRAM

Center for Defense Information. "Russian Nuclear Arsenal" (7/30/08). Available online. URL: http://www.cdi.org/friendlyversion/printversion.cfm?documentID+2967. Accessed September 7, 2007. A chart listing Soviet ICBMs, long-range air-launched cruise missiles, SLBMs, aircraft, and nonstrategic and defensive weapons.

GlobalSecurity.org. "Russia develops defense program against high-precision strikes." Available online. URL: http://www.globalsecurity.org/wmd/library/news/russia/2008/russia-080429-rianovosti02.htm. Accessed July 4, 2008. A report on Russia's new plan for a unified national defense against high-precision missile attacks.

Harding, Kyle. "Yeltsin's Nonproliferation Legacy: Two Steps Forward, Now Two Steps Back" (5/08/07). Henry L. Stimson Center. Available online. URL: http://www.stimson.org/pub.cfm?ID=537. Accessed July 18, 2008. An evaluation of the positive and negative aspects of the nuclear policies of former Russian president Boris Yeltsin.

Holloway, David. *The Soviet Union and the Arms Race.* New Haven, Conn.: Yale University Press, 1983. The standard work on the Soviet arms buildup during the cold war.

———. *Stalin and the Bomb.* New Haven, Conn., and London: Yale University Press, 1994. The most thorough overview available on Soviet nuclear weapons policy in the years immediately after World War II by the leading authority in the field. Holloway demonstrates that the Soviet Union made the commitment to build thermonuclear weapons several years before the United States and would have developed those weapons regardless of what the United States said or did.

Julian, Hana Levi. "Russia Sells S-300 Anti-Aircraft Missile Defense System to Iran." Arutz Sheva IsraelNationalNews.com. Available online. URL: http://www.israelnationalnews.com/News/News.aspx/124719. Accessed October 1, 2008. A news report on the Russian announcement that it will sell the advanced S-300 air defense system to Iran.

National Nuclear Security Administration. "NNSA Announces the End of Plutonium Production in Seversk, Russia" (6/5/08). Available online. URL: http://nnsa.energy.gov/news/2041.htm. Accessed September 30, 2008. An announcement from the NNSA that the second of two plutonium-producing nuclear reactors in Seversk (formerly the secret Soviet city called Tomsk-7) has been shut down. The first reactor was shut down in April.

Norris, Robert S., and Hans M. Kristensen. "Russian Nuclear Forces, 2008." *Bulletin of the Atomic Scientists* (May/June 2008). A detailed accounting of the Russian nuclear arsenal as of 2008, based on publicly available sources. Includes a chart that breaks down the arsenal by type of weapon.

———. "Russian Nuclear Forces, 2009." *Bulletin of the Atomic Scientists* (May/June 2009). A detailed accounting of the Russian nuclear arsenal as of 2009, based on publicly available sources. Includes a chart that breaks down the arsenal by type of weapon.

Nuclear Threat Initiative. Russian Profile. Available online. URL: http://www.nti.org/E_research/profiles/Russia/index.html. Accessed July 8, 2008. An overview of the Soviet/Russian nuclear, biological, chemical, and missile programs.

Nuclear Weapon Archive. "*Big Ivan,* The Tsar Bomba ('King of Bombs')." Available online. URL: http://nuclearweaponarchive.org/Russia/TsarBomba.html. Accessed September 28, 2008. A report on the largest nuclear device ever exploded, a monster known to its designers as "Big Ivan."

———. "Soviet Nuclear Test Summary." Last updated October 7, 1997. Available online. URL: http://nuclearweaponarchive.org/Russia/Sovtestsum.html. Accessed September 30, 2008. A summary of all the Soviet nuclear tests, broken down by category into a series of charts.

———. "The Soviet Nuclear Weapons Program." Available online. URL: http://www.nuclearweaponarchive.org/Russia/Sovwpnprog.html. Accessed July 14, 2008. A concise history of the Soviet nuclear weapons program, including sections on the program to 1949, the first atomic explosion, the thermonuclear weapons program, and the super-secret Arzamas laboratory, sometimes called the Soviet Los Alamos.

"One plutonium production reactor in Seversk to be shut down." Russian Strategic Nuclear Forces. Available online. URL: http://russianforces.org/blog/2008/04/one_plutonium_production_react.shtml. Accessed September 30, 2008. Report that the first of two nuclear reactors in Seversk will be shut down. An update on April 20 reports on the shutdown and adds that the second reactor in Seversk will be shut down in June. The report notes that Russia has three such reactors and that the third, in the city of Zheleznogorsk (formerly Krasnoyarsk-26), will operate until 2010.

Podvig, Pavel. "The Russian Nuclear Arsenal" (November 2005). Center for International Security and Cooperation, Stanford University. Available online. URL: http://www.ciaonet.org/casestudy/case003/case003/html. Accessed September 7,

2008. A detailed overview of the Russian nuclear arsenal. This case study includes an introductory section on the Soviet program inherited by Russia, a survey of Russian-U.S. arms negotiations beginning with START I (actually signed with the Soviet Union in July 1991), and the status of Soviet nuclear forces—including defensive forces—as of 2005.

"Report: Russia Shuts Down Nuclear Reactor Producing Weapons-Grade Plutonium." FoxNews.com. Available online. URL: http://www.foxnews.com/story/0,2933,351880,00.html. Accessed April 20, 2008. A news report on the shutting down of the first of two plutonium-producing nuclear reactors in the city of Seversk (formerly Tomsk-7).

Russianforces.org. Russian strategic nuclear forces. "Current Status." Available online. URL: http://russianforces.org/current. Accessed September 7, 2008. Statistics on Russia's nuclear arsenal as of June 2008. Russianforces.org is the Web site for the Russian Nuclear Forces Project, which was started by a group of Russian scientists in 1991.

"Russia Test-Fires Topol Missile, Georgia Desperately Cries for NATO Membership." *Pravda* (6/28/08). Available online. URL: http://english.pravda.ru/print/russia/politics/106240-russia_topol_missile-0. Accessed September 30, 2008. News article on the most modern Russian ICBM.

"Russia to Deploy S-400 Air Defense Systems around Moscow Aug. 6." RIA Novosti. Available online. URL: http://en.rian.ru/russia/20080121/97447013.html. Accessed October 1, 2008. A news report on Russian plans to deploy an advanced new air defense system with the ability to destroy aircraft, cruise missiles, and ballistic missiles.

"Sibirskii khimicheskii kombinat zaglushil atomnyi reaktor ADE-4" (Siberian chemical enterprise closed the atomic reactor ADE-4; 4/20/08). Tomsknews.com. Available online. URL: http://tomsknews.com/news/?id=5189. Accessed September 30, 2008. News report on the closing down of the first of two plutonium-producing nuclear reactors in the city of Seversk. The report adds that the second reactor will be shut down in June.

"System 135." MISSILETHREATcom. Available online. URL: http://www.missilethreat.com/missiledefensesystems/id.7,page.1,css.print/system_detail.asp. Accessed October 1, 2008. A description of the defensive missile system currently deployed by Russia to defend Moscow. The system has three components: a long-range Gorgon interceptor, a short-range Gazelle interceptor, and an advanced radar system.

THE UNSTABLE MIDDLE EAST

Bergman, Ronen. *The Secret War with Iran: The 30-Year Clandestine Struggle against the World's Most Dangerous Terrorist Power.* New York: Free Press, 2008. Bergman chronicles the abject failure of the world's democratic countries to prevent Iran from developing nuclear weapons. Of particular interest are sabotage operations that actually have delayed Iran's program. The author chronicles the crucial role Pakistan and Abdul Qadeer Khan played in providing vital resources to the Iranians.

WEAPONS OF MASS DESTRUCTION

Broad, William J., and David Sanger. "Iran Said to Have Nuclear Fuel for One Weapon." *New York Times* (11/20/08). Available online. URL: http://www.nytimes.com/2008/11/20/world/middleeast/20nuke.html?_r=1& ref=todayspa. Accessed November 20, 2008. Newspaper article on a report by the IAEC.

Cordesman, Anthony H. "Iran, Israel, and Nuclear War." Available online. URL: http://www.csis.org/media/csis/pubs/071119_iran.is&nuclearwar.pdf. Accessed December 10, 2008. Projections on what could happen if a nuclear war breaks out in the Middle East, illustrated by charts, graphs, and maps. Cordesman hold the Arleigh A. Burke chair in Strategy at the Center for Strategic and International Studies, whose site hosts this publication.

GlobalSecurity.Org. "Dimona Nuclear Research Reactor." Available online. URL: http://www.globalsecurity.org/wmd/world/israel/dimona.htm. Accessed October 26, 2008. History and description of Israel's heavy-water reactor at Dimona. Includes an estimate of the size of Israel's nuclear arsenal and a list of the 10 facilities that make up the Dimona complex.

James Martin Center for Nonproliferation Studies. "Egypt: Weapons of Mass Destruction Capabilities and Programs." Available online. URL: http://cns.miis.edu/research/wmdme/egypt.htm. Accessed May 24, 2008. A chart showing Egypt's nuclear, chemical, biological, ballistic missile, and cruise missile resources, along with other information.

———. "Iran: Weapons of Mass Destruction Capabilities and Programs." Available online. URL: http://cns.miis.edu/research/wmdme/iran.htm. Accessed May 24, 2008. A chart showing Iran's nuclear, chemical, biological, ballistic missile, and cruise missile resources, along with other information.

———. "Reported Conventional Military Attacks on NBC Facilities in the Middle East." Available online. URL: http://cns.miis.edu/research/wmdme/prempt.htm. Accessed May 22, 2008. A chart showing attacks made on nuclear, biological, and chemical weapons facilities in the Middle East between 1980 and 1998.

———. "Reported Use of Chemical Weapons, Ballistic Missiles, and Cruise Missiles in the Middle East." Available online. URL: http://cns.miis.edu/research/wmdme/use.htm. Accessed May 24, 2008. A comprehensive chart on the use of chemical weapons and missiles in the Middle East.

———. "Syria: Weapons of Mass Destruction Capabilities and Programs." Updated April 2006. Available online. URL: http://cns.miis.edu/research/wmdme/syria.htm. Accessed May 24, 2008. A chart showing Syria's nuclear, chemical, biological, ballistic missile, and cruise missile resources, along with other information.

———. "Weapons of Mass Destruction in the Middle East: Libya." Updated April 2006. Available online. URL: http://cns.miis.edu/research/wmdme/libya.htm. Accessed July 5, 2008. A chart with information on Libya's chemical, biological, and nuclear programs and on its arsenal of ballistic and cruise missiles.

Mansharof, Y., and A. Savyon. "Iran." MEMRI E-mail Newsletter (6/6/08). Translations of genocidal public statements regarding Israel by Iranian leaders including President Ahmadinejad, Supreme Leader Ali Khamenei, and Foreign Minister Manuchehr Mottaki.

Raphaeli, Nimrod. "The Middle East Ventures into Nuclear Energy." MEMRI Inquiry and Analysis Series—No. 467. Available online. URL: http://www.memri.org/bin/latestnews.cgi?ID=IA46708. Accessed October 9, 2008. In response to Iran's nuclear programs and the threat they could pose to security, several Arab states in the Middle East are trying to develop nuclear energy. These programs, supposedly for peaceful purposes, could be used to produce nuclear weapons.

Rubin, Michael. "Iran's Global Ambition." *Middle Eastern Outlook* (March 2008). Available online. URL: http://www.aei.org/outlook/27658. Accessed November 1, 2008. An alarming overview of Iran's global ambitions by one of the leading experts on Iran.

Sciolino, Elaine. "Atomic Monitor Signals Concern Over Iran's Work. *New York Times* (5/27/08). A newspaper article summarizing an IAEA report on Iran's nuclear weapons program. The IAEA report accuses Iran of noncooperation.

———. "Nuclear Agency Says Iran Has Improved Enrichment." *New York Times* (9/16/08). A newspaper article on Iran's progress in its effort to enrich uranium. The report also notes the IAEA reported for the first time that foreign experts may have helped Iran develop a detonator that can be used in an implosion-type nuclear weapon.

Teitelbaum, Joshua. "Analysis: Iran's talk of destroying Israel must not get lost in translation." *Jerusalem Post* (6/22/08). Available online. URL: http://www.jpost.com/servlet/Satellite?cid=1213794429523&pagename=JPost52FJPArtic. Accessed June 22, 2008. An analysis of Iranian president Mahmoud Ahmadinejad's public remarks about Israel and their clear genocidal implications.

"Wipe Israel 'Off the Map' Iranian Says." *International Herald Tribune* (10/27/05). Available online. URL: http://www.iht.com/articles/2005/10/26/news/iran/php. Accessed October 10, 2008. Newspaper report on some of the incendiary and hateful remarks by Iran's president.

ISRAELI CHEMICAL AND BIOLOGICAL WEAPONS PROGRAMS

Cohen, Avner. "Israel and Chemical/Biological Weapons: History, Deterrence, and Arms Control." *Nonproliferation Review* (Fall/Winter 2001): pp. 39–40. A detailed history of Israel's efforts to develop chemical and biological weapons and how they have played a role in Israel's strategy of deterrence. Israel developed WMD to insure its national survival. Ultimately, nuclear weapons became the backbone of Israel's deterrence strategy, and Israel cut back its chemical and biological weapons programs and focused mainly on defensive research in these areas.

Katz, Yaakov. "Gas Mask Handout Delayed to Late 2009." *Jerusalem Post.* Available online. URL: http://www.jpost.com/servlet/Satellite?cid=1222017545320&pagename=JPost%2FJPArticle%2FShowFull. Accessed October 16, 2008. A news article on Israel's program to provide gas masks for its entire civilian population.

Nuclear Threat Initiative. Israel Profile. "Biological Chronology." Available online. URL: http://www.nti.org/e_research/profiles/Israel/Biological/3652.html. Accessed

October 14, 2008. A chronology of Israel's biological weapons program from the 1940s to December 2003.

———. "Biological Overview." Available online. URL: http://www.nti.org/e_research/profiles/Israel/Biological/index.html. Accessed October 12, 2008. A history and overview of Israel's biological weapons program. Fear of what Saddam Hussein might do as dictator of Iraq probably was the most important factor for the growth of Israel's defensive biological warfare program.

———. Israel Profile. "Chemical Overview." Available online. URL: http://www.nti.org/e_research/profiles/Israel/Chemical/index.html. Accessed July 17, 2008. A history and overview of Israel's chemical weapons program. NTI concludes that Israel has produced chemical weapons but that it probably does not have an offensive chemical warfare program today. However, because of the threat it faces from its Arab neighbors, Israel probably has an ability to retaliate with chemical weapons and continues to develop advanced knowledge in that field.

ISRAELI NUCLEAR WEAPONS PROGRAM

"American crews will control US FBX-band radar granted Israel." DEBKAfile (8/19/08). Available online. URL: http://www.debka.com/headline.php?hid=5518. Accessed August 21, 2008. News article from a Web site based in Israel specializing in intelligence and military matters.

Cohen, Avner. *Israel and the Bomb.* New York: Columbia University Press, 1998. The first detailed and scholarly account of Israel's nuclear weapons program. Cohen begins around 1950, when the program was established, and traces the story until 1970, when the United States accepted Israel's status as a nuclear power. He explains why Israel adopted the policy of ambiguity: that is, not formally stating that it was a nuclear power. In writing the book, Cohen drew heavily on American and Israeli documents that were not declassified until the 1990s.

Farr, Warner D. "The Third Temple's Holy of Holies: Israel's Nuclear Weapons." Available online. URL: http://www.fas.org/nuke/guide/israel/nuke/farr.htm. Accessed June 10, 2008. This 1999 paper, a detailed history of Israel's nuclear program, was written for the United States Air Force Counterproliferation Center at Maxwell Air Force Base by a lieutenant colonel in the U.S. Army.

Federation of American Scientists. WMD Around the World. "Nuclear Weapons." Available online. URL: http://www.fas.org/nuke/guide/israel/nuke. Accessed July 9, 2008. A historical overview of Israel's nuclear weapons program. It includes a graph showing the growth of Israel's arsenal according to three different estimates, which place Israel's stock of nuclear warheads at between 70 and 400 as of 2006. FAS believes that actually the number is closer to the lower estimate.

"Israel, U.S. reportedly close radar deal." Jewish Telegraphic Agency (8/19/08). Available online. URL: http://www.jta.org/cgi-bin/iowa/breaking/109991.html. Accessed August 19, 2008. News article on the U.S. decision to supply Israel with an advanced radar system for its Arrow II antiballistic missile defense system.

James Martin Center for Nonproliferation Studies. "Israel: Weapons of Mass Destruction Capabilities and Programs." Updated April 2006. Available online. URL:

http://cns.miis.edu/research/wmdme/israel.htm. Accessed May 24, 2008. A chart with information on Israel's arsenal of nuclear warheads, chemical weapons program, biological weapons program, ballistic missiles, cruise missiles, other delivery systems (including aircraft), and unmanned aerial vehicles. CNS estimates that Israel has between 100 and 200 warheads, some of which may be thermonuclear.

Karpin, Michael. *The Bomb in the Basement: How Israel Went Nuclear and What That Means for the World.* New York: Simon and Schuster, 2007. Karpin, a journalist and documentary filmmaker, updates and expands on Anver's Cohen's *Israel and the Bomb.* Many of his insights are based on exclusive interviews with key figures in Israel's nuclear program. This is the most up-to-date history of Israel's nuclear program currently available.

Nuclear Threat Initiative. Israel Profile. "Israel Nuclear Facilities." Available online. URL: http://www.nti.org/e_research/profiles/Israel/Nuclear/3583.html. Accessed October 19, 2008. An overview of Israel's major nuclear facilities and the Israel Atomic Energy Commission.

———. Nuclear Threat Initiative. Israel Profile. "Missile Overview." Available online. URL: http://www.nti.org/e_research/profiles/Israel/Missile/index.html. Accessed October 19, 2008. Information on Israel's arsenal of ballistic missiles, including the Jericho II missile and the Arrow antiballistic missile defense system.

———. Israel Profile. "Nuclear Overview." Available online. URL: http://www.nti.org/e_research/profiles/Israel/Nuclear/index.html. Accessed October 19, 2008. An overview of Isreal's nuclear program from its origins in the 1950s through the 1967 and 1973 wars to the present.

Spector, Leonard, and Avner Cohen. "Israel's Airstrike on Syria's Reactor: Implications for the Nonproliferation Regime." Arms Control Association. Available online. URL: http://www.armscontrol.org/act/2008_07-08/SpectorCohen. Accessed October 29, 2008. News article on the international reaction to Israel's air raid that destroyed a nuclear reactor being built in Syria.

"U.S. Defense Department Pledges Financial Support for Arrow 3." *Jerusalem Post* (8/8/08). Available online. URL: http://www.jpost.com/servlet/Satellite?cid=1215331213785&pagename=JPArticle%2FShowFull. Accessed August 6, 2008. News article on the U.S. commitment to support development of the Arrow 3, which will exceed the Arrow 2 in terms of range, speed, and altitude.

THE CHEMICAL AND BIOLOGICAL WEAPONS PROGRAMS OF INDIA AND PAKISTAN

Nuclear Threat Initiative. India Profile. "Biological Overview. Available online. URL: http://www.nti.org/e_research/profiles/India/Biological/index.html. Accessed October 17, 2008. Covers the history and current status of India's biological weapons program. At present there is no clear evidence of an offensive program. Instead, India is focusing on defensive measures against biological attack.

———. India Profile. "Chemical Overview." Available online. URL: http://www.nti.org/e_research/profiles/India/Chemical/index.html. Accessed October 17, 2008.

Covers the history and current status of India's chemical weapons program. At present India is destroying its stock of chemical weapons. It has a defensive program run by the Ministry of Defense.

———. Pakistan Profile. "Biological Overview." Available online. URL: http://www.nti.org/e_research/profiles/Pakistan/Biological/index.html. Accessed October 17, 2008. Overview of Pakistan's biological weapons program.

———. Pakistan Profile. "Chemical Overview." Available online. URL: http://www.nti.org/e_research/profiles/Pakistan/Chemical/index.html. Accessed October 17, 2008. Overview of Pakistan's chemical weapons program.

THE NUCLEAR WEAPONS PROGRAMS OF INDIA AND PAKISTAN

Corera, Gordon. *Shopping for Bombs: Nuclear Proliferation, Global Insecurity, and the Rise and Fall of the A. Q. Khan Network*. New York: Oxford University Press, 2006. Gordon, a British journalist, has unearthed a great deal of new information about how the Khan network operated and how the CIA and Britain's MI6 intelligence agency finally broke up that network. His book also provides insights into Iran's nuclear ambitions.

Economist.com (1/03/08). "The Spider's Stratagem." Available online. URL: http://www.economist.com/books/displaystory.cfm?story_id=10424283. Accessed November 29, 2008. Review of the book *The Nuclear Jihadist,* by Douglas Frantz and Catherine Collins, that details the nuclear proliferation activities of Pakistan's Abdul Qadeer Khan.

Federation of American Scientists. WMD Around the World. "Nuclear Weapons." Available online. URL: http://www.fas.org/nuke/guide/india/nuke/. Accessed October 17, 2008. Includes a historical overview, a section on the tests of May 1998, an estimate of India's nuclear arsenal, and a summary of India's nuclear doctrine.

———. "Pakistan Nuclear Weapons." Available online. URL: http://www.fas.org/nuke/guide/pakistan/nuke/. Accessed October 17, 2008. Includes a chart of Pakistan's May 1998 nuclear tests and an estimate of Pakistan's nuclear arsenal as of 2004.

Joshi, Sharad. "India and Pakistan Missile Race Surges On." *WMD Insights* (October 2007). Available online. URL: http://www.wmdinsights.org/I19/I19_SA2_MissileDev.htm. Accessed October 17, 2008. A survey of the continuing India-Pakistan race to develop new and more accurate missiles. Both sides have made advances. The author points out that India may be developing a missile with a range of 3,000 miles (5,000 km). This is so it can target China's major cities, several of which—including Beijing, Nanjing, and Shanghai—are currently out of range of missiles based in southern India, where India prefers to base missiles aimed at China. *WMD Insights* is published by the U.S. Defense Threat Reduction Agency.

Norris, Robert S., and Hans M. Kristensen. "India's Nuclear Forces, 2007." *Bulletin of the Atomic Scientists* (July/August 2007): 74–77. The authors estimate that India has produced enough plutonium for about 100 warheads and has about 50–60 assembled warheads. The article includes a chart of India's missiles and aircraft that can deliver nuclear weapons.

———. "Pakistan's Nuclear Forces, 2007." *Bulletin of the Atomic Scientists* (May/June 2007): 71–74. A comprehensive assessment of Pakistan's nuclear arsenal as of 2007. Includes a chart on the aircraft and missiles Pakistan has for delivering nuclear weapons.

Nuclear Threat Initiative. India Profile. "Missile Overview." Available online. URL: http://www.nti.org/e_research/profiles/India/Missile/index.html. Accessed October 17, 2008. A detailed summary of India's missile program and capabilities. Includes a historical overview, an assessment of the current status of India's missile forces, and other information, including a table with specifications on all of India's ballistic and cruise missiles.

———. India Profile. "Nuclear Overview." Available online. URL: http://www.nti.org/e_research/profiles/India/Nuclear/index.html. Accessed October 17, 2008. Includes a historical overview, estimate of India's capabilities, and a summary of India's nuclear use doctrine. NTI states that India does not maintain its nuclear forces on a heightened state of alert but instead relies on plans to ready them rapidly in an emergency or crisis.

———. Pakistan Profile. "Missile Overview. Available online. URL: http://www.nti.org/e_research/profiles/Pakistan/Missile/index.html. Accessed October 17, 2008. A comprehensive summary of Pakistan's ballistic and cruise missile programs. Includes information on each missile in the current Pakistani arsenal.

———. Pakistan Profile. "Nuclear Overview. Available online. URL: http://www.nti.org/e_research/profiles/Pakistan/Nuclear/index.html. Accessed October 17, 2008. A summary of the development of Pakistan's nuclear weapons program.

Nuclear Weapon Archive. "India's Nuclear Weapons Program. The Beginning: 1944–1960." Available online. URL: http://nuclearweaponarchive.org/India/IndiaOrigin.html. Accessed October 17, 2008. Traces the history of India's nuclear weapons program from its origins in the 1940s to 1960, when India's heavy-water Cirus reactor began operation.

———. "India's Nuclear Weapons Program. India as a Nuclear Power: 1998–2001." Available online. URL: http://nuclearweaponarchive.org/India/IndiaNPower.html. Accessed November 27, 2008. Focuses on India's formal declaration of its status as a nuclear power by issuing its nuclear doctrine in 1999.

———. "India's Nuclear Weapons Program. The Long Pause: 1974–1989." Available online. URL: http://nuclearweaponarchive.org/India/IndiaPause.html. Accessed November 27, 2008. An overview of the period of uneven progress and delay in India's nuclear weapons program between 1974 and 1989.

———. "India's Nuclear Weapons Program. The Momentum Builds: 1989–1998." Available online. URL: http://nuclearweaponarchive.org/India/IndiaMomentum.html. Accessed November 27, 2008. An overview of the period when India developed and stockpiled a few dozen operational nuclear bombs.

——. "India's Nuclear Weapons Program. On to Weapons Development: 1960–1967." Available online. URL: http://nuclearweaponarchive.org/India/IndiaWDevelop.html. Accessed October 27, 2008. Traces India's nuclear weapons program from 1960–1967, pointing out how that program was in part driven by concerns regarding China.

——. "India's Nuclear Weapons Program: Operation Shakti: 1998." Available online. URL: http://nuclearweaponarchive.org/India/IndiaShakti.html. Accessed November 27, 2008. A detailed description of the five nuclear tests India conducted in May 1998.

——. "India's Nuclear Weapons Program: Present Capabilities." Available online. URL: http://nuclearweaponarchive.org/India/IndiaArsenal.html. Accessed November 27, 2008. Includes a historical summary, an overview of India's arsenal as of April 2001, a summary of India's nuclear force planning, specifications on India's ballistic missiles, and an overview of India's nuclear facilities.

——. "India's Nuclear Weapons Program. Smiling Buddha: 1974." Available online. URL: http://nuclearweaponarchive.org/India/IndiaSmiling.html. Accessed November 27, 2008. Chronicles India's first nuclear test, the supposedly peaceful "Smiling Buddha" test of 1974.

——. "Pakistan's Nuclear Weapons Program. 1998: The Year of Testing." Available online. URL: http://nuclearweaponarchive.org/Pakistan/PakTests.html. Accessed November 27, 2008. Chronicles the background and preparation for the series of tests in May 1998 and also provides extensive information on the tests themselves.

——. "Pakistan's Nuclear Weapons Program. Present Capabilities." Available online. URL: http://nuclearweaponarchive.org/Pakistan/PakArsenal.html. Accessed November 27, 2008. An estimate of Pakistan's nuclear arsenal as of 2001. Includes a chart summarizing specifications of Pakistan's missiles.

NORTH KOREA'S CHEMICAL, BIOLOGICAL, AND NUCLEAR WEAPONS PROGRAMS

BBC News. "Q&A: N. Korea Nuclear Stand-off" (10/11/08). Available online. URL: http://bbc.co.uk/2/hi/asia-pacific2340405.stm. Accessed December 12, 2008. Short article on the negotiations between North Korea and the United States as they stood in the fall of 2008.

Center for Defense Information. "Fact Sheet: North Korea's Nuclear Weapons Program." Updated January 23, 2003. Available online. URL: http://www.cdi.org/nuclear/nk-fact-sheet.cfm. Accessed June 16, 2008. A survey of the North Korean nuclear weapons program as of 2003.

Institute for Science and International Security. "North Korea." Available online. URL: http://www.isis-online.org/mapproject/country_pages/northkorea.html. Accessed December 12, 2008. Estimates on the North Korean stocks of fissile material and nuclear warheads as of 2004.

Nikish, Larry A. "CRS Issue Brief for Congress: North Korea's Nuclear Weapons Program." Updated May 25, 2006. A summary of the North Korean nuclear weapons program as of 2006 and the effort of the Bush administration to get the program dismantled.

Nuclear Threat Initiative. North Korea Profile. "Biological Overview." Available online. URL: http://www.nti.org/e_research/profiles/NK/Biological/index.html. Accessed December 2, 2008. NTI finds that there are varying assessments regarding North Korea's secretive biological weapons program, which exists in violation of North Korea's obligations as a member of the Biological Weapons Convention.

———. North Korea Profile. "Chemical Overview." Available online. URL: http://www.nti.org/e_research/profiles/NK/Chemical/index.html. Accessed December 12, 2008. NTI concludes that North Korea has one of the largest chemical weapons arsenals in the world, although it is unclear how well the North Koreans can manufacture nerve agents such as sarin, soman, and VX.

———. North Korea Profile. "Nuclear Facilities: IRT-2000 Nuclear Research Reactor." Available online. URL: http://www.nti.org/e_research/profiles/NK/45_552.html. Accessed December 10, 2008. Specifications and other information on the small nuclear reactor North Korea received from the Soviet Union in the 1960s.

———. North Korea Profile. "Nuclear Facilities: "5MW(e) Experimental Reactor." Available online. URL: http://www.nti.org/e_research/profiles/NK/45_551.html. Accessed December 10, 2008. Specifications and other information on the nuclear reactor that produced the plutonium for North Korea's first nuclear weapons.

———. North Korea Profile. "Nuclear Overview." Available online. URL: http://www.nit.org/e_research/profiles/NK/Nuclear/index.html. Accessed December 2, 2008. Covers the background to the program, the failed October 1994 Agreed Framework, the breakdown of the six-nation talks after 2003, and North Korea's 2006 nuclear test.

Nuclear Weapon Archive. "North Korea's Nuclear Weapons Program." Available online. URL: http://nuclearweaponarchive.org/DPRK/index.html. Accessed December 27, 2008. A historical survey of North Korea's nuclear program and description of North Korea's nuclear test on October 9, 2006. This article includes an estimate of the yield of that test.

Wright, David C. "An Analysis of the North Korean Missile Program" (November 2000). Available online. URL: http://www.fas.org/irp/threat/missile/rumsfeld/pt2_wright.htm. Accessed December 10, 2008. The author stresses that North Korea has demonstrated considerable ability in missile engineering. The author is a senior staff scientist with the Union of Concerned Scientists and a research fellow with the Security Studies Program at the Massachusetts Institute of Technology.

11

Chronology

Ancient Times to 1900

- ***429 B.C.E.*** Spartans create poisonous fumes by igniting a mixture of pitch and sulfur during the Peloponnesian War.
- ***1346:*** Mongols attacking the city of Kaffa on the shores of the Black Sea use catapults to hurl corpses infected with bubonic plague over the city walls.
- ***1763:*** British troops give smallpox-infected blankets to Native Americans. Earlier in the century Native Americans may have tried to poison the water supply of a British military force.
- ***1863 (April 24):*** U.S. War Department issues General Orders 100, based on the Leiber Code, banning the use of poisons in warfare.
- ***1899 (July 29):*** Hague Convention Respecting the Laws and Customs of War on Land (first Hague Convention) bans "poison or poisoned weapons" in warfare.
- ***1907:*** Second Hague Convention reaffirms the prohibitions of the Hague Convention of 1899.

1915

- ***April 15:*** Nine months into World War I, Germany uses chlorine gas against French troops for the first time near the Belgian town of Ypres, killing more than 600 and severely injuring many others.
- ***September 25:*** Britain uses chlorine gas against German forces for the first time.
- ***December 9:*** Germans fire artillery shells filled with phosgene against British troops.

1916

- ***February:*** The French attack German troops with phosgene.

1917

- ***July 12–13:*** The Germans use mustard gas for the first time against Allied troops. This attack, at Ypres, causes 20,000 casualties.

Chronology

1918

- ***February 26:*** Germany uses phosgene against American troops. It is the first time American troops are attacked with chemical weapons.
- ***June:*** U.S. troops use chemical weapons in combat for the first time.
- ***June 28:*** United States establishes the Chemical Warfare Service. In 1920, it becomes a specialized branch of the U.S. Army. In August 1946, its name is changed to the U.S. Army Chemical Corps.

1925

- ***June 17:*** Protocol of the Prohibition of the Use in War of Asphyxiating, Poisonous, or Other Gasses, and of Bacteriological Methods of Warfare (Geneva Protocol) adopted by the League of Nations. The United States ratifies the protocol in 1975.

1936

- ***December 23:*** The German chemist Dr. Gerhard Schrader isolates a chemical with deadly properties that eventually is called tabun. Schrader discovers sarin in 1938.

1938

- ***December:*** The German chemists Otto Hahn and Fritz Strassmann achieve nuclear fission. Their achievement opens the possibility that a nuclear bomb can be built.

1939

- ***August 2:*** Albert Einstein sends a letter to Franklin D. Roosevelt warning that it is possible to build an atomic bomb and that Nazi Germany may try to do it.
- ***November 1:*** A committee appointed by Roosevelt recommends investigating the possibility of building an atomic bomb.

1942

- ***Summer:*** Britain tests anthrax on Gruinard Island off the coast of Scotland. The experiments demonstrate that airborne anthrax spores are extremely infectious.
- ***August 13:*** The Manhattan Engineering District, which soon will be called the Manhattan Project, is established to build an atomic bomb.
- ***September:*** General Leslie Groves takes command of the Manhattan Project. Within days Groves has the federal government buy 52,000 acres in Tennessee, which is used to build the Oak Ridge facility for enriching uranium. That site will contain a gaseous diffusion plant that is the largest building in the world at the time.

- ***October:*** Groves appoints J. Robert Oppenheimer to head the laboratory that will design and build the atomic bomb.
- ***December 2:*** The Manhattan Project's Metallurgical Laboratory (Met Lab), headed by Enrico Fermi, achieves a controlled chain reaction.
- ***December 21:*** Dr. Ira Baldwin takes his post as the head of the newly established U.S. biological warfare program. He chooses an abandoned airfield about 50 miles northeast of Washington as the site for building the facilities necessary for that work. Today that site is called Fort Detrick.
- ***December 28:*** Roosevelt approves the enormous construction projects necessary to build the atomic bomb. These facilities are built during 1943.

1943

- ***January:*** The U.S. government purchases 500,000 acres in Hanford, Washington, to be used to build the facilities for producing plutonium for a nuclear bomb.
- ***January–March:*** The Soviet Union makes the decision to begin a small atomic bomb project. The physicist Igor Kurchatov is appointed the scientific director of the project on March 10.

March 15: U.S work on the atomic bomb begins at a new laboratory established at Los Alamos.

- ***April:*** Following a decision by the State Defense Committee, the body chaired by Stalin that is managing the Soviet war effort, a secret instruction is issued by the Soviet Academy of Sciences establishing what is cryptically called Laboratory No. 2. Laboratory No. 2 is the facility headed by Igor Kurchatov whose task is to work on an atomic bomb.
- ***Winter:*** Working for the Manhattan Project, the mathematician John von Neumann designs the explosive arrangements for an implosion system for a nuclear bomb that works in theory.

1944

- ***Spring:*** While working for the German army on tabun and sarin, the Nobel Prize–winning German chemist Richard Kuhn discovers soman. The documents detailing his work are hidden in a mineshaft but are later found by Soviet forces.

1945

- ***January 20:*** Oak Ridge separates its first U-235.
- ***March:*** At Los Alamos, the chemist George Kistiakowsky builds and tests the implosion system necessary for a plutonium bomb.
- ***May 31:*** Secretary of War Henry L. Stimson comments that the development of the atomic bomb marks "a new relationship of man to the universe."

- ***July 16:*** The United States successfully tests the first atomic bomb, a plutonium device that explodes with the force of 18,000 tons of TNT, at the Alamogordo bombing range in the New Mexico desert. Robert Oppenheimer named the test Trinity for reasons that have never been clear.
- ***July 26:*** The United States, Britain, and China issue the Potsdam Declaration, warning Japan to surrender or face total destruction. The statement also promises Japan that after a period of occupation and reform its sovereignty will be restored under a government chosen by the people.
- ***July 28:*** Japan rejects the Potsdam Declaration.
- ***August 6:*** The United States drops an atomic bomb on the city of Hiroshima.
- ***August 9:*** The United States drops an atomic bomb on the city of Nagasaki. Japan surrenders five days later.

1946

- ***April 13:*** The Soviet Union's Design Bureau No. 11 is established about 240 miles (400 km) east of Moscow in the small town of Sarov, which until then had been best known for its monastery. The name of the town was changed to Arzamas-16, and it promptly disappeared from all Soviet maps. Design Bureau No. 11, which consisted of a number of research and development units, was the most important Soviet atomic weapons facility. It designed and built the Soviet Union's first atomic and hydrogen bombs. The design bureau also was called Arzamas-16, and, hence, in a play on words invoking the Los Alamos laboratory in the United States, the Soviet Union's "Los Arzamas."
- ***April 18–20:*** A conference—called the Super Conference—of top physicists is held at Los Alamos with 31 participants. Among them are Edward Teller, Stanislaw Ulam, and the Soviet spy Klaus Fuchs. A report issued by the conference in June concludes that it is possible to build a thermonuclear bomb and that it will work.
- ***December 25:*** Soviet scientists achieve a controlled chain reaction.
- ***December 31:*** Igor Kurchatov writes a memo indicating that Soviet scientists have received information on American thinking about thermonuclear weapons. This information could only have come from a spy network. Earlier that year the Soviets began working on a thermonuclear bomb.

1948

- ***May:*** The chemist Ephraim Katchlalsky—who many years later as Ephraim Katzir will become president of Israel—is appointed commander of the Israel Defense Forces (IDF) Science Corps (known as HEMED).
- ***August:*** Israeli prime minister David Ben-Gurion appoints the organic chemist Ernst David Bergmann as scientific director of the Israel Defense Forces.

- ***September:*** Andrei Sakharov proposes what he calls in his memoirs the "First Idea," the layer cake design that will eventually become the basis of the first Soviet hydrogen bomb. Sakharov had been working on his concept since July. It supplants an earlier concept worked out during the summer of that year.

1949

- ***January:*** Sakharov begins working at Arzamas-16, the Soviet Union's atomic weapons nuclear weapons research and development center.
- ***August 29:*** Soviet Union successfully tests an atomic bomb. Thanks to successful spying on the Manhattan Project, the Soviet bomb is a copy of the bomb the United States used against Nagasaki in August 1945.
- ***September 3:*** A U.S. weather plane flying off the coast of Siberia detects the radiation that quickly is identified as coming from a Soviet nuclear test.

1950

- ***January 31:*** President Truman orders that the United States proceed with the development of the hydrogen bomb.
- ***February:*** After an extensive review process, President Truman approves an extension of the U.S. retaliation-only policy regarding chemical, biological, and radiological weapons.

1952

- ***June 13:*** Israel secretly establishes its Atomic Energy Commission; its founding is not announced until 1954. The organization is headed by Ernst David Bergmann, who in 1952 also organizes the Israel Institute for Biological Research (IIBR), an institute that absorbs HEMED BEIT and continues its work.
- ***October 3:*** Great Britain tests its first atomic bomb.
- ***November 1:*** The United States successfully tests a thermonuclear device. Because of its immense size, it is not a deliverable bomb. The yield is 10.4 megatons. The test, code named "Mike," completely vaporizes the atoll of Elugelab.

1953

- ***August 12:*** The Soviet Union tests a layer cake hydrogen bomb, which explodes with a force of 400 kilotons. Unlike the device tested by the United States in 1952, the layer cake is not a fully two-stage thermonuclear bomb. It is, however, a deliverable bomb.
- ***December:*** The United States begins producing offensive biological agents at the Pine Bluff Arsenal in Arkansas. At least seven different agents will be produced there until 1967, including anthrax.

Chronology

1954

- ***March 1:*** United States tests its first deliverable thermonuclear bomb. This test, code-named "Bravo," has an explosive yield of 15 megatons, three times what was expected. The Bravo test remains the most powerful nuclear explosion ever set off by the United States.

1955

- ***November 22:*** The Soviet Union tests its first fully thermonuclear bomb, which has an explosive yield of 1.6 megatons.

1957

- ***October 4:*** The Soviet Union launches *Sputnik*, the world's first artificial satellite. This achievement demonstrates that the Soviets have developed the world's first ICBM, a rocket capable of carrying an atomic bomb from the Soviet Union to the United States.
- ***November 8:*** Great Britain tests its first hydrogen bomb, which explodes with a force of 1.8 megatons.

1958

- ***October–November:*** Great Britain, the United States, and the Soviet Union all announce moratoriums on nuclear testing. The three countries are conducting negotiations on a treaty to ban nuclear testing.

1960

- ***February 13:*** France tests its first atomic bomb, which explodes with a force of more than 60 kilotons.

1961

- ***April 18:*** Soviet Union rejects the U.S.-British proposal for a treaty banning nuclear tests.
- ***August 30:*** Soviet Union announces it will resume nuclear testing.
- ***September 1:*** Soviet Union resumes nuclear testing. It conducts 15 tests, all in the atmosphere, before the United States resumes testing with an underground test two weeks later. The Soviet tests continue through November.
- ***September 15:*** United States resumes underground nuclear testing.
- ***September 26:*** United States establishes the Arms Control and Disarmament Agency.
- ***October 30:*** Soviet Union tests a 57-megaton thermonuclear bomb, the largest man-made explosion in history. Soviet tests continue through November 4. By then they have conducted almost 60 tests since they resumed testing two months

earlier. Only one of those tests is underground. One is underwater and two are in outer space. The rest are in the atmosphere.

1962

- ***April 25:*** The United States resumes nuclear testing in the atmosphere.
- ***October:*** Cuban missile crisis, the closest the United States and the Soviet Union ever come to nuclear war.

1963

- ***August 5:*** The United States, the Soviet Union, and Great Britain sign the Limited Nuclear Test Ban Treaty. It bans nuclear tests in the atmosphere, underwater, and in outer space.

1964

- ***October 16:*** The People's Republic of China tests its first atomic bomb.

1966

- ***November:*** Israel probably completes the process of "cold testing" that gives it the ability to build a nuclear weapon.

1967

- ***May:*** As Israel fights the combined forces of Egypt, Syria, and Jordan during the Six-Day War, its scientists and technicians assemble two atomic bombs.
- ***June 17:*** The People's Republic of China tests its first thermonuclear bomb in a desert region in the northwestern part of the country.

1968

- ***July 1:*** The Nuclear Nonproliferation Treaty is signed in Washington, London, and Moscow. The treaty enters into force in 1970.
- ***Summer:*** The United States conducts its only biological warfare tests using live agents near a coral atoll about 1,000 miles southwest of Hawaii. Aircraft release the pathogens in powdered form over barges on which monkeys are caged. About half of the monkeys die.
- ***August 24:*** France tests its first hydrogen bomb. The bomb explodes with a force of 2.6 megatons.

1969

- ***November 25:*** President Richard Nixon announces that the United States is renouncing the offensive use of biological weapons and will keep chemical weapons for retaliatory purposes only.

Chronology

1970

- ***February 14:*** President Nixon extends the policy announced in November 1969 to specifically include toxins.

1972

- ***April 10:*** Biological Weapons Convention is signed in Washington, London, and Moscow. It enters into force in 1975. The United States signs the BWC in April 1972 and ratifies it in 1975.
- ***May 26:*** SALT I ABM treaty is signed by the United States and the Soviet Union in Moscow.
- ***May 26:*** SALT I interim agreement on strategic offensive arms is signed by the United States and the Soviet Union in Moscow.

1973

- ***April 23:*** Biopreparat is established, headed by an army general.

1974

- ***May 18:*** India tests its first nuclear device, describing it as being for peaceful purposes.

1979

- ***April 2:*** Outbreak of anthrax in the Soviet city of Sverdlovsk kills more than 60 people. The Soviet government claims the cause of the outbreak is tainted meat, but in fact the cause is a release of aerosol from a biological weapons laboratory. The lab is located within a military complex called Compound 19. It takes until 1992 before Russian president Boris Yeltsin, who in 1979 was the Communist Party official in charge of Sverdlovsk, admits the true cause of the outbreak.
- ***June 18:*** The United States and the Soviet Union sign the SALT II treaty. The treaty limits each side to a total of 2,400 ICBMS, SLBMs, and long-range bombers. Of those, 1,320 can have multiple warheads. The treaty is never ratified and therefore never entered into force.
- ***September 22:*** An America VELA spy satellite detects a mysterious flash in the Indian Ocean, probably a nuclear test carried out by Israel in cooperation with South Africa.

1981

- ***June 7:*** Israel bombs and destroys Iraq's Osirak nuclear reactor, which would have produced plutonium for an Iraqi nuclear bomb.

1983

- ***March 23:*** President Ronald Reagan proposes a missile defense system he calls the Strategic Defense Initiative. Critics, who believe it is impossible to build such a system, give it the name "Star Wars," after the popular science fiction movie.
- ***August:*** Iraq begins using mustard gas against Iranian forces in the Iran-Iraq war.

1985

- ***December 12:*** North Korea joins the Nuclear Nonproliferation Treaty but does not complete the required safeguards agreement with the International Atomic Energy Agency.

1986

- ***February:*** The largest documented use of chemical weapons by Iraq during the Iran-Iraq war. The Iraqis use mustard gas and tabun, injuring as many as 10,000 Iranians.

1987

- ***December 8:*** INF Treaty between the United States and the Soviet Union is signed in Washington. It enters into force in June 1988.

1988

- ***March 16:*** Iraqi warplanes under orders from dictator Saddam Hussein attack the Kurdish town of Halabja with mustard gas and nerve agents, killing an estimated 4,000 people.
- ***Spring:*** Soviet scientists are ordered to dispose of anthrax bacteria, which is stored near the Siberian city Irkutsk, by decontaminating it and then burying it on Vozrozhdeniye Island in the middle of the Aral Sea. The work is done in great haste and secrecy. The anthrax—enough to kill the world's population many times over—is put into stainless-steel containers, shipped 1,000 miles by train, treated with bleach to render it harmless, and buried in deep pits. This process fails to decontaminate the anthrax, which remains a deadly threat until decontaminated by the United States 14 years later.

1989

- ***May:*** Matthew S. Meselson, a Harvard University biologist and leading consultant to the U.S. government, who had argued that the Soviets were telling the truth about the 1979 anthrax outbreak in Sverdlovsk, tells the U.S. Senate that the Soviet Union does not have a stockpile of biological or toxin weapons.
- ***October:*** Vladimir Pasechnik defects from the Soviet Union to Great Britain, exposing the existence of Biopreparat.

Chronology

1990

- ***October 24:*** The Soviet Union conducts its last nuclear test.

1991

- ***July 31:*** The United States and the Soviet Union sign the START I treaty, which calls for substantial reductions in their nuclear arsenals.
- ***September 27:*** President George H. W. Bush announces that the United States will end the deployment abroad of all land-based and naval tactical nuclear weapons. About 100 of those weapons had been based in South Korea. It is a unilateral decision not dependent on what the Soviet Union does. Within eight days Soviet president Mikhail Gorbachev reciprocates.
- ***October 1:*** Russian chemical weapons scientist Vil Mirzayanov publishes an article in the Moscow newspaper *Kuranty* exposing the Soviet Union's secret Foliant chemical weapons program.

1992

- ***April:*** Russian president Boris Yeltsin admits that the 1979 anthrax outbreak in Sverdlovsk was caused by an accident in a Soviet military research facility. He also admits that from the 1970s onward the Soviet Union had a biological warfare program, in violation of the Biological Weapons Convention, to which the Soviet Union had been a party since the treaty entered into force in 1975.
- ***May:*** Russian officials announce that all tactical weapons of the former Soviet Union based in Ukraine, Belarus, and Kazakhstan have been moved to Russia.
- ***August 29:*** The Cooperative Threat Reduction Program is established. It is often called the Nunn-Lugar Program after its two main sponsors in the Senate, Richard Lugar and Sam Nunn.
- ***September:*** Kanatjan Alibekov—who later Americanizes his name to Ken Alibek—defects from Russia, confirming and expanding upon the revelations of Vladimir Paschnik about Biopreparat.
- ***September 23:*** The United States conducts its last underground nuclear test.

1993

- ***January 3:*** The United States and Russia sign the START II treaty in Moscow. The treaty is intended to reduce the Russian and American arsenals of nuclear warheads to 3,000–3,500 each. Although it is ratified by the United States Senate in 1996 and by the Russian Duma in 2000, it never enters into force because of conditions set by the Russians requiring the United States to remain a party to the 1972 ABM treaty.
- ***January 13:*** Chemical Weapons Convention pronounced ready for signing. It enters into force on April 29, 1997.

- ***February 9:*** Based on evidence of cheating on the NPT, the International Atomic Energy Agency demands to inspect two sites where it is believed North Korea stores nuclear waste. North Korea refuses the request.
- ***July 22:*** Belarus becomes a party to the NPT.

1994

- ***January:*** The Central Intelligence Agency says that North Korea may have produced one or two nuclear weapons.
- ***February 14:*** Kazakhstan becomes a party to the NPT.
- ***October 21:*** The United States and North Korea accept the Agreed Framework under which North Korea will freeze and eventually eliminate its nuclear program in return for substantial foreign aid.
- ***December 5:*** Ukraine becomes a party to the NPT.

1995

- ***April 25:*** Kazakhstan completes the transfer of all former Soviet strategic nuclear weapons to Russia and is officially declared nuclear free.
- ***August:*** Lieutenant-General Hussein Kamal, a son-in-law of Saddam Hussein and formerly in charge of Iraq's WMD programs, defects to Jordan. This sets in motion events in which Iraq finally gives up information on its biological weapons program—which had been successfully kept secret until then—and on the vast extent of its nuclear program. None of this information—documents stored in 150 crates hidden on a chicken farm belonging to Kamal Hussein—had been uncovered by UN inspectors in more than four years of effort. Kamal later returns to Iraq and is executed.

1996

- ***June 1:*** Ukraine announces that the last of the strategic nuclear weapons of the former Soviet Union have been transferred to Russia.
- ***September 24:*** The Comprehensive Nuclear Test Ban Treaty is opened for signature, two weeks after being adopted by the UN General Assembly. A total of 71 countries sign the treaty that day, including the United States, Russia, Britain, the People's Republic of China, and France.
- ***November 23:*** The last strategic weapons of the former Soviet Union are transferred from Belarus to Russia.

1998

- ***April 17:*** The United States imposes sanctions on North Korea and Pakistan after North Korea transfers missile technology and components to Pakistan.

- ***May 11:*** India conducts its first nuclear weapons tests. India conducts three tests that day and two additional tests on May 13.
- ***May 28:*** Pakistan conducts its first nuclear weapons tests. It conducts five tests that day.
- ***October 1:*** The Defense Threat Reduction Agency is established to consolidate all the agencies in the Department of Defense charged with responding to threats posed by weapons of mass destruction. It is given an annual budget of $1.9 billion.

1999

- ***April 11:*** India tests an upgraded version of its intermediate-range Agni ballistic missile, which can carry a nuclear warhead.
- ***April 13:*** Pakistan tests its Ghauri ballistic, which can carry a nuclear warhead.
- ***August 17:*** India issues a draft report of its nuclear doctrine, declaring a policy of no first use. It formally adopts this statement as its nuclear doctrine in 2003.

2000

- ***April 23:*** President Putin formally approves a new Russian nuclear doctrine, which accepts the possible first use of nuclear weapons to deter a massive attack with conventional weapons.

2001

- ***January 17:*** India tests an Angi-2 intermediate-range missile, capable of reaching any part of Pakistan and also part of western China.
- ***September 11:*** The World Trade Center in New York City is destroyed and the Pentagon in Washington, D.C., damaged in an attack by Islamic terrorists who crash hijacked passenger aircraft into the buildings. Almost 3,000 people are killed.
- ***Fall:*** Envelopes containing anthrax spores are sent to several prominent political and media figures in the United States. They include Senate Majority Leader Thomas Daschle and NBC journalist Tom Brokaw. Twenty-two are infected, including several postal workers; five people die.
- ***October:*** Israel's Institute for Biological Research announces it has developed an anthrax vaccine that requires only a single injection.
- ***December 13:*** President George W. Bush gives notice that the United States will withdraw from the 1972 ABM treaty, beginning the six-month timetable required by the treaty for that withdrawal to become effective.

2002

- ***May 24:*** The United States and the Russian Federation sign the SORT treaty, or Treaty of Moscow, under which each country pledges to reduce its nuclear arsenal to between 1,700 and 2,200 warheads in 10 years. Both countries ratify the treaty in 2003.

- ***June 13:*** The United States withdrawal from the 1972 ABM treaty, announced six months earlier, takes effect.
- ***June 14:*** Russia withdraws from START II, meaning that the START process will end as of December 2009.
- ***Summer:*** A team from the U.S. Defense Threat Reduction Agency successfully decontaminates the anthrax on Vozrozhdeniye Island in the Aral Sea. The anthrax had been left behind by the Soviet biological weapons program, whose scientists unsuccessfully attempted to decontaminate it in 1988.
- ***November 25:*** The Department of Homeland Security is established by the Homeland Security Act. The act consolidates 22 government agencies and 180,000 employees in a new agency to better protect the country against a variety of threats, including WMD attacks.

2003

- ***January 10:*** North Korea withdraws from the Nuclear Nonproliferation Treaty.
- ***December 19:*** Libya agrees to give up its nuclear weapons program. It does so during 2004.

2004

- ***July 21:*** President George W. Bush signs the law establishing Project BioShield.

2005

- ***May:*** The U.S. Reliable Replacement Warhead (RRW) program is established.
- ***September 19:*** The final American MX Peacekeeper missile is decommissioned.

2006

- ***September 9:*** North Korea conducts a nuclear test.

October 13: President George W. Bush signs the Security and Accountability for Every Port (SAFE) Act, designed to keep nuclear, biological, and chemical weapons out of the 11 million shipping containers that enter the United States every year.

2007

- ***March 2:*** The Lawrence Livermore National Laboratory is selected as the lead laboratory to design the first warhead for the Reliable Replacement Warhead program.
- ***August 1:*** President George W. Bush signs bill mandating the scanning of all sea cargo and all air cargo on passenger planes entering the United States. The 100

percent requirement for sea cargo—to be scanned before it is loaded onto vessels—is to be achieved in five years. All air cargo on passenger planes is to be scanned within three years.

- ***August 30:*** The U.S. Army announces it has destroyed half of the U.S. chemical weapons stockpile. That represents more than 1.7 munitions including bombs, rockets, mortars, spray tanks, and other munitions filled with nerve agents (including sarin and VX) and blister agents (including mustard gas).
- ***September 6:*** Israel bombs and destroys a nuclear reactor being built in Syria. The reactor, which would have produced plutonium, was being built with North Korean technical assistance and Iranian funding.

2008

- ***July:*** The United States completes the removal of 550 tons of yellowcake natural uranium from Iraq. This operation eliminates the last major remnant of Saddam Hussein's nuclear program. It involved a secret two-week operation involving an airlift and then the shipping of the yellowcake by sea to Canada, where it will be used by Canadian power reactors to produce electricity.
- ***August 1:*** Bruce E. Ivins, a biodefense researcher suspected in the anthrax mailings case of 2001, commits suicide. The U.S. Justice Department was about to file criminal charges against Ivins in connection with the anthrax mailings of 2001.
- ***August 6:*** The U.S. Department of Defense announces it will help Israel develop and finance the Arrow 3 missile defense system.
- ***September:*** The United States delivers its advanced FBX-T radar to Israel to be used with the Arrow 2 to defend Israel against a missile attack from Iran.
- ***October 16:*** Israel announces that the distribution of gas masks to the entire population, originally scheduled for January 2009, will not take place until late in the year.
- ***November 29:*** The International Atomic Energy Agency reports that Iran has produced enough low-enriched uranium to build a nuclear bomb.

2009

- ***March 4:*** The United States announces that the IAEA has found "significant" evidence that the Syrian facility bombed by Israel in 2007 was a nuclear reactor.
- ***April 24:*** Reports emerge that various intelligence agencies and the IAEA have concluded that North Korea has developed nuclear warheads small enough to mount on medium-range missiles.
- ***May 6:*** The IAEA announces it has detected traces of weapons grade uranium in Egypt, as it did in 2007.
- ***May 25:*** North Korea conducts its second nuclear test.

- ***September:*** Iran admits the existence of a second secret nuclear enrichment plant, this one being built into a mountain near the city of Qom. Its size and configuration are suited only for enriching uranium for an atomic bomb, removing any lingering doubt about the goals of Iran's nuclear program.
- ***December 4:*** START I expires. The United States and Russia agree to observe the treaty's terms as they continue negotiations on a new treaty.

12

Glossary

agent toxic material (biological or chemical) that goes into weapons.

anthrax a contagious bacterial disease that in nature can spread from animals to humans. Anthrax is one of the most favored poisons in biological weapons. Anthrax BACTERIA live in soil, water, and vegetation and can infect the lung, intestinal, and nervous systems.

antibiotic a drug used to treat diseases caused by BACTERIA or other microorganisms.

atomic bomb a bomb in which the explosive power comes from the release of energy that occurs with the FISSION of uranium or plutonium. This term sometimes is applied to any bomb that gets its power from the release of nuclear energy and, hence, to THERMONUCLEAR bombs.

bacteria single cell or multicell living creatures. Bacterial diseases often can be treated with antibiotics.

ballistic missile a missile that upon launch is powered upward by a rocket engine. When a ballistic missile reaches the apex of its flight trajectory, its engine shuts off and the missile is brought down to its target by gravity, reaching enormous speeds as it descends. Long-range, or strategic, missiles leave the atmosphere during their ascent and reenter it as they move toward their target.

binary chemical weapon a weapon designed to use two nontoxic or less-toxic AGENTS that are combined after the weapon is fired to produce a highly toxic chemical agent for release on a target.

biological agent a microorganism or TOXIN derived from a microorganism that can cause a disease in a human or animal.

biological weapon a device that projects, disperses, on in other ways spreads a biological AGENT to harm soldiers or civilians. It can take many forms, such as a missile WARHEAD or bomb.

blister agent a CHEMICAL AGENT that burns or blisters the skin, eyes, or lungs on contact. It can take the form of a gas or liquid spray.

WEAPONS OF MASS DESTRUCTION

blood agent a CHEMICAL AGENT that is absorbed into the circulation system and carried to body tissues, depriving them of oxygen. The brain is especially susceptible to this kind of agent.

botulism a food poisoning caused by the botulinum TOXIN. One gram of the botulinum toxin is capable of killing thousands of people by destroying the nervous system. The botulinum toxin has been investigated by various biological warfare programs, but it is difficult to produce in large quantities and turn into an effective aerosol.

bubonic plague a bacterial disease spread by flea bites that has caused some of the worst epidemics in human history. Japan attempted to use bubonic plague as a weapon in China during World War II by putting plague-infected fleas into bombs. Another form of plague, pneumonic plague, is spread through the air and is 100 percent fatal if not treated with antibiotics.

cascade a large number of connected GAS CENTRIFUGES used to enrich uranium (*see* GAS CENTRIFUGE PROCESS).

centrifuge *See* GAS CENTRIFUGE.

chain reaction the process in which neutrons from an initial FISSION reaction are released, cause additional atoms to fission, and thereby keep the process going. When a chain reaction is controlled so that the number of neutrons remains constant, the process technically is called a critical chain reaction. In a nuclear reactor a chain reaction is kept under control by varying the fraction of neutrons that escapes from the reactor or by introducing control rods, which usually have boron or cadmium—elements that absorb neutrons—and decrease the number of neutrons moving through the reactor. In a NUCLEAR WEAPON, an uncontrolled chain reaction—or supercritical chain reaction—releases energy in the form of an enormous explosion.

chemical agent poisonous chemicals that are used to kill, immobilize, or incapacitate civilians or military personnel.

chemical weapon a device that projects, disperses, or in other ways spreads a toxic chemical AGENT to harm soldiers or civilians.

choking agent a chemical agent that attacks lung tissue, making it impossible to breathe.

conventional weapons weapons such as tanks, artillery, or aircraft that use nonnuclear explosives to attack and damage targets.

critical mass the amount of FISSILE MATERIAL required to sustain a CHAIN REACTION. The amount required in turn depends on the purity, density, shape, and other qualities of the fissile material involved. *See also* SUPERCRITICAL MASS.

cruise missile a pilotless aircraft with a conventional or nuclear WARHEAD powered by a jet engine. Cruise missiles have guidance systems that enable them to avoid enemy defenses by flying low and following the terrain. They can hit targets with very high accuracy.

deuterium the hydrogen ISOTOPE (H_2) that contains one proton and one neutron. It is a key part of the fuel of a THERMONUCLEAR BOMB. It is present in the bomb as the solid lithium deuteride.

dirty bomb a device made from radioactive nuclear waste and explosives. When a dirty bomb is exploded, radioactive waste is carried into the atmosphere, where it is dispersed by wind and rain. The goal is to contaminate a target area so as to cause radiation-related diseases and/or the abandonment or destruction of a contaminated area.

dual-use material or equipment a chemical or biological AGENT or piece of equipment that has both civilian and military uses. This category includes precursor chemicals, or chemicals that have civilian uses but can be combined to produce toxic chemicals, as well as equipment that has civilian uses but also can be used to produce chemical, biological, or NUCLEAR WEAPONS.

electromagnetic isotope separation (EMIS) a method for enriching uranium developed by the Manhattan Project during World War II. EMIS relies on electromagnetic devices called calutrons, which were installed in the Y-12 plant at Oak Ridge, Tennessee. The Y-12 plant, using uranium that had been enriched to about 23 percent U-235 by GASEOUS DIFFUSION (and before that to 2 percent by thermal diffusion, another process developed by the Manhattan Project), produced the weapons-grade uranium for the Hiroshima bomb. That uranium was about 84 to 89 percent U-235. However, because the EMIS used so much electricity, the United States abandoned it in favor of gaseous diffusion after the war. Decades later, Iraq hid its enrichment program by using EMIS. This effort was successful because U.S. and other intelligence observers, believing EMIS was obsolete, did not look for signs that the Iraqis might be using it.

enrichment with regard to NUCLEAR WEAPONS, the process of increasing the percentage of U-235 in a given quantity of uranium. Uranium in its natural state is less than 1 percent (.7 percent) U-235, the ISOTOPE needed for nuclear FISSION. LOW ENRICHED URANIUM (LEU), which is used in power or research reactors, is less than 20 percent U-235. The uranium in power reactors typically is between 3 to 5 percent U-235. HIGHLY ENRICHED URANIUM (HEU) has more than 20 percent U-235. WEAPONS GRADE URANIUM, the material best suited for nuclear weapons, is today typically more than 90 percent U-235.

entry into force the point at which a treaty becomes binding on the countries that have become party to it. Often that is defined as when a certain number of countries or certain countries in particular have ratified the treaty in question.

fissile material elements that FISSION readily when bombarded with neutrons. When the nuclei of these elements undergo fission, they give off neutrons. If enough neutrons are given off additional atoms fission and the result is a CHAIN REACTION. U-235 and Pu-239 are fissile materials.

fission the process in which a neutron splits a nucleus into two or more lighter nuclei. This process releases huge amounts of energy in the form of heat and radiation, as well as additional neutrons.

fission bomb *See* ATOMIC BOMB.

fusion the process when two nuclei from lighter elements are merged to form the nucleus of a heavier element. This releases an enormous amount of energy. In fusion bombs, which generally are referred to as THERMONUCLEAR BOMBS or hydrogen bombs, hydrogen atoms are fused to produce helium.

fusion bomb *See* THERMONUCLEAR BOMB.

G-agents the American name for TABUN, SARIN, and SOMAN, NERVE AGENTS developed from pesticides by German scientists between 1936 and 1944. After World War II even more deadly nerve agents were developed (*see* V-AGENTS).

gas centrifuge cylindrical machines made of high-tech metal alloys and composite materials that rotate at extremely high speeds. Gas centrifuges are used to enrich uranium (*see* GAS CENTRIFUGE PROCESS).

gas centrifuge process an advanced system for enriching uranium that is widely in use today for producing HIGHLY ENRICHED URANIUM. The system relies on high-tech GAS CENTRIFUGES that are connected to each other to form what are called CASCADES. The uranium is present in the form of a gaseous compound, uranium hexafluoride. As the centrifuges spin at extremely high speeds, the gaseous uranium hexaflouride with the isotope U-238 moves toward the outer cylinder walls, while the lighter gas with U-235 gas collects in the middle of the cylinder, from where it can be withdrawn from the centrifuge.

gaseous diffusion a system for enriching uranium originally developed by the Manhattan Project. The world's first gaseous diffusion plant, K-25, was built in Oak Ridge, Tennessee in 1943–45. Gaseous diffusion was successfully used to produce HIGHLY ENRICHED URANIUM by the Manhattan Project and is still used to enrich uranium today, although mainly to produce LOW ENRICHED URANIUM. The gigantic K-25 plant that went into operation in January 1945 operated with only normal maintenance for decades after World War II.

gun-type fission bomb the design for the uranium bomb used at Hiroshima. It is the simplest type of ATOMIC BOMB. A SUPERCRITICAL MASS and explosion are achieved when a small piece of weapons-grade uranium is fired down the barrel of a small cannon into a larger piece attached to the canon's muzzle.

heavy water water whose atoms contain deuterium atoms, or heavy hydrogen (H_2), rather than regular hydrogen. Heavy water is present in regular water in a proportion of about 1 to 6,500. It is produced by an industrial process that creates 99.75 percent, or "reactor grade," heavy water. Heavy water is a desirable moderator in nuclear reactors used for producing electricity because it permits the use of natural uranium as fuel.

highly enriched uranium (HEU) uranium in which the percentage of U-235 has been increased to at least 20 percent. Only seven-tenths of 1 percent of naturally occurring uranium is U-235. Virtually all the rest—there are naturally occurring traces of U-234—is U-238. The uranium used in U.S. NUCLEAR WEAPONS is usually enriched so that it is at least 93 percent U-235. *See also* WEAPONS GRADE MATERIAL.

hydrogen bomb *See* THERMONUCLEAR BOMB.

implosion-type fission bomb a bomb in which a SUPERCRITICAL MASS is achieved by compressing the nuclear material in a precisely calibrated series of conventional explosions. An implosion system was developed under severe time limits by scientists of the Manhattan Project after it was discovered that plutonium could not be used in a GUN-TYPE FISSION BOMB because of spontaneous FISSION.

intercontinental ballistic missile (ICBM) a BALLISTIC MISSILE that is land based and can carry a nuclear WARHEAD for at least 3,400 miles (5,500 km).

isotope a variant of an element whose nucleus has a different number of neutrons than other forms, or isotopes, of that element. While all isotopes of a given element have the same atomic number, they have a different atomic mass and different physical properties. Thus the isotope U-235, which has three less neutrons than U-238, is fissile, while U-238 is not.

kiloton a measure of explosive force equal to 1,000 tons of TNT. The term is used to describe the explosive power of NUCLEAR WEAPONS in comparison to the explosive power of dynamite.

low enriched uranium (LEU) uranium that has been enriched to less than 20 percent U-235. LEU of about 3 to 5 percent U-235 is used in civilian light water nuclear reactors that produce electricity, and LEU of about 12 to 20 percent commonly is used in civilian research reactors.

megaton a measure of explosive force equal to 1 million tons of TNT. The term is used to describe the explosive power of NUCLEAR WEAPONS.

multiple independently targeted reentry vehicle (MIRV) a high-tech structure with two or more WARHEADS inside, each of which can be guided to a specific target once the BALLISTIC MISSILE has reached the top, or apex, of its flight pattern. A MIRV contains computers and other equipment designed to release each individual warhead at an exact time and angle so it can reach its target. Both INTERCONTINENTAL BALLISTIC MISSILES and SUBMARINE-LAUNCHED BALLISTIC MISSILES can be MIRVed. A MIRV can also contain decoy warheads designed to defeat anti-missile defensive systems.

mustard gas a blister agent that can cause severe damage to the eyes, respiratory system, and internal organs. Mustard gas was used widely during World War I.

nerve agent the most powerful and fast acting of all chemical warfare agents. Nerve agents act like pesticides and in fact were discovered by scientists working to develop new pesticides. *See also* V-AGENTS, G-AGENTS.

neutron bomb also called an enhanced radiation weapon (ERW), a neutron bomb is a very small THERMONUCLEAR WEAPON. It is designed for tactical, or battlefield, use against tanks and infantry formations. When detonated, it produces a minimum amount of blast and large quantities of radiation, the goal being to kill enemy soldiers but not destroy surrounding buildings and other structures. It is considered a weapon especially suited for use against large tank formations. Even the radiation from a neutron bomb will kill in only a small area, sparing civilians in cities and towns near a battlefield.

no first use policy a policy by which a nuclear power undertakes not to be the first combatant to resort to NUCLEAR WEAPONS in a future conflict. It will use nuclear weapons only in retaliation for a nuclear attack.

nonproliferation the prevention of the spread of NUCLEAR WEAPONS and nuclear weapons technology to nations that presently do not have them.

nuclear weapon a missile, rocket, artillery shell, or other device armed with a nuclear WARHEAD.

pathogen a biological organism that causes disease. This term less commonly can refer to a harmful chemical.

poison a substance that can cause severe injury or death if ingested, breathed in, or absorbed through the skin.

PU-239 the ISOTOPE of plutonium that is formed in nuclear reactors from U-238 and is suitable for use in NUCLEAR WEAPONS.

Pu-240 an ISOTOPE of plutonium that FISSIONS spontaneously at a rate that makes it impossible to use in a gun-type ATOMIC BOMB. Since it is not practical to separate Pu-240 from Pu-239, fission weapons made of plutonium must be brought to a supercritical (explosive) state by implosion. This problem was discovered at Los Alamos in 1944.

radioactivity the process by which an unstable atomic nucleus spontaneously decays, emitting energy in the form of subatomic particles.

ricin a powerful TOXIN made from the waste produced when processing castor beans. A weapons grade of this toxin was developed by the Soviet Union and used by one of the Soviet Union's satellites in Eastern Europe to assassinate defectors.

rickettsiae microorganisms with characteristics of both BACTERIA and VIRUSES. Although larger than bacteria, rickettsiae are similar to bacteria in that they have metabolic enzymes and cell membranes and use oxygen. They resemble viruses in that they can only grow inside living cells.

rogue state a state that does not abide by generally accepted international norms, such as states that aid international terrorist groups. The most notable current examples are North Korea and Iran.

sarin a chemical agent developed in Germany in 1936. Colorless and odorless, it is 20 times more deadly than cyanide gas. A droplet the size of a pinprick can kill a person.

smallpox a virulently infectious disease that has killed enormous numbers of people throughout history. It is caused by the variola VIRUS. Smallpox was eradicated in nature in the late 20th century but has been investigated by biological warfare programs. The Soviet biological warfare program Biopreparat weaponized the smallpox agent for delivery by INTERCONTINENTAL BALLISTIC MISSILES.

soman The last and most deadly of the NERVE AGENTS developed by German scientists in the 1930s and 1940s. If soman is released in the air, people can absorb it through their skin and eyes or take it in by inhalation. Soman mixes easily with water and therefore can be used to poison water supplies. It is clear, colorless, and tasteless.

spent nuclear fuel radioactive material that has been removed from a nuclear reactor because it can no longer sustain a CHAIN REACTION. This fuel contains Pu-239, which can be separated from other waste materials and used in NUCLEAR WEAPONS.

spontaneous fission the tendency of atoms to FISSION on their own but not fast enough to cause a CHAIN REACTION. Spontaneous fission became a serious problem for the Manhattan Project when it was discovered that plutonium—actually, Pu-240, which could not be separated from Pu-239—fissioned spontaneously and therefore could not be used in a GUN-TYPE FISSION BOMB. The problem of spontaneous fission was overcome by the development of the implosion process (*see* IMPLOSION-TYPE FISSION BOMB).

strategic nuclear weapon a long-range missile, either an INTERCONTINENTAL BALLISTIC MISSILE or SUBMARINE-LAUNCHED BALLISTIC MISSILE, or a long-range bomber. The latter can carry either bombs or CRUISE MISSILES with nuclear WARHEADS. *See also* TACTICAL NUCLEAR WEAPON.

subcritical mass an amount of fissile material that cannot sustain a fission chain reaction because it is too small in volume or lacks the necessary geometric characteristics.

submarine-launched ballistic missile (SLBM) a BALLISTIC MISSILE capable of carrying a nuclear WARHEAD that can be launched from a submarine.

supercritical mass the amount of FISSILE MATERIAL that has the required purity, density, shape, and other qualities necessary to produce an explosive, or supercritical, CHAIN REACTION. *See also* CRITICAL MASS.

tabun a chemical warfare NERVE AGENT first produced in Germany in 1936. Tabun is a clear, colorless, tasteless liquid, but it does have a slight odor. If released into the air it can be inhaled or absorbed through the skin. It mixes easily with water and therefore can be used to poison water supplies.

tactical nuclear weapon a short-range NUCLEAR WEAPON such as an artillery shell or short-range missile. Tactical nuclear weapons are used in battlefield situations. *See also* STRATEGIC NUCLEAR WEAPON.

thermonuclear bomb an advanced NUCLEAR WEAPON in which intense heat from a FISSION explosion is used to cause the FUSION of atomic nuclei, in turn releasing enormous amounts of energy.

TNT 2,4,6-trinitrotoluene. An extremely powerful and useful explosive with many uses, both civilian and military. With proper precautions, TNT can be manufactured and handled reasonably safely. It does not explode when bumped or jarred, and must be set off by a detonator. These qualities, and because it melts at a low temperature and does not react with metal, allow it to be put into bombs and artillery shells. TNT's importance as an explosive made it the standard for measuring the far greater power of nuclear weapons. A kiloton is equal to the explosive power of 1,000 pounds of TNT; a megaton is equal to the explosive power of 1 million tons of TNT.

toxin a poisonous substance derived from living plants, animals, or microorganisms. Some toxins can be produced or changed by chemical means. Toxins have a relatively simple biochemical makeup and, unlike microorganisms, cannot reproduce. In many ways they are comparable to CHEMICAL AGENTS.

tritium the hydrogen ISOTOPE (H_3) that contains one proton and two neutrons. It is an important part of the fuel in a THERMONUCLEAR BOMB. It is formed in the bomb after the FISSION explosion causes the lithium in the bomb to fission into helium, tritium, and energy.

U-235 the ISOTOPE of uranium found in nature that readily FISSIONS and therefore can be used in NUCLEAR WEAPONS. It accounts for .7 percent of all natural uranium.

U-238 the most common form of uranium found in nature, accounting for almost 93 percent of all naturally occurring uranium. Unlike U-235, U-238 does not FISSION readily and is not usable for NUCLEAR WEAPONS. However, in a nuclear reactor it is converted to PU-239, which does readily fission and therefore is suitable for use in nuclear weapons.

V-agents nerve agents developed during the 1950s by British scientists that are more deadly than TABUN, SARIN, and SOMAN (*see* G-AGENTS). The "V" stands for "venomous."

virus an organism that can only reproduce inside a living cell. Viruses produce diseases that usually cannot be treated with antibiotics.

VX a NERVE AGENT first developed in Great Britain during the 1950s. It is considered to be the most potent of all nerve agents. An oily liquid, after being released into the air it can be absorbed through the skin or eyes or inhaled. VX evaporates very slowly, which means that any surface contaminated with this agent will remain hazardous for a long time.

warhead the front of a ballistic or CRUISE MISSILE that carries its explosive charge, be it conventional or nuclear. Warheads can also be packed with CHEMICAL AGENTS or BIOLOGICAL AGENTS. The structure of a MIRVed (*see* MULTIPLE INDEPENDENTLY TARGETED REENTRY VEHICLE) BALLISTIC MISSILE that holds multiple warheads is called a warhead bus.

weapons-grade material nuclear material that has a sufficiently high concentration of PU-239 or U-235 to make it suitable for use in a NUCLEAR WEAPON. In the United States, that generally means plutonium that is at least 94 percent Pu-239 or highly enriched uranium that is at least 93 percent U-235.

weapons of mass destruction (WMD) weapons capable of inflicting massive destruction to populations and/or property using chemical, biological, and especially nuclear material.

Index

Page numbers in **boldface** indicate major treatment of a subject. Page numbers followed by *b* indicate biographical entries. Page numbers followed by *c* indicate entries in the chronology. Page numbers followed by *f* indicate figures. Page numbers followed by *g* indicate glossary entries.

B

C

Index

Index

N

Index

Index